THOSE MUST BE THE GUARDS

OSPREY
PUBLISHING

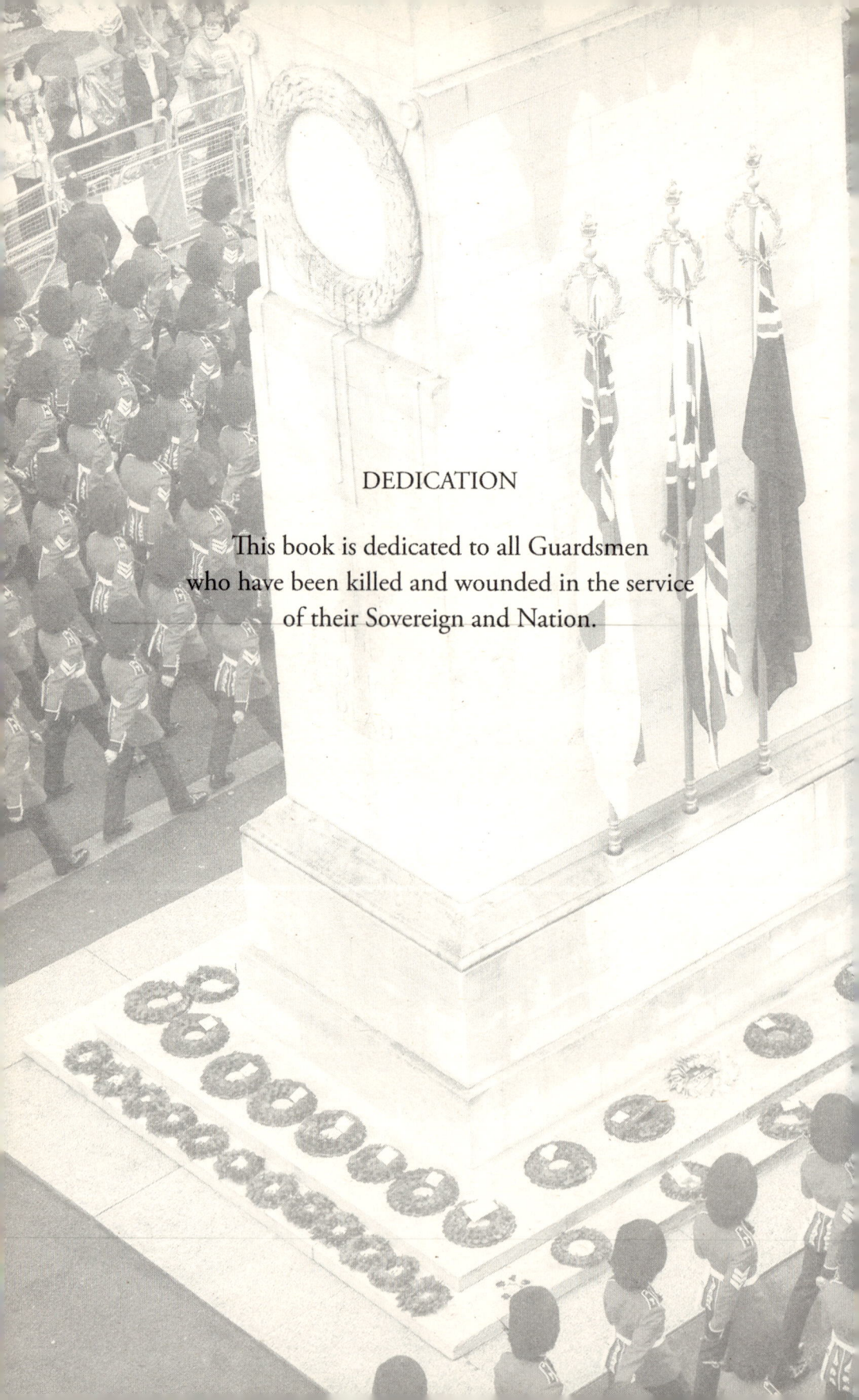

DEDICATION

This book is dedicated to all Guardsmen
who have been killed and wounded in the service
of their Sovereign and Nation.

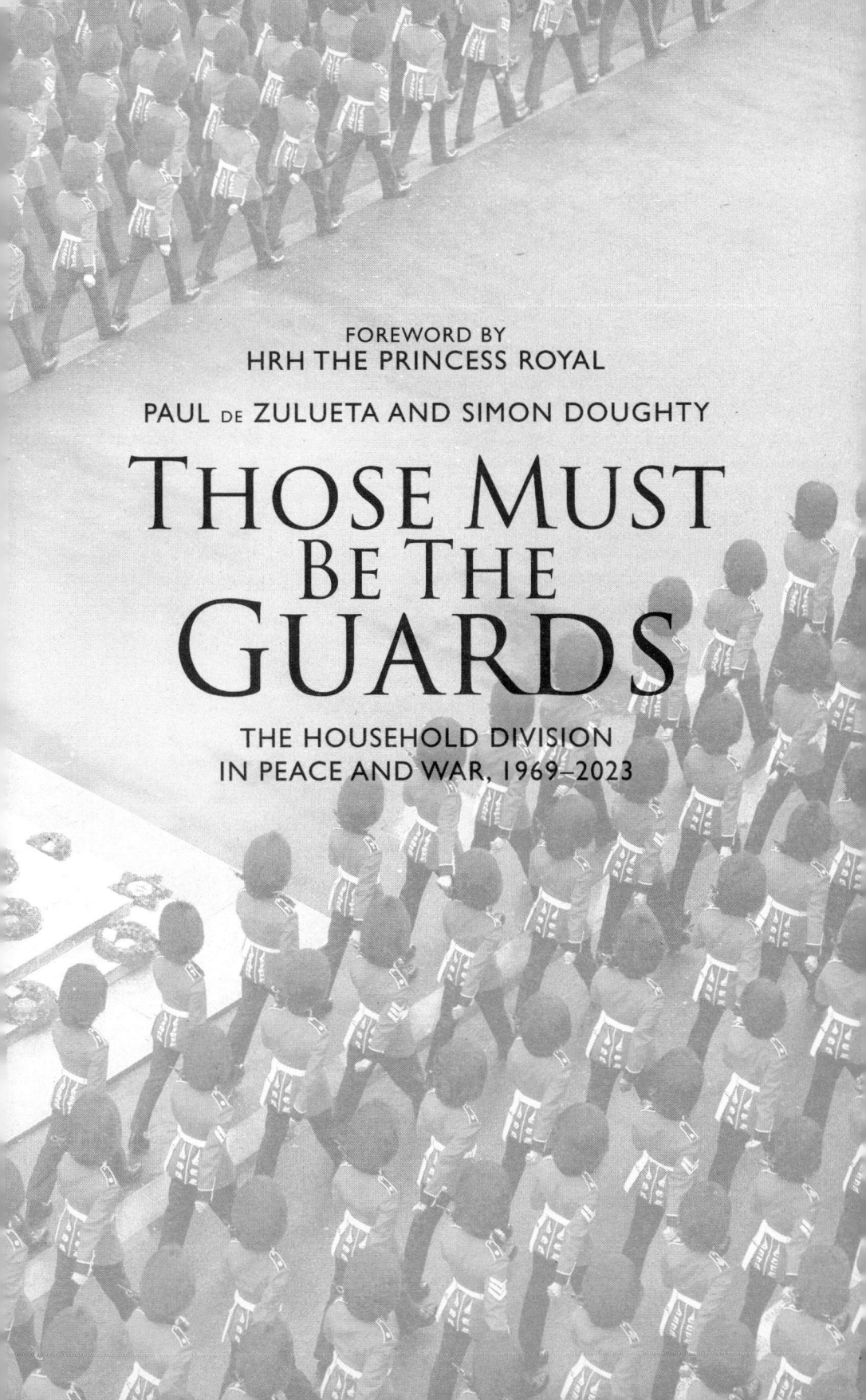

FOREWORD BY
HRH THE PRINCESS ROYAL

PAUL DE ZULUETA AND SIMON DOUGHTY

THOSE MUST
BE THE
GUARDS

THE HOUSEHOLD DIVISION
IN PEACE AND WAR, 1969–2023

OSPREY PUBLISHING
Bloomsbury Publishing Plc
Kemp House, Chawley Park, Cumnor Hill, Oxford OX2 9PH, UK
29 Earlsfort Terrace, Dublin 2, Ireland
1385 Broadway, 5th Floor, New York, NY 10018, USA
E-mail: info@ospreypublishing.com
www.ospreypublishing.com
OSPREY is a trademark of Osprey Publishing Ltd

First published in Great Britain in 2024

ISBN: HB 978 1 4728 6364 5; eBook 978 1 4728 6366 9; ePDF 978 1 4728 6367 6; XML 978 1 4728 6368 3

24 25 26 27 28   10 9 8 7 6 5 4 3 2 1

Map by www.bounford.com
Index by Zoe Ross

Typeset by Deanta Global Publishing Services, Chennai, India
Printed and bound in Great Britain by CPI (Group) UK Ltd, Croydon CR0 4YY

Contents

BUCKINGHAM PALACE

It is now nearly fifty years since Julian Paget's *The Story of the Guards* was published, a period as demanding as any since Sir John Moore spoke those famous words at the Battle of Corunna in 1809: *'Those Must be The Guards'*. This latest book takes the story to the present day, covering events that are part of our national story. Throughout this time, the Household Division has been on active service at home and overseas, while also taking a leading role in all the great state and ceremonial occasions so central to our constitution. In all of these roles, embracing both challenge and change while never compromising their pursuit of excellence, the Guards have never wavered.

I am delighted that this book recognises the Guards' loyal and outstanding service to the Nation and the Crown. Her Majesty Queen Elizabeth, as Princess Elizabeth, became Colonel of the Grenadier Guards in 1942, and from 1952 Her Majesty was Colonel-in-Chief of the seven regiments of the Household Division. It is therefore entirely appropriate that this book should cover such a long period of a glorious reign.

Those Must Be The Guards is a tribute to the Guardsmen who have served and, in particular, to those who have lost their lives and suffered life-changing injuries. I hope this book will rekindle proud memories among former and current members of the Household Division and their families. It is an extraordinary story to inspire the next generation as it faces an uncertain and challenging future.

Anne

Preface

The Household Division of 1969 would seem a very different place to the officer or soldier of 2023: more regiments and battalions, a wholly different approach to training, more stations worldwide from which to operate, more activity which would be viewed today as superfluous and the threat from the Warsaw Pact as the pacing threat. The one thing, however, which both the Guardsman or Trooper of 1969 and the one of 2023 would recognise instantly would be the search for excellence, for being better than the rest and retaining the Division's reputation whether conducting state ceremonial duties or on operations; and in the 50 or so years covered by this book, there have been plenty of both.

Whether as individuals, companies, or squadrons, or as formed units, the Household Division has been in the centre of almost every operation the Army has conducted over the last 50 years. Northern Ireland, the Falklands, the Balkans, Iraq and Afghanistan to name some, but there are others of lesser profile in which Guardsmen have also served. In whichever way the Household Division has been involved, it has performed in an exemplary manner. From calm individual courage, unseen by most but a triumph of will to the individuals concerned, to the well-publicised acts of gallantry, the record of operational professionalism is an enviable one. Most of the operations have evolved over time. The Northern Ireland of 1969 was a world away from the violence of the later 1970s and 1980s; the heavy fighting of the 2006–12 period in Helmand was unimaginable during the initial foray to Kabul in 2001. Like all world-class organisations, however, the Household Division has adapted with the changing circumstances, often at great speed, to meet the new challenges. In each case, it has emerged changed and ready to deliver high-quality operational service, underpinned by professionalism and self-discipline.

The qualities which mark the soldiers of the Household Division out on operations are identical to those which ensure the same high standards when delivering state ceremonial and public duties. These duties, of the highest profile, are the way in which the country marks significant events: State Visits, the State Opening of Parliament, the Birthday Parade, funerals and coronations, as well as the daily guard mounting outside royal residences. The parades are an outward symbol of the respect and loyalty the Household Division owes to the monarch and the close relationship between the Sovereign and their household troops. All the parades are delivered with faultless precision. In this they have much in common with some other ceremonial troops in the world. The difference, however, is that these duties are conducted with dignity and gravitas, symbolic of a personal relationship to the Sovereign by those who also risk their lives on operations in pursuit of the same values, and that is something unique which has not changed for as long as the Household Division has existed.

The passing of over 50 years has seen many positives: improved living and working conditions for soldiers, better equipment, and improving professional standards with time. There have been the disappointments: the reduction in pure numbers, with consequences for those available for public duties, the end of the Guards Depot and, with it, some long-held customs. It is hard to know if our forebears over the centuries, looking over 50 years of change, would have reflected similarly with the same admission of positive and negative. It is likely that they would have done so, and pondered that the life of a soldier is not always easy, yet full of challenge and reward.

Through all these challenges, the one thing that has sustained Guardsmen has been those with whom they have shared both triumphs and setbacks. The Household Division is nothing without its people. Whether transiting the Division for a few years of service or as a career soldier, lucky or unlucky, this story is one of people with a common heritage as Guardsmen determined to deliver the highest standards in whatever situation they find themselves. At the heart of soldiering, in whatever form, lies the loyalty and cohesion of the group; for Guardsmen, the sense of loyalty is heightened by centuries of tradition, example, and excellence.

We have been extremely fortunate that in Simon Doughty and Paul de Zulueta we have two authors who, as well as serving in the Household Division personally, have drawn out the themes of operations and state ceremonial through a remarkably chequered half-century of soldiering. They have demonstrated how times have changed and yet the central characters in the story – the men and women of the Household Division – have remained true to a set of values that would be just as familiar to those of 1969 as they are today.

Major General Sir Christopher Ghika
KCVO CBE
Major General Commanding the Household Division
Horse Guards, July 2023

List of Illustrations and Maps

PLATE SECTION

32. Guards Independent Parachute Company Families' Day, July 1975. (Robert Corbett)
33. Dragon boat racing in Hong Kong, 1976. (© Regimental Headquarters Grenadier Guards)
34. Major General John Acland, CBE, and Richard Metaure in Rhodesia (now Zimbabwe), 1980. (Crown Copyright)
35. Members of ZANLA before voting in 1980. (Crown Copyright)
36. After the IRA bomb attack on The Queen's Life Guard on 20 July 1982. (PA Images/Alamy Stock Photo)
37. The Queen's Company at Windsor Castle on 19 April 1983. (Crown Copyright)
38. HM Queen Elizabeth during the Queen's Birthday Parade, 15 June 1985. (Crown Copyright)
39. HM Queen Elizabeth accompanied by the President of Poland, Lech Wałęsa, on 23 April 1991. (Crown Copyright)
40. The Queen's Birthday Parade, Windsor Castle, 13 June 2020. (Crown Copyright)
41. The funeral of HRH The Duke of Edinburgh. Windsor Castle, 17 April 2021. (Crown Copyright)
42. Meeting to discuss Operation *London Bridge*, 8 September 2022. (Crown Copyright)
43. The Garrison Sergeant Major and members of the Royal Family during HM Queen Elizabeth II's State Funeral, 19 September 2022. (Crown Copyright)
44. The bearer party from the Queen's Company carry the coffin of HM Queen Elizabeth. (Crown Copyright)
45. Moments before HM The King stepped onto the terrace of Buckingham Palace. (Crown Copyright)
46. 1st Battalion Grenadier Guards on Op *Granby*. (© Regimental Headquarters Grenadier Guards)
47. The Life Guards Command Team on Op *Granby*, 1991. (Crown Copyright)
48. Company Sergeant Major Ric Howick and Lance Corporal 'Lennie' Lenthall with Iraqi prisoners of war. (© Regimental Headquarters Coldstream Guards)
49. C Company, 1st Battalion Scots Guards, during Op *Granby*. (© Regimental Headquarters Scots Guards)

MAPS

Northern Ireland

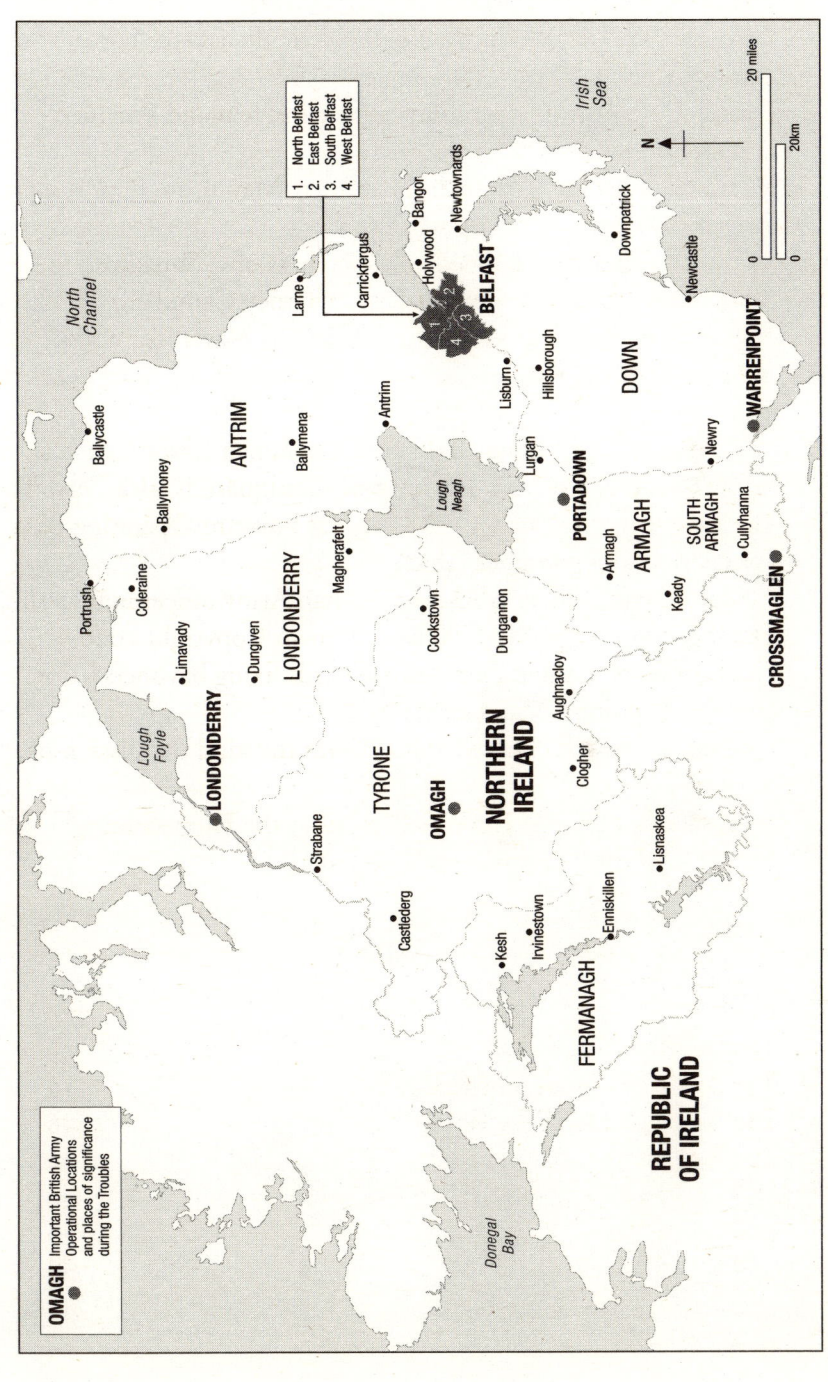

Irish Sea

North Channel

1. North Belfast
2. East Belfast
3. South Belfast
4. West Belfast

20 miles
20km

N

Bangor
Newtownards
Holywood
Downpatrick
Carrickfergus
Larne
BELFAST
Newcastle
WARRENPOINT
Lisburn
Hillsborough
DOWN
Antrim
Ballymena
Lough Neagh
Lurgan
Newry
PORTADOWN
ANTRIM
Ballycastle
Armagh
ARMAGH
SOUTH ARMAGH
Cullyhanna
Keady
CROSSMAGLEN
Ballymoney
Portrush
Coleraine
Dungiven
LONDONDERRY
Limavady
Magherafelt
Cookstown
Dungannon
Aughnacloy
LONDONDERRY
Strabane
TYRONE
OMAGH
NORTHERN IRELAND
Clogher
Lough Foyle
Lisnaskea
Castlederg
Kesh
Irvinestown
Enniskillen
FERMANAGH
REPUBLIC OF IRELAND
Donegal Bay

OMAGH Important British Army Operational Locations and places of significance during the Troubles

The Falkland Islands

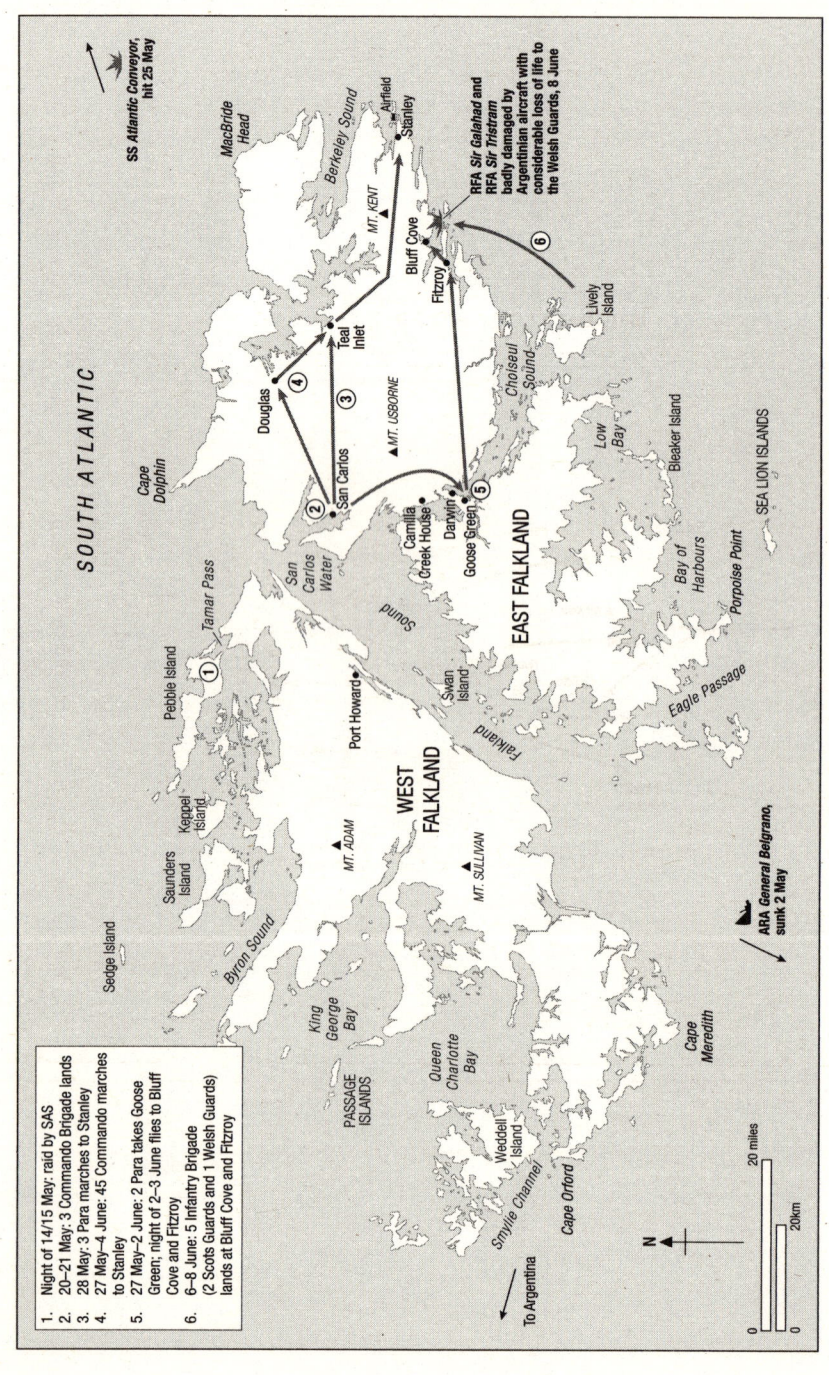

SOUTH ATLANTIC

SS *Atlantic Conveyor*, hit 25 May

MacBride Head

Berkeley Sound

Airfield

Stanley

▲MT. KENT

RFA *Sir Galahad* and RFA *Sir Tristram* badly damaged by Argentinian aircraft with considerable loss of life to the Welsh Guards, 8 June

Bluff Cove

Fitzroy

⑥

④ Teal Inlet

③

▲MT. USBORNE

Douglas

Choiseul Sound

Lively Island

② San Carlos

⑤

Camilla Creek House

Darwin

Goose Green

Low Bay

Breaker Island

Cape Dolphin

San Carlos Water

EAST FALKLAND

Bay of Harbours

Porpoise Point

SEA LION ISLANDS

Tamar Pass

Sound

Pebble Island

①

Falkland

Swan Island

Eagle Passage

Port Howard

WEST FALKLAND

Saunders Island

Keppel Island

▲MT. ADAM

▲MT. SULLIVAN

ARA *General Belgrano*, sunk 2 May

Sedge Island

Byron Sound

King George Bay

Queen Charlotte Bay

PASSAGE ISLANDS

Weddell Island

Cape Meredith

Smylie Channel

To Argentina

Cape Orford

N

20 miles

20km

0

0

1. Night of 14/15 May: raid by SAS
2. 20–21 May: 3 Commando Brigade lands
3. 28 May: 3 Para marches to Stanley
4. 27 May–4 June: 45 Commando marches to Stanley
5. 27 May–2 June: 2 Para takes Goose Green; night of 2–3 June flies to Bluff Cove and Fitzroy
6. 6–8 June: 5 Infantry Brigade (2 Scots Guards and 1 Welsh Guards) lands at Bluff Cove and Fitzroy

THE BATTLE OF MOUNT TUMBLEDOWN

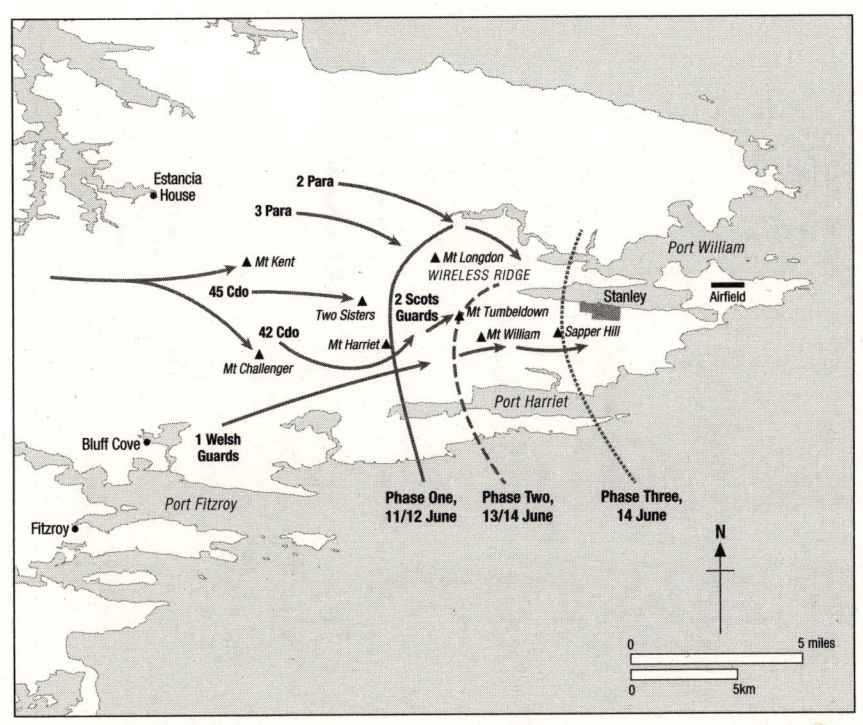

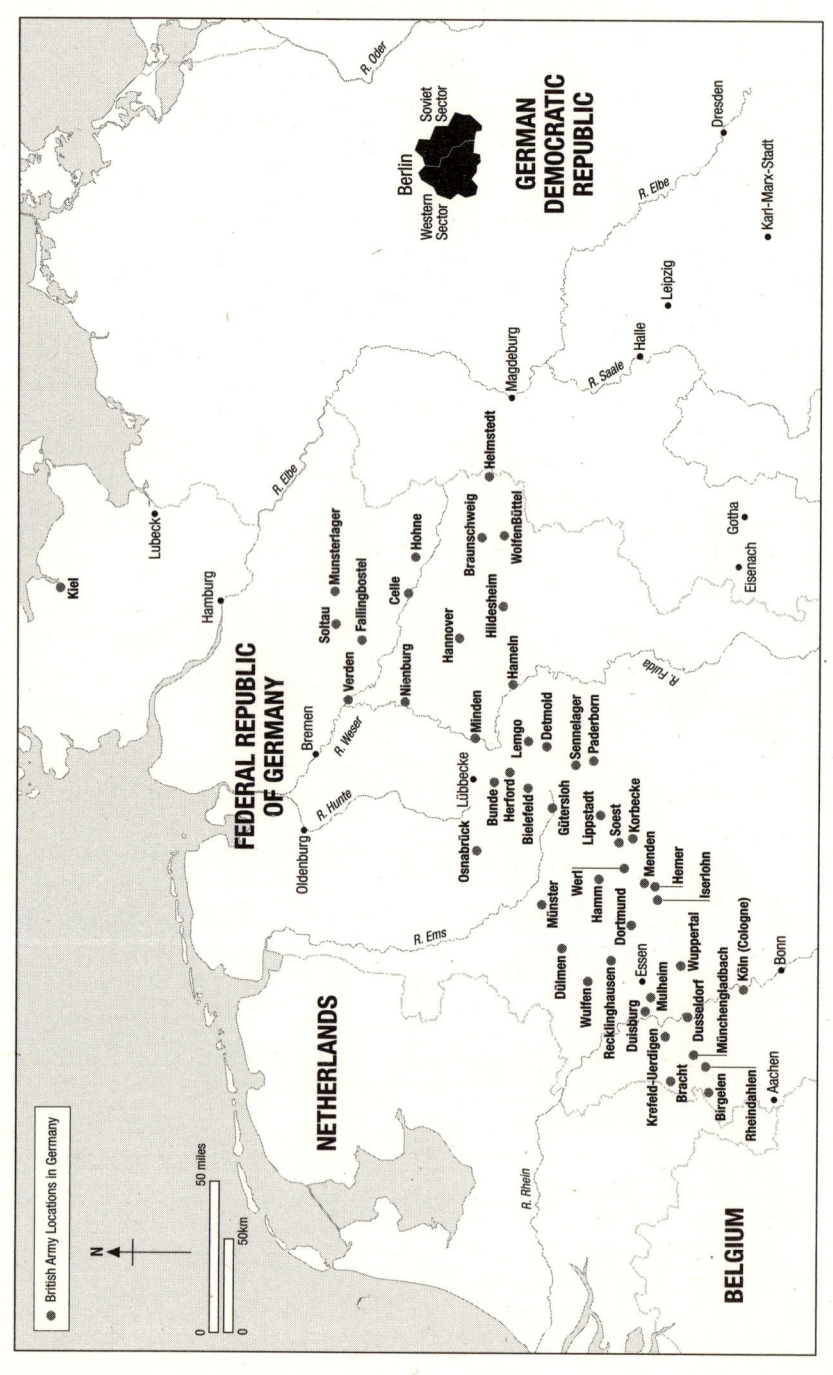

R. Oder

Berlin
Western Sector
Soviet Sector

GERMAN DEMOCRATIC REPUBLIC

Dresden

Karl-Marx-Stadt

R. Elbe

Leipzig

Halle

Gotha

R. Saale

Eisenach

Magdeburg

Helmstedt

R. Elbe

Lübeck

Kiel

Hamburg

Munsterlager
Soltau
Fallingbostel
Verden
Celle
Hohne
Braunschweig
WolfenBüttel
Hannover
Hildesheim
Hameln

FEDERAL REPUBLIC OF GERMANY

Nienburg

R. Weser

Bremen

R. Hunte

Minden
Lemgo
Detmold
Sennelager
Paderborn

R. Fulda

Oldenburg

Osnabrück
Lübbecke
Bunde
Herford
Bielefeld
Gütersloh
Lippstadt
Soest
Korbecke

Werl
Münster
Hamm
Dortmund
Menden
Hemer
Iserlohn

R. Ems

Dülmen
Wulfen
Recklinghausen
Duisburg
Essen
Mülheim
Wuppertal
Düsseldorf
Köln (Cologne)
Mönchengladbach
Krefeld-Verdigen
Bracht
Birgelen
Rheindahlen
Aachen

Bonn

NETHERLANDS

R. Rhein

BELGIUM

● British Army Locations in Germany

50 miles

50km

N

● British Army Locations in Germany

The Balkans

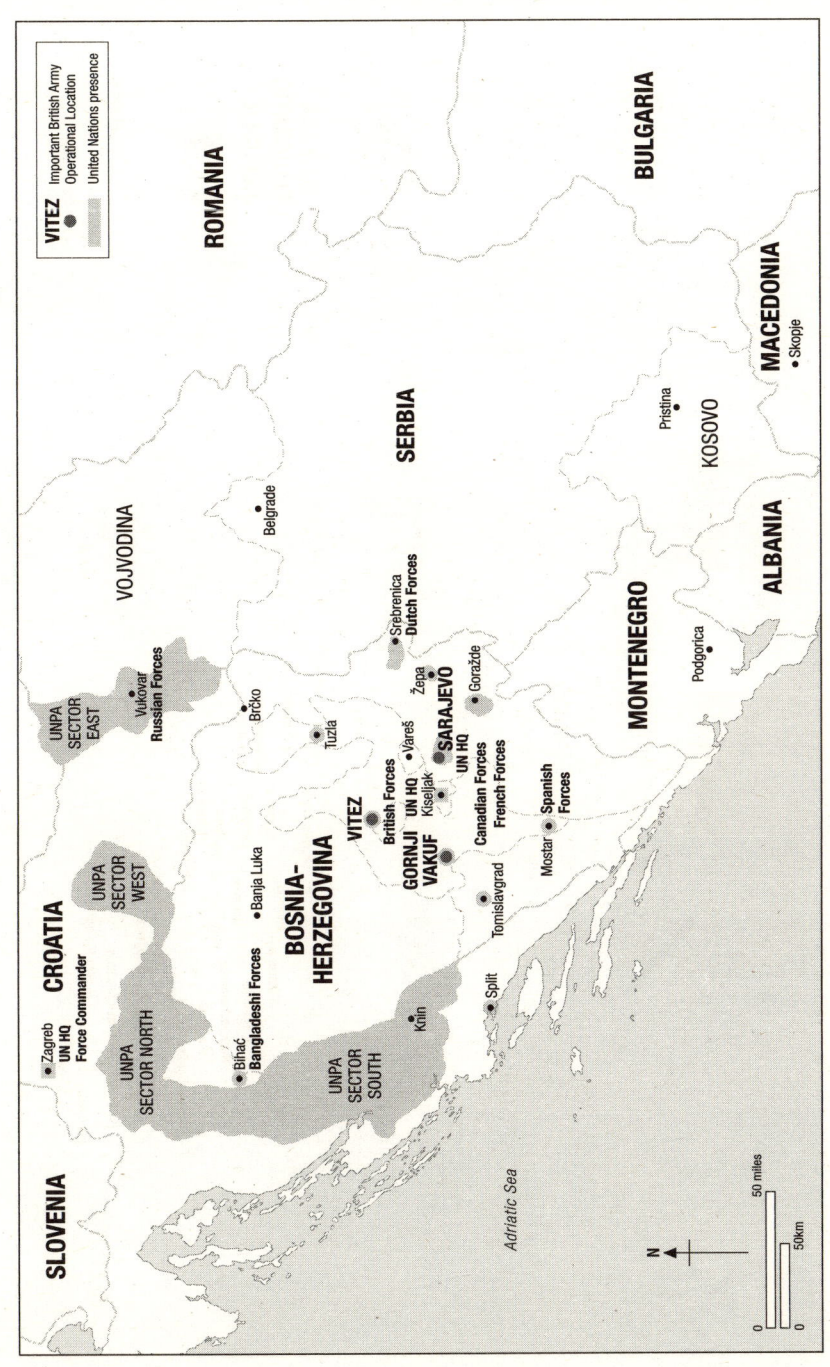

The First Gulf War

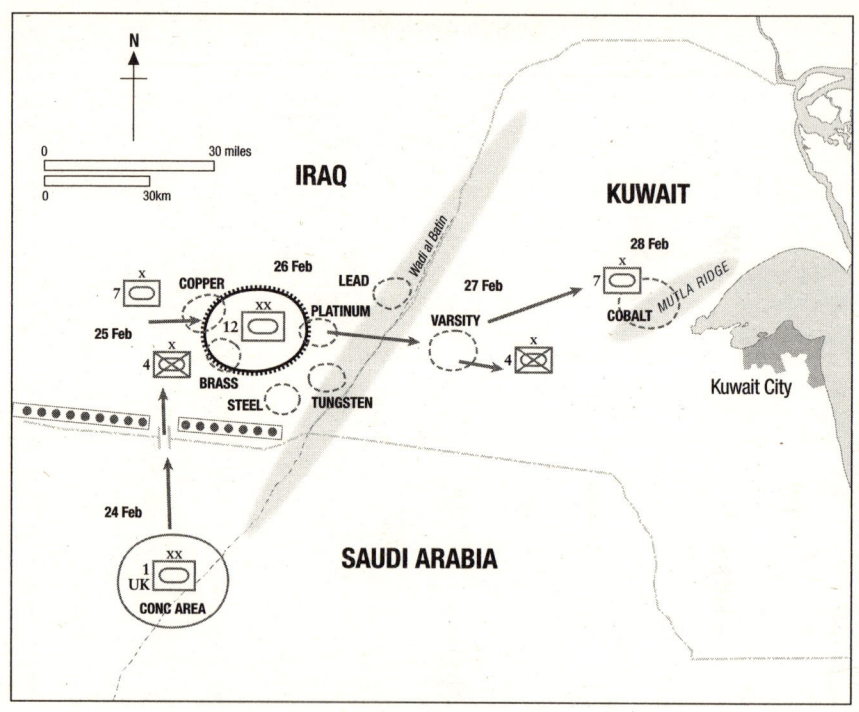

Basra, Iraq

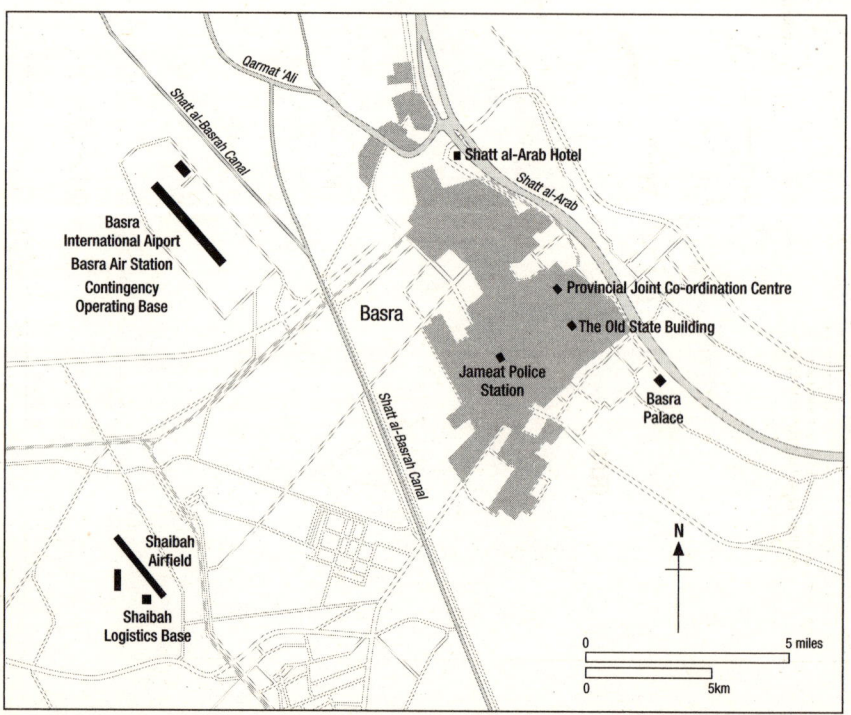

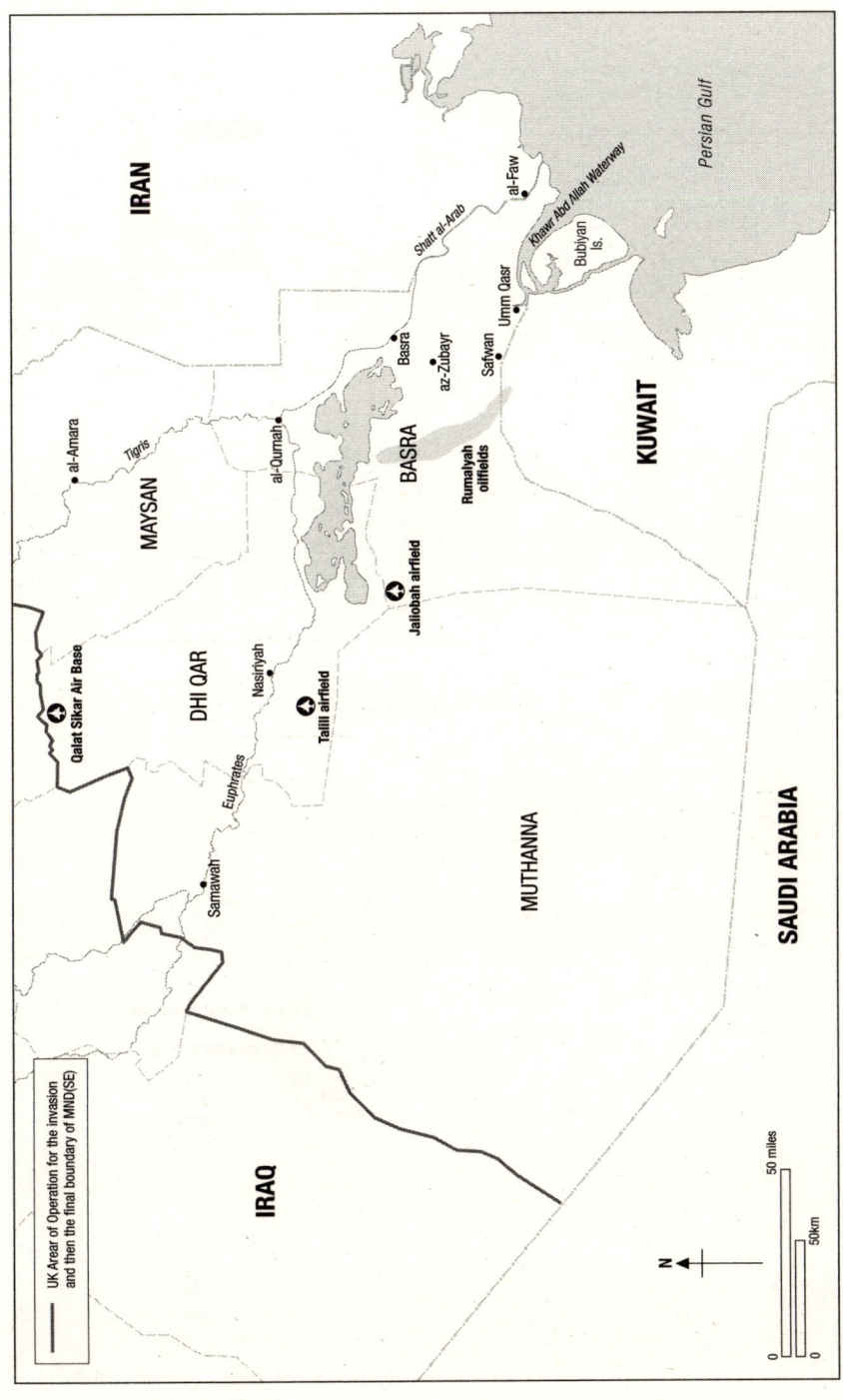

IRAN

Persian Gulf

Shatt al-Arab

al-Faw

Khawr Abd Allah Waterway

Bubiyan Is.

Basra

az-Zubayr

Safwan

Umm Qasr

BASRA

KUWAIT

al-Amara

Tigris

MAYSAN

al-Qurnah

Rumaylah oilfields

Jalibah airfield

DHI QAR

Nasiriyah

Qalat Sikar Air Base

Talili airfield

Euphrates

Samawah

MUTHANNA

SAUDI ARABIA

IRAQ

UK Arear of Operation for the invasion
and then the final boundary of MND(SE)

N

50 miles

50km

0

0

Helmand Province, Afghanistan

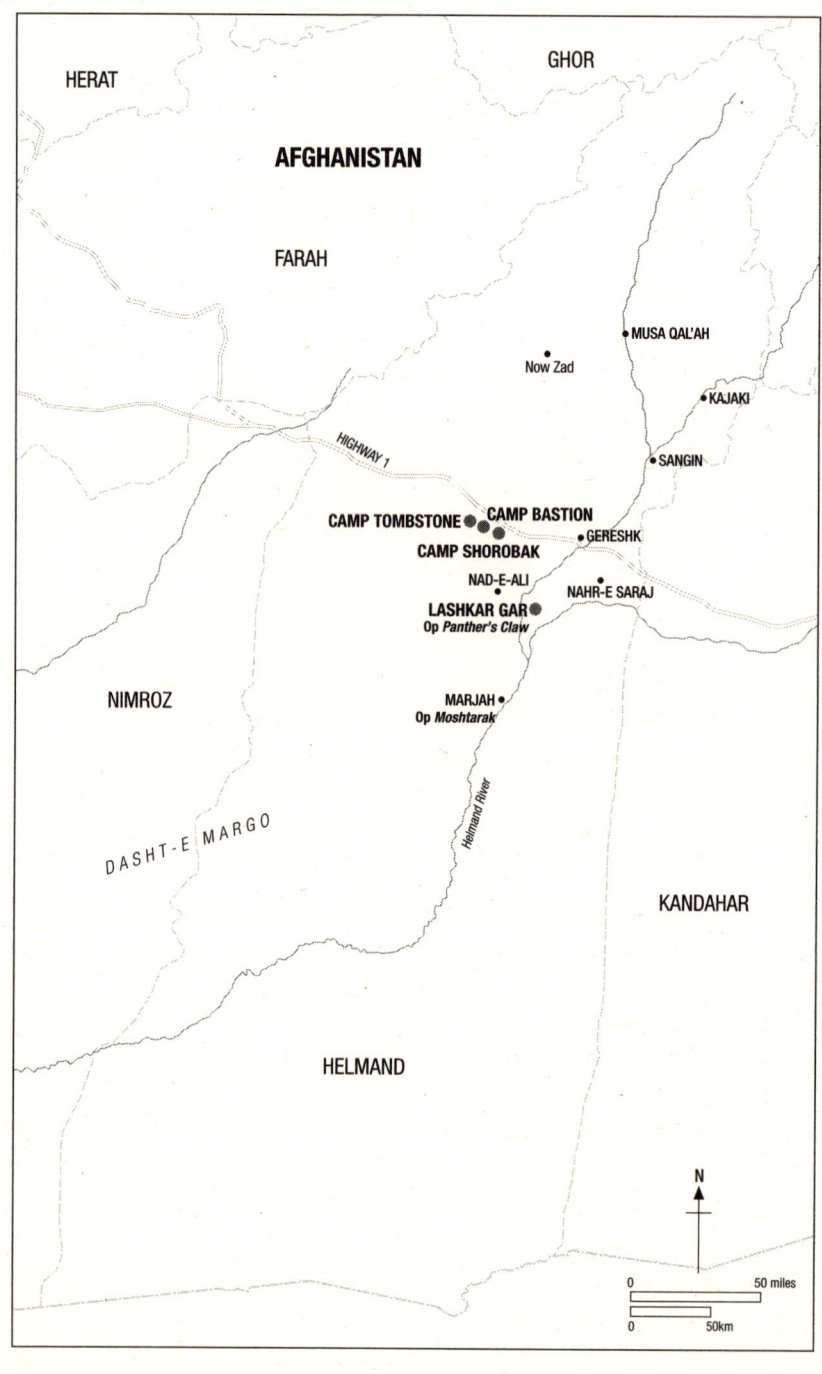

GHOR

HERAT

AFGHANISTAN

FARAH

• MUSA QAL'AH

Now Zad

• KAJAKI

HIGHWAY 1

• SANGIN

CAMP TOMBSTONE ●● **CAMP BASTION**

● GERESHK

CAMP SHOROBAK

NAD-E-ALI •

NAHR-E SARAJ

LASHKAR GAR ●
Op *Panther's Claw*

NIMROZ

MARJAH •
Op *Moshtarak*

Helmand River

DASHT-E MARGO

KANDAHAR

HELMAND

N

0   50 miles

0   50km

Prologue

L/Cpl James Ashworth VC was the bravest of soldiers and the best of men. His tenacity and selfless commitment served as an example to us all. He will continue to inspire soldiers in the Grenadier Guards for many years to come.

LIEUTENANT COLONEL JAMES BOWDER,
GRENADIER GUARDS

A little after first light on 13 June 2012, Lance Corporal James Ashworth of the 1st Battalion Grenadier Guards raced 300 yards with his fire team into the heart of a Taliban-dominated village in the Nahr-e-Saraj district of Helmand Province. A fierce firefight broke out. Ashworth took cover behind a wall and inched his way forward to within a few yards of an insurgent's position. He calmly took out a grenade, although enemy bullets were tearing up the ground around him. He did not shrink back. As he was about to throw his grenade, he was hit by enemy fire and died at the scene.

Just under a year later, on 22 May 2013, Her Majesty The Queen at a private audience in Buckingham Palace presented the Victoria Cross to James Ashworth's family. As Ashworth's mother, Kerry, steeled herself to receive her son's Victoria Cross from the Queen, she found it hard to suppress her emotions, a mixture of enormous pride and blind grief. As she was later to remark, "no words can describe how you feel when you are told that your son is the bravest of the brave."

There is no record of the Queen's sentiments on that day. But she must have felt a particular warmth towards the Ashworth family, not only for their loss, but also because their son had fought with a Regiment for whom she had an abiding affection. The Queen, as Princess Elizabeth, had been Colonel of the Grenadier Guards from 1942 until her accession to the throne. His Royal Highness The Prince Philip, Duke of Edinburgh succeeded as Colonel in 1975, a role he was to carry out with great style and spirit for 42 years.

Nelson Mandela said that courage was not the absence of fear, but the triumph over it. Courage, both physical and moral, is clothed in many forms, but Mandela's maxim holds true in the light of the heroic action that took place on 13 June 2012. By mid-June, the Grenadier Guards were six months into their nine-month operational tour.

Enemy snipers exert a powerful grip on a soldier's psyche. The task given on that fateful day to the Grenadier Guards' reconnaissance platoon was to destroy a Taliban sniper team operating at will from a small hamlet in the Nahr-e-Saraj district. It was a task that the platoon must have viewed with a mixture of anticipation and apprehension. The operation was planned for first light. Apart from the principle of surprise, the ferocious heat in Afghanistan, where the temperature rarely dropped below the mid-40s during the day, meant that heat exhaustion and, worse, heat stroke were an acute threat.

The planning for the operation lay largely in the hands of the platoon commander, Captain Michael Dobbin. Dobbin, a Cambridge graduate and an officer of great gifts, had the respect of everyone with whom he served. If the British Army's experience in Belfast, the Balkans, and Basra had dulled its warrior spirit, Afghanistan created a new generation of army officers, acutely aware of protecting innocent lives but unafraid of aggressive action.

If the sun was merciless, the topography was just as harsh. The fields of maize and poppy were abundant, but there was pitifully little cover apart from the walls of the outbuildings and the drainage ditches which crisscrossed the area. The hamlet which sheltered the Taliban sniper team was a maze of mud brick buildings, labyrinthine alleyways, and clusters of small clumps of bushes and trees with fleeting shade. The defender had the upper hand.

There is a striking photograph of Lance Corporal Ashworth taken a few months into the tour. It is striking because he is looking directly at his fellow Guardsman taking the photograph, revealing a natural calmness and composure; a soldier at ease with himself and his professionalism. There is no hint of bravado. Even though he is sitting down, his height,

6 feet 8 inches, and reassuring physical presence are plain to see. If you were ever to find yourself in a tight spot, he looks just the man you would want at your side.

Soldiering and the spirit of adventure were in Ashworth's blood. He had been brought up in Corby in Northamptonshire, a town famous for its steelworks, and infamous for their brutal closure in 1979 with the loss of 11,000 jobs. Despite the town's regeneration and renewal in the 1990s, prospects for meaningful work were still hard to come by. In 2006, aged 17, Ashworth, a natural sportsman with a commanding appearance, joined the British Army, following his father, Duane, who had served in the Grenadier Guards.

The formative period of Ashworth's career was spent in the Guards Parachute Platoon which is part of the 3rd Battalion The Parachute Regiment. The Household Division and the Parachute Regiment have long had a close affinity. The discipline and steadfastness of the Guards has always complemented the aggression and fighting spirit of the Parachute Regiment. The two other Victoria Crosses awarded during the campaign in Afghanistan were awarded to members of the Parachute Regiment. It was these qualities that Ashworth was to display with such fortitude on 13 June.

The action in which Ashworth was to win the Victoria Cross is recorded in the *London Gazette* dated 22 March 2013. The language used in the *Gazette* is peculiar to gallantry awards, slightly old-fashioned, where grenades are 'posted' rather than thrown. But feats of extraordinary courage are difficult to convey with mere words. There is no dignified way of describing the death of a soldier killed in action.

Major Chris Sargent, a Welsh Guards officer seconded to the Grenadiers, was only too familiar with the raw emotions that soldiers experience when they lose a brother in arms: "I could see the reactions in those with whom he fought and served when he died. Devastation, fear, loss, heartbreak." A friend and fellow Guardsman said, "He put his life on the line for us, we're all so proud that we knew him."

Captain Michael Dobbin, commander of the platoon, who was awarded the Military Cross for repeated courage throughout the operational tour, said about Ashworth, "His professionalism under pressure and ability to remain calm in what was their chaotic situation is testament to his character. Lance Corporal Ashworth was a pleasure to command and I will sorely miss his calming influence on the battlefield. Softly spoken, he stepped up to every task thrown in his direction."

After his death, Ashworth's body was taken to Camp Bastion and then repatriated to the United Kingdom. He was then buried in Shire Lodge Cemetery, Corby, with full military honours.

Recognition and affirmation of what we have done in our lives is a natural human need. Medals for gallantry, battle honours emblazoned on a regiment's Colours, a regiment's collective memory handed down through the ages are what sustains a soldier in battle.

It was to be nine months before Ashworth received the recognition his feat of courage deserved.

The Victoria Cross is awarded for "most conspicuous bravery or extreme devotion to duty in the face of the enemy". The word 'conspicuous' is critical because the recommendation for such an award is subject to rigorous scrutiny. There have to be at least three close witnesses to the action; the phrase "in the face of the enemy" has, therefore, a particular resonance.

It is the highest and most prestigious award of all British honours and outranks all other orders, medals, and decorations. It is the one decoration or honour that can never be forfeited.

On 16 March 2013, the Ministry of Defence announced the award. The citation was read out at the Grenadier Guards barracks in Aldershot. All those present, officer and Guardsman alike, as they listened to the citation's words felt just that little bit taller. They wondered at Ashworth's actions that day, thinking perhaps whether they too were made of the right stuff if the time came. Lieutenant Colonel James Bowder, Ashworth's commanding officer at the time, said, "I speak for the whole Regiment, the Regimental family and the broader Army, we could not be more proud that this brave, capable young man has received national recognition."

In Corby, the Ashworth family received the news with those emotions that are difficult to reconcile, pride and grief. The town of Corby, which had seen its fair share of suffering during its industrial decline, was visibly proud. A parade was held to honour a heroic son, the streets were thronged, parade standards were dipped, the national anthem was sung to the echo and a two-minute silence observed. A town square, the 'James Ashworth VC Square', was later named after him. His mother, Kerry, said, "He is part of history, he is part of regimental history, his memory will go on forever."

A life should leave deep tracks. The passage of Ashworth's life, a span cut short in its prime, left a lasting legacy. Not only to his own blood family but also to his regimental family and the six other regiments, '*Septem juncta in uno*' (seven joined in one) of the Household Division.

The Household Division, like any institution, has had to adapt to a world of accelerating change. When Sir Julian Paget wrote *The Story of the Guards* in 1975, not much had changed in the previous 25 years. And without change, complacency sets in. Tradition becomes hidebound. Tracks can quickly become ruts. The last 50 years have been witness to profound change, driven as much, if not more so, by social values as by technological advances. The Household Division has adapted because of its grounding in ceremonial and because of men like James Ashworth who showed the very best of the human spirit.

Three days after James Ashworth's heroic action in Helmand Province, spectators at Trooping the Colour witnessed discipline and duty of a different nature. Few present would have made the connection between Helmand and Horse Guards Parade. But what had taken place 4,500 miles away in the bare and arid plains of Afghanistan had its origins on Horse Guards Parade. The strength and steadfastness that James Ashworth had shown that fateful day had been born out of his experience in ceremonial.

Military parades tell you a lot about the character and conceit of a nation: the fervent cries of adoration for North Korea's Supreme Leader, Kim Jong-un; the Russian Victory Day Parade in Moscow's Red Square with 12,000 troops coinciding with military exercises on its borders; the National Day of the People's Republic of China in Tiananmen Square where President Xi spoke on 1 July 2021 of "cracking heads" of those who oppose China's vaunting ambitions.

True to the pragmatic and calm nature of the British, the only annual military parade in London is a celebration of the Sovereign's birthday by the Household Division. The Birthday Parade has always been a typically British mixture of immaculate ceremonial with a human and personal purpose. There are no displays of military might or the blur of dignitaries in passing cars; just the intimate and colourful spectacle of riding down the Mall at a walking pace to the gentle murmur of applause, and the March Past in front of the Sovereign to music that evokes patriotism but never nationalism.

Tradition matters. Shared memories and the collective unconscious of a regiment passed down over generations are what sustains a soldier in battle. In the 18th century, when the Colours of a regiment were carried in the confusion and mist of battle, soldiers needed a rallying point. But the Colours had to be known and recognised and, for that reason, they were marched, 'trooped' slowly along the ranks.

Every Birthday Parade is special to those who take part but 2012 had a unique significance. It was Her Majesty's Diamond Jubilee 1952–2012. Britain was hosting the 2012 Olympics. After close to five years of 'austerity' following the 2008 financial collapse, Britain had cause to celebrate. Tens of thousands of rain-soaked spectators watched with good humour on 3 June as the Queen's 1,000-boat Diamond Jubilee pageant meandered down the Thames. A celebration of the Queen's 60-year reign through music was held at Buckingham Palace on 4 June. The eyes of the world were on us and not without a hint of envy for a nation seemingly at ease with itself.

The 2012 Troop was to be the completion of these celebrations. Many of those officers, senior non-commissioned officers and Guardsmen taking part in the parade had fought in Afghanistan. In Afghanistan they had experienced and learnt to deal with anxiety and nerves in sometimes extreme circumstances. On Horse Guards Parade, their nerves would be of a different nature but no less palpable. The self-awareness they had developed on active service would see them stand resolute, flinching never a shade.

1st Battalion Coldstream Guards Trooped the Colour in 2012. Their motto *'Nulli secundus'* (Second to none) holds true. They are the oldest continuously serving regiment in the British Army. The parade commander that day was Lieutenant Colonel Robin Sergeant, Coldstream Guards, a talented officer who had made his reputation commanding his brigade's reconnaissance force in Helmand Province. The Major General Commanding the Household Division was George Norton, a Grenadier, who had served three tours of duty in Afghanistan as a staff officer and commander.

Ceremonial without music is merely drill. The music chosen for the 2012 Troop was rich and varied. George Norton, a Cambridge graduate who had also attended the German Military Academy in Hamburg, knew that well-chosen music was integral to mood, *esprit de corps*, and a sense of excitement. He had only just returned from Afghanistan where he had served as deputy commander of the Helmand Task Force. He had helped create close bonds between all the regiments of the Household Division and the United States Marine Corps (USMC).

The music George helped to choose that day was a reflection of those close bonds. The music combined the USMC March 'Semper Fidelis' by Sousa, 'Anchors Aweigh' by Charles Zimmerman and the USMC hymn. Richard Mills, a USMC general and George's senior commander in Helmand, was a guest at the parade. The Coldstream Guards, whose Colour was being trooped, marched past to a beautiful march, 'The Milanollo'. Perfect in time and tempo, it never fails to raise the spirits of all those who march to its beat.

If there was one man who had cause for nerves it was Second Lieutenant Hugo Codrington. Scion of a distinguished Coldstream family who had served Crown and country from Waterloo to the Second World War, Hugo had been selected to carry the Queen's Colour. Hugo, on hearing the news from his commanding officer, Lieutenant Colonel Robin Sergeant, that he had been selected, remembered feeling "thrilled but slightly terrified". The next four weeks were a blur as the Battalion's Regimental Sergeant Major and drill sergeants prepared him for the task. What little free time Hugo had was spent on building his physical strength. The Queen's Colour weighs close to 13 pounds. A strong gust of wind swirling round Horse Guards would see Hugo in full sail across the parade ground.

Hugo recalled just one moment of blind panic. Just before an important rehearsal, he noticed his sword was not in its scabbard. "How on earth could I have forgotten it?" he thought to himself. A friend and fellow ensign from the Grenadiers owned up to the prank minutes before the rehearsal began to the great amusement of all. Hugo's only concern on the day was a warning from the police that the activist group Fathers 4 Justice would try to pull off a stunt to derail the parade.

In typical British understatement, the weather forecast for the day was described as 'uncertain'. Nothing less than excellent is expected of the Queen's Birthday Parade but there are shades of excellence, and 2012 was considered one of the finest. Some would say it was a reflection of the importance attached to the Queen's Diamond Jubilee year; other, more wiser heads, would point to the operational experience in Afghanistan of those on parade.

There is an unbreakable link between the grounding in ceremonial and operational experience. If the Household Division's role was purely ceremonial, its members would become stage actors like the Swiss Guard outside the Vatican, or the Chinese Guard of Honour at the handover of Hong Kong, all over 6 feet and seemingly identical in jaw line and fixed gaze, not unlike the female dancers at Paris's Folies Bergère. Without active service, ceremonial becomes meaningless.

As Her Majesty's Guards marched down the Mall at the parade's end, Irish and Welsh and Scot, Coldstream and Grenadier, spectators would cheer Guardsmen from every corner of the Union. They would admire the twinkle, glitter, and flash of the Sovereign's Escort from The Life Guards and The Blues and Royals, the two most senior regiments of the British Army. Many of them had also recently returned from active service in Afghanistan in their operational role as a brigade reconnaissance regiment.

Less than 18 months later, Hugo Codrington deployed to Afghanistan with his Battalion. Hugo was later to remark that his role as the Ensign on the 2012 Queen's Birthday Parade had given him the self-confidence to face up to the rigours of active service. He had learnt to manage himself and the burden of pressure. He felt that he was now equipped to manage and lead others on operations. Operational service does not necessarily depend on ceremonial to make better soldiers, but ceremonial becomes meaningless if it is carried out by soldiers who have no other role.

Setting the Scene: The Guards, 1969–2023

The Guards are the litmus test for the Army – if we get it right the
Army gets it right.
MAJOR GENERAL SIR EVELYN WEBB-CARTER

The Household Division has a unique and dual role. Like all members of the Armed Forces, Guardsmen swear an allegiance to the Sovereign. The words are simple and direct: to "honestly and faithfully defend His Majesty, his heirs and successors in person, crown and dignity, against all enemies". Implicit in these words is a readiness to fight and, if necessary, kill while accepting the risk of being killed or seriously injured, in defence of the nation's interests. The liability for those who serve their nation in the name of the Sovereign is unlimited.

For Guardsmen, this allegiance is even more personal, and the clue is in the title 'Guardsman', granted by King George V shortly after the end of the First World War. Soldiers, on completion of their training to join the Household Division, are given the rank of Guardsman (or Trooper for the Household Cavalry); however, this is a title that, in a more general sense, applies to all members of the Household Division, regardless of their actual rank. This also goes some way to explaining why there is such a close bond across the seven regiments, to the extent that to serve with a sister regiment is regarded as a privilege rather than a penance. It is both the similarities and the differences between these regiments that make the Guards special.

Before the reign of Queen Victoria, the Guards, as the soldiers closest to the Sovereign, were responsible for the physical safety of the King and Queen, wherever they went. While this is no longer the case in all respects, on State occasions it is Guardsmen who are always closest to the Sovereign: riding next to a carriage, providing guards of honour, and lining the routes of a royal procession, always ready to 'close ranks' to protect the Sovereign if necessary. This special responsibility to 'guard the Sovereign' is not only an obligation and a duty, it is an honour. In recognition of this special relationship, the Sovereign is the Colonel-in-Chief of each of the seven regiments of the Household Division.

Her Majesty Queen Elizabeth II's long and close relationship with the Guards began formally in the Quadrangle at Windsor Castle when Princess Elizabeth, on 21 April 1942, her 16th birthday, inspected the Grenadier Guards on becoming their Colonel. From then on and throughout a long reign, the Guards served their Colonel-in-Chief loyally. In the most public and obvious way, this loyalty was demonstrated every year on the Queen's Birthday Parade, the State Opening of Parliament, State Visits, at the Garter Service, during the four Jubilees of Queen Elizabeth's reign, and at more regular events such as the guarding of royal palaces.

The precise moment when the Household Division carried out its last symbolic duty to Queen Elizabeth was during the closing moments of the committal service in St George's Chapel, Windsor, following the Queen's funeral in Westminster Abbey on 19 September 2022. The Queen's coffin was placed on the catafalque below the High Altar in St George's Chapel by the bearer party of Guardsmen from the Queen's Company, 1st Battalion Grenadier Guards. During the service that followed, Her Majesty's Crown, Orb, and Sceptre were removed from the coffin and handed to the Dean of Windsor who laid them on the High Altar. The Regimental Lieutenant Colonel of the Grenadier Guards then stepped forward to hand the Camp Colour of the Queen's Company, a small and simple rectangular cloth flag, to the King, who placed it on the coffin, where it will remain in perpetuity. The Lord Chamberlain then ceremoniously broke his wand of office, signifying the end of his service to the Queen, laying the wand upon the Camp Colour. Moments later, as the Dean of Windsor read the final prayers, the Queen's coffin descended into the private vault below the chapel.

The Household Division had fulfilled its last and solemn duty to its former Colonel-in-Chief, Her Majesty Queen Elizabeth II.

The Guards' loyalty to the new Sovereign was clear from the day of the accession, and began formally in 1975 when Prince Charles, as Prince of Wales, became Colonel of the Welsh Guards. The Household Division's loyalty to King Charles was most obviously demonstrated during the Coronation on 6 May 2023, when the Guards played a prominent part in the procession to and from Westminster Abbey, and during the service itself. Six weeks later, on 17 June, the Household Division was again centre stage, conducting the first King's Birthday Parade since 1952.

However, the Guards' role is not solely as ceremonial or household troops. Their existence and credibility lie in their dual role as soldiers, capable of taking on the many tasks expected of a modern army. The key to this is that while being ceremonial troops is a special privilege, it is not a displacement activity for the other roles that soldiers fulfil. The agility required to step from the sands of Iraq onto Horse Guards Parade has never been more important. Gone are the days when the Foot Guards spent months if not years exclusively on the 'blue line' conducting ceremonial duties, and so the time available to prepare for large state events is much reduced.

Back in 1969, where this book begins as a sequel to *The Story of the Guards* by Julian Paget, there was almost certainly more time, more people and, for a short while, less going on. However, this was just a transitory moment in the long history of the Guards, soon to change. Excluding 2023 up to the point of this book going to print, 1968 and 2016 are the only two years since the Second World War when a British soldier has not been killed on operations.

This is not to suggest that Guardsmen serving in 1969 or before had enjoyed an easy or quiet time, although during National Service (which ended in 1963) it had sometimes been possible to spend 18 months on public duties or sitting in a barracks in West Germany. Bamber Gascogne, a National Serviceman who served in the Grenadiers in the 1950s, interviewed on *Desert Island Discs* in 1987, recalled "the first six months being bashed around on the Square" as being "pretty unpleasant"; followed by "an extraordinary six months dancing with debs in London, and guarding the Queen at Buckingham Palace on my off moments"; then a posting to Berlin "which was extremely interesting"; followed by Headquarters 4th Guards Brigade, "which was perfect for weekends in Paris"!

The post-war period had been an era of small campaigns and insurgencies, a consequence of Britain's retreat from the days of empire. More importantly, it was the Cold War that remained the main preoccupation for the British Army until the early 1990s, a huge commitment in the name of deterrence, and one in which the Household Division played an important role. For the later generation of Guardsmen who all joined after 1990, the Cold War is not even a distant memory; it is part of history, and obscured by all that has happened in the last 30 years. For those Guardsmen who were born in the closing decade of the 20th century, many will now have completed their careers and left the Army.

In 1969, the senior Guardsmen of staff and general rank, as well as some of the commanding officers, senior majors, quartermasters, and long-service warrant officers, had joined the Army before or during the Second World War. The 'War' defined most of the tactics of the British Army in 1969 and for several decades thereafter, adapted for the NATO Central Front as part of the British Army of the Rhine. When, in the early 1980s, there was a re-think about NATO strategy in West Germany, this was heavily influenced by the tactics of the Second World War.

The Guardsmen joining the Army in 1969 and the early 1970s were the 'baby boomers', a generation forming an unusually large percentage of the population, growing up in a period of increasing affluence, free medical care, social security, improvements in education, relatively low inflation, high employment, and better standards of living. Harold Macmillan, Prime Minister in the late 1950s and early 1960s (a former Grenadier and veteran of the First World War), claimed in 1957 that Britain "had never had it so good", and if that's the case, it would not last. By the mid-1970s, unemployment was on the increase, and by 1975 there was a wage-price spiral resulting in an all-time high of 25 per cent inflation. It was a good period for recruiting, but not for military pay, nor for defence spending, which was to see a steady decline over the decades that followed.

If the late 1960s and 1970s were a period of change in the wider society, a consumer age in which the 'pop culture' was centre stage, it is unlikely that there was anything quite as dramatic happening in the Army or the Guards. Traditionally, the Armed Forces are rarely if ever in the vanguard of social trends, and while the Guards certainly led the way as soldiers, setting high standards both on ceremonial duties and operations, coming to terms with social change was lower on the agenda. Notwithstanding, there have been significant changes over the last half-century, although fundamentally the Household Division has remained the same in its purpose and composition, just smaller now than it was then.

In 1969 the Household Cavalry had two service regiments, The Life Guards and The Royal Horse Guards (The Blues); the latter amalgamated with the 1st Royal Dragoons in March 1969 to form The Blues and Royals. In London the Household Cavalry Mounted Regiment, a composite regiment of both Life Guards and Blues, carried out ceremonial duties. For the Foot Guards, there was the 1st and 2nd Battalions of the Grenadier, Coldstream, and Scots Guards; the 1st Battalion Irish Guards, and the 1st Battalion Welsh Guards. There was also Headquarters 4th Guards Brigade in Germany, in which the commander and staff were Guardsmen with, routinely, two Guards battalions under command; the Guards Depot at Pirbright, training Adult Recruits and Junior Guardsmen; the 1st Guards Independent Parachute Company in Aldershot, the 'Pathfinders'; G Squadron 22nd Special Air Service Regiment in Hereford; and the Guards Company, Infantry Junior Leaders' Regiment in Oswestry.

The Royal Military Academy Sandhurst and the Officers' Cadet School Mons (which merged with Sandhurst in 1972) trained the next generation of officers for the entire Army. Although these establishments have never been 'under command' of the Household Division (a suggestion that would amuse non-Guardsmen), there can be no doubt that, in almost every functional way, they were run by the Guards. At Sandhurst, the Academy Adjutant, College Adjutants, the Academy Sergeant Major, the College Sergeant Majors, and the majority of platoon colour sergeants were Guardsmen and, over half a century on, there is still a strong Guards presence. In 1969, and in the years that preceded and followed, young officer cadets learned drill from a Guards drill instructor who was also an important influence on them throughout their commissioning course. Although in the intervening years Sandhurst has become more cosmopolitan in its selection of training staff, the Guards still predominate in the important task of training young officer cadets. Ask any officer or former officer who their Sandhurst colour sergeant was; the likelihood is that he was a Guardsman, and his name will not have been forgotten.

In 1969, the seven regiments were based in England (London, Windsor, Caterham, Pirbright, and Tidworth) and West Germany (Münster), with one battalion on an unaccompanied nine-month posting to Sharjah (now part of the United Arab Emirates). This was to be the pattern for much of the next 45 years. Guards regiments garrisoned both at home and overseas, in an era of accompanied service with service families 'following the flag'; together with an increasing pace of unaccompanied four- and later six-month operational tours to Northern Ireland, the Balkans, Iraq, Afghanistan, and elsewhere, including United Nations peacekeeping tours in Cyprus (sometimes two-year accompanied tours). The only significant change, other than one of scale, is that a reserve battalion, the London Guards, is now based in London.

By the end of the first decade of the 21st century, the British Army had become a predominately expeditionary army, with units living at home and deploying, without their families, worldwide, sometimes for extended periods. 1st Battalion Scots Guards was the last Household Division regiment to serve overseas on an accompanied tour: the Battalion returned from Münster, Germany to Catterick in the summer of 2008, while concurrently on an operational tour in Iraq. From then on, Guards regiments continued to deploy overseas on operations and exercises, and in many forms, but never again with their families. The nature of these deployments has also evolved and changed in both shape and purpose, providing multiple opportunities for sub-units, platoons, and small teams to be despatched on new and challenging missions.

In the period covered in this book, the first few months of 1969 were the last moments of relative calm. All changed in August of that year when, at short notice, B Squadron The Life Guards and 1st Battalion Grenadier Guards deployed onto the streets of Belfast and Londonderry to restore order and stop the sectarian fighting that the police were no longer capable of preventing. From then on, until 2007, the Household Division conducted many emergency tours, and sometimes longer residential tours in Northern Ireland as part of Operation (Op) *Banner*. Just as Iraq and Afghanistan became the main operational commitment in the early 2000s, for the 'baby boomers' who joined in the 1960s and 1970s, it was Northern Ireland, time and again, that dominated their operational lives.

In April 1982, Argentina invaded the Falklands Islands. 2nd Battalion Scots Guards and 1st Battalion Welsh Guards, with a troop of The Blues and Royals, were soon on the long sea-journey south as part of the Task Force. For a while, there was a chance that war would be averted, but in the event, the Guardsmen marched with their heavy loads, dug trenches, 'closed with the enemy', and fought with rifle and bayonet in a way that would have been familiar to their forefathers.

In the autumn of 1990, not long after the fall of the Berlin Wall, the British Army began deploying to Saudi Arabia following the Iraqi invasion of Kuwait in August that year. The Household Division was well represented but not in the time-honoured way that units march off to war. Op *Granby* proved to be something of a 'numbers game' from the outset, with an unprecedented level of political control, heralding a new 'task-orientated' approach for conducting military campaigns that appeared to undermine the well-established regimental structures that had worked well in the past. In the years that followed, attempting to explain the hybrid structure of a regimental 'battle group' to a veteran of former wars, or indeed a commanding officer from the more recent past, was never easy. Some senior Army commanders even questioned the value of the 'regimental system', a notion that made little sense to Guardsmen, both past and present.

The British government announced its *Options for Change* defence review in July 1990 following the end of the Cold War. As part of the reductions that followed, the Household Cavalry formed a 'union' of its two service regiments, The Life Guards and The Blues and Royals (an amalgamation that retained regimental identities); and the 2nd Battalions of the Grenadier, Coldstream, and Scots Guards went into suspended animation, with each regiment forming an incremental company based in London. Even more worrying at the time was the decision to close the Guards Depot, since this was the place where all Guardsmen joined the Army and where they were trained, by Guardsmen. There were later reductions to the size of regimental bands and greater threats that were somehow resisted, prompting Max

Hastings to claim in 2018 that "nobody dares to axe a Foot Guards battalion, because the Guards Division remains a powerful trades union", a suggestion that many would reject since Guardsmen have never been complacent about their continuing existence.

The British Army's long commitment to Bosnia began in 1992, with 1st Battalion Coldstream Guards deploying the following year, the first of many Guards regiments to serve there. Op *Grapple* and the NATO-led peace enforcement operations in the Balkans were very different from the benign peacekeeping that many Guardsmen had experienced latterly in Cyprus. This was a real conflict, in which British troops were placed at the centre of a maelstrom, a human tragedy, with genocide on a shocking scale, and strict 'rules of engagement' that created new legal and moral challenges for commanders and soldiers alike.

In 2003, Britain joined a US-led coalition to invade Iraq, dismantle its military arsenal, and, in effect, remove Saddam Hussein's regime. The Guards were part of Op *Telic* from the beginning and continued to be involved in what became one of the longest operational commitments of the past century. Twenty years on, there are still British Army units serving in Iraq in supporting and training roles. To take just one example: the Queen's Company 1st Battalion Grenadier Guards was on Operation *Shader* in Iraq when its Company Commander, Her Majesty Queen Elizabeth II, died on 8 September 2022. Within days members of the company were back in London training for the funeral on 19 September, accompanying and bearing the Queen's coffin from Westminster Abbey to its last resting place in St George's Chapel, Windsor. Within just a few days, the Queen's Company was back in the desert.

The international commitment in Afghanistan began following 9/11 (the attack of the World Trade Center in New York on 11 September 2001); however, it was not until 2006 that the British commitment increased significantly as part of Op *Herrick*, principally in Helmand Province. Unexpectedly, and certainly unplanned, this coincided with continuing counter-insurgency operations in Iraq, leading to an intensive period of deployments. For the next decade, Afghanistan was centre stage for the Household Division, but never at the exclusion of all else. Combat operations ceased in 2014, and in 2018 the Guards left Afghanistan for the final time, when the Welsh Guards completed their tour on Op *Toral*, training the Afghan Army and providing protection to NATO advisers in Kabul.

Northern Ireland, the Falklands, Iraq, the Balkans, and Afghanistan. These were the operational highlights of the Household Division over the last 54 years; however, they were not neatly sequential, with one following the next. There were occasions when regiments were committed to more than one operation at a time; difficult to believe but true. For each operational deployment there is a lead time of intensive training; an overseas commitment is never just a six-month tour with some leave at the end – it is much more. There is also a human cost; many Guardsmen were killed and more were injured during these operations.

Every army trains for war even when it is not sure of the precise threat or requirement. During the Cold War, it was a case of training for 'the' war, but for the last 30 years military training has become multifarious, and consequently more demanding. Exercises alone, both small and large, would fill any diary. So too would the commitment to state ceremonial and public duties, together with the training required to maintain the excellence that everyone expects.

However, much else was going on throughout this last half-century, with the Household Division actively involved in many roles and tasks in support of the UK's interests, both at home and overseas. Here are just a few examples of activities that probably hover in the margins of history but nevertheless deserve to be remembered.

Guardsmen drove Green Goddess fire engines and fought fires during national fire service strikes in 1977–78 and 2002. For example, from November 1977, over a two-month period that ended in January 1978, 450 Guardsmen from the Guards Depot, many of them Adult Recruits from Caterham Company, acted as firemen, climbed ladders, grappled with massive water hoses, and helped to save people from blazing fires. The London operation was run by Headquarters London District, and many officers and soldiers from across the Household Division were involved, from manning control centres to fighting fires. Not surprisingly, the idea of Guardsmen as firemen provided much amusing 'copy' for newspaper cartoonists. In one cartoon by JAK of the *Daily Express*, an officer in red tunic and smouldering bearskin is seen standing nervously at the entrance to a Guards officers' mess: "*Well Fanshawe! What's your excuse this time?*" By the end of the strike, the military in London had attended to over 2,500 fires, some small and some of considerable size and ferocity. On one occasion, 19 Green Goddesses were deployed to a single incident, with the fire burning for several days.

In 1989–90, Guardsmen drove and manned ambulances during a protracted national ambulance strike, with London becoming the focus for the strike action. During its six-month duration, over 62,000 tasks were completed with the support of personnel from London District, some 30 per cent of them Guardsmen and musicians. The press doubted the military's ability to cope with being ambulance drivers and medics. One 'news' outlet even set up an observation post in a multi-storey block overlooking Chelsea Barracks to find out whether Guardsmen were up to it; they were proved wrong. While the challenges were of course starkly different to those for which regimental medics are trained, they managed well: carrying elderly patients from high-rise buildings where the lifts did not work; attending to highly infectious patients; or, more happily, delivering babies.

During the Covid-19 pandemic of 2020–21, Headquarters London District set up a Joint Military Command Headquarters in London, and individual units were tasked to run Covid-19 testing centres in support of the government's efforts to minimise infection rates and reduce deaths and illness. It was an extraordinary period, engendering much fear and uncertainty amongst the population, like a terrorist campaign where the enemy is elusive, unpredictable, and deadly. Soldiers do not join the Army to fight pandemics, but their skills proved to be well matched to all the uncertainties that Covid-19 created. Well used to being concerned about their own safety and that of their comrades on operations, soldiers were now worrying about their parents and elderly grandparents. *Stay Home, Protect the NHS, Save Lives* was the guidance to follow; however, for the emergency services, including the Army, staying at home was rarely an option.

Sometime during the first lockdown in the spring of 2020, a letter from a member of the public was received at Horse Guards, and the words speak for themselves:

> Many of the civilian staff at the testing centre clearly did not want to be there. By contrast, a group of soldiers wearing Household Division flashes were friendly, encouraging, and polite, even empathetic to the people receiving the intrusive test. A credit to the Guards and to the Army. It is really encouraging to know that our people are performing so well in their duties and making the ordeal easier for us all.

The Guards' deployments during the Covid-19 pandemic were sometimes many miles from London. In September 2020, No 1 Company 1st

Battalion Irish Guards, commanded by Major Charlie Sprake, recently returned from South Sudan, were conducting a 'green skills training exercise' back home when rumours circulated of a new government initiative in the fight against Covid-19: 'whole city testing', codenamed Op *Moonshot*. No 1 Company, among other units, was sent at short notice for a ten-day deployment to Liverpool that soon extended to nearly nine weeks. Living in a Pontins holiday camp, with few facilities, and no mobile phone coverage (it had been better in South Sudan), this was to be far from a holiday. The 'Micks' focused on the job: conducting lateral flow tests in a population of 100,000. The stakes were high; much was resting on the success of this initiative, in a period before vaccines had appeared on the horizon. The Micks lived in a lockdown bubble, deploying in pairs to test sites around the city, carrying their picnic 'haverbag' to sustain them 'in the front line'. Soldiers were now 'service providers', calming the fears of the locals and answering nervous questions about their role. Were they, for example, conducting 'DNA testing for the government'? Their approach was 'no nonsense' but equally "empathetic, sympathetic, understanding, and gracious", employing less-familiar soldierly skills: probing with a swab up people's noses and down their throats. And they did it extremely well, interacting with their 'target' in an entirely different way to the one they might have expected when they joined the Army.

———

Are Guardsmen different now, in 2023, than they were during the decades that have passed since 1969? Remarkably, there have been four defined generations since the 'baby boomers' who joined the Army in the 1960s and 1970s, and the Millennials who joined around the turn of the 21st century have now left or are well into their military careers. What has not changed is that the Guardsmen of today have fundamentally the same human qualities, the same high standards, as they have always done. The Army is certainly a more complex and diverse institution than it was 50 years ago and is no longer immune from the social change that surrounds it. The digital age and the multiple and often hidden threats that nations and their armies face have led to changes that our forefathers might have difficulties grasping. However, it is the similarities that unite generations rather than the differences that divide; and this will always be the case in an institution that has traditions, standards, and a collective memory that takes pride in past achievements while focusing on the next challenge and never accepting anything less than excellence. Every generation can talk about falling standards ("It wasn't like that in my time") but their views and prejudices do not always stand up to close scrutiny.

Warrant Officer (Class One) Ray Huggins, the Academy Sergeant Major at Sandhurst in the 1970s, a Grenadier who joined in 1945, and one of the most distinguished Guardsmen of his generation, always addressed the officer cadets on the evening before their commissioning parade, and not just those joining the Guards. He would talk about his first platoon commander, Lord Erskine, who carried a gold-nibbed fountain pen and leather-bound notebook in which he recorded information about his Guardsmen: details about their families, their interests, their aspirations, their prospects. He admired Lord Erskine enormously, a wartime soldier, an officer and a gentleman who had all the human qualities that Ray Huggins wished his officer cadets to emulate. When Ray Huggins spoke to the cadets in March 1976, he was clear about what he expected of these soon to be commissioned officers: "You are leaders of men," he said, and "you have now entered the top five per cent of the nation", rather alarming words for his young audience. And then some advice on appropriate dress: "I would not wear jeans to do my gardening in, so I never expect to see any of you gentlemen wearing them, ever." Ray Huggins was also very clear about the tribal nature of the Army. There were clearly young officer cadets in the room that day that would not have been suitable candidates for the Grenadier Guards, or indeed any other Household Division regiment, although they had all earned their commissions. Indeed, Ray Huggins made that point very clear in his speech, and by no way of criticism. To be a Guards officer, they had to be of a certain type, recruited from a narrow and close-knit strata of society, and in those days there seemed no reason for this to change because it worked.

The most important aspects of being an 'officer and a gentleman' apply equally wherever an individual serves, but there are other social factors which help to determine who joins which regiment. In 1969, all Guards officers who joined the Army as officer cadets were privately educated, mostly in a boarding school, and while this statistic has hardly changed in the last half a century, regiments now take a broader view about their recruiting. One important change, however, is that many more officer cadets have now been to university than those of 50 years ago. Family connections remain an important source of recruiting; a study of surnames in back-copies of regimental magazines will reveal familiar and reassuring repetitions; like the old school roster, names just keep reappearing as each generation gives way to the next. However, they do not guarantee a hallowed place in the Regiment; potential and quality are equally important.

In any event, places for officers in the Household Division are always at a premium, and it is not only the officers who take a view about whom they want in their regiments. So too do the warrant officers and the other ranks, and sometimes their standards and judgements are more demanding and unforgiving than the officers' perspective. It is a brand of elitism that works, at every level.

Another aspect that has changed over the past 50 years is that there are now more opportunities for commissioning from the ranks. These have always existed, with quartermaster and late entry commissions; however, now these officers, with their wealth of experience and talent, can apply for many more mainstream appointments, in competition with that other tribe, the officers who join from Sandhurst in their early 20s.

Equally important in the Household Division is the tight-knit sense of being part of an extended family which transcends all social classes. It was this that helped the Welsh Guards to endure the shocking and long-term effects of the tragedy that took place on the *Sir Galahad* on 8 June 1982, during the Falklands War, when 32 Welsh Guardsmen died and many more were injured with severe burns, including Simon Weston, who became well known in the years that followed for his charity work.

Was the Household Division ethnically diverse in 1969 or keen to recruit from ethnic minorities? The prejudices over 50 years ago existed not just in the Guards and the Army, but across society, attitudes which are now wholly unacceptable. For the Armed Services, there was nothing new here, however shocking this might seem today. When the National Service Act was passed in 1949, it was decided, unofficially, not to conscript black and Asian British men, and consequently, only a small number served in the ranks during the 12 years of National Service, and there were no officers at all.

Attitudes began to shift in the 1970s, with some parts of the Army recruiting significant numbers from the ethnic minorities, while elsewhere, and particularly in the Household Division and the Scottish regiments, there continued to be resistance to recruiting from these groups. Indeed, there were subtle and sometimes not so subtle ways of avoiding the recruiting of any ethnic minorities at all. The prejudice existed not just among some of the officers, but also among the other ranks. The general reasoning was based on the misguided belief that ceremonial troops had to be universally white, ignoring the reality that Britain by the 1970s had become a multi-racial country. Increasingly, the Guards were out of step with the rest of the Army, while also becoming a high-profile target for campaigners.

The newspapers frequently reported on an institutional bias in the Guards that appeared to make it impossible for any young man from an ethnic background to apply and have any prospect of getting through the training. In 1986, the Prince of Wales (now King Charles III) expressed serious concern about this policy. In the same year, Richard Stokes, a black teenager who had been adopted by a white couple, joined the Grenadier Guards because his father had seen Prince Charles's comments being reported at the time and encouraged his son, who had always been keen on an Army career. But Prince Charles's "moral leadership" (Richard Stokes's words) in raising the issue would not, at a stroke, sweep away years of deeply set prejudices that had existed at every level. There was also an element of institutional inertia from the Ministry of Defence, who refused on several occasions to produce statistics on ethnic recruiting for a House of Commons Select Committee.

Guardsman Stokes was certainly bullied and given an extremely unpleasant time at the Guards Depot. He somehow endured it, and in 1988 became the first black Guardsman to be on guard at Buckingham Palace. He left the Army two years later, ostensibly because of racist bullying, and was certainly not the only Guardsman to be subjected to this kind of treatment. 'Why the Guards give blacks their marching orders' was the title of an article that appeared in the *Sunday Telegraph* in early 1990. Written by a former Welsh Guards officer, Marcus Scriven, the article seeks to explain rather than merely point the finger: "The Guards have no monopoly on bigotry. Their resistance to black people may instead have been due more to the unyielding conservatism of some in its ranks, for whom change is tantamount to capitulation." It seemed, said Scriven, that the belief that the "Guards don't have blacks is now so widely and deeply held throughout the Army that it has become self-perpetuating." He concludes with the view that "many of the youngest sergeants, the men who will shape attitudes within the Army, more than any Ministry of Defence directive, believe that it is simply a matter of time before there are many more blacks in the ranks."

In June 1995, the Commission for Racial Equality (CRE), reported that the Household Cavalry was excluding people from ethnic minorities from enlisting or transferring in from other units. While there was no active recruiting of ethnic minorities during this period, and evidence to suggest that there was discrimination in the Guards regiments, the story was often distorted by single incidents of bullying rather than something more substantive. In the *Sunday Times*, 17 June 1995, the day after the Queen's Birthday Parade, the same article that reported the CRE findings about the Household Cavalry also observed that in the past all the soldiers on parade would have been white but that now there were indeed "black and Asian faces ... among the ranks". But clearly not that many. 'Deadline set for Guards to recruit black officer', a *Daily Telegraph* headline that appeared in October 1997, was just one of many media reports highlighting the lack of ethnic minorities in the Household Division. And the Household Cavalry was under particular scrutiny, with a warning that if it had not satisfied the CRE by March 1998 that it had made utmost efforts to increase the numbers of ethnic minorities, then it would risk the serving of a Non-Discrimination Notice.

Positive action was required. When Major General Evelyn Webb-Carter became the Major General Commanding the Household Division in the summer of 1997, he was determined to focus his efforts on the problem. With the full support of the Chief of the General Staff, General Sir Charles Guthrie, he worked closely with the CRE to recruit more ethnic minorities to the Guards and also to end the culture of discrimination. Early in his appointment, he met Bob Purkiss from the CRE in the Major General's office overlooking Horse Guards. Purkiss, a former merchant seaman, was the Transport and General Workers' Union's equality officer and CRE commissioner responsible for the Armed Forces. His advice to the Major General was to "go and meet people" from ethnic minority communities, including activists and community leaders in Bristol, Brixton, Bradford, Tiger Bay in south Wales, Birmingham and Nottingham, where he visited churches, temples and mosques to "start a dialogue".

The experience had a profound effect on Evelyn Webb-Carter, as he told Seumas Milne, a *Guardian* journalist, in 'General goes to war on racists in the Guards' (20 July 1999). Milne wrote: "The experience, he says – fresh from a night of manoeuvres on Salisbury Plain and an hour trying to enthuse hundreds of mainly black teenagers in a west London town hall about life in the army ... taught him an enormous amount." He quoted Webb-Carter as saying: "The image was pretty bloody awful and if I was black British I wouldn't have joined. I'd have thought the army was dodgy and the Guards, you must be joking. I think I was probably racist in the past without realising it. I thought of blacks as completely different."

Evelyn Webb-Carter's plan was radical but simple, and it worked. The second-in-command of the Welsh Guards, Major Crispin Black, a staff college graduate recently returned from a tour in South Armagh, was brought in to assist with the overall plan. As he recalls, "It was quite hard work at first but a hugely positive experience. I can remember to this day the Major General, in full-service dress and Sam Browne, promising community leaders at various locations all over the country that we were absolutely serious about this. And nearly all were convinced; if the Major General says it's going to happen then we'll help get the message out. Numbers in the training pipeline soon began to rise rapidly."

Colonel Simon Falkner, who had just returned from South Africa where he had been working on the integration of black soldiers into the new National Defence Force, and was now commanding the Household Cavalry, was given the task by Evelyn Webb-Carter of tackling the problem of racial discrimination in his own two regiments. He recalls having lunch with Bob Purkiss and being immensely impressed by his attitude. Not only did Purkiss understand the challenges ahead, but he was also a great supporter of the Army, and sympathetic. Falkner remembers saying to him, "if the CRE label us, as it has, as guilty of institutional racism, then how can we ever hope to recruit anyone from these minorities?" Bob Purkiss agreed entirely, as did John Reid, the Minister for the Armed Forces.

Considerable efforts were being made to recruit officers and soldiers from ethnic minorities, not just in the Household Cavalry but across the Household Division. Extra recruiters were appointed in areas where there were a higher proportion of these groups. The Household Cavalry went one step further, so important was the issue, by declaring that the recruitment of ethnic minority officers and soldiers was second only to operations as its highest priority. The CRE concern was duly lifted and this helped enormously with getting the right message out and forging a more inclusive attitude, not just among the more senior people, but also among the soldiers themselves. However, it all took time.

Evelyn Webb-Carter made "quite a thing" about tackling attitudes and behaviour that was actually completely alien to the ethos of the Household Division. "Sometimes there is a slight intake of breath ... but our tradition of discipline means that if I say something, that goes ... Some people say I'm politically correct. I defy that. It's straight common sense. It's their army as much as it's ours."

Nearly a quarter of a century later, and the changes have been significant. There are many more black and Asian Guardsmen serving in the Household Division, as almost any image from Her Majesty Queen Elizabeth's funeral and His Majesty The King's Coronation will testify. While a few might not like the idea of a Sikh Guardsman on parade wearing his turban, their views are no longer relevant, nor do they reflect the prevailing views of those who serve. As Evelyn Webb-Carter was quoted as saying in 1999: "When I speak to some of the old comrades, the old and bold, there are mutterings and some think I've gone pinko. But I don't ask for their support, I demand it. If we don't do it, we'll be damned."

There was a time when the issue of homosexuality in the Armed Forces appeared to be a much greater problem than it ever was in reality, although for the Guards in London there were often the salacious newspaper reports or indeed the occasional amusing anecdote. There is the story of Winston Churchill, when Prime Minister in the early 1950s, being woken one freezing February morning by a Downing Street aide with the shocking news that a Tory Member of Parliament had been caught with a naked Guardsman in St James's Park. "Makes you proud to be British," came Churchill's response, acknowledging the arctic-like conditions which somehow had not deterred the activities of these two offenders.

Homosexual acts, in private and between consenting males over the age of 21, were decriminalised in England and Wales in 1967 (Scotland

and Northern Ireland followed in 1980 and 1981). However, there was no lobby to remove the ban in the Armed Forces until the mid-1980s, the Armed Forces themselves arguing for the 'right to be different' in the name of operational efficiency. Any admission from a serviceman of being gay led to immediate dismissal. The reality was that there had always been gay soldiers across in the three Armed Services, and for many years they had been forced to live a secret life, open to discrimination, intimidation, and dismissal.

At a 'Military and Society' conference, held at Glasgow University in the early 1990s, a panel of Ministry of Defence speakers, among them Colonel Sebastian Roberts, an Irish Guardsman, was asked some sharp questions about the morality of maintaining the ban on gay soldiers in the Army. The senior officer, a major general, was obliged to present the official Ministry of Defence line about operational efficiency and the potential dangers of employing gay soldiers, while Sebastian Roberts took an entirely different stance. "Look," he said, "my regiment is like a family, and you don't throw out a member of your family because he is gay. And for us, all that matters is that the individual is a good soldier who knows the rules about decency and respect for others; whether a soldier is gay or not is really not the issue."

The ban on gay people in the military was finally lifted by the British government in January 2000, mainly due to a challenge in the European Court of Human Rights in Strasbourg. The Ministry of Defence introduced a new general code of sexual conduct which was similar to a policy adopted in the Australian Defence Forces eight years earlier, a sensible and pragmatic approach to behaviour, regardless of sexual orientation. Active policies to recruit gay people evolved over the years that followed, and there were few if any dissenters.

In 2009, a photograph of Trooper James Wharton of The Blues and Royals appeared on the front cover of *Soldier*, the British Army's in-house magazine. Inside were two articles, one about two female officers in the Royal Army Medical Corps who were enjoying successful military careers as a married couple, and the other about James Wharton, who was openly gay and had served in his regiment for six years. His experience had been a good one. Wearing his Iraq medal, awarded for his service on Op *Telic* 10, he conceded that there were some "people who are set in their ways and aren't in favour of the changed policy, but the whole attitude is different. I think there is room for improvement because there are still people who can't accept the changes, but it's 1,000 times better than ten years ago."

As the editor of the *Guards Magazine* commented at the time of this interview: "Trooper Wharton's comments lead one to believe that the British Army has demolished an artificial barrier and has successfully faced up to its irrational fears about the place of homosexuals in the military. We should indeed be proud that a member of the Household Division has stood up to represent this brave new world of equality and diversity." Now, nearly 25 years on from the lifting of the ban, there can be no doubt that this was indeed an 'artificial barrier' and not one that needs further debate or discussion. Just one small but important indicator of the long journey, and many changes, which have taken place over the past half century.

The Army's gradual change in its attitude towards the employment of women began in 1992 with the disbandment of the Women's Royal Army Corps. This led to women directly joining other parts of the Army, but restricted to support functions, not combat roles. The Ministry of Defence held the view that women serving in the front line would undermine 'unit cohesion', but by 2015, this policy had changed, and by 2018, all restrictions on the employment of women in the Armed Forces had been removed. For some years now, there have been women serving in the Household Division Bands, but more recently they are being recruited into all parts of the Guards, as officers and soldiers. Their uniforms, in all orders of dress, including ceremonial, are remarkably similar. Women are now serving alongside men in all seven regiments of the Household Division. Hardly a revolution, just a change which has been generally accepted and welcomed without a fanfare.

Anthony Sampson, who wrote *The Anatomy of Britain* in 1962, updating it several times over the next 40 years, observed that the Guards "remain what they are supposed to be, a superb fighting force, and it is in the Army that tribalism and lack of social mobility, so damaging in other fields, have their greatest justification." Sampson's views about the Guards did not change much in his various revisions of the book, and apart from trivial and amusing observations about officers not using public transport, or not living south of the river, or never using the word 'cheers', or always wearing hats, his broader point remains valid. In fairness, however, much *has* changed since 1969, and also much has happened since 1969, as the following pages of this book will show.

2

Commendable Restraint:
The Troubles, 1969–2007

I have always been proud of the way the Household Division
conducted itself during the Troubles in Northern Ireland. I would
summarise this as commendable restraint.
FIELD MARSHAL LORD GUTHRIE OF CRAIGIEBANK

On 21 December 1978, Sergeant Richard Garmory of the 1st Battalion Grenadier Guards was leading his four-man patrol in Crossmaglen, South Armagh. It was Thursday, market day, but the streets and town square were eerily quiet. An experienced former Army junior leader with several Northern Ireland (NI) tours behind him, Garmory sensed the worst.

As the patrol rounded a bend in the road, Garmory saw what he thought was a British Rail parcel delivery van parked partly on the pavement facing away from the patrol. As he pressed his magnifying sight to his eye, time seemed to momentarily freeze. In a fraction of a second, the patrol came under raking fire from three Armalite rifles and a Kalashnikov. A burst of rounds had passed through the sleeves of Garmory's smock but the remainder of his patrol were not so lucky. Guardsmen Graham Duggan, Kevin Johnson, and Glen Ling were all killed.

The immediate aftermath was distressing for the Grenadiers. Guardsman Saunders saw a priest walking from the Parochial House to the church. He asked the priest if he could help and give succour to the dying men. The priest turned away, as did a fellow priest a few minutes later. The company commander, Major Charles Woodrow, also recalled asking a priest to help. With not even a backward glance, the priest walked away. Woodrow thought of the parable of the Good Samaritan: "Now by chance a priest was going down that road; and when he saw him, he passed by on the other side."

The Troubles in Northern Ireland exert a powerful grip on the memories of Guardsmen who served there. Op *Banner*, as it became known, was the longest operation in the Army's history. Over a period of 38 years, some 300,000 troops served there. A total of 763 were killed and 6,116 wounded and maimed. The Army had its greatest loss of life in one day since the Korean War at Warrenpoint on 27 August 1979 when 18 soldiers were killed and 20 seriously injured in a Provisional IRA (PIRA) ambush. On the same day, the PIRA assassinated Lord Mountbatten. Northern Ireland was to become one of the Army's most formative experiences since the Second World War.

Op *Banner*'s legacy to the Army and all who served in Northern Ireland was profound. It taught generations of Household Division officers and non-commissioned officers a good deal about the profession of arms at a tactical level. And it did so within the gimlet eye of politicians and the media. The Household Division carried out close to 50 operational tours during the Northern Ireland 'Troubles', the longest and most trying in the Army's history.

The 2nd Battalion Grenadier Guards was the first Household Division battalion to serve in Northern Ireland. Its experience on its first tour was quite unlike that experienced by the 1st Battalion in South Armagh in 1978 when Sergeant Richard Garmory lost three men from his patrol in the devastating PIRA ambush.

"Welcome to Londonderry, put your watch back 300 years," were the first words to greet a Grenadier officer as he disembarked from the LSL *Tristram* (ironically the same vessel that was to carry Guardsmen in the Falklands campaign) in Londonderry docks on 24 August 1969. The General Officer Commanding (GOC), Sir Ian Freeland, who met the 2nd Battalion Grenadier Guards at the docks, inquired of the young officers whether they had brought their shotguns and fishing rods with them. It is an endearing characteristic of many British Army officers that when things are potentially fraught with danger, sporting analogies are brought into play to reduce tension.

The Major General Commanding the Household Division, Michael Fitzalan-Howard, remarked to the Grenadiers' commanding officer, Philip Haslett, that he did not expect the Battalion to be there for more than six weeks. It was to be five months before they returned to Chelsea Barracks.

In Ireland, history casts the darkest of shadows. The Grenadiers, like pretty well everyone else in mainland Britain, were unfamiliar with the province's history, oblivious of Ulster's injustices towards the minority Catholic community.

There was undoubted discrimination towards the Catholic minority in housing and jobs and education. Poverty and social deprivation meant that Londonderry was the poorest city in the UK with the highest unemployment. A great many of the Catholic population were housed in Victorian slum estates outside the city walls in areas called the Bogside and the Creggan. Their names alone paint a grim picture. Families of 12 to 14 lived in dwellings of just three to four rooms. Children aged five were often found wandering the streets at 2am to allow sleeping in shifts.

Many of the Grenadiers were appalled by the squalor and conditions in which the Catholic population had to live. They were equally taken aback by the bigotry and narrow-mindedness of both communities. It was in this emptiness of hope that the PIRA were to find willing recruits to their cause.

At that time, the Royal Ulster Constabulary (RUC) was regarded as nothing more than the paramilitary arm of the Unionist Party. Any Catholic civil rights protests were brutally crushed, if not by the RUC, then by the thugs who followed the Rev Dr Ian Paisley, the messianic and fiery leader of the Democratic Unionist Party.

The conflict began during a campaign by the Northern Ireland Civil Rights Association to end discrimination against the Catholic/Nationalist minority by the Protestant/Unionist government and local authorities. In August 1969, tensions between the two communities boiled over. Harold Wilson, the Prime Minister, ordered British troops to keep the peace between the Catholic and Protestant communities.

Patrick Holcroft, then a platoon commander and about to go to university, remembered the first two months well:

> We arrived in Londonderry, green about the gills after a rough crossing. There was an air of excitement as we drove to our billets at Magilligan Camp on the River Foyle estuary. Some of the officers, mindful of the GOC's encouraging words, tried duck flighting on the estuary. We began training for internal security almost immediately but it all seemed based on Colonial experience, marching troops, drill movements, "banner men" to help comms and recognition, and the use of gas and aimed shots if authorised. It was to prove wholly inadequate. At the outset, both Catholic and Protestant communities greeted us as their friends, particularly the Catholics who had lost faith, if they ever had any, in the RUC. Many of my platoon were given garlands of flowers and endless cups of tea and sandwiches. Our task was to watch, wait and reassure. This "softly, softly" approach and the innate self-discipline of a Guards Battalion seemed to work.

Philip Wright, a company commander, had similar memories: "It was all fairly relaxed, the Regimental Band came for a concert, we were entertained by our Colonel, Allan Adair [Adair commanded the Guards Armoured Division in 1944/45] at his house in NI, my wife visited me, and Giles, the celebrated cartoonist, drew a cartoon of Guardsmen in tunics and bearskins playfully chasing children stealing apples from an orchard."

In early September, the Battalion less the Inkerman Company deployed to Belfast where the two communities were now entrenched behind barricades. The period of relative calm where the Army was seen as neutral was coming to an end. Guardsmen were not policemen and with the RUC manifestly on the side of the Protestant community, it was inevitable that, as the Army sought to keep the peace, it would be seen as the ally of the Northern Ireland government at Stormont. Extremists on both sides sought to exploit the ambiguity.

Lieutenant Colonel Philip Haslett was later to remark after the Battalion returned to London, "We were all saddened of how it all turned out. We were there to keep the peace and we did so. No British soldier was murdered until 1971 when 43 were killed."

The Household Division was to carry out a further 42 Op *Banner* tours. The 2nd Battalion Grenadier Guards tour was in the opening or 'honeymoon' phase of the Troubles. There were further, more murderous phases until everyone tired of the killing.

During the late summer of 1970, the descent from rioting into violence took on a momentum of its own. By early 1971, the PIRA had become the principal threat to law and order in the province. By late spring there were 10–15 serious incidents per month. The first soldier to be killed was on 6 February. Incendiary attacks and the use of anti-personnel mines were becoming commonplace.

In March 1971, the Welsh Guards began their first operational tour of Northern Ireland. Major Charles Guthrie, commanding The Prince of Wales Company in North Belfast, and later to become the first Household Division field marshal since Alexander of Tunis, remembered the tour with both its gentler, humorous times and its grimmer moments. "I'm not sure we knew what to expect, the training for NI didn't amount to much in the early days of the conflict. I just remember one rather earnest brigadier briefing us, after which he asked whether we had any questions. A brother officer and good friend to this day, Jamie Robertson, raised his hand and said, 'Sir, are you by any chance wearing a toupee?'"

Guthrie went on:

Our brigade commander, Frank Kitson, was a gritty and controversial figure who had made his name during the Mau Mau uprising in Kenya in the late 50s. He was laconic, forensic, and unnerving to those who did not know their profession. Still, if he didn't suffer fools, the Catholic community did not suffer him. The lessons of Kenya were far removed from North Belfast in 1971, but at least he got a firm grip on gathering hard intelligence.

I was determined to remain non-partisan, however, and that The Prince of Wales Company should earn a reputation for impartiality. In this we succeeded and suffered no casualties except for the usual cuts and bruises. I recall coming across that rabble-rouser, Ian Paisley, bellowing through a tannoy, doing his best to stir his fellow unionists up. As one Guardsman said to me, "Fuckin drama merchant, that bloke Paisley ain't he." It was 40 years before he was to show signs of statesmanship.

I had the impression that both sides enjoyed a good riot, an antidote to long stretches of unemployment. We had to put down a major riot by the Protestant community in the unlikely named Snugville Street, just off the staunchly unionist enclave of the Shankill Road. It was chaotic, a cacophony of noise, confusion, petrol bombs, bottles, rocks and assorted missiles. My views were confirmed a week or so later when a man came up to one of my platoon commanders and said, "Was it youse Welsh boys involved in that dust-up we had last week on the Shankill? Fockin great fight, that was. Enjoyed that, so we did."

Guthrie, not for the first time in his distinguished military career, realised that in a febrile atmosphere, poor political decisions were often made. The decision to introduce internment without trial in the summer of 1971 was a public relations disaster. The move seemed to be directed solely against the Catholic community. That decision, combined with the introduction of 'deep interrogation techniques', ensured that the Army was seen as one with the Unionists and the partisan RUC. Trust was irrevocably lost with the Catholic community. The US with its influential Irish diaspora, Europe, and the Republic of Ireland looked on with a cold eye.

The impact of internment was quickly and harshly felt. Before internment, 31 people were killed in 1971; after internment, another 185 were to lose their lives in the last four months of that year.

On return from Sharjah, the 1st Battalion Scots Guards under the redoubtable Murray de Klee were sent at short notice to North Belfast. Another distinguished Scots Guardsman and major general, Murray Naylor, wrote in his history of the Scots Guards *Among Friends*, "training for the tour was inadequate, something which might have been avoided had those responsible for dispatching the Battalion at such short notice been better informed on the situation on Belfast's streets."

The Scots Guards under de Klee and some fine company commanders and senior non-commissioned officers learnt their trade quickly. A tour which had started gingerly ended on a high operational note. Nevertheless, they were to lose five Guardsmen and 48 all ranks wounded by sniper fire or explosions.

But worse fortune was to come with Bloody Sunday on 30 January 1972 when the Parachute Regiment, whose tradition, 'Far, fast and without question' was to serve them so well in the 1982 Falklands campaign, shot dead 13 Catholic civilians. The PIRA now had a 'legitimate' reason for war, to fight the Army out of Northern Ireland. And it was to do so with the overt support, or at least tacit approval, of the majority of Nationalists. "Bloody Sunday," as Prime Minister David Cameron was to say to Parliament 40 years on, "was a tragedy for the bereaved and wounded, and a catastrophe for the people of Northern Ireland."

After Bloody Sunday and the grave mistake of internment without trial, the Army and political establishment were now on the back foot. This allowed the PIRA to regroup, retrain, and reorganise behind 'no-go' areas in the Bogside, the Creggan, and the Falls Road in Belfast. Shooting incidents rose fast, from 399 in March 1972 to 2,718 in July. There were 95 deaths in July alone. The Army had to regain the initiative and launched Op *Motorman* on 31 July 1972.

Today it is hard to comprehend that 28,000 soldiers were deployed on *Motorman*. Their objective was to clear the 'no-go' areas established by the PIRA earlier in the summer. The Household Division was in the thick of it with one palpable advantage, the reprieve from execution of the 2nd Battalion Scots Guards who had been placed in suspended animation in March 1971. Northern Ireland was draining troops and resources. It was no time for ill-judged cutbacks. The decision to suspend 2nd Battalion Scots Guards was revoked and under the leadership of Tony Boam, the 2nd Battalion re-formed and joined the fray for *Motorman* in Londonderry.

'The Thin Red Line'. No truer is this figure of speech than in looking at the record of 1st Battalion Coldstream Guards who carried out three tours of duty in Belfast and Londonderry within 18 months. Their first deployment under Michael Hicks in December 1970 was to keep the peace in Londonderry and prevent bands of PIRA crisscrossing to and from the border in Donegal. The Coldstream were back again in December 1971 as Province Reserve. 'Reserve' implies a time of inactivity. It was far from it. The Battalion was shot at 1,047 times, fired 1,661 baton rounds in riot control and, to keep its spirits up with egg and chip butties, consumed 40 tons of potatoes and 160,000 eggs. Nor did the Guardsmen take their travails lying down, when Second Lieutenant Andrew Jacques and five Guardsmen flushed out a PIRA gun team under their own initiative. Jacques won the Military Cross and all the Guardsmen were Mentioned in Dispatches. The Battalion left Northern Ireland in late February 1972, only to return with 24 hours' notice in July to reinforce Op *Motorman*.

The 2nd Battalion Coldstream Guards were equally in the thick of it after the honeymoon period that had characterised 1970. They had deployed to West Belfast in July 1970 under the command of Lieutenant Colonel Colin Wallis-King. During their tour they had fired not one round of ammunition or CS gas. They had drunk around 17,000 cups of tea given to them by friendly locals of both denominations. They had arrested one pony and one donkey. But all was to change utterly as sentiment swung against the Army after 'Bloody Sunday'.

West Belfast 1972/73. The 2nd Battalion, now under the command of Lieutenant Colonel Denis Lewey, found itself in Springfield Road RUC Station and the four companies in areas of Belfast which had become distinctly hostile. Fortunately, Colonel Denis could count on company commanders whose names would resonate in the Regiment's history: Majors Neville Howard, Miles Frisby, Martin Maxse, Sir Brian Barttelot Bt, and Richard Macfarlane. Cups of tea by friendly locals had been replaced by rockets and sniper fire and well-planned ambushes. Five Guardsmen were killed by snipers.

Andrew Parker Bowles, who commanded B Squadron, The Blues and Royals on *Motorman* in Londonderry, and was held in great affection by all those who served with him, remembered the atmosphere at the time.

We were fortunate in having Pat MacLennan, a Coldstreamer, as our brigade commander with Colin Wallis-King, another Coldstreamer, as his deputy. Pat was calm and level-headed when, frankly, a few senior officers were getting a bit hot under the collar. We had nine infantry battalions in Londonderry, a bit over the top I thought. The night before Motorman was the Padre's blessing as though it was going to be a re-run of the Somme! Mind you, pretty well the whole Squadron attended the blessing which few did five months later when we had a Christmas church service in Cyprus.

Needless to say, nobody was at the barricades, they'd all fled across the border. We had eight or nine serious injuries during the tour. My real concern was reigning in my troop commanders who, typical of young officers throughout the army's history, were fearless if not foolhardy, firing off their sub-machine guns at the slightest of shadows. Fun to be with though.

Op *Motorman* was a turning point in the Troubles. The spiral of violence which had so characterised the last few months of 1971 and the first half of 1972 began to unwind. The loss of life never returned to 1972 levels. The classic insurgency campaign which the IRA had sought to mount with more or less formed bodies of soldiers and an almost recognisable military structure drew to a close. British Army operations at brigade, divisional, even close to corps level, witness *Motorman*, were never to be repeated.

For many Guardsmen who served in the early years of the Troubles, lost opportunities for a lasting peace were a matter of regret. There was a good chance that the Troubles could have been ended earlier in 1971. Even after 1972, the bloodiest of years, there was a glimmer of optimism that with good leadership, firmness of purpose and even handedness, things could improve. There was no better example of this than in the 2nd Battalion Grenadier Guards tour of Belfast from July to November 1973.

The Battalion was commanded by Richard Besly, described by his then Adjutant, Evelyn Webb-Carter, as an "immensely human person, intensely loyal to his officers and Guardsmen whose wellbeing were of much greater interest than his own." In Oliver Lindsay's book *Once a Grenadier*, Besly wrote:

> We took over the Shankill (Loyalist) and Ardoyne (Nationalist) areas of Belfast. The previous but one battalion had lost six killed and their commanding officer had a nervous breakdown. We took over from 3 Para, tough as usual but they made few friends. I had three outstanding company commanders, Martin Smith, Sam Coleridge and Henry Hanning. It was important to get them in the right place according to their strengths. My Adjutant was Evelyn Webb-Carter who became a first-class operations officer. The men's welfare and overall administration was in the capable hands of the Senior Major, Andrew Duncan, and the wonderful Quartermaster, Peter Lewis, who fed the men properly, getting rid of endless fry-ups and junk food.

Besly also remarked, "A good proportion of our arrests and finds of ammunition and explosives were from Protestant areas which did not endear us to the RUC and local authorities." It was a prescient statement.

Besly knew his officers and senior non-commissioned officers and who was suited to a particular role. It was a lesson not lost on future Household Division commanding officers before a tour of Northern Ireland. Before returning to England in November 1973, Besly was sent for by the head of the local Catholic community who said, "Our people have found that your Guardsmen have behaved in a gentlemanly and courteous fashion, and we thank you for it."

Internment without trial and Bloody Sunday were, however, a catastrophe from which the Army could not recover.

What replaced the classic insurgency of the early to mid-70s was something a great deal more nuanced, more vicious and a lot more draining on the psyche of Guardsmen and local people. The Troubles had now become a counter-terrorist operation which was to test the resilience of every Household Division battalion and regiment right up to the Good Friday Peace Agreement in the spring of 1998.

Following *Motorman*, the PIRA had to evolve to reflect the Army's growing effectiveness and it did so by adopting the classic cell structure. This was a form of organisation successfully developed by the Viet Cong in the Vietnam War. A small group of terrorists would know the identities of people only in their cell. They would not be familiar with who was who in their higher ranks or people in other cells. It made the cell extremely difficult for military intelligence to penetrate. More importantly, the cell structure lent itself to the PIRA's almost unbreakable bonds of kith and kin. They would sniff out an outsider as quickly as a bloodhound picks up the scent of a fox.

If the Troubles exert a powerful grip on the recollections of Guardsmen who served in Northern Ireland, then those who served in South Armagh retain the most vivid of memories. South Armagh was branded as 'Bandit Country', but this suggests that it was a place merely of casual lawlessness. It was a great deal more murderous than that. Any drop in concentration, however innocent, would result in tragedy. All Household Division battalions served there at some stage, but it was the exacting five-year period 1978–83 that saw Guardsmen draw on their innate strengths of resilience and self-discipline.

In South Armagh, the PIRA had many factors in their favour. First, there was the topography of the land and its proximity to the border with the Irish Republic. The British Army had few friends there including their police, the Garda. Terrorists could spirit across the border with ease.

Second, the countryside, framed by blackthorn hedges, was hard going and concealment was nigh impossible. The local farmers would notice any change in vegetation; dogs would bark from a quarter of a mile away; cows would meander over to where a patrol was hiding, proof enough to a farmer or local 'spotter' that soldiers were there; and Guardsmen would get no help from the local population who, if not actively supporting the PIRA, would never give away information. The mere suspicion of being a 'tout', or informer, would result in a grisly end.

Finally, there was the PIRA's South Armagh cells made up of the 'fighting men of Crossmaglen'. Their blood ties of kith and kin were bound by myths and grievances handed down from generation to generation. Names such as Murphy, Caragher, McMahon and McCabe were a mirror to the same names published as outlaws and cattle-thieves in the early 18th century. Some just went by their nicknames, 'The Undertaker' or 'The Surgeon'.

Smuggling, given the proximity to the border, was a serious business and inextricably linked to PIRA strategy. A good deal of money was made and it funded arms, explosives, and bribes. If they had had iPhones or laptops in the late 1970s and 1980s, it would have made no difference to intelligence gathering. The PIRA only communicated face to face, usually across the border in a safe house or in a staunchly Republican bar in Dundalk.

It was against this unnerving background that the Household Division battalions had to operate, their wits sharpened in the knowledge that a quarter of all soldiers were murdered or maimed in South Armagh.

The 1st Battalion Grenadier Guards tour of South Armagh in the winter of 1978/79 started as it continued, ferocious and friendless. Just a few days after the Grenadier advance party arrived to take over from 42 Commando, a mixed patrol of Grenadiers and Marines were drawn into a bomb attack. A Marine was killed.

The Battalion was commanded by Michael Hobbs, fizzy, energetic, ambitious, and with a remarkable ability to remember the name of every man in his Battalion. Similar to Richard Besly, he knew his officers' strengths and where to place them.

Lord Valentine Cecil was operations officer for the tour and recalled with affection Hobbs's willingness to allow his less experienced officers to grow in the job. Cecil was thrown in the deep end at the tour's outset and asked to write the Battalion's Standard Operating Procedures and, with assistance from brigade headquarters, the operational plan to move 2,000 tons of engineer stores to the Base at Forkhill and a similar amount to Crossmaglen. Movement by road was nigh impossible in such a hostile and unforgiving area.

Bessbrook, the headquarters of battalions serving in South Armagh, was the busiest heliport in Western Europe. But to move such an amount of heavy material by helicopter was undoable. Twenty-one convoys moved the stores by road, the main supply route guarded by two battalions from the Light Infantry and Royal Anglian Regiment.

Later, as Michael Hobbs reflected on the tour which had cost the lives of three Grenadiers, one Marine, six wounded, and two killed in a helicopter crash, he said: "In South Armagh, more than anywhere else in NI, the task of the Battalion was largely reactive. The complete hostility of the population, the professionalism of the terrorists meant there was little intelligence available to regular soldiers on the ground."

As a postscript to the Catholic priests in Crossmaglen who walked on by as the three Grenadiers lay dying, Michael Hobbs went to see Cardinal Tomás Ó Fiaich, the Catholic Primate of all Ireland and Archbishop of Armagh. Michael Hobbs, a convert and devout Catholic, sought an explanation. There is no record of their conversation. Ó Fiaich had been brought up in Crossmaglen and was considered to be less critical of militant republicanism than others in the Irish Catholic hierarchy. He would lamely cite his wider pastoral responsibilities. The two priests who had shamefully forgotten their calling on 21 December 1978 were later to visit the Crossmaglen base to offer their apologies.

In the history of the Household Division during the Troubles, and the savagery of the PIRA in South Armagh, the exceptional courage of

Captain Robert Nairac, Grenadier Guards, merits more than a mere footnote. The murder of Captain Nairac by the IRA in County Louth, across the border from South Armagh in the Republic of Ireland, on 14 May 1977 has always attracted controversy. But controversy is a common enough bedfellow with those who pass judgement without knowing what took place or who succumbed to their own prejudices. And if there remains controversy, there is no doubt about Nairac's extraordinary courage. He was awarded the George Cross two years after his death.

Nairac has been the subject of endless speculation over the years. If Nairac himself has receded into the shadows of the Troubles, the memory of those who knew him remains undimmed.

Julian Malins KC, a contemporary of Nairac's at Oxford, said of him, "Even against the backdrop of the swinging sixties, Robert stood out. Fights with local Oxford boneheads, dalliances with LSD. He was, nonetheless, the most handsome of his generation. He had a terrific aura. No one could be in his presence without feeling better for it. That is a great and rare gift."

Amongst his Grenadier contemporaries, there was a sense of trouble beneath his glittering presence. Nairac served his first tour of duty in Northern Ireland in 1973. He involved himself with 'hearts and minds' initiatives and teaching boxing at local youth clubs. When the Battalion returned to London with a glamorous tour of Hong Kong to look forward to, Nairac volunteered for special duties in the province. He became a liaison officer between covert Army Intelligence units and the RUC Special Branch in South Armagh.

To the dismay of many of his colleagues, he would visit Republican bars, engaging IRA sympathisers in conversation and singing rebel songs. He used the name of Danny McAlevey. He must have known that Ampleforth, Oxford, and the Grenadiers did not stand up to too much scrutiny, least of all in the tight Republican tribes of South Armagh. Whatever his motivation, and it is here that controversy and conspiracy theories abound, Nairac had a clear idea of how he wished to live his life.

He was an Englishman in a long tradition, the brave Catholic soldier prepared to die for a cause. That cause was peace and the end to needless violence. Nairac may have felt sympathy for the Catholic peoples of Northern Ireland and their suffering under centuries of blatant discrimination; but he hated the IRA's twisted logic, their patent criminality, and indiscriminate brutality.

If the Army was concerned about Nairac's freelance activities, it was prepared to indulge him. It needed a reliable and knowledgeable liaison officer.

On Saturday 14 May, Nairac left the Army base at Bessbrook Mill. He made his way to the Three Steps Inn in Drummintree. We will never know why he went there. He struck up conversation with several men at the bar and sang songs with the band to loud applause.

When he left the bar, a number of men were waiting for him. He was given a brutal beating and kicking. Knowing he was going to be killed, he asked for a Catholic priest and said a final prayer. Liam Townson, who shot him dead, said on his arrest a fortnight later, "He never told us anything, he was a great soldier."

His mortal remains have never been found. But that divine spark that made Nairac the man he was still shines brightly in the minds of those who knew him. His portrait stands proudly in the Grenadier officers' mess to this day.

Five months after the Grenadier tour under Colonel Michael Hobbs ended, the IRA assassinated Lord Mountbatten and members of his family. The same day, 18 soldiers from 2nd Battalion The Parachute Regiment and the Queen's Own Highlanders were murdered at Warrenpoint.

Lieutenant Colonel Charles Guthrie, commanding the Welsh Guards, deployed with his Battalion to South Armagh a month later. He was determined to get on the front foot from the outset. He understood and was sympathetic to Hobbs's view that, because of a lack of intelligence, battalions were largely forced to be reactive. But in the light of Warrenpoint and the high casualty rate in South Armagh, he knew that the Army's approach had to change.

Guthrie said:

Things were at a low ebb when we arrived in South Armagh. I was determined, however, not to accept that the Welsh Guards were there just to keep PIRA at bay. If your strategy was to play safe and keep a clean sheet, then you had no business to command. Mike Hobbs whom I knew to be a first rate commanding officer was dead right about intelligence. We had no signals or electronic intelligence. We relied entirely on human intelligence. The trouble was, informers, or anyone suspected of passing information, just passing the time of day with a friendly Guardsmen, might meet a grisly end.

Some commanding officers kept the RUC at arm's length. This was a mistake. The RUC felt under the cosh and unloved, particularly after Mountbatten's assassination. But they were born and bred in the Province and had a feel for things which the Army did not. Guthrie made sure his relationships were as strong as possible. It paid dividends as well as Guthrie's recognition that winning 'hearts and minds' of the locals was a false prophet in South Armagh. Similar to the 2nd Battalion Grenadier Guards tour in 1973, the Guardsmen won the grudging respect – though in South Armagh no more than that – for their unfailing courtesy and discipline.

Good PR was, however, a winnable battle. Guthrie invited two journalists from the *News of the World* to 'embed' themselves in Crossmaglen. It was a successful initiative, generating a lot of positive PR for the Army and keeping the Welsh Guards in the public eye.

Guthrie realised that it took a few weeks for a battalion to 'acclimatise' so that good infantry skills learnt by every recruit at the Guards Depot became second nature. He was determined to take the fight to the IRA once the timing was right, and, in spite of the foul and unforgiving winter, he launched Op *Voluble*, a period of incessant patrol activity by night and day but with no obvious pattern, to create uncertainty in the PIRA's minds. It worked. After the loss of Guardsman Paul Fryer at the tour's beginning there were no further casualties.

The tour was considered a great success. The initiative had been wrestled back from the PIRA and it offered a template for operations in South Armagh. Guthrie had just one regret, namely that he did not do enough to support the young officer who led the patrol in which Paul Fryer was blown up. The officer led a troubled life after the tour and died prematurely.

By now, the Army had fully grasped what it took mentally and physically to undertake a successful tour of South Armagh and how to minimise casualties while keeping the PIRA guessing. The tour by 1st Battalion

Coldstream Guards over the autumn and winter of 1982/83 was another example of the Household Division's commendable restraint and resilience.

The Battalion, commanded by Lieutenant Colonel Sir Brian Barttelot, Bt, was on its fourth tour of Northern Ireland but its first in South Armagh. Colonel Brian, engaging, level-headed, and calm, had no greater ambition than to command his Battalion and to put the interests of his officers and men first. He was also a courageous man, or at least a man who did not believe in fate, as his father, grandfather, and great-grandfather had all been killed in action for Queen, King, and Country.

Like Hobbs and Guthrie, Colonel Brian was frustrated by the lack of intelligence, which he felt had become the preserve of the Special Air Service (SAS), Special Branch and a few laconic chameleons who drifted in and out of Army bases. He also made it his business to get on well with the police and, in doing so, was introduced to the Garda sergeant from Dundalk who was friends with the RUC commander in Newry.

Colonel Brian's natural bonhomie and a bottle of Bushmills more than made up for the lack of hard intelligence. He would don his farmer's gear and meet the Garda sergeant at one of the 43 officially recognised border crossings. Barttelot gleaned little information from these meetings except as to who, of the known PIRA operatives, were frequenting Dundalk's bars. As this was generally where all their planning took place, it at least gave some indication that something might be afoot.

Unpredictable tactics, irregular patterns of patrolling, and covert observation posts (OPs) kept the PIRA confused. The Battalion's approach paid off, though good fortune played its part, sometimes through plain luck, but more often through the ever-watchful eye of a Guardsman. Lance Corporal Smallpage, as part of a multiple patrol commanded by the Coldstream mortar platoon officer, Captain G.W. McLean, saved his own and many lives when he spotted the drips from a catgut trip wire leading into a wall near the Dublin road railway bridge. The device hidden in the wall contained 100 pounds of explosive. A PIRA sniper hit a Guardsman from the distance of half a mile. He was saved by his chest armoured plate measuring just 4 inches by 6.

In a letter to his wife during the tour, Colonel Brian wrote:

The Guardsmen are still doing a wonderful job. I see them off by night at the helipad in bitter cold and often driving rain, clambering aboard the Wessex helicopters, loaded down with stores and equipment to last them for two or three days. They head off with grinning blackened faces, get dumped in some inhospitable field and then head off to establish a 'lie up' position in some rain sodden ditch under a dripping blackthorn hedge from where they can observe terrorists crossing the border. Their resilience, restraint and endless good humour has made these five months by far the most rewarding time of my 22 years as a Coldstreamer.

The Prime Minister, Mrs Thatcher, accompanied by her husband Denis, visited the Coldstream just before Christmas as she had done two years before when the Welsh Guards were in South Armagh. It was just six months after the victorious Falklands campaign and she was on top of her game, at ease with herself but concerned about the Guardsmen's welfare. They warmed to her immediately. She agreed to officiate over the Christmas Draw, blissfully unaware that the first prize was a box of 500 condoms. "Make the most of your prize, I'm sure you'll put it to good use," she remarked to the winning Guardsman. Denis, who had been tipped off, smiled sagely, adding, "hear, hear."

It had been a remarkably successful tour with no loss of life, although one Guardsman lost his eye in a bomb attack. As the Coldstream left the main base at Bessbrook, the Royal Scots guarded the route to the airport to ensure safe passage. They occupied trenches dug by Guardsmen who had done the job, much to Sir Brian's surprise, with great enthusiasm. It was only when the 'Wee Jocks' jumped into their trenches and disappeared from sight that he allowed himself a wry smile.

Colonel Brian, whose estate in Stopham, West Sussex, had been in his family's hands since 1379, knew that whatever his future Army career held for him, nothing would give him as much pleasure as his period in command. He served a further nine years, during the last five of which he set up and ran the new Headquarters Foot Guards. As Colonel Foot Guards, he replaced the five full-time Regimental Colonels. This was a delicate assignment which he carried out with his characteristic good sense and tact. He retired from the Army in 1992, a loss to the Army, but perhaps a relief to his family whose antecedents had all given their lives in service.

The assassination of Lord Mountbatten and members of his family, and the murder of 18 soldiers at Warrenpoint in the late summer of

1979, had been the low point of the war against the terrorists. It now became a steady war of attrition on both sides. The 1980s may have witnessed a gradual drop in violence and loss of life, but there was little change in the all-pervasive climate of fear.

By the mid-1980s the Army had grown sufficiently confident to extend tours from four to six months and to station battalions for two years with their families. 'Force protection' by both tactical and technical means had become a priority. But leadership of a different calibre is needed if a regiment is to thrive in an accompanied posting where the environment is still far from benign.

The 2nd Battalion Grenadier Guards posting to a deserted air base in Ballykelly on the southern shores of Lough Foyle in the north-west of the province was to last for over two years. The commanding officer, Lieutenant Colonel Charlie Woodrow MC QGM, made no great claims for himself though his record spoke otherwise. Woodrow had won the Queen's Gallantry Medal in Londonderry in 1974 and the Military Cross in the 1978/79 tour of South Armagh.

Hugh Robertson, a Life Guards officer attached to the Grenadiers, who was later to become Minister of Sport and Minister for the Olympics, held Woodrow in high regard:

As was common at that time, many officers served with Household Division Battalions and Regiments apart from their own. I filled in with 2nd Battalion Grenadier Guards for six months while they were completing a two-year residential tour in NI based at the old Ballykelly airfield. The Battalion was commanded by Charles Woodrow, small, wiry and with great charisma, Woodrow had remarkably won the Military Cross and Queen's Gallantry Medal on previous tours.

I was attached to Number 2 Company commanded by Lord Valentine Cecil who dispensed with the usual briefings but sent me down to look over the border and our Tactical Area of Operations (TAOR) in his own private plane.

Intelligent, kind and loyal, Valentine had a highly individual approach to leadership. I remember one night after a particularly arduous period of patrolling, he suspended all activity for a night and arranged for us to watch Doctor Zhivago accompanied by a wonderful hamper of goodies sent over from his mother, Lady Salisbury, at Hatfield House. The Grenadiers as befits the senior regiment of infantry in the British Army, have a formidable reputation. To be frank, I was a little in awe on my arrival but they could not have been more welcoming. On my last day, Colonel Charles thanked me with the present of a print to remind me of my time with them. He said to me, "we haven't bothered much with you, Hugh, because as far we're concerned, you're just part of the great family that is the Household Division." It certainly felt that way.

Ballykelly in the grip of winter looks forbidding but on a clear summer's evening it is as beautiful a place as any in the UK. The Donegal hills lie to the east across Lough Foyle, bright flecks of colour, light and shade, forever changing.

Colonel Charlie established an operational cycle which gave the Guardsmen and those with families plenty of variety, excitement, and time at home. Woodrow knew that a successful battalion defines itself not only through operational success but also through sporting achievement. The Battalion won the UK Land Forces skiing, athletics, and basketball championships as well as coming runners up in the cricket league and reaching the finals in the Army Sevens.

On the operational side, the Grenadiers earned a reputation for impartiality and fairness. The July Loyalist (Protestant) marches were always a source of tension between the two communities. After the Anglo-Irish Agreement in 1985, an important step in the peace process which gave the Irish government an advisory role in Northern Ireland affairs, the Loyalist factions had become unruly, hell bent on stirring things up. The Loyalists complained that the Grenadiers were neutral and insisted on searching both sides.

On any lengthy tour of duty, a battalion needs a hinterland to which it can escape and where a normal life can be led. The Battalion bought a boat which families could charter and deep freezes kept humming with hake, haddock, and mackerel. The Wives' Club was active and many became 'Greenfinches', signing up for the Ulster Defence Regiment, an infantry regiment of the British Army established in 1970 for the defence of life and property in Northern Ireland against armed attack or sabotage.

This may have all seemed small beer to an outsider who knows little about the trials of Army life. But it has always been a hallmark of the Household Division that the small things matter. A regiment has only to be 5 per cent better at everything to be 100 per cent better overall.

The Grenadiers lost no one through terrorist action. In March 1988, Colonel Charlie said his farewells to the whole Battalion. Few remembered the occasion with anything but a sense of sadness.

The 1st Battalion Scots Guards six-month tour of West Belfast in May 1992 had a significance beyond its length. Commendable restraint had been a characteristic of the Household Division throughout the Troubles. But restraint, laudable though it is in efforts to keep the peace, was always going to be tested in the face of stopping acts of violence.

Senior officers in Northern Ireland at the time had come under strong political pressure to create conditions for a peaceful settlement; the Peace and Reconciliation Group, established across the religious divide in 1976 to promote a peaceful and inclusive society for Northern Ireland, had grown in influence. "We need to broker an accommodation with PIRA" had become the watchword.

The Battalion's commanding officer, Tim Spicer, had won his spurs as the 2nd Battalion's operations officer in the Falklands campaign. The campaign had taught Spicer to be uncompromising on the need for utmost professionalism and the traditional infantry skills of physical fitness, shooting, and tactical discipline. The Battalion arrived in Belfast in good shape. A company from the Paras were attached to the Scots Guards. As Spicer remarked: "They were bloody good, as they had been in the Falklands, but best kept on a tight leash. I used to think of them in a glass case with a sign saying 'in case of war, break glass.'"

Belfast City Centre had been bombed to not quite rubble. People were fearful of going shopping. Spicer had learnt the lessons of previous Household Division commanding officers and got off to a good start with the police. They were keen to regenerate the city centre and, against Spicer's better judgement, asked the Battalion to man permanent vehicle checkpoints. These established a dangerous pattern which played into the PIRA's hands. Army vehicles were also told to stop at red lights. A stationary vehicle was a target for snipers. This led directly to the death of Guardsman Shackleton who was shot dead as he provided top cover in a vehicle travelling down the Antrim Road.

Spicer's training of his Battalion paid off in a way which he may not have expected at the time. A patrol led by Second Lieutenant Ben Wallace apprehended a terrorist active service unit which had positioned itself to bomb his patrol as it passed through a narrow defile. Wallace was Mentioned in Despatches. His name is probably more familiar today as a former Secretary of State for Defence. As an aside, former Scots Guards officers have been remarkably successful in their subsequent careers in business and in public service, with Alex Younger as head of MI6 and Christopher Geidt (enlisted but not commissioned) as the highly regarded Private Secretary to The Queen, as was Sir Robert Fellowes; Sir Charles Mayfield as Chairman of the John Lewis Partnership; Sam Vestey, Master of the Horse to Her Majesty The Queen; and Michael Scott, the first lay Complaints Commissioner to the Bar.

Another incident in May 1992 bore witness to the Battalion's professionalism and high degree of training. On the 16th, a joint RUC and reconnaissance platoon mobile patrol was engaged by a Mark 12 mortar concealed in the back of a car in the Beechmount area of Belfast. Quick reaction during the follow-up, led by Lance Sergeants Burgess and Goodman, resulted in an IRA active service unit being arrested. For his consummate courage and swift action Lance Sergeant Goodman was awarded The Queen's Gallantry Medal.

On 4 September, an incident occurred in the New Lodge area when a terrorist suspect, seen to be acting suspiciously, was apprehended, whereupon he tried to run away. Shots were fired and the man later died. The incident remains mired in controversy. What took place started innocently enough. A joint Army/police patrol was tasked in serving a summons on a suspected criminal. It was a time of high terrorist activity, in particular the use of coffee-jar bombs which were easy to carry and hide. The patrol apprehended Peter McBride, whom they suspected of concealing such a device. McBride broke away and vaulted over a garden wall. Guardsmen Wright and Fisher gave chase. The patrol commander ordered Wright and Fisher to stop him. McBride continued to run off and was shot dead.

It was a politically sensitive time and the Army's Commander Land Forces ordered Wright and Fisher to be arrested. Spicer and his Regimental Sergeant Major interviewed the two men and, to this day, believe they were telling the truth. Others did not and they were convicted of 'wrongful judgement'. They served six years in gaol.

Wright and Fisher were released in December 1998 under the terms of the Good Friday Agreement. They were reinstated in the Army and one went on to serve in Kosovo.

The Army Board decision to reinstate them stuck in the craw of the McBride family and Republican sympathisers. But Prime Minister Tony Blair's decision to release prisoners convicted of murder under the terms of the Good Friday Agreement infuriated Unionists and soldiers who had served, or were serving, in Northern Ireland.

Irish soldiers from the Republic and the wider Irish diaspora have long been a mainstay of the British Army. And often a heroic one at that. Because of the Troubles, particularly the prospect of Irish soldiers having to conduct operations in their home towns and villages, the Irish Guards were not allowed to serve in Northern Ireland. It was an understandable political decision, though politicians should not have feared. The Irish Guards' good humour, natural courtesy, and willingness to engage with both sides of the community served them and the British Army well.

The changing political situation and the slow but gradual process towards a lasting peace settlement saw the Irish Guards' first deployment to Fermanagh, under Lieutenant Colonel Christopher Langton, from November 1992 to May 1993; the second deployment, under Lieutenant Colonel Sebastian Roberts, was in East Tyrone from June to December 1995. Captain Rupert Uloth, a Life Guards officer attached to No 1 Company in Fermanagh, remembered his time with the Micks with affection:

> The Micks needed an officer at short notice for someone who was on compassionate leave. I leapt at the chance to join them as an ops officer and watchkeeper. The company commander was Charlie Knaggs who could not have been more welcoming as were all the officers and Guardsmen. It was the first time the Irish Guards had been deployed to NI and it was fascinating to listen to the views of the soldiers, a third of whom were from the Republic. They were proud Irishmen, even prouder Irish Guardsmen, and heartily sick of what had taken place. One Lance Sergeant was particularly pleased to stop and search the Sinn Fein leader, Gerry Adams.

I enjoyed the foot patrols, not something I was used to as a cavalryman, and got to know the local towns and their people pretty well. Memories were still fresh of the appalling Remembrance Day bombing at Enniskillen. The locals were genuinely pleased to have the presence of Irish Guardsmen, offering cups of tea and a friendly chat.

I remember one Guardsman had a meltdown and had to be restrained by his mates. It brought home to me that, despite the relative quiet in County Fermanagh compared to the ever-present anxiety in South Armagh, soldiers were always under strain. I've retained a great affection for the Micks.

Both tours were largely uneventful. It would be fanciful to think that the PIRA did not want to take on Irish Guardsmen. The East Tyrone PIRA were effective and ruthless. And their strategy at the time was to murder as many RUC and Ulster Defence Regiment men and women as possible, while avoiding deliberately attacking the British Army.

Langton wrote in his post-tour report, "The one characteristic across the Battalion which stands out as a key ingredient in the success of the tour has been the sense of humour. Given some of the hardships and appalling weather this has been remarkable."

It was a sentiment echoed in the second Irish Guards tour. Roberts wrote in the *Guards Magazine* about the "unexpected connections" of kith and kin and the goodwill of farmers, councillors, journalists, and priests towards the Regiment. Father Denis Faul, no apologist for the British Army and with strong Republican instincts, was one of the first to visit the Micks. Denis Faul was an Irish Roman Catholic priest and civil rights campaigner. He was best known for his role in trying to bring to an end the 1981 Irish Republican hunger strike in the Maze Prison. He spoke of his affection for his uncle, Terence Ó Beirne, who had fought with the Irish Guards in the Great War. A total of 270 attended a reception hosted by the Regiment.

The Irish Guards held an open day at Ballykinler to encourage recruiting. On the day, 350 turned up, of whom 96 applied to join the Army, 41 to join the Micks. Fifty came from Dublin. If it was a testament to unemployment, it was also a witness to the strength of the historical ties between Ireland and the British Army. The Irish Guards Association (Eire Branch) dinner was attended by the Irish Army's Chief of Staff, Lieutenant General McMahon.

It wasn't all beer and skittles. And there was undeniably a certain unease about the Irish Guards' approach on their second tour under Roberts from those who recognised the importance of sustaining a firm operational footing. It was effective in terms of 'hearts and minds' but there was still a job to be done, as events in South Armagh were to prove for many Household Division battalions.

Things turned for the worse in South Armagh in 1993. The South Armagh active service unit had perfected its sniping operations. Seven soldiers were killed in nine .50-calibre single-shot attacks. The active service unit would use a van which contained an armour-plated shield with an aperture behind which they would fire the fatal shot. Road signs reading 'Sniper at Work' were unnerving, to say the least, for soldiers on patrol.

Good infantry skills mattered, and after the murder of the three Grenadiers in December 1978, the Household Division suffered just one further casualty from snipers in South Armagh: Daniel Blinco, a 6-foot 6-inch-tall Guardsman serving with the Queen's Company 1st Battalion Grenadier Guards, who was shot dead on 30 December 1993.

The indifference of the locals, similar to that shown towards the killing of the three Grenadiers exactly 25 years before, shocked the Battalion. Flowers which were placed on the pavement where Blinco was murdered were found kicked down the street 20 minutes later.

It was the Grenadiers' final tour of Northern Ireland. The commanding officer, Lieutenant Colonel Edward Bolitho, had some 830 all ranks under his command including platoons and individuals from the Coldstream, Scots Guards, Household Cavalry and Irish Guards. Colonel Edward observed, "It was 15 years since my last tour. Much had changed. We were better equipped, more professional in the sense we were better trained and clued up as to what to expect. But the terrorists were as wily as ever. After all, they had had 24 years to watch us."

The Grenadiers were able to watch the terrorists as well. Hilltop observation towers had been constructed by the Royal Engineers to cover much of South Armagh. For Republicans they became the symbol of British military occupation; for the Army they were isolated fortresses surrounded by mines, wire, and trip flares and tied down a company of men. Resupply was by air only.

The six-month tour ended on 29 March 1994, five months before the 31 August ceasefire. The Battalion received an exceptional number of honours and awards.

Guardsman Blinco was the last sniper casualty before the August 1994 ceasefire, a ceasefire fiercely opposed by the South Armagh terrorists. On 12 February 1997, a month before the Welsh Guards' deployment, Lance Bombardier Stephen Restorick was shot dead. Restorick was the last soldier to be killed by terrorist activity during the Troubles; his death caused particular sadness and shame.

Mrs Lorraine McElroy, whose driving licence Restorick was checking when he was shot, said: "I sat there in that ambulance and watched a man die. My strongest emotion was shame. I felt ashamed that we were going to be tarred with the same brush as the IRA. They don't speak for us. They are themselves alone."

'Sniper at Work' was to continue to cast a long shadow over South Armagh until the end of the Troubles. It became the focal point of the Welsh Guards tour from March to September 1997. The 1994 ceasefire had given the Army and RUC time to study the PIRA sniper tactics in detail. The Army response, slightly to the consternation of battalions deployed in South Armagh, was to use a tactic known as 'the tethered goat'. This meant that soldiers on the ground were sometimes used as decoys to smoke the sniper out. At the heart of this tactic lay good intelligence, something hitherto in short supply. By now, however, the Army had become pretty adept at analysing the PIRA's patterns of behaviour and how they used ground.

There was the occasional nasty fright for the Welsh Guards. On 29 March 1997, a sniper squeezed off a clear shot at the Forkhill Army base. The PIRA were able to do so by using 'dead ground', ground the Army could not observe. This was the sitting room of an innocent local family, the Sheridans, who found themselves under PIRA armed guard for three and a half hours. Constable Ronnie Galwey, accompanying the Welsh Guards patrol, nearly lost his leg, the bullet striking his right hip.

The Welsh Guards' low-level tactics began to pay off. Establishing patterns of behaviour was to invite a terrorist response. Their approach to keep the PIRA guessing was to plan carefully and constantly reassess patrol activity. The terrorists found it nigh impossible to nail the Battalion down. Ironically, it was something the Army had to relearn in Afghanistan a decade later. There it faced a different kind of foe but a foe who were not too dissimilar to the PIRA.

The Welsh Guards also knew they were part of a much bigger operation to track down and capture the South Armagh sniper team. On 7 April 1997, the sniper team was holed up in a farm complex on the Cregganduff Road waiting to strike. Welsh Guards platoons were tasked to patrol in an imaginary box around the complex. An SAS team was to swoop on the farm complex and restrain and hand over the terrorists to the RUC. A decade earlier they would have been shot dead, but a sustainable peace was within reach. Four Republican martyrs would not have helped.

The operation was a qualified success. It was a triumph in the sense that all four terrorists were caught and brought to justice. A Barrett .50-calibre rifle was found along with AK-47 rifles, live rounds, and spent ammunition. Three months after the arrests, the IRA called another ceasefire. At last, they were on the back foot. Whatever feelings of vulnerability the Welsh Guards might have felt as 'tethered goats' were tempered by the operation's success.

It was qualified success, however, because although the four members of the sniper team would receive life sentences in March 1999, they were able to laugh and joke as they left the dock, "See you in 18 months" to supporters in the public gallery, a chilling reference to the early release scheme agreed in the Good Friday Agreement signed on 10 April 1998.

The Welsh Guards had had a successful tour under their commanding officer, Lieutenant Colonel Sandy Malcolm, whose father and grandfather had also commanded the Regiment. Malcolm had built a good team; two of his company commanders, Major Robert Talbot-Rice and Major Ben Bathhurst, were to become generals and Major Simon Treadgold proved himself as a company commander who was respected and much liked by the Guardsmen under his command. Captain Rupert Thorneloe was to show extraordinary promise, attached to the Brigade Intelligence Cell. Even then, it was clear that the highest reaches of the Army were within Thorneloe's grasp. He was killed in action in July 2009 commanding the Regiment in Afghanistan.

Colonel Sandy, who had great sensitivity as a Welsh Guardsman, was to face a challenge of a different nature on the news of the tragic death of Diana, Princess of Wales, on 31 August 1997. It would naturally fall to the Household Division to take part in and plan the funeral which was to take place just a week later at Westminster Abbey. The Major General, Evelyn Webb-Carter, a veteran of the Troubles and in particular South Armagh, decided in good faith that the Scots Guards based in London should escort the coffin from Kensington Palace to the Abbey.

Colonel Sandy, quite rightly, was having none of it; the Welsh Guards, he said, should accompany the Princess of Wales's coffin. He telephoned Lieutenant Colonel Alexander Matheson, the Brigade Major at Headquarters London District, who conveyed Colonel Sandy's feelings to General Evelyn. General Evelyn was entirely sympathetic but explained the challenge to Colonel Sandy of such a short time span for a battalion on operations. The logistics alone, rehearsals, availability of flights to the UK, all seemed insurmountable. Malcolm stuck to his guns. The Royal Air Force rose to the occasion and allowed the use of Chinook helicopters to ferry the cortège party back to Chelsea Barracks. The backdraft blew the windows out, an acceptable case of collateral damage under the circumstances.

All was well. Excellence in ceremonial derives much of its sinew from battlefield discipline. Twelve Guardsmen were taken out of Crossmaglen along with the Regimental Sergeant Major and Drill Sergeant Cunliffe. On Saturday 6 September, the Welsh Guard bearer party under Captain Richard Williams MC accompanied the Princess of Wales's coffin, draped in the Royal Standard, for one hour and 47 minutes from Kensington Palace to Westminster Abbey. No Guardsman would forget the experience. It was an emotional trial as well as a physical test. One million people lined the street, flowers rained down on the coffin, 2.5 billion people watched worldwide.

In November that year General Evelyn called Colonel Sandy to say that, despite the success of the Welsh Guards operational tour, no medals were to be awarded. The Prime Minister, Tony Blair, did not want to 'militarise' the Army's contribution to the peace process. Only Warrant Officer (Class Two) Cunliffe, the senior non-commissioned officer on the funeral cortège, received a citation.

The Good Friday Agreement, which ended most of the violence of the Troubles, was signed on 10 April 1998. A quarter of a century has now passed, and it is hard to believe or remember how the Troubles dominated not only politics but also British society during those tumultuous 30 years. But human nature has a great capacity to forget, or at least dull in the memory the more harrowing experiences. There had been 500 'IRA incidents' in England during the Troubles, mostly in London. Fifty people had been killed on the mainland. The bombings were particularly shocking and shook the country to its core. Few will ever forget the images of the Hyde Park and Regent's Park bombing in July 1982 which killed 11 Household Cavalrymen and Royal Green Jackets, including seven horses.

The Household Division was to carry out any number of tours after the Good Friday Agreement, but the worst was over with no further loss of life. Those battalions who found themselves in Londonderry, Belfast, or South Armagh putting in cordons, policing marches, or keeping the lid on public order well into the early 2000s may have found the experience wearisome but worthwhile in keeping an edge in training and operational discipline.

Op *Banner* gave the Household Division something it had never before quite enjoyed: public recognition that they were foremost operational soldiers. The more discerning would have also seen that they had also operated on the whole with commendable restraint and discipline. This was true of most of the Army, though 'Bloody Sunday', the Ballymurphy massacre from 9 to 11 August 1971 in which 1 Para killed 11 civilians as part of the operation to introduce internment without trial, and other occasions where regiments or individuals lost self-control, were a stain on the Army's reputation.

Successive Major Generals Commanding the Household Division since the Falklands campaign had wrestled with the challenge of ensuring that battalions and regiments were able to train effectively while meeting their ceremonial commitments. There was a steady improvement in pre-Northern Ireland training over the course of Op *Banner*, and this was supported by a more systematic approach to training in the Army generally. It was important to ensure that battalions serving in London District were able to train annually at company level as a minimum in order to provide the basis for successful pre-operational tour training. It took some work from Headquarters London District to obtain the time and resources required, but it was achieved, along with recognition that battalions in London District needed to be trained for operations as well as ceremonial duties.

The Household Division had unquestionably shaken off the complacency of the post-war years. The British Army of the Rhine might have been seen as the bigger deal for career progression, but Northern Ireland was the true proving ground for junior leadership. Guardsmen and junior officers would afterwards fill senior command appointments in their own regiments and their hard-won experience in Northern Ireland contributed to operational success at a tactical level in subsequent conflicts.

But it was to be short-lived. The lessons of counter-insurgency were soon lost. By the mid-1990s, it was no longer a topic for study at the Staff College. This cost the Army dearly in the early years of the Afghanistan campaign. Later on in the campaign, from 2009 onwards, 'courageous restraint' and winning the support of the local population became the campaign's focus. It played to the Household Division's strengths and with interest.

———

On 25 November 2022, Guardsman David Holden, 53, was convicted of the manslaughter in February 1988 of Aidan McAnespie by gross negligence. McAnespie was shot in the back after walking through an Army checkpoint in County Tyrone. Guardsman Holden was serving with the 2nd Battalion Grenadier Guards at the time. Holden's defence was that although the general purpose machine gun was cocked, it was wet and his finger slipped, loosing off a round. Mr Justice O'Hara, who heard the case without a jury, found against Holden. Holden was the first veteran to be convicted of an historical offence since the Good Friday Agreement, which released all terrorists convicted of murder.

3

National Renewal: The Falklands Campaign, April–June 1982

We fought well because we were among friends.
MAJOR GENERAL MICHAEL SCOTT

In the early hours of 14 June 1982, Captain Tim Spicer, operations officer of the 2nd Battalion Scots Guards, was huddled in the lee of a rocky crag at the bottom of Goat Ridge to the west of Mount Tumbledown with his commanding officer, Lieutenant Colonel Mike Scott. They were just a bound behind G Company, commanded by Major Iain Dalzell Job. Colonel Mike considered it to be a good place from which to conduct a fighting withdrawal in contact should the attack falter.

An epic battle was about to begin against a well-prepared enemy of Argentine Marines sited on dominating and often insurmountable crags. The night was dark and cold with temperatures below zero. Snow was falling horizontally.

Ten weeks before that fateful night, Captain Spicer's surroundings could not have been more different. He was Captain of the Tower of London Guard. Spicer was avidly reading the day's newspapers and the alarming accounts of the Argentinian invasion of the Falklands. Spicer felt a growing sense of frustration. A Sword of Honour winner at Sandhurst and former instructor at the School of Infantry in Brecon, he took his soldiering seriously.

Spicer had already completed an operational tour of Northern Ireland but here was a chance to put everything he knew into practice. It was an opportunity that seemed to recede by the hour as he read that 3 Commando Brigade was to spearhead the fight to take back the Falklands. Whatever anticipation and excitement he had felt as the news of the invasion broke now gave way to gloomy feelings of a spring and summer on public duties watching from the sidelines as the action unfolded.

Captain Spicer need not have worried. He received a telephone call from his commanding officer, Mike Scott. Colonel Mike, calm of temperament and self-effacing, could barely disguise the excitement in his voice. "Tim, we're on for the South Atlantic, how and when I don't know, the Adjutant is arranging for someone to take over from you on Tower Guard, but I want you back here within the hour."

Argentina had long laid claim to the Falkland Islands. The year 1983 would be the 150th anniversary of British rule. With mounting economic problems and social unrest, the Argentine military junta believed an invasion of the Falklands would take people's minds off the dire state of affairs at home and release a wave of patriotic jingoism. On that they were right. The wild scenes in the Plaza de Mayo in Buenos Aires in early April 1982 were witness to the patriotic fervour sweeping the country.

The Ministry of Defence had been ambiguous in the messages it had sent. The Defence Review of 1981 recommended selling off one-third of the Royal Navy's surface fleet. There was speculation in the press that the Royal Marines were to be cut. The decision to withdraw the ice patrol ship HMS *Endurance* from the South Atlantic and not replace it sent yet another signal to the junta that Britain had given up on its South Atlantic territories. Although the British Military Attaché in Buenos Aires had warned the Foreign Office that an invasion was likely, he was ignored. In the event, the junta's invasion of the Falklands on 2 April 1982 came as a complete strategic and tactical surprise.

On news of the invasion, the British military and political establishment dithered. But as the Falklands campaign so heroically demonstrated, there were enough people made of the right stuff to realise that Britain's future was not worth contemplating if Britain did not retake the islands. The First Sea Lord, Admiral Sir Henry Leach, later described in the documentary series *History of Modern Britain* as Mrs Thatcher's 'Knight in Shining Gold Braid', was asked by Thatcher if retaking the islands was possible. He replied, "Yes, we can recover the islands, because if we do not, or if we pussyfoot in our actions and do not achieve complete success, in another few months we shall be living in a different country whose word counts for little."

The British Army was now on high alert, anxious to know how the fight was to be joined. Lieutenant Colonel Johnny Rickett, commanding 1st Battalion Welsh Guards, a man of infectious enthusiasm, wasted no time reminding people that the Battalion had just come off Op *Spearhead*, Britain's quick response force, and was ready to go. He put in a call to Christopher Airy, a former Grenadier who later commanded the 1st Battalion Scots Guards and who was now a senior staff officer at Headquarters UK Land Forces. Later that day, Colonel Johnny was told to report to Headquarters 5 Infantry Brigade at Aldershot and prepare his Battalion for action.

The decision to send the Scots Guards and the Welsh Guards, both on public duties, was viewed with dismay and a degree of jealousy by other infantry battalions who considered themselves more combat-ready. This was disingenuous. The Army thought at the time that the Marines and Parachute Regiment with the Royal Navy would do all the fighting and, once victory was won, the only role left would be the unpalatable one of garrison troops.

The decision to dispatch the Scots and Welsh Guards may have been both emotional and political. Three serving members of Prime Minister Thatcher's government at the time of the invasion had served in the Household Division: William Whitelaw (Scots Guards), Michael Heseltine (Welsh Guards), and Lord Carrington (Grenadier Guards). It was a decision much like the desire of the Chief of the General Staff, Sir Edwin 'Dwin' Bramall, to use 7th Duke of Edinburgh's Own Gurkha Rifles in the campaign. Bramall had served alongside the Gurkhas in Borneo. He was also Colonel of the 2nd Battalion King Edward VII's Own Gurkha Rifles. Mrs Thatcher remarked to Bramall when he told her that he was sending a Gurkha battalion, "Really, only one?" If the Falklands campaign was going to be the last roar of the British Lion, then the roar had to reverberate across Britain and the wider world.

The Scots and Welsh Guards were, nonetheless, under no illusions as to the challenge they faced. Tim Spicer, the Scots Guards operations officer, said:

> We knew we had to catch up and fast. I had a number of concerns, we hadn't had the opportunity to train as a battalion headquarters, 5 Brigade to whom we were assigned had been cobbled together and could not compare with 3 Commando Brigade who had worked together, knew each other, trained together with a clear focus on operating in harsh conditions like the Arctic with the right kit and winter clothing.

Spicer went on:

> Our kit was awful, 58 pattern webbing with a large pack. The first thing I did was to call up a mate in Berghaus, the outdoor gear specialists, and get hold of some proper bergens. Helly Hansen also, great windchill smocks, a lot of private purchases. It was negligence really by the MOD [Ministry of Defence] and unfair on the Guardsmen. It took the MOD a long time to respond to the level of events for the conditions we would face.

Colonel Mike Scott remarked, "We were issued with civilian bergens which we painted and arctic socks, together with extraordinary rubber over-boots. Our shiny bayonets were replaced by gunmetal ones which we duly sharpened. The best thing I invested in was a breathable waterproof sleeping bag cover for £70." He continued, "as there was no armoured threat, we converted our anti-tank platoon to .50 heavy machine gunners. The platoon was commanded by Captain Jeremy Campbell-Lamerton who'd played rugby for Scotland and spoke fluent Spanish. Our radios weren't up to it so we borrowed new ones, believe it or not, from the Territorial Army."

Second Lieutenant Crispin Black, then a platoon commander in The Prince of Wales's Company Welsh Guards, was equally dismayed at the dismal equipment for 5 Brigade: "rubbish boots, polyester army-issue socks, spray-proof wetproofs, leaky sleeping bags devoid of any warmth, bergens bought from camping shops, difficult radios. And we were less well fed. All the units of 3 Commando Brigade enjoyed Arctic rations stuffed with treats and amounting to 4,000 calories per man per day. 5 Brigade had standard NATO rations at 2,500 calories per day." Ironically, according to Mike Scott, this was not a view shared by 3 Commando Brigade, who were sick of dehydrated Arctic rations and could not wait to get their hands on the standard NATO rations and the old certainties of sausage and beans and beef stew.

Colonel Mike felt that, from the outset, there was confusion as to 5 Brigade's role:

There was a feeling that 5 Brigade were going to be garrison troops once 3 Commando Brigade and the Royal Navy had wrapped the whole thing up. It was easy in hindsight for other battalions to feel they should have been sent but they didn't push for it at the time. The thought of garrisoning the islands didn't appeal and many were either preparing for a tour in Northern Ireland, or just returning. But Dwin Bramall, the Chief of the General Staff (CGS) made it pretty clear when he said to me, "you're in reserve, you will be used." I wasn't sure I believed him. The Gurkhas were unemployable in NI or British Army of the Rhine, so were "spare". And who better than two Guards Battalions to be garrison troops after the war finished; paint everything Blue-Red-Blue and do double sentry outside Government House.

Scott remarked:

Command and control initially was a mess. Northwood was the controlling headquarters for the campaign but it was the headquarters of the Commander-in-Chief Fleet and not the Permanent Joint Headquarters for the Services that it is today. There was no in-place command structure to mount and direct a tri-service operation. I was concerned about who gave me direct operational orders and to protect the Battalion from any silliness.

There were immediate reservations about 5 Brigade Headquarters. The Brigadier, Tony Wilson, was a showman. He wore a maroon beret, to which he was not entitled, to the Parachute Regiment's contempt. When he started wearing 'Red Sea rig' in the evenings on the *Queen Elizabeth 2* (*QE2*) as the Task Force sailed south, there were many who wondered about his temperament and constitution. Admittedly, he'd had a good record to date but as the investment warning says, "Past performance is no guarantee of future results." One officer was to remember later an Orders Group when Wilson stood up and said, "The Intelligence will be so good that you'll know the names of every Argentinian soldier in every trench."

Johnny Rickett put it as succinctly: "Wilson was good with the pen but not with the sword." As 5 Brigade was ruefully to find out, the best intelligence came from the BBC World Service. Accompanying the force on the *QE2* was Brigadier John Waters. His official role was ground force deputy to Major General Jeremy Moore, a Marine appointed as Commander Land Forces. He had an order, in writing, from the Chief of the General Staff to take over command of 5 Brigade if Wilson failed. Waters was liked by 2nd Battalion Scots Guards and Colonel Mike found him a good deal easier to talk to than Wilson.

Crispin Black, who was later to become a lieutenant colonel in the Defence Intelligence Staff and a Fellow of Chatham House and BBC commentator, wrote a controversial book on the Falklands campaign, published on its 40th anniversary, *Too Thin for a Shroud*. Black believed that what was needed was a strong hand to make sure the two brigade commanders worked well together. Scott felt that there were Army generals who would have done better: "once ashore it was an Army operation with two brigades, artillery, two troops from The Blues and Royals and logistics. If it had been an opposed landing requiring expert amphibious advice, fine, but it wasn't. Moore should have made it clear to Wilson that 5 Brigade were in support of 3 Cdo [Commando] Brigade."

5 Brigade started training in earnest in mid-April at Sennybridge in the Brecon Beacons in south Wales. Bleak and windswept with one of the highest rainfalls in the country, it had a certain similarity to the topography of the Falklands. But in the late spring of 1982, the weather was unseasonably hot. The conditions would bear no resemblance to the Falkland Islands winter. General Sir Frank Kitson, his usual peppery and forensic self, who commanded UK Land Forces, was sardonic in his praise of the Welsh and Scots Guards at Sennybridge, remarking, "Well, the Guards know they've got a hill to climb."

James Stuart, aged just 20, had joined the Scots Guards as a second lieutenant just two months before in February 1982. James recalled that, during his time at Sandhurst training to be an officer, he had been given just one command appointment. He arrived in the Battalion looking forward to gently 'playing himself in' during a summer of public duties. Not even in his wildest imagination did James think that just over three months later, he would be leading his Guardsmen with bayonets fixed in one of the bitterest battles of the Falklands campaign.

James Stuart would be the first to admit that, though he was short on experience, he knew he had joined something much greater than he was. He was now part of an ethos passed down from generation to generation of Guardsmen. That *esprit de corps* would somehow see him through. It was a belief that was borne out in the battle for Mount Tumbledown.

For the first three weeks of April, the junta clung to the belief that Britain was engaged in an enormous game of bluff. They believed their invasion of British Sovereign territory would be settled by diplomatic means. Al Haig, President Reagan's Secretary of State, sought to broker a peace settlement. But Britain and its Prime Minister, Margaret Thatcher, were in no mood for a shoddy compromise. Britain had to make an emphatic statement of intent. Just after sunset on 1 May, HMS *Conqueror*, a Churchill-class nuclear-powered submarine, fired three torpedoes and sank the *General Belgrano*, the Argentine Navy cruiser.

The junta would have been wise to have remembered Mrs Thatcher's words at the Conservative Party conference in October 1980, "You turn if you want to, this lady's not for turning." After the sinking of the *Belgrano*, there was indeed no turning back. The world sat up and took notice. A cartoon in a German newspaper showed a proud, but mangy old lion with a ferocious paw still able to inflict a killer blow. It was an emblematic image.

On 2 May, 3 Commando Brigade had already begun to steam south from Southampton. As the only realistic military option with any chance of retaking the Falklands was to put a landing force ashore, it was clear that the three Commandos, 40, 42, and 45, would spearhead the assault. The 2nd and 3rd Battalions of the Parachute Regiment were attached to 3 Commando Brigade. Two Troops from The Blues and Royals were also sent as part of 3 Brigade. This raised some eyebrows but, if it did, it was replaced by unalloyed respect by the campaign's end.

Some ten days later, on 12 May, 5 Brigade set sail from Southampton on the *QE2*. There was to be much talk and rumour as the Brigade sailed south as to what their orders would be. But few were under any illusion that they would not have to fight. John Kiszely, the company commander of the Scots Guards 'Left Flank' (the Scots Guards name their companies in the old Marlburian fashion), and who was later to win the Military Cross, said to his platoon commanders and senior non-commissioned officers that they should commit to seeing action as soon as they stepped on board the *QE2*.

The voyage south played to every conceivable emotion. The stark contrast between the splendour of the sleek and slim *QE2* with its sundecks and sumptuous interiors and what lay ahead must have been hard to reconcile. The departure from Southampton, with crowds cheering, the docksides bristling with bunting and regimental bands playing, was not unlike the wave of patriotism as troops entrained at Victoria Station in August 1914. Only a handful of the men on board kept their own counsel as to what the future might hold. A Soviet spy ship bristling with communications kit trailed the *QE2* all the way south.

The *QE2*'s ten decks thundered all day as the officers and Guardsmen tried to keep themselves fit and their minds focused. The elegance of their surroundings did not help. Julian Sayers, special operations officer for the Welsh Guards, remarked, "All the supplies on board the *QE2*, wine, champagne, food were as you would expect in a luxury cruise from Southampton to New York. The weather was wonderful and quite a few of us felt we'd get as far as the Bay of Biscay, a peace settlement would be brokered, and we'd all return in high spirits to the UK, a bit like 1914 and back for Christmas I suppose."

As they cruised south, the mood perceptibly changed. Sayers went on, "A good barometer of how people began to feel was the daily church service. When we set sail, it was a pretty desultory turnout. By the time we got to the equator, the congregation had increased fourfold, and as we approached the Falklands there was standing room only. There were any number of 'foxhole' conversions."

In Argentina, the glee and rush of patriotism that had swept the Argentine Pampas gave way to alarm and gloom. They had misjudged Britain. They had misjudged the people's mood. Britain was sick of the sense of decline that had so suffocated the country in the 1970s.

They wanted their voice to be heard again across the globe and, in Mrs Thatcher, they had found their mouthpiece.

Britain's newspapers, with the odd exception, were warming to a patriotic if not a downright jingoistic theme in their coverage of events. The *Sun*'s headline after the *Belgrano*'s sinking on 2 May and the loss of 323 lives, 'Gotcha', was in questionable taste. There was no doubt, however, that Britain was up for a fight. Photographs of 'ripped' Royal Marines, stripped to the waist, exercising on the decks of the SS *Canberra*, played out on the front pages.

Dwin Bramall, the Chief of the General Staff, who had played cricket for the Army, remarked that "We've put our first XI into bat." The assault force of 3 Commando Brigade, numbering some 7,000 men, comprised some of the fittest, best trained and highly motivated troops in the world. Mike Scott, commanding the Scots Guards in 5 Brigade, whose regimental motto was '*Nemo me impune lacessit*' (No one provokes me with impunity), merely remarked of his own Regiment, "we just don't do defeat".

For the Parachute Regiment, it was an opportunity to show their true worth, 'far, fast and without question'. The Troubles in Northern Ireland had badly stained their reputation, particularly after the Ballymurphy massacre in August 1971, and Bloody Sunday on 30 January 1972. But the political and strategic environment in Northern Ireland was never the campaign to demonstrate the courage and aggression which the Falklands campaign would demand of them.

The final players selected for the 'first XI' were two Troops from B Squadron, The Blues and Royals. The Blues and Royals, formed in 1969 from the merger of the Royal Horse Guards, 'the Blues', and 1st Dragoons, known as 'the Royals', were stationed at Combermere Barracks in Windsor from where, almost 170 years ago, they had ridden to fight at the Battle of Waterloo.

When 3 Commando Brigade assembled in Plymouth in early April, the Marines and Paras must have looked at The Blues and Royals with curiosity. The feeling was mutual. Regiments in the British Army and the Royal Marines may have a healthy regard for one another but they also like each other to conform to type.

A picture in *The Guards* by Anthony Edgeworth at the Guards Polo Club, Windsor, in 1980 showed officers of The Blues and Royals at the Guards Polo Club lounging by their motor cars, Bentleys and Aston

Martins to a man, standard issue black or brown labradors by their side, and all looking remarkably untroubled by life.

By the end of the campaign, 3 Commando Brigade had enduring respect for The Blues and Royals and vowed that, if they were ever to find themselves in a tight spot again, they would always like to fight alongside them. This respect, hard won, owed much to the leadership of two young troop commanders, Mark Coreth and Lord Robin Innes-Ker, and an outstanding senior non-commissioned officer, Paul Stretton.

The British Army has always embraced original characters who go against the grain. Mildly eccentric, strongly artistic, and with no apparent warrior instincts, Coreth possessed courage, resilience, and an ability to think differently. Coreth, today a distinguished sculptor and artist, commanded No 4 Troop of B Squadron. With a shock of black hair, slight and wiry of build, and precise in his manner of speaking, Coreth was a natural leader. He never tried to pass himself off as an Army officer with an overdeveloped sense of urgency. But he took the trouble to master his profession and understand the men under his command.

Innes-Ker was the younger son of the ninth Duke of Roxburghe. His elder brother, Guy, had won the Sword of Honour at Sandhurst and had also been commissioned into The Blues and Royals. Brought up at Floors Castle in the Scottish Borders with its 55,000 acres, Innes-Ker had a natural affinity with the countryside and the country sports of hunting and shooting.

This gave him a flair for fieldcraft, how to judge distance and move across rough terrain in poor conditions. He had grown up with many of the estate workers and knew instinctively how to bring out the best in his Troopers. Authority sat easily with him. Despite the privations of combat, he felt at home as much as anyone could reasonably expect to do in the Falklands, where the topography was not unlike the Cheviot Hills which overlooked his family estates.

The two Troops under Coreth and Innes-Ker settled into a routine on board *Canberra* under their guardians, 3 Para. Coreth remarked that the Paras expressed surprise that they did not want to join them running around the *Canberra*'s decks 25 hours a day. But each regiment builds its own *esprit de corps*. The Blues and Royals had other priorities: signals, gunnery theory and practice, aircraft recognition and, more importantly, making sure their vehicles were in good shape for what was likely to be heavy going over the virtually trackless, peat-sodden ground of the Falklands.

They also took time to brief 3 Commando Brigade on their capabilities and how they could support the Brigade in combat. One of the Brigade's attached engineers was dismissive of the Troops' ability to cover the sodden quagmires they were likely to encounter. Coreth replied that the ground pressure of their light tanks, the Scorpion and Scimitar, was less than a human foot. Few were convinced, but Coreth proved true to his word.

It was extraordinary that the two Troops did not have their squadron headquarters, commanded at the time by the able and experienced Major Tim O'Sullivan. Neither the Marines nor the Paras knew what to do with The Blues and Royals as neither had served with armoured support before. If there had been two more Troops with a squadron commander who was able to tell senior officers what they were capable of, it would have made a significant difference to both brigades' firepower.

General Menendez, the Argentine commander, described by an SAS officer who had met him socially some years before as "soft skinned and soft faced", had a simple strategy. Menendez knew that the vital ground in the Falklands was the capital, Port Stanley, with its airfield and harbour. If he could hold this ground for long enough, it was his belief that the British resupply line would break down.

Menendez had a point. A logistics system stretching over 8,000 miles was fraught at best. The Argentine Navy, with four submarines, an aircraft carrier, and a number of Exocet-equipped warships, had the ability to attack the Task Force well north of the islands. Of course, once the Argentine cruiser *Belgrano* was sunk, the Argentine Navy stayed in port.

The Fuerza Aerea Argentina (FAA), Argentine Air Force, had 120 high-performance combat jet aircraft, all seemingly flown by pilots who modelled themselves on the legendary Argentine racing car driver, Juan 'El Maestro' Fangio. If the FAA and the Navy could seriously degrade the British supply chain and the ships protecting it, then Admiral Woodward, who confided to his diary, albeit later on in June, "We are now on the cliff edge of our capability" would have been proven right.

On 2 May, in retaliation for the sinking of the *Belgrano* the day before, the FAA fired two Exocet missiles, one of which smashed into HMS *Sheffield*. The ship was abandoned later that day, the first warship the Royal Navy had lost to enemy action since 1945. The stakes had risen. A fearful battle of attrition had begun between the Royal Navy and its Sea Harrier aircraft, and the Argentine Navy and the FAA.

Failure to win this battle of attrition would have meant 3 Commando Brigade, the amphibious Task Force, would be doomed to failure. In its rich, courageous, but chequered history, the British Army had any number of unpleasant memories of opposed landings to unsettle the nerves of the Task Force: Gallipoli in 1915; Dieppe in 1942; D-Day on 6 June 1944.

The momentum in the air and naval battle slowly swung towards Britain. During the campaign, in the period between 21 and 25 May, Argentine air attacks sank or damaged eight warships and transports, including the *Atlantic Conveyor*. This 28,000-ton container ship was loaded with supplies. More importantly, it had three Chinook and six Wessex heavy-lift helicopters. The loss of the *Atlantic Conveyor* was to weigh heavily on the Task Force.

The Argentine attacks on 25 May were the high water mark of Argentina's air campaign. Throughout the campaign, the FAA were to lose 45 aircraft in the air and 21 on the ground. 3 Commando Brigade was able to secure unopposed the beachhead at San Carlos Bay on East Falkland, 50 miles from the vital ground of Port Stanley. Dwin Bramall, the Chief of the General Staff, whose wartime experience of opposed landings had made him pretty jittery, could rest more easily. At least for the time being.

But it was the War Cabinet and politicians who were now beginning to flap. Diplomatically, things were moving in Argentina's favour, not helped by the Republic of Ireland which had called for an immediate ceasefire. Brigadier Thompson, commanding 3 Commando Brigade, was under pressure to push forward to Stanley. But the loss of the *Atlantic Conveyor* had removed at a stroke pretty well all his transport. In 1982, there were still any number of politicians with war experience who remembered the Germans bottling up established beachheads in Normandy and Anzio in Italy.

Pressure for action was building up. The Paras and Marines were tired of waiting. They were dug in with freezing rain dripping down their necks on the hillsides of Sussex Mountain. They were raring to go, 'fast, furious and without question'. Brigadier Thompson was given clear orders from Headquarters Northwood to attack Goose Green, which had a garrison of 1,400 men, with close support from Puccara aircraft, the only credible threat to the land operation's overall success and the advance on Stanley. The attack was a success. The Parachute Regiment of some 650 men forced the surrender of an Argentine force of more than 1,000 soldiers.

It was a considerable feat of arms. In hindsight, the attack on Goose Green was a political necessity, not a military one. The Argentine heavy-lift helicopters had been destroyed so the garrison at Goose Green could not be resupplied. They weren't going anywhere and could have been contained by a battalion on Sussex Heights, preferably the Gurkhas who, through reputation alone, would have made the Argentine Garrison pretty jumpy. The remainder of 5 Brigade could then deploy, as was originally intended, as reserve to reinforce 3 Commando Brigade when required.

Dwin Bramall's words to 5 Brigade, "You're in reserve, you will be used", were about to ring true. 5 Brigade had transferred to the SS *Canberra*, now at South Georgia and out of harm's way from Argentine air or naval attack. Johnny Rickett, commanding the Welsh Guards, remembered the approach to the Falklands: "As we made our way through the Roaring Forties, I began to feel distinctly queasy as we bounced up and down on waves whose size I had never witnessed before, but as we sailed through the fleet, Aldis lamps flashing signals, helicopters buzzing all around us, I was filled with confidence."

Tony Wilson, 5 Brigade commander, and his staff began to make a number of serious misjudgements. In fairness to Wilson, those armchair critics at home forgot that 5 Brigade was cobbled together and untrained in the complexity of amphibious operations. Wilson knew he had to keep level with 3 Commando Brigade's breakout, or 'yomp', across country towards Stanley as Brigadier Thompson was determined to maintain momentum. With 2 Para on the Wickham Heights protecting his left flank, he planned to march 35 miles to Fitzroy. It was never doable for the simple reason that troops would have to carry their heavy equipment, Browning machine guns, mortars, and all the ammunition. The Brigade had no transport, let alone helicopters to support them. The loss of the *Atlantic Conveyor* had seen to that.

Colonel Mike Scott, ever the realist, worked out that they would do well to manage 5 miles a day and would lose a number on the way through lack of the fitness needed for what would have been quite a challenge.

Johnny Rickett was not a man to sit still and wait for the wheel of good fortune to turn his way. He was only too aware of the damaging effect on morale and momentum that waiting in San Carlos would have on the Guardsmen. They were there to help win the war, not wait vainly in a defensive position for the perfect conditions to advance. He suggested to Wilson that the best way to get out of San Carlos was to start walking with his Battalion towards Darwin. Wilson agreed on the understanding (and promise) that Snowcats (small tracked vehicles) would be made available to lift the 81mm mortars, anti-tank launchers, bergens, ammunition and Browning heavy machine guns.

No Snowcats were forthcoming. To push on, separated from crucial arms and ammunition, would be to court disaster. Rickett called a halt to the march. Regrettably, this played into the hands of those carpers who, for some reason or another, were only too keen to criticise a Guards battalion. Rickett was only doing what any infantry battalion should do in war: do their utmost to close with and engage the enemy. Colonel Mike Scott had a point about the level of challenge. As he observed the Welsh Guards walking towards Darwin, he remarked to Major Richard Bethell, one of his company commanders, "Shouldn't we be doing something?" Bethell replied, "No. Preserve the fighting edge."

3 Commando Brigade was now far forward with its superior logistical support, but its right flank was vulnerable to enemy attack from the Stanley/Goose Green track. With a clever sleight of hand and the use of the only Chinook available to 5 Brigade, 2 Para, now under command of 5 Brigade, managed to get itself to Fitzroy.

5 Brigade's 'leap forward', led by 2 Para, along the southern flank towards Fitzroy and Bluff Cove, was probably the most controversial aspect of the campaign. It was done without the knowledge of Headquarters Land Forces and Headquarters 3 Commando Brigade. It opened up the southern flank while there was scarcely any logistical support to assist a two-pronged approach to Stanley.

The speed of 2 Para's move caught Moore by surprise. With 2 Para so far forward and without support, it meant 5 Brigade was off balance. Moore had to re-allocate resources to 5 Brigade. Moore, understandably, was keen to maintain momentum and, if possible, attack Stanley on 6 June. On 4 June, Moore asked Commodore Michael Clapp, who was responsible for troop transportation and landing plans, to get Wilson's brigade forward. Clapp's formal title was Commodore Amphibious Warfare (COMAW). It was Clapp, amongst others, whose decisions were to attract the most attention after the war had ended.

The decision was made by Commander Land Forces that 2nd Battalion Scots Guards and 1st Battalion Welsh Guards would move forward from San Carlos to Bluff Cove by sea. On the first night, 5/6 June, most of 2nd Battalion Scots Guards would embark in the Landing Platform Dock (LPD), HMS *Intrepid*, to sail south around East Falkland to just off Elephant Island, where they would cross-deck into *Intrepid*'s four Landing Craft Utility (LCU) boats for the final part of the voyage to Yellow Beach at Bluff Cove.

The next night, 1st Battalion Welsh Guards in HMS *Fearless*, the other LPD, would take the same route, except that not only would they have the four LCUs in *Fearless*, but, after they had dropped off 2nd Battalion Scots Guards at Bluff Cove, the four LCUs from *Intrepid* would rendezvous with HMS *Fearless* so that the whole Battalion and a considerable amount of stores could be moved in one lift. Major Ewen Southby-Tailyour, the amphibious warfare officer, would sail in *Intrepid* and then take the LCUs to Yellow Beach at Bluff Cove the following night. He would then bring the LCUs back to rendezvous with *Fearless* for the Welsh Guards.

For each journey, the LPDs would launch the LCUs off Elephant Island. This was 13 nautical miles from Bluff Cove and, at 7 knots, a journey of two hours.

There was a problem with Falklands Islands' charts. There were too few and many of them dated from the 1830s. LCUs were a low priority for charts as they operated within line of sight of an LPD. Off-shore navigation largely depended on Ewen Southby-Tailyour. He was a man of considerable sailing experience and, on his own initiative, had charted the waters in 1978 when he commanded the Royal Marines detachment. But, given the speed of the planned operation, he had no time to collect his notes, which were on HMS *Fearless*.

When Ewen Southby-Tailyour boarded the *Intrepid*, the captain, Captain Peter Dingemans, informed him that, contrary to the orders from Commodore Michael Clapp, Commander Amphibious Warfare (COMAW), he considered it too dangerous for *Intrepid* with its escorting frigate to sail further than a point south-west of Lively

Island. The LCUs would have to sail 35 rather than 13 nautical miles in deteriorating weather. Southby-Tailyour protested but to no avail: "We are about to launch 600 men in four small, very lightly armed and unprotected craft ... we are going to transit hostile waters along enemy-held shores in the dark ... we do not have updated charts and no log for speed and distance, a steering compass with at least 30-degree error through an area of known magnetic anomalies."

Captain Dingemans assured Southby-Tailyour that he had been told by COMAW that there would be no Royal Navy ships nearby. That was to prove wrong.

2nd Battalion Scots Guards embarked with Southby-Tailyour in the four LCUs from *Intrepid* at 2.30am. The weather was good; visibility less so. The weather, however, soon began to worsen with heavy rain and water pouring over the bows, soaking the Guardsmen to the skin. If that wasn't unpleasant enough, star shells were fired over the LCUs by HMS *Cardiff* which was on the gun line to shell the environs of Stanley. It was a shocking lack of communication as HMS *Cardiff* had not been informed of the LCUs. The captain of the *Cardiff*, Captain Michael Harris, had his wits about him. If he had engaged with high explosives rather than star shells, the Scots Guards would have been destroyed. The history of combat is littered with 'blue-on-blue' incidents, and this was a potentially catastrophic oversight on behalf of the Royal Navy, saved only by Captain Harris's foresight to identify the LCUs.

After seven desperately trying hours at sea with remarkable navigation by Southby-Tailyour, encouraged by two of Colonel Mike's officers, Ian Mackay-Dick and John Kiszely, both qualified ocean-going yachtsmen, the LCUs arrived at Yellow Beach at Bluff Cove. Everyone was in a poor state. It took them 24 hours to dry their kit and recover from the ordeal. Captain Tim Spicer, the operations officer and as resilient as anyone, remarked, "it was quite the worst night of my life, to this day I have difficulties with the circulation in my hands."

The plan for the Welsh Guards was to sail on HMS *Fearless* on the night of 6 June. It began well enough. Jeremy Larken, the captain, was determined to drop the Welsh Guards closer to their destination than the Scots Guards the previous night. Larken believed he could get the Battalion to the Elephant Island RV to meet *Intrepid*'s landing craft by 2am on the morning of 7 June.

No such landing craft appeared. Poor weather was given as the excuse but the reality was more sinister. A Parachute Regiment officer, brandishing a pistol, 'persuaded' the landing craft coxwains to ferry 2 Para to Bluff Cove. This was against Southby-Tailyour's direct orders, "to remain where they were for future operations."

With only two integral landing craft on *Fearless*, Rickett was faced with the dilemma of splitting his Battalion. Jeremy Moore assured him that the remaining half of his Battalion would be brought up to Bluff Cove the following night (8/9 June).

"Everything involving 5 Brigade is going wrong," remarked Colonel Ian Baxter, a logistics officer on Jeremy Moore's staff. Michael Clapp tried to put Baxter's mind at ease but much later was to tell Rickett, "The problem was to find an available Landing Ship Logistic (LSL) and the only one available was the *Sir Galahad* which was due to arrive from Teal inlet. I was not happy about sending her as she had been badly bombed but was seaworthy."

The remainder of Rickett's Battalion embarked on the *Sir Galahad* but was forced to anchor offshore because of the weather conditions. If the weather changed for the better, she would become an easy target for marauding Pucara aircraft from the FAA.

The forthcoming disaster on the *Sir Galahad* then began to take on a momentum of its own. Communications between COMAW's headquarters and 5 Brigade were non-existent. The three landing craft eventually appeared, but not at Bluff Cove. And finally, the weather gave way to a bright blue sky and almost perfect flying conditions for the FAA.

The Welsh Guards were now fatally exposed to air attack. The *Sir Galahad* had slid quietly into Port Pleasant Sound but nobody ashore was expecting it and 5 Brigade was unaware of what was happening. The senior operations officer at 5 Brigade did not even know that only half of Rickett's Battalion had been landed. The overriding concern of the two Welsh Guards company commanders on the *Sir Galahad* was to rejoin the rest of the Battalion as quickly as possible at Ridge Camp. They did not know that the bridge at Fitzroy had been repaired and decided they should remain on the *Sir Galahad* to be taken by sea to Bluff Cove.

Ewen Southby-Tailyour and Ivar Hellberg, commanding the Commando Logistic Regiment, tried to convince the Welsh Guards company commanders to get off the *Sir Galahad* with all speed. But they were unpersuaded. They had their orders and were determined to honour Rickett's wishes based on the available intelligence.

Finally, at around midday on 8 June, 5 Brigade gave the message to disembark. But who, how, and in what order was unclear. Once again, and this time with appalling consequences, 5 Brigade's lack of amphibious experience began to tell. HMS *Exeter*, the picquet (early warning ship), had sounded 'air raid warning red', but the message did not reach the *Sir Galahad*. The ship's radio was either not working or on the wrong frequency.

At around 3pm, the *Sir Galahad* came under attack from five A4 Skyhawks flying low with 500-pound bombs and 30mm cannon fire. The *Sir Galahad* was hit at least twice. The effects were devastating: a fireball ripped through the ship's interior. The Battalion lost 38 men killed and 80 badly wounded.

There will always remain conjecture as to why such a tragedy took place. Crispin Black, however, in *Too Thin for a Shroud*, unearthed evidence in the National Archives (DEFE 69/26 Annex G) that the Navy passed the buck for the *Galahad* disaster entirely onto 5 Brigade's shoulders. The Navy claimed that 5 Brigade was in tactical control of the landing craft that day. This was a deceit and a complete departure from naval doctrine and the rules and regulations under which the Navy operates. Whether this was true or not remains a matter of some controversy.

Some three weeks before, on 21 May, the two Troops of The Blues and Royals attached to 3 Commando Brigade were making their mark. They slipped ashore at San Carlos in the early hours, the night still bible black. Naval gunfire was in support. At first light, they engaged the first of many FAA sorties seeking to disrupt and destroy the Brigade landing.

It was Robin Innes-Ker's birthday and his Troop decided to give him a treat of roast beef from a beautifully skinned cow they had come across. The meat, however, was past its best and the Troop found themselves dancing the 'Falklands Foxtrot' for the next 36 hours.

The gainsayers who had confidently declared that the CVR(T) could not move on the Falklands terrain were proved wrong. On their way to protect 3 Brigade's north-east flank, Coreth's Troop stumbled across a farmer, his tractor up to its axles in liquid mud. Using a terrific piece of kit, the kinetic energy rope, the tractor was catapulted out with some ease. The CVR(T) was resting on a slither of peat.

The real star was the Rarden 30mm gun. The Rarden with its flat trajectory, six-shot capability, and pinpoint accuracy could swiftly overwhelm a target. Target acquisition with a superb night sight was effortless. Captain Roger Field, Blues and Royals, who was attached to 5 Brigade as a liaison officer/watchkeeper but found himself later on in the campaign commanding a Scimitar and 'firing in' the Paras assault on Wireless Ridge, said, "We played a little game: a short burst of machine gun fire would attract an Argentinian response but of course giving away their position. The Rarden would then target the source of the enemy tracer. Deathly silence followed from the enemy position." Roger's book *Scimitar into Stanley* paints a colourful and exacting portrait of the CVR(T)'s impact on the Falklands campaign.

Fuel was precious and hard to come by. Once 3 Commando Brigade saw the value of The Blues and Royals, the two Troops were hard pressed to meet their commitments. 'Beg, borrow, and steal', the mantra of any army whose logistical tail was floundering, became the Troops' watchword. The Engineers soon discovered they were missing 28 jerry-cans.

The two Troops' mission remained constant: to assist 3 Commando Brigade in closing with and destroying the enemy at Port Stanley. They formed the fire base for 3 Para's successful assault on Mount Longdon and found themselves under consistent mortar and artillery fire. The Argentine mortar and artillery observers knew the Troops' CVR(T)s were a prize target, but the Troops' clever use of ground gave them clear passage.

Both the Marines and the Paras continued to be surprised by the Troops' versatility and ability to cover distance at speed. No 3 Troop under Innes-Ker took six hours to complete an arduous journey; the Marines with their Snow Cats took 17 hours to cover the same distance.

Given their operational flair, it was predictable that the two Troops were ordered to cross the central mountains and join 5 Brigade at Fitzroy. The locals considered this stretch of terrain to be nigh impassable. Coreth was later to remark, "This was our most gruelling test in dense fog but, by then, we had learnt never to follow another vehicle's tracks but to make your own."

The 'experts' told Coreth and Innes-Ker to plan on 48 hours to get to Fitzroy. They completed the journey in six and were met with a stunned welcome by Wilson and his staff. Coreth said, "Well, Brigadier, we're here in good order and way before time. May I suggest our men find a comfortable barn, some good tucker and a few drams, a hot bath, 12 hours kip and then we're all yours." Wilson could only but agree.

The short rest from what had been a relentless few weeks was more than welcome. Their biggest test was to come as the battle for Port Stanley reached its final days.

On 9 June, Brigadier Wilson, his nerves now somewhat frayed after the disaster on the *Sir Galahad*, ordered the Scots Guards to capture Mount Tumbledown. Tumbledown was part of the Argentine outer ring of defence to Port Stanley. It was key to the Argentine defensive ring.

Mount Tumbledown was a daunting challenge. It stretches nearly a mile west to east. Its northern flank is an escarpment. It rises sharply from the south with deceptive summits at its centre and to the east. Peat bogs and crags dominate the ascent.

Mount Tumbledown had been occupied by 5th Marine Infantry Battalion since early April. The Battalion had been based in Tierra del Fuego in Argentina's deep south. Its members, numbering some 650 men, were used to hostile conditions. They were well led by Commander Hugo Robacio. A photograph of Robacio taken at the time shows him to be a man of proud and forthright bearing. Of all the Argentine forces on the Falklands, his Battalion was as well trained as any. And they were well armed with eight heavy-calibre machine guns, 24 sustained fire machine guns, 22 mortars of varying calibre, and 12 artillery 105mm pieces.

They would take some dislodging.

On 9 June, Brigadier Wilson summoned Colonel Scott to give him his plan for the advance on Port Stanley. Scott was told that the Gurkhas would take Mount Tumbledown by patrols. And his Battalion was to conform to the Commando Brigade by advancing along the main track to Stanley in daylight on 12 June. If the Gurkhas had not managed to take Tumbledown, he was to swing his Battalion to the left and assault Tumbledown from the south, uphill. The Welsh Guards were then to advance on Sapper Hill, which, after the trauma of the *Sir Galahad*, was a credit to their resilience.

Very unhappy with this, Scott returned to Bluff Cove to consult his command team. They were horrified. It would entail breaching the minefield across the Stanley track, which their patrols had identified, in the dark. This would take all night. They would then be exposed in daylight to direct enemy fire from any defenders on the other side of the minefield, and heavy machine-gun fire, within range, from the southern slope of Tumbledown. They would also be subjected to observed indirect fire from mortars and artillery.

Scott and his team then conceived a new plan. This was to attack Tumbledown by night from the west. The Battalion would establish its fighting formation in the ground held by the Marines. This was in the dead ground to the immediate west of Goat Ridge and Mount Harriet. From here, they would launch their attack. Major Richard Bethell would lead a diversionary attack, with a Troop of The Blues and Royals, on the predictable track, stopping short of the minefield.

Scott's job was to persuade the Brigadier of their alternative plan. Major John Kiszely had this to say much later:

An important factor to be considered here is institutional culture. The armed forces are, by necessity, hierarchical organisations which depend on an acceptance of authority, particularly in war and on operations. Even more damaging than an over authoritarian hierarchy in the armed forces is one which places no limits on dissent or challenge to authority.

The optimum solution is, of course, a balance. And a balance that requires fine judgement. As a company commander in the Falkland Islands conflict of 1982, I was fortunate enough to have a commanding officer who struck this balance skilfully. When it came to orders, it was clear: orders are orders; but on other occasions, he was happy for alternative ideas to be put forward and self-confident enough to allow his opinion to be challenged.

Before the Battle of Mount Tumbledown, he gathered his company commanders and key staff officers together to discuss the brigade plan for the attack and to share his misgivings. Suffice to say that after an open discussion, led by him, he formulated a very different plan, and returned to brigade headquarters that evening to speak truth to power, pointing out the inadequacy of the brigade plan to the brigade commander. Fortunately, his plan was accepted. To give the brigade commander his due, he did not treat this as a challenge to his authority, and allowed logic and common sense to prevail.

There was then a pause while the Commando Brigade took its objectives. Late in the afternoon on 12 June, Scott was summoned to brigade headquarters to be told by Wilson, "Tonight's the night." This was for the Scots Guards to attack. Scott was appalled. It would mean ferrying the Battalion, by helicopter, in the dark to their assembly area. This was unlikely to be completed before midnight. They would then have to shake out into formation and attack over unseen ground. On top of that, Scott's gunner had told him that the ammunition for the supporting artillery was in extremely short supply having been used up in the Commando attacks. It was a recipe for disaster.

Scott explained the difficulties and asked for a 24-hour delay. Wilson immediately agreed, without consulting General Jeremy Moore. Scott then, with two hours of daylight left, rushed back to his headquarters and took his company commanders up to the saddle between Goat Ridge and Mount Harriet from where they could see Tumbledown. The company commanders followed this up with their platoon commanders the next day when the Battalion took up its position in the assembly area and forming up point for the attack. It was an important and masterly stroke as it gave everyone the confidence in what was expected of them and what they had to do.

Scott was fortunate in his officers. John Kiszely who commanded Left Flank had a true warrior spirit and was a fine trainer of men. Richard Bethell was an imaginative and colourful officer who thought laterally when faced with a challenge. Scott's operations officer, Tim Spicer, was tactically highly competent, a brilliant instructor, and enjoyed Scott's complete confidence. Ian Dalzell-Job, commanding G Company, was an old-style Guards officer who took great care over his men's welfare. Simon Price, who commanded Right Flank, was unassuming and steadfast. Lastly, Scott's second-in-command, Ian Mackay-Dick (later to become the Major General Commanding the Household Division 1994–97), affectionately known as 'Major Small Points', was guaranteed to raise important issues that no one else had thought about. He was also Scott's heir apparent if Scott was killed in action. Wisely, they kept well apart in the assault lest either one was killed.

Scott knew 5 Brigade was a hollow affair with no experience in logistics. He relied heavily on Ewan Lawrie, his technical quartermaster. Lawrie, who started his career as a Guardsman and ended it as Lieutenant Colonel with an OBE, was as canny as he was brave. He kept the Battalion going with whatever it needed. One plus point, and one at odds with the Army's usual experience, was that the radios borrowed from the Territorial Army worked extremely well.

Scott and his officers took a long, cool look at Wilson's plan in a dingy, poorly lit attic and dismissed it as at best unworkable, and at worst suicidal. Artillery ammunition was running out fast and what little there was seemed to be earmarked for 3 Brigade. Scott had great faith in his mortar platoon led by Peter Farrelly but the softness of the peat ground meant that the mortar base plates sank, rendering the mortars pretty well useless.

It was Bethell who unlocked the dilemma with a plan for a diversionary attack which he would lead with a mixture of Guardsmen and non-commissioned officers largely taken from the Battalion's administrative support and the reconnaissance platoon. Coreth's Troop from The Blues and Royals were to give direct fire support.

H-Hour (the time for attack) was set for 9pm. It was to be a four-phase silent night attack with the three rifle companies advancing from Goat Ridge to seize Tumbledown. Bethell's diversionary attack was to confuse the Argentine Marines and draw fire away from the main thrust of the attack. The password, amusingly, was 'Heh, Jimmy'. Spanish speakers can never say their Js: 'Heh Himmy' would attract a burst of machine-gun fire.

Bethell's diversionary attack with direct fire support from Coreth's CVR(T)s had to provoke the Argentine Marines into thinking that the main attack was coming from the south. This would allow the main Scots Guards thrust to gain a strong foothold on Tumbledown. The fighting was close quarter. It took Bethell and his men nearly two hours to fight through 11 positions. They lost two men, including the much-loved and respected Drill Sergeant Danny White. Because of the heartfelt loss of White, the diversionary attack attracted some controversy. But it was a brave and courageous attack carried out with imagination and boldness. Strategically, it was a success. The Argentine Marines were convinced that the main attack was from the south. Some years later, Scott saw Colonel Robacio's map, which showed the whole of the Welsh Guards Battalion advancing along the track of Bethell's diversionary attack.

Three hundred years of fighting reputation, from Waterloo to the Somme to Salerno, were now at stake. It was that collective memory, absorbed by every officer and Guardsman, that got the Scots Guards to the top of the mountain. The fighting was bitter, close quarter with bayonets fixed. There were moments of stalemate in the freezing cold. There was a ghostly half-light as fleeting clouds obscured the moonlight. But as a Guardsman in Left Flank shouted to John Kiszely, "Aye, Sir, I'm fucking with you!", there was little chance that the Scots Guards would be thrown off Tumbledown.

The Guardsman's brave and heartening words were typical of a Scots Guardsman recruited at that time from the Gorbals area of Glasgow. If you came from the Gorbals – a notoriously tough and deprived area on the south bank of the River Clyde – the Scots Guards was the first place you had three square meals a day and your own bed. It was either the army or Barlinnie Prison.

Spicer, the operations officer, was later to remark, "In the end it came down to a simple and classic strategy – a short barrage followed by an aggressive fire and manoeuvre infantry attack. Ironically, it was something that a Guardsman in the Second World War would have recognised, old-fashioned perhaps but effective. And in Kiszely, commanding Left Flank, we had a cool headed and rational officer who knew his profession."

Mike Scott kept his thoughts to himself: "If we hadn't taken Tumbledown by dawn, I would have had to conduct a fighting withdrawal still exposed to the Argentine Marines who had good sangar positions and indirect artillery fire from Stanley; coordination would be diabolical. Thank goodness, the radios worked extremely well. But that would have been about it in our favour."

Kiszely, huddled next to his radio operator, said, "Curiously, I felt a sense of detachment, apparently not uncommon among people in extreme danger, but it became increasingly apparent to me that if the artillery couldn't get its act together, we would have to take the risk and begin our final assault without fire support. Eventually, in my mind I gave them ten minutes. They must have been psychic because five minutes later artillery rounds arrived on target."

James Stuart, commanding 13 Platoon in Left Flank, had lost his platoon sergeant, Sergeant John Simeon, in the battle's opening firefight. For an officer fresh from Sandhurst, who would have relied heavily on Simeon's experience, it must have been an unnerving moment. As he and his platoon fought their way up a steep gully, James felt unusually calm. He was later to remark: "I never thought for a moment we were going to lose, the confidence I got from our 300 years of history enshrined in the Regiment's Colours, the Guardsmen, granite tough from Glasgow's turf wars, well, how on earth could we falter? Now I think back on it, it was probably the bravado of youth but I felt it all the same."

It was a sentiment mirrored by an 18-year-old Guardsman, Mark Cape, in Left Flank: "No matter how much you train for war, nothing quite prepares you for lying down waiting for the order to advance towards a well dug in enemy position. Victory was never in question, it was just how long would we the Scots Guards take to root out the enemy on Mount Tumbledown."

'Once a Guardsman, always a Guardsman' is an overused phrase, but on the morning of 14 June it had more than a kernel of truth. Captain Sam Drennan, a former Scots Guardsman, had transferred to the Army Air Corps and was now flying a Scout helicopter in the campaign. Sam had been forbidden to fly that morning because of 'other priorities', but Sam knew the Scots Guards had been in the thick of it and there were certain to be casualties who needed immediate casevac. Time and time again, Sam flew to Tumbledown to pick up the wounded. He had not forgotten the obligations of kith and kin and where his loyalties lay. He was awarded the Distinguished Flying Cross.

The cost to the Scots Guards was high, eight killed and 43 wounded. Half of the casualties were officers, warrant and non-commissioned officers. Leadership from the front. Even in death, the Guardsmen retained their unflinching discipline. Guardsman Ronald Tabini died telling the redoubtable Company Sergeant Major Bill Nichol of Left Flank, "I've been shot, Sir."

The advance on Port Stanley drew strength and inspiration from the Scots Guards' success. The final Argentine domino to fall was Wireless Ridge. 2 Para, whose performance at Goose Green had given the Task Force such confidence, was given the job. Robin Innes-Ker's No 3 Troop The Blues and Royals was in support. A platoon commander in 2 Para said, "It was reassuring to hear the roar of the Scimitars and Scorpions arriving to support our attack."

Extraordinarily, there was only one major engine failure suffered by The Blues and Royals during the entire campaign, a reflection of expert crew maintenance and the CVR(T)'s robustness.

Wireless Ridge fell to a four-phase night attack from the north supported by all the firepower and artillery support that 3 Commando Brigade could bring to bear. The Argentine 7th Infantry Regiment, holding the ridge, had been decisively defeated. Once again 2 Para, now under command of David Chaundler, who had replaced 'H' Jones 'killed in action', proved itself to be a formidable fighting force.

An army close to defeat is a pitiful sight. By dawn on 14 June, the 5th Marine Battalion and the 7th Infantry Regiment were falling back to Stanley. Stumbling, filthy, tired to the point of exhaustion, dragging themselves along with their wounded, it was a bittersweet moment for even the most hardened of British soldiers to observe.

The Welsh Guards, stoical after the *Sir Galahad* tragedy, had begun to pick themselves up. Rick Jolly, who commanded the Field Hospital at Ajax Bay, commented on the Welsh Guardsmen who had been badly wounded, "I cannot praise them enough, that sense of family and deep friendship which you find in a Regiment like the Welsh Guards. A Guardsman, badly burnt, said to me, 'Sir, treat my mate first, he needs it more than me.'"

There would be a time for grieving. Johnny Rickett quickly recognised the importance of reconnecting to some sense of meaning. And that of course was to get the Battalion on the move again to do whatever it could to bring about the Argentine surrender.

Brigadier Thompson also saw the need for the Battalion to get back on its feet and attached two Commando companies from 40 Commando as replacements for The Prince of Wales's and No 3 Company. The Battalion was now under command of 3 Commando Brigade. As Rickett said, "It was such a joy to be in an HQ which breathed professionalism and confidence."

The comforting embrace of 3 Commando Brigade was not for long. For the final battle for Stanley, the Welsh Guards were once again under Wilson and 5 Brigade. Their final task was to capture Sapper Hill. It was to be a daylight attack without artillery support. This was the stuff of the Great War and Rickett wasted no time in making his feelings clear to Wilson. Nevertheless Colonel Rickett realised the importance of the task, not only to turn around the Battalion after the *Sir Galahad* disaster, but also to maintain the momentum of the final assault on Stanley. And he was to do so with remarkable success and courage as the leading elements of the Battalion stood on the windswept summit of Sapper Hill.

Rickett need not have worried unduly. White flags were now appearing over Stanley. The Argentine commander, Mendoza, wanted to accept a ceasefire and surrender.

Wellington's famous phrase, "Nothing except a battle lost can be half so melancholy as a battle won", could not have been truer of the scenes that faced British soldiers in Port Stanley.

The detritus of despair. The streets were littered with abandoned weapons and ammunition. The smoke from burning documents and destroyed material filled the air. Argentine officers were allowed to keep their side arms lest they were attacked by their men, mutinous, angry and hungry. A bitterly cold wind and freezing rain swept through the town. An elderly couple asked a Royal Marine to be gentle with the prisoners, "After all they are so young and confused."

Port Stanley was also without water. An epidemic spreading through 8,000 prisoners of war did not bear thinking about. British soldiers had to guard against booby traps and the hundreds of plastic anti-personnel mines scattered without rhyme or reason.

3 Commando Brigade were first in, and it was only right that they should be first out. Johnny Rickett became garrison commander and the Welsh Guards took on the immense task of the clean-up and repatriation of the Argentine prisoners. Christopher Drewry, No 2 Company commander, took on this responsibility with strict instructions from Johnny Rickett to "Tell the Captain of the *St Edmund* [the ship designated to repatriate Argentine POWs] to get a move on because when you get back, we'll all pile on and go home."

One further tragedy was to befall the Welsh Guards. A Harrier Jet, skidding on the ice, let loose a sidewinder missile. Eleven Welsh Guardsmen were badly injured. Many lost limbs.

After the loss of life on the *Sir Galahad*, it was another grievous blow for the Battalion to endure. Good fortune and disaster are two sides of the same coin in war, but Welsh Guardsmen must have felt unduly hard done by the vagaries of fate.

In Johnny Rickett, however, the Battalion had a commanding officer whose stoicism and care of his men was clear for all to see. Johnny's infectious optimism could easily be misread for bravado. Journalists who did not take the time to look at the true human being, or had an axe to grind about the Guards, could be unfairly critical. But as Mike Scott, commanding the Scots Guards, said, "I had the utmost admiration for Johnny, I'm not sure how I would have coped with the losses he had to endure."

The Scots Guards were sent to West Falkland and were the last combat troops to leave the islands. It was six weeks after the Argentine surrender that they were finally flown back home. Ironically, the forced delay to their return was something of a blessing. It helped the Battalion which had fought so hard at Tumbledown to 'decompress'.

'Decompression' was an expression first coined by US Troops in Vietnam, but was not common currency in the British Army until after the Falklands campaign. Even then it didn't really take hold as a way of helping soldiers getting back on their feet after the trauma of combat until the Afghanistan campaign.

Those who sailed back from the Falklands seem to have done a lot better than those who flew back. They had more time to 'decompress', air their feelings, and unwind in the company of men with shared memories. The barriers between officers and Guardsmen, often quite stark on public duties in London, no longer existed. Comradeship in adversity and in a tough, shared endeavour had strengthened the bond between officers and men.

Forty years on, James Stuart, a platoon commander with Left Flank on Tumbledown, remarked, "Everyone in my platoon with just one exception aimed and fired their weapon that night; for better or worse they were intimately engaged in the battle's outcome and were none the worse for it. Sometimes, I think it must have been a lot harder in Afghanistan where you could witness shocking scenes like the after effects of an IED but never face the enemy directly."

Scott was understandably concerned about the length of time they had to spend in Port Howard, West Falkland, before returning to the UK.

It was bad for morale, the average age of the Guardsmen was 22, they'd given their all, Brigade HQ had pushed off and it was quite a challenge keeping men engaged and motivated for close to two months after the last battle. We managed it pretty well; Padre Angus Smith and our medical officer did a great job. We were able to live in some style and comfort after the privations of the campaign. But frankly, it wasn't till the arrival of General David Thorne, as Commander of British Forces in the Falklands, that the MOD got a well-deserved rocket and we were on our way to the UK, the last of us returning on 18 Aug.

David Thorne, to the day he retired from the Army, kept mounted on his desk a broken bayonet which had been owned by a Guardsman killed in action.

As Tim Spicer looked back on the Falklands campaign, he remarked that it had been "a transitional war". An officer or Guardsman fighting in the Great War or the Second World War, he argued, would have noticed little difference in how they were expected to fight in the battle to retake the islands. The final assault on Tumbledown was classic infantry: artillery support, fire and manoeuvre, enemy trenches and sangars cleared one by one.

It was also transitional as the first war since Korea 1950–53 that involved air, sea, and land with the added dimension of strategic intelligence and intercept.

But the Falklands campaign was not 'transitional' in terms of the qualities of leadership and courage needed by officers and Guardsmen alike in the campaign.

After the campaign, the Household Division would look at itself and the rest of the Army through a different prism. The day of the gentleman amateur, a lingering hangover from the doldrums of the 1960s and early 1970s, was over. The rest of the Army had caught up. For too long, in the decades after the Second World War, the Household Division had rested on its laurels, relying on its nuanced relationship with the establishment and popularity with the public through its mastery of ceremonial. It also recognised the importance of public relations and controlling the narrative. There has always been more than a hint of envy towards the Guards, any number of naysayers looking for Guardsmen to trip up.

5 Brigade Headquarters might have been a muddle but it was a muddle that brought the Household Division up sharp. Ceremonial excellence and operational soldiering complement each other, but commanding officers were now acutely aware that they had to work doubly hard if the two were to march in step.

Nevertheless, despite the prejudicial view of some commentators who knew no better, the Household Division could draw comfort from much of its performance during the campaign, particularly at an individual level. Discipline and resilience, the hallmarks of Her

Majesty's Guards, were evident to see. The Blues and Royals more than made their mark. After their union with The Life Guards in 1992 where they became the Household Cavalry Regiment, they quickly emerged as exceptional at operations as they were at ceremonial.

The Troubles continued to exercise the professionalism of the officers and men of the Household Division. It was the Balkans conflict, however, that was to highlight their innate strengths. Both campaigns highlighted the Household Division's hallmarks of discipline, professionalism, and commendable restraint. Sir John Moore at Corunna in 1809 was not the last general to remark on seeing Household Division troops, "Those must be the Guards."

On 13 July 1982, General Sir Edwin Bramall, Chief of the General Staff, wrote to the Major General:

> I want to place firmly on record the magnificent way in which all three regiments of the Household Division performed which was in the best traditions of the Brigade of Guards and the Household Cavalry. The Scots Guards carried out an attack on the key objective of Tumbledown where the enemy were well trained, well equipped and determined, and consisted of Argentine crack troops, their Marines. It was a long, hard fight, It was only by the utmost determination, courage and gallantry that, despite considerable casualties, they ultimately took their objective. It really was a magnificent achievement. They have earned the admiration of all of us for their professionalism, courage and spirit and shown to the world the incomparable quality of the Household troops and the strength of the regimental system.

Controversy will continue to surround the Falklands campaign. More books will emerge with a different take on the events that took place. As the Great Duke of Wellington remarked, "The history of a battle is not unlike the history of a ball. No individual can recollect the order in which, or at which, events occurred where the battle was lost or won."

In June 2022, the 40th anniversary of the Falklands campaign took place. It was overshadowed by the celebrations for Her Majesty The Queen's Platinum Jubilee, but for those of the Household Division who had fought for Crown and Country in the campaign this would not have troubled them for a moment.

4

The Household Division in Germany: The British Army's Latter Day 'Raj', 1969–2008

Like all model organisations, the Army in Germany regulates its life according to the season.
IRISH GUARDS REGIMENTAL UPDATE, 1953

A lull in a 'battle' on Sunday 17 October 1982 provided a fleeting opportunity for a Household Division lunch party in Schloss Schenke, a village *Gasthaus* on the North German Plain. Exercise *Quarter Final*, the largest field training exercise of the year, had been running for a week. For the troops deployed, serving with the British Army of the Rhine (BAOR) the most challenging task to date had been to move from their barracks to their notional 'general deployment positions', an important and challenging exercise in itself.

At the lunch party were 30 Guards officers, representing all seven regiments and the three main elements of the exercise: the 'Blue' (Friendly) forces, the 'Red' (Enemy) forces, and the Umpires, easily recognisable with their white armbands. Two brigade commanders, Brigadier Charles Guthrie (the host) and Brigadier Murray Naylor, were there, as was the commanding officer of the 1st Battalion Irish Guards, Lieutenant Colonel Robert Corbett. There were key staff officers present from all the deployed headquarters, and from the exercising units: The Life Guards ('Blue' forces, equipped with Chieftain tanks), 2nd Battalion Coldstream Guards (Umpires and with a company of 'Red' forces in their FV432 armoured personnel carriers), and 1st Battalion Irish Guards (Umpires). Schloss Schenke, on that Sunday afternoon (a rest day for all), was a temporary 'no man's land', a place to relax away from the 'exercise play' that would resume sometime later that day.

The exercise had begun several days earlier with long queues of tracked and wheeled vehicles crawling along deployment routes. It rained incessantly, reducing mobility and off-road activity as it might have done in a real war. During the second week the weather improved, as the troops, still concealed in their concentration areas, conducted low-level training prior to the final big attack, the climax of the exercise. This would see armoured forces emerging from their 'hull-down' hides in forests and farmyards for a fast-moving trial of the new 'counterstroke' tactics designed to strike at the flank of an advancing Soviet army. Tactical concepts were changing from the old static and defensive posture that had prevailed since the mid-1950s, even if the equipment had not kept pace with the ideas. Just a few months earlier, in the South Atlantic, the British had won the Falklands War, and this victory was contributing to a renewed confidence in Germany. Could NATO fight and possibly win a war on the Central Front or at least delay a Warsaw Pact ground attack, thus avoiding an escalation to nuclear annihilation?

With over 20,000 troops and many armoured and tracked vehicles deployed, Exercise *Quarter Final* was conducted on an impressive scale. Few restrictions existed in 1982, and although equipment reliability was a problem, at least there was no shortage of hardware, and troops could go virtually anywhere on the exercise area that their tactical plan required. Advancing across a field of standing crops, or reversing tanks into farmyards or barns, was an accepted part of a field training exercise during this period.

This was not surprising, since the threat from the Warsaw Pact was a real one and, with the Russian invasion of Afghanistan in 1979, there seemed no prospect of the Cold War ending soon. In East Germany alone, there were three Soviet tank armies and two motorised armies, comprising some 370,000 troops, 7,000 tanks, 2,350 infantry fighting vehicles, and 300 helicopters, supported by an air force of some 900 combat aircraft. And this was not accounting for the East German Army, regarded as one of the most effective Warsaw Pact armies. Furthermore, although the likelihood of an attack across the Inner German Border seemed remote to many, it was deterrence at every level, not just the threat of nuclear retaliation, that provided NATO forces with a clear professional purpose: to be ready for war in order to avoid war. Although it might not have been obvious to the soldiers deployed on Exercise *Quarter Final*, this was an important demonstration of NATO resolve.

The first BAOR formed in 1919 as an army of occupation in the aftermath of the First World War and was disbanded in 1929 when the British Army withdrew from Germany. The second was formed in August 1945 with Germany now occupied by the four Allied powers: the United States, Britain, the Soviet Union, and France, each with their own zone of occupation. Berlin, the old German capital, was also divided and now deep in the Soviet-controlled sector that was to become East Germany.

This occupation soon evolved with the emergence of the 'Iron Curtain' (as described by Winston Churchill in his famous Fulton, Missouri, speech on 5 March 1946), whereby the Soviets now faced the three Western Allies with a new threat from the East. In June 1948, the Soviets blockaded all land access to West Berlin to force the Western Allies to leave but they failed because of the US-led Berlin Airlift. In 1949, shortly after the Soviets finally backed down in Berlin, the North Atlantic Treaty Organisation (NATO) was formed by the US, Britain, and ten other Western nations. In 1952, the East Germans closed the Inner German Border, and in 1955 the Warsaw Pact between the Soviet Union and seven other Eastern Bloc socialist republics of Central and Eastern Europe was signed. Germany joined NATO in 1955, and the alliance continued to grow with a total of 31 members by 2023. In 1961, the East Germans built the Berlin Wall, closing the last escape route to the West.

Until 1990, the BAOR mission was to defend a 40-mile-wide sector of the North German Plain, from Hanover to the northern edge of the Harz Mountains. At its height in the early 1960s, BAOR comprised some 80,000 troops, a number that steadily declined over the next three decades. Facing the British troops, just across the Inner German Border, was the Soviet 3rd Shock Army, sitting on an axis with Berlin.

In the early days, NATO's *Forward Defence* policy was to defend West Germany along its border with the Warsaw Pact, accepting that any ground war would soon lead to a massive nuclear response. For a while, this seemed the only politically acceptable option, and it was also a cheaper one for NATO, avoiding the need to match the Warsaw Pact's conventional forces, an almost impossible task. However, it also placed a heavy reliance on the nuclear deterrent, which by the mid-1960s was becoming a less credible option because its use would lead almost certainly to a state of 'mutually assured destruction'. The NATO strategy of *Flexible Response*, introduced in the late 1960s, was designed to address these weaknesses; however, this required stronger conventional forces capable of fighting a sustained battle on the Central Front rather than an early use of nuclear weapons. This approach was welcome news for the British Army because it provided a renewed emphasis for BAOR to have better equipment and training.

The Household Division served in Germany throughout the Cold War and afterwards until 2008, when the Scots Guards finally left Münster. It had been a long association. In early April 1945, Münster was liberated by 6th Guards Brigade (with battalions of Grenadier, Coldstream, and Scots Guards under command), and so it can be said that the Scots Guards were among the first British troops to arrive there as well as the last to leave.

Cold War soldiering was a new experience; however, there were at least two aspects that suited the Guards extremely well. Firstly, armoured soldiering was not new to them: the Guards Armoured Division was formed in 1941, with a Household Cavalry armoured car reconnaissance regiment, and tank and motor battalions from each of the five Foot Guard regiments.

The Guards adapted quickly to the new demands – vehicle driving and maintenance, gunnery, signals, and armoured tactics – and although the Guards Armoured Division was disbanded in 1945, these skills were to remain and develop in the post-war period. The ease and flair with which the Household Division embraced these new challenges surprised those outsiders who regarded the Guards as far too regimented and rigid to adapt to the conditions of armoured soldiering. To quote Lord Carrington, a wartime Grenadier who retired from the Army in 1949 and was later to be the NATO Secretary-General: "Comradeship in war obviously has an effect on you and how you think. Any social divisions disappear when you share your life with three other people in a tank. I'll never forget the brave splendid people I served with."

Secondly, life in Germany relied upon discipline, leadership, the maintenance of morale, and a focus on training and readiness, all facets of soldiering that had always served the Guards well. The challenge was clear, since only a few British soldiers ever saw the potential enemy, albeit at a distance: along the Inner German Border, in Berlin, or as part of the British Commanders'-in-Chief Mission to the Soviet Forces in Germany (BRIXMIS). For the rest, it was the hard and often laborious grind of vehicle maintenance, together with all the specialist skills required for armoured and armoured infantry soldiering. Not least among these was the training required to survive a nuclear, biological, or chemical attack; gas masks and protective clothing being the most basic requirement. Much of this individual training was augmented by low-level unit exercises on local training areas and ranges, building up for the annual field training exercise in BAOR or a live-firing tactical exercise in Canada. Although the big set-piece exercises like *Quarter Final* were very different from the chaos of real war, they did have a purpose for those taking part, as a test for commanders and soldiers at all levels, and as a demonstration of readiness.

For the Household Division, life in Germany was different because prior to the Second World War the Guards were not normally garrisoned with their families on overseas postings; the only time they were abroad was on operations: fighting wars. In the post-war period Guards battalions were often overseas in garrisons, serving alongside other units of the British Army, mostly in Germany but also in Hong Kong, Cyprus, and Northern Ireland. This was to bring the Household Division closer to other British Army units because there was more integration in these garrisons, both professionally and socially, than existed in London District, where the focus on state ceremonial and public duties was a distinctly different role.

All Household Division regiments served in Germany, interspersed with periods of public duties in or close to London. From the early 1970s and throughout the next 35 years, the Guards were frequently deployed on operational tours from their peacetime bases in Germany, most frequently in Northern Ireland and then later in the Balkans, the Gulf, and Afghanistan, leaving their families behind. The local German population were usually supportive, and the Mayor of Münster (the home of Guards battalions for many years) often wished British troops farewell and a safe return as they departed overseas to fight someone else's war. Occasionally, however, there were demonstrations, as happened in 1990 when British units deployed to the Gulf, for a war that was not supported by all. One Grenadier wife recalled Arab scarves left in phone boxes, white sheets hung over balconies near the Grenadiers' barracks, and white doves, symbolising peace, painted on buildings.

The two Household Cavalry regiments, The Life Guards and the Royal Horse Guards, served in Germany as reconnaissance regiments, equipped with armoured cars until, in 1969, The Blues and Royals was formed, and the new regiment took on the armoured role equipped with main battle tanks, based in Detmold. For the next 20 years, the two regiments exchanged postings every five years between Windsor and Detmold until moving to Sennelager in 1986. The Life Guards finally left Germany in 1992 when both regiments merged in a 'union' in Windsor.

The Foot Guards normally had two battalions in Germany, as mechanised and later armoured infantry, serving with 4th Guards Armoured Brigade until its disbandment in 1976, based first at Hubbelrath, then at Iserlohn, and finally at Münster. Thereafter, there was always at least one battalion in Germany, and sometimes two, with Berlin as another posting in the infantry role.

To take the example of just one Foot Guards regiment, the Irish Guards: following the disbandment of the Guards Armoured Division in 1945, the Regiment was reduced from three battalions to one, seeing service in Palestine before being posted to Germany in 1951 for two years. Thereafter, when not in England, usually close to London on public duties, the Battalion served in the Suez Canal Zone, and in Cyprus during the EOKA campaign, returning to Germany in 1961 for three years. In 1966 it deployed to Aden for a year, and in 1970 it was posted to Hong Kong for two years, returning to Germany in 1974 to become a mechanised infantry battalion. During the early 1980s, the Micks saw service in Rhodesia and Belize, and then, from 1982, were in Germany for a four-year tour. Following a short tour in Belize in 1988–89, they were posted to the British Zone in West Berlin, arriving as the Berlin Wall was being torn down, marking the end of the Cold War. When the British Army withdrew from Berlin in 1992, the Irish Guards were one of the last units to leave. The following year, the Battalion deployed to Northern Ireland for its first operational tour there. It was back in Germany in 1998, just in time to deploy to the Balkans in 1999, serving in Macedonia and Kosovo. In 2003 the Micks fought in the Second Gulf War. They left Germany for the final time later that year and in 2004 were back in Northern Ireland for their second tour.

Prior to October 1976, Guards battalions served in 4th Guards Armoured Brigade, which was always commanded by a Guardsman, and most of the brigade staff were also Guardsmen. Supported by dedicated artillery, engineer, logistics, and signals units, it was a tightly knit and cohesive formation, in which the 'blue-red-blue' culture was imbued in all. (The blue-red-blue derives from the Guards Colours as displayed on flags, the Guards' tie, and elsewhere.) The Brigade had an impressive reputation and a long history, with some coveted battle honours to its name, including the little-known action at Hazebrouck in France in April 1918 when the Brigade held a German advance just 45 miles short of the Channel ports.

As Brigadier Christopher Wolverson, the Brigade Major in the mid-1970s, recalls: "Many of us who served in the Guards Brigade appreciated serving together with other Guardsmen, as indeed did our families. Besides setting a standard for the rest of the Army, we had fun together. It was often said that the cream of specialist officers were attached to us: Royal Signals, REME, etc."

In February 1975, the British government, struggling with an "economic situation ... now more serious than at any time over the last 25 years", announced defence cuts that sought to maintain its commitment to NATO and BAOR's overall troop levels. To make savings, among other measures, the government decided to remove the brigade level of command across the Army's order of battle. 4th Guards Armoured Brigade was now to be known as Task Force Charlie, losing both its special link with the Household Division and all its essential logistic support. It seemed an odd decision, predicated upon a belief that these savings could actually add to efficiency. Apart from amusement about the frivolous new name, the actual purpose of these changes was difficult to understand. A small headquarters would still exist in an administrative and garrison role, but without direct command of the fighting units.

There is an irony to this story, because the genesis of the idea about removing the brigade level of command was in 1961, when Harold Macmillan, the Prime Minister and a former Grenadier Guardsman, attending the annual officers' regimental dinner in London, expressed his concern at the cost of BAOR, wondering how savings might be found without compromising the NATO commitment. Brigadier John Nelson, commanding 4th Guards Brigade at the time, and sitting next to Macmillan at the dinner, suggested that BAOR could be cut by "10,000 men and made more efficient by cutting out brigade headquarters". Macmillan immediately seized on the idea, asking Nelson to write a paper personally for him on the subject, promising, in Nelson's words, that "he would make it clear to the Chief of the Imperial General Staff that it was by his order that I was producing the paper directly to him and not to have me shot". The idea was not taken forward, but 14 years later it was picked up by another Grenadier, General Sir David Fraser, the Vice Chief of the General Staff, and this time it was implemented.

Brigadier Desmond Langley, an officer in The Life Guards who later commanded the Household Division, was the last to command 4th Guards Armoured Brigade, taking over early in 1976, just before the implementation of the government's reductions. By this time the Brigade, now based in Münster, had become a 'square brigade' consisting of two armoured regiments from the Royal Tank Regiment and two Foot Guard mechanised infantry battalions, each equipped with 80 FV432 armoured personnel carriers: 1st Battalion Scots Guards and 1st Battalion Irish Guards.

By the time Desmond Langley arrived in 1976, all the decisions about the future of the Brigade had been taken, and so he focused his mind on the disbandment parade which was to take place on 1 October. It was to be a grand send-off, with the entire Brigade represented on the square with armoured vehicles, while the Brigade staff were mounted on horses with, as Christopher Wolverson recalls, "the trepidation of some". Horses arrived from London, and an Andover of the Queen's Flight delivered guests from England, including the Major General and his staff as well as other senior officers and former commanders of the Brigade. Although a sad day, it was also an opportunity for reminiscences about happier times. Christopher Wolverson recalls Major General Sir George Burns, the Colonel of the Coldstream Guards, "arriving puffing away and dusting ash off his service dress and asking whether the BAFSVs he was clutching were still valid". The British Armed Forces Special Vouchers (each with a cover value) were issued after the war for use in the British Zone; they were still in use in Berlin in the early–mid 1970s in a decimalised form, and were phased out in the early 1980s.

Another former 4th Guards Brigade commander there for the parade was Major General Lord Michael Fitzalan-Howard, who had commanded 2nd Battalion Scots Guards when George Burns was the brigade commander in the 1950s, and who became Colonel of The Life Guards in 1979. A story told by General Sir Michael Gow, also a former brigade commander and future Commander-in-Chief BAOR, was fondly remembered when they all gathered on the day of the disbandment parade in 1976. Back in the mid-1950s, during Exercise *Summer Sales*, a recurring exercise in which communications and staff procedures were practised, the message went around the radio nets that the commanding officer of 2nd Battalion Scots Guards had been "sacked for dereliction of duty". Michael Gow, a major at the time, made discreet enquiries. "Oh yes," he was told, "and all so very sad – and Colonel Fitzalan-Howard was such a promising officer. Brigadier Burns asked him about a vital bridge in the Scots Guards sector and you wouldn't believe it. He had not even bothered to recce it … so he has been sacked on the spot." There was an inference that Buckingham Palace had been informed and 'there had been consternation' from all quarters. Given the Guards' close relationship with the Royal Family, was it possible for a senior Guardsman to be sacked without first informing Her Majesty The Queen?

George Burns's explanation was simple:

Usually the traffic for signals exercises goes through the 'G' [operations] channels. This occasion, I thought, was a good opportunity to give the 'A' [admin] channels a run, so I sacked the Commanding Officer and asked for a replacement, as good an exercise signal as any other. Little did I think it would be taken seriously. The Adjutant General was in a flap. The GOC [General Office Commanding] hunted me down and asked me very seriously what had happened. Unwittingly I had produced one of the best military leg pulls of my life!

The disbandment parade in 1976 was indeed on a grand scale. The Commander-in-Chief BAOR, General Sir Frank King, inspected the assembled soldiers and vehicles and a Drumhead Service followed at which the brigade flag, with its *Ever Open Eye*, was lowered for the last time while the pipes of the Scots Guards and Irish Guards played a lament. Desmond Langley, mounted on a Household Cavalry horse, led the Brigade, followed by his staff. Six Sioux helicopters from 662 Army Air Corps Squadron flew past in a V formation, trailing blue-red-blue smoke. Detachments of the 1st Battalion Irish Guards marched past, followed by a mechanised platoon of the 1st Battalion Scots Guards. The last vehicles to move were the Chieftains of 2nd Royal Tank Regiment, slowly advancing in line, halting 25 yards in front of the spectators, fading their engines and dipping their guns in a final salute.

In General King's address to the parade, he expressed the hope that everyone would understand that "changes are good for the Army ... however much they may cut across the individual feelings and the emotions ... In this particular restructuring you will leave the tight family enclave of your Brigade and after this parade you will find yourselves in the much larger family of Divisions." He also predicted that in the future the "Corps Commander ... will have more tanks ... more guns ... far more armoured reconnaissance vehicles ... stronger air defence ... better equipped against tanks than any other ... in history." He suggested that if ever the British Army was to go to war, then perhaps these Guards battalions would find themselves "as the only Guards unit in a very strange division. But remember that this too is an opportunity to spread and display your regimental talents on a much wider stage."

Eloquent words, but everyone knew that these changes had been prompted by defence cuts and savings rather than by a desire for more equipment. There was also a suspicion, not for the first or last time, that the wider Army didn't much like the idea of dedicated fiefdoms in which all the key appointments were tied to one small elite. The truth, however, was that this reorganisation was merely part of a much larger one. And in another ironic twist of history, the Commander-in-Chief's comments about "regimental talents on a much wider stage" were similar to those used by Guardsmen in 1915 in an attempt to resist the creation of a Guards Division because they believed that it was better for the Guards' high levels of training and discipline to be distributed across the British Expeditionary Force as an example for all. Not long after the disbandment parade, Desmond Langley conveyed some of his frustrations and sadness while briefing journalists about the reorganisation. "Last week," he began, "I would have introduced myself as Commander 4th Guards Armoured Brigade. Today, I am simply Commander Task Force Charlie."

A few weeks after the parade, Task Force Charlie found itself deployed on an exercise designed to prove the new concept, and it was soon clear that some 'non-exercise' concessions were needed, since the pared-down headquarters could not function without some dedicated administrative support. A platoon of the Mixed Service Organisation (MSO) was pressed into service, and, as Christopher Wolverson recalls, this comprised a "a splendid body of men, many former prisoners-of-war of the Germans or refugees from Eastern Europe, dressed in blue battledress, they served as drivers and guards". The MSO was tasked to establish the officers' mess which was to be set up "surrounded by barbed wire and white tape" since this was "NOT part of the exercise!" Christopher Wolverson also remembers visiting the divisional headquarters, which had similarly been affected by these unwelcome changes. Here he found Major General Frank Kitson's aide-de-camp collecting the General's "supper" in a mess tin. Back in the Task Force Charlie officers' mess, behind the white mine tape, Wolverson "reported this to the Brigadier over a glass of port who then, ever hospitable, invited the General to dinner with us the following night". On the day after the dinner, the aide-de-camp turned up to borrow a table, a table cloth, two chairs, knives, forks, spoons, etc. "and maybe even the food so the General could reciprocate our entertainment".

These early field trials merely confirmed the earlier criticisms of the plan to remove brigade headquarters altogether. The 1977 Defence White Paper tried a face-saving spin by creating 'tactical command posts' commanded by brigadiers to oversee ad hoc groups of units that had not trained together in the way that the old brigades had done. The reductions had gone too far and so, in 1983, the brigade level of command was re-introduced in Germany. Nevertheless, there was to be no reprieve for 4th Guards Brigade, or indeed for any operational formations that might occasionally find themselves with two or more Guards units under command. Under the old rules dating back to 1853, this might have constituted grounds to form a Guards Brigade; however, times had changed. The 4th Guards Armoured Brigade disbandment parade in 1976 really did mark the end of an era when Guards units could train together and expect to fight together. The only exception, albeit in a different operational environment, is in London, where Household Division units train together to provide and deliver the military component of both public duties and state ceremonial events.

The experience of living and working in West Germany changed in the 1970s; indeed there were times when the conditions were better than back home. Germany had been a bleak place in the 1950s and 1960s as it struggled with the aftermath of the Second World War, a period when NATO's defensive strategy was static and professionally undemanding. By the 1970s, there had been a renaissance, with an economic miracle in West Germany in stark contrast to life in Britain, with its endless strikes, the 'Three Day Week', the IMF financial crisis, the 'Winter of Discontent', and indiscriminate IRA bombing on the mainland. In contrast, a posting to BAOR was interesting and rewarding. The end of National Service in the 1960s and changes in NATO strategy had given BAOR a more professional edge. On the political level, this was the era of *détente*, an attempt to lower tensions and the risks of war, a period that lasted until the Soviet invasion of Afghanistan in 1979.

West Germany was a place where officers and soldiers, and their families, could enjoy fringe-benefits, like duty free cars, alcohol, cigarettes, cheap petrol, and holidays in Europe. As Christopher Mackarness, a former Coldstream officer, recalls from his time as a subaltern in the early 1970s, "we bought BFG petrol coupons which cost us substantially less than about £0.25p per gallon" and while "beer was expensive, a double gin and tonic was about £0.10p and 20 cigarettes about £0.20p". The Local Overseas Allowance, with its complicated criteria, was designed to guarantee the same standard of living as back home, although with all the other benefits included it often helped to put more money into a soldier's pocket rather than less.

Germany was a well-ordered life where most activities and tasks were governed by a 'forecast of events' that rarely changed. Regiments and battalions were often busy, but there was always time for fun and recreation. But for young soldiers, often living away from home and overseas for the first time, the scourge of alcohol and other temptations were ever-present; leadership and organised activities, both on and off duty, were vital. Lieutenant Colonel Evelyn Webb-Carter, commanding 1st Battalion Grenadier Guards when they moved to Münster in early 1986, placed special emphasis on this in his training directives. Life must be fun, the 'giggle factor' was important: "Let us 'play hard and work hard' and above all be optimistic in approach and enjoy it," he wrote, concluding one directive with the words: "Laugh and the world laughs with you; weep and you weep alone." Germany presented different challenges to a posting back home or an operational tour. It required strong leadership, imaginative training, and an acknowledgement that life overseas, particularly for single soldiers living in barracks, was not as exciting as it might seem.

This had been a comfortable peacetime existence until the early 1970s when BAOR units began to conduct operational tours in Northern Ireland. For those based in Germany, each garrison had all the facilities expected in a medium-sized English town, including supermarkets selling popular UK food brands and fresh bread from a Royal Army Ordnance Corps bakery, with duty free alcohol and tobacco, schools teaching the UK curriculum, medical centres, hospitals, cinemas, and recreational and sporting amenities. Another world existed beyond the garrison, but not everyone ventured there. These were enclaves: a British way of life, with many more attractions further afield for those few who sought them.

Sport was an important part of the routine and in Germany there was often more flexibility for units to focus their efforts on big fixtures, with representative teams and individual sportsmen getting plenty of time to train. Skiing in the Harz Mountains, Bavaria, and the Alps (Exercise *Snow Queen*) was a major pursuit during the winter months, and there was also adventure training throughout the year and sailing in the Baltic, activities enjoyed by all ranks.

Guardsmen have been riding the Cresta Run, a unique toboggan course in St Moritz in Switzerland, for many years. Back in 1971, when Captain Johnny Moss was canvassing support in the *Guards*

Magazine, a fee of £6 covered entry and the first five rides, with £1 a ride thereafter. In early 1985, the Cresta marked its centenary, and the Pipes and Drums of the 1st Battalion Scots Guards were there to help celebrate the event. As a sport, the Cresta attracted soldiers of all ranks, and particularly in more recent years. It is an amateur sport, requiring skill acquired through practice, a considerable element of risk and injury, and courage. Over the years, Guardsmen have had considerable success. To name just two: Major James Kelly, Scots Guards, a past captain of the Army Cresta team and overall champion in 1999; and Captain Lord Wrottesley, Grenadier Guards, world record-holder with the fastest time for the course. They were both in the six-man Army Cresta team in 1993, along with two other Guardsmen. In the 1997 season, the Scots Guards team strategy was simple: "to ride faster than we had ever ridden before or crash in the process, a dangerous but potentially rewarding policy".

The Weser Vale Bloodhounds is a hunt formed in 1969 by three officers of The Blues and Royals serving in Detmold. Foxhunting was banned by Hitler in 1934 but had a brief revival after the war when the British were an army of occupation. Once German sovereignty was reinstated in 1955, so too was the foxhunting ban. The British Army then began hunting with the 'clean boot', whereby the hounds follow the scent of a man. In an article published in the *Daily Telegraph* and later in the *Guards Magazine*, in 1989, Willy Poole described a day with the Weser Vale, across the Sennelager Training Area, close to Paderborn. The 'prey', Lieutenant Andrew Wilkinson, bounded along as the "booming cry of the hounds got louder" and they "came surging across the open heath and stopped to eye me speculatively" before they "harooshed and boomed away", casting "a critical eye on the mounted followers as they made the most of the jumps which are scattered about the heath". The hunt ended with the 'prey' being "covered in muddy paw marks [with] a severely licked face". Poole concluded by saying that the "members of the Weser Vale Hunt are some of the best ambassadors the British Army has among the German people", and he was right. The Household Cavalry left Germany in 1992, when the Weser Vale Bloodhounds were handed over to a group of keen German supporters. The Weser Vale Hunt continues to prosper, with its blue and red *honi soit qui mal y pense* badge. Certainly, one of the more tangible legacies of the Household Division's time in Germany.

———

In the background to this peacetime routine, there was always the possibility of war, but for most of those serving in Germany this all seemed very remote, even in West Berlin, an 'island' 100 miles behind the Iron Curtain. Lieutenant General Sir John Kiszely (one of those at that convivial lunch in 1982), a Scots Guardsman who served as the aide-de-camp to the General Officer Commanding Berlin (Major General David Scott-Barrett) in the early 1970s, recalls that the realities were never far away, but life went on. "There was certainly a sense of tenseness about it ... you were at something of the sharp end ... I don't think that we really thought that there was a very high chance of deterrence failing at the time I was in Berlin but that didn't stop the feelings of tenseness ... there was a wall around you and people were being shot trying to escape from it."

The stakes had always been higher in Berlin, beginning in 1948–49, when the US-led Berlin Airlift defeated the Soviets' attempt to force West Berlin into submission. The Soviets tried again in 1958 by giving the Western powers six months to withdraw, but they refused and again the Soviets backed down. In response, the Allies established a tripartite military planning group, codenamed LIVE OAK, for contingency planning in the event of any further threats against West Berlin. Then, in August 1961, the East Germans began to build the Berlin Wall through the centre of the city, surrounding it with barbed wire and checkpoints. For the next 28 years, this was the place of daring escapes, intrigue, spying, and potential confrontations that might just have escalated to war.

It was edgy being in Berlin and, partly because of this, it was an exciting and interesting place to be, a popular posting. Everyone, the civilian and military population alike, lived for the moment, isolated and surrounded, and for those officers and soldiers who wished to venture into East Berlin, this was allowed under the Four Powers agreement, provided they were in uniform. Mess kit was the preferred dress for the Berlin State Opera on the Unter den Linden, and service dress for the frequent 'flag tours' around Berlin and the perimeters of the wall.

The US, British, and French brigades based in West Berlin were well trained and equipped; they co-operated closely in all their contingency planning, and had a good relationship with the civilian population and police. In the event of any attack, they would have employed all the street-fighting tactics that they frequently practised, backed-up by the LIVE OAK plans to relieve Berlin from the West. However, as everyone knew, this was all highly problematic. To quote Major General Peter Williams, who served with the Coldstream Guards in Berlin in the 1970s and then again with BRIXMIS in the 1980s and 1990s, the role of the British Infantry Brigade, along with the "US and French garrisons ... was largely political ... a sacrificial military tripwire [that] might just have gained the politicians valuable hours, if not days, within which diplomacy might have managed to de-escalate a major Cold War crisis".

All the Household Division regiments, except for the Scots Guards, served in Berlin, mostly on full residential tours or on short sub-unit tours to help relieve those away on training elsewhere. The Grenadiers were the first to be based there in 1945, the 5th Guards Brigade served in West Berlin for a short tour in 1946, and the Irish Guards were there just after the Berlin Wall came down in 1989 and were one of the last British Army regiments to leave in 1992.

Many Guardsmen served in Berlin, either in command or on the staff. Three Guardsmen commanded the Berlin Infantry Brigade and eight held the appointment of General Officer Commanding and Commandant of the British Sector. One of them was Major General Robert Corbett who, as a young Irish Guards officer in 1961, experienced a hair-raising journey on the British Military Train to Berlin just after the Berlin Wall was built, and was to return in early 1989, just a few months before the Wall was torn down.

Serving in West Berlin, particularly for those in command, required special qualities of leadership and diplomatic skills. Major General Roy Redgrave, who had served in the Royal Horse Guards during the war and was the British commander in Berlin during the mid-1970s, saw his role as keeping up "the morale of the Berliners by ensuring that our tenuous lines of communication with West Germany stayed open and, together with our French and American allies, to try to defuse as quickly as possible every diplomatic crisis that arose between ourselves and the Soviet Union".

Roy Redgrave recalls being visited one morning by a Russian colonel to discuss the bartering of cap-badges and magazines between British and Russian soldiers at Checkpoint Bravo, the western entry point into the British sector. In good English, the colonel explained that: "My soldiers do not have wives or girlfriends like yours in Germany ... [and] so *Playboy* and *Penthouse* mean a lot to them. Imagine their feelings when they discovered that from the middle of each magazine the double-page picture of a beautiful naked lady was missing. This is simply not cricket." The solution for Redgrave was very simple: a quick call to the commanding officer of the infantry battalion concerned, and "the missing pages were delivered to the Russians that afternoon ... thus yet another international crisis was swiftly averted." A trivial event that could so easily and unnecessarily have added to the strains of a delicate relationship had it been handled differently.

Regular duties for the troops in Berlin included 'flag tours', conducted throughout the year by each of the Four Powers. For the Western Allies this was an opportunity to show the civilians in both East and West Berlin that they were still there, honouring their responsibilities and their right to move freely while also observing any changes in Soviet deployments that might indicate unusual or worrying activities. The British patrols were conducted by intelligence sections and reconnaissance platoons of the units under command. As Peter Williams recalls, "in order to avoid giving any impression of hostile intent the members of these patrols [normally two per vehicle] wore service dress, were unarmed and, in the British case, normally travelled in Morris 1100 staff cars. Whatever else the Morris 1100 may have been, it could never have been mistaken for an aggressive or warfighting vehicle!" He also remembers the contrast between "the frantic bustle of West Berlin's roads and the comparatively deserted streets of East Berlin", although on one occasion during the oil crisis in the winter of 1973–74, the reverse was true: a total ban on vehicle movements in West Berlin while on the other side something that looked like a "rush hour in London in comparison to the fogbound traffic-free streets of the much more prosperous western part of the city. Berlin never ceased to surprise us."

One of the other special duties assigned to the four contingents in Berlin was to take their turn to guard Rudolf Hess, 'Prisoner Number 7', the former Deputy Führer who had flown to Britain in May 1941 in a self-styled peace mission. Following the Nuremberg Trials in 1945–46, seven Nazi prisoners had been held in Spandau Prison. However, by 1966, all had been released, except for Hess who had now become the victim of a cynical diplomatic game. Spandau was in the British sector, and for as long as there was a prisoner there, the Russians had a right of access, taking their turn to guard this one prisoner. On many occasions the three Western Allies had advocated Hess's release or at least a move to a more appropriate place of confinement, and every time the issue was raised, it was vetoed by the Russians.

Each of the four contingents provided a guard of 34 soldiers to man the watchtowers for three months every year, in three one-month blocks. Inside the prison, and quite separate to the perimeter guards, were four teams of six warders and four prison governors from each contingent. At the beginning of each three-month guarding period, a formal parade took place outside the gates of Spandau Prison, all part of this strange ritual which involved so many soldiers to guard one single prisoner. Rarely did any of the military guards ever see Hess although occasionally they would catch a glimpse of an old man, wearing a collarless shirt and loose-fitting jacket, walking in the garden. On one occasion, in 1979, Hess was moved to the British Military Hospital in Berlin for medical treatment. An entire floor of the hospital was closed, with 1st Battalion Grenadier Guards mounting an 'emergency guard', providing "many Guardsmen with the unique opportunity of seeing him [Hess] face to face", something which rarely happened in Spandau Prison.

One of the duties of the four sector commandants was to visit Rudolf Hess in his cell. Roy Redgrave remembers visiting him with the Russian prison governor and his interpreter. When Redgrave introduced himself to Hess, in German, he said that he must have met many British commandants. "Fourteen," came the reply, "but you are the first to speak to me in my own language." In his subsequent visits, Redgrave's linguist skills became a frustration to the Russian prison governor, since Hess could also speak French and English, and it was difficult to keep up with what was being said, and Redgrave would usually check what Hess was reading before beginning a conversation. Redgrave also tried hard to get improvements in Hess's living conditions. Many of the rules, all agreed by the Allies in 1946, had now become unnecessary and irrational, like the censorship of newspapers given to Hess and his own letters to his family. Every time the Western commandants raised the issue with the Russians, they rejected any changes, although occasionally there were small concessions. Hess had once seen a television in the British Military Hospital and asked Redgrave whether both he and his warders might be allowed to watch one. Redgrave had already been warned by his US and French colleagues "to stop rocking the boat by always asking for improvements after each visit" so he tried a different tack: asking the warders what they needed to improve their conditions, in the hope that Hess might benefit. The Russians countered with the 'technical problems', the fact that television signals would never penetrate the thick walls of Spandau Prison. Redgrave concurred: "Look Colonel, he is such an old man that he will never understand or believe our reasons. Why not let us demonstrate to him that with so much metal around there will never be good reception?" A few days later, with some 'amateur dramatics' thrown in, the Chief Signals Officer in the British sector laid on a demonstration for the four governors outside Hess's cell. When the television was switched on, there was no sound, the picture was very distorted, and the Russians began to smile, having seemingly made their point. Then, as the Chief Signals Officer put on a frantic show, with "a bit of deft finger work, he gradually achieved perfect reception". Soon there was a television in an adjoining cell "where censored programmes relieved the monotony for warders as well as for Prisoner Number 7".

The one concession that the Western Allies never achieved was Rudolf Hess's release. Following at least two attempts at suicide, he hanged himself in 1987 with a length of electrical cable while unobserved by his civilian warders in the summer house in the prison garden. He was 93 and had been a prisoner since 1941. For the British troops in Berlin, including those of the Household Division, their guard duties at Spandau Prison were certainly not onerous, nor interesting in any professional sense, but they were memorable because of the strange circumstances. The Brigade of Guards had escorted Hess from the Tower of London to Mytchett Place ('Camp Z') in Surrey in 1941, and then provided the perimeter guard there until he was moved to a military hospital in Monmouthshire where he remained until his return to Germany and finally Spandau. In the long post-war period until 1987, every Guards battalion that served in West Berlin spent time guarding Spandau Prison, a bizarre duty that few could forget, and one of the many odd legacies of the Cold War.

The real enemy in West Berlin was not an old former Nazi who was now in poor physical and mental health, but the Soviet forces that surrounded the city and the East German secret police, the Stasi, who helped to maintain an oppressive regime to the east. The immediacy of this threat, given its close proximity, was much more obvious here than in West Germany; in Berlin, everyone needed to be ready for battle at a moment's notice. Berlin was also a place where British troops, along with their US and French allies, honed their skills in fighting in built-up areas, a technique known as FIBUA. The Grenadiers placed special emphasis on this training during their tour in the early 1980s, developing new tactics, and while thankfully there was never any real fighting in Berlin, the training was to be extremely useful in other operational theatres, notably the Balkans and the Gulf.

The British Commanders'-in-Chief Mission to the Soviet Forces in Germany (BRIXMIS) was a special unit based in the East German town of Potsdam, just outside the perimeter fence around Berlin. It was formed in 1946, along with similar missions from each of the other occupying powers, and its main purpose was to maintain a liaison with the Soviet forces in Germany. The word 'liaison' was a suitably vague one, never clearly defined because the real purpose of BRIXMIS was to conduct intelligence collection patrols on its potential enemy, the Soviet forces in East Germany. The normal *modus operandi* was for BRIXMIS personnel, in teams of three, to 'tour' East Germany in clearly identified vehicles, in uniform, and unarmed. The aim was to evade the Soviets and East Germans, including the Stasi, in order to enter out-of-bounds areas and gather intelligence and photographs. Tours normally lasted two to three days, with the teams living 'off their vehicles' in concealed places like wooded areas. In the 44 years of its existence there was not one single day when a BRIXMIS patrol was not on the ground somewhere in East Germany.

The Guards were well represented in BRIXMIS, with members of all the seven regiments, both officers and non-commissioned officers, serving with this small but important unit prior to its disbandment on the eve of German reunification in October 1990. Brigadier Miles Fitzalan-Howard, Grenadier Guards, later the Duke of Norfolk, who commanded

BRIXMIS in the late 1950s, was the youngest brigadier to hold the post, and had been specially selected for his leadership and diplomatic skills following the departure of his predecessor, who had been declared *persona non grata* by the Soviets. Soon, however, Fitzalan-Howard was enjoying the challenge of the mission's unofficial role to spy on the Soviets, and pushing the boundaries wherever he could; he was frequently stopped by the Soviets while on tour, but never detained. "Great characters, the Russians, rather like Irish Guard sergeants," he was quoted as saying, also observing that "we got close enough to the Russians to respect them as people as well as to photograph their military secrets".

Serving with BRIXMIS was not without its risks. Vehicles were often shadowed by Stasi 'narks' or East German units, security personnel, often armed with loaded weapons. Being detained for a short while or being escorted away from sensitive areas was a frequent occurrence. In the late 1970s, Captain Christopher Langton, Irish Guards, was the subject of a deliberate laser attack by the Soviets while he was observing artillery training near Potsdam. A hole was burned into the shutter of his Nikon camera, and he was fortunate not to have been seriously injured.

Captain Peter Williams, Coldstream Guards, serving with BRIXMIS in 1982, in the first of two tours, was given the task of escorting the new commander, having been told to "take the Brigadier out, give him a feel for what we get up to, and bring him back in one piece!" After they found themselves close to an East German early warning site that they did not know existed, their tour vehicle, an Opel saloon, was rammed broadside by a Tatra 10-ton truck. "The noise was incredible as the truck ploughed into us as we braced ourselves for the deadly roll that I knew would certainly kill us. The side of the Opel caved in as it was violently shunted off the road sandwiched between the truck and a fruit tree." They were lucky to survive, and as the two officers and their driver emerged from the wreckage, a group of heavily armed personnel and plain-clothed Stasi agents surrounded them. Calmness under these circumstances was always a BRIXMIS byword, and so while they patiently awaited the arrival of the *Komendant*, they made themselves a cup of coffee. Many years later, when Williams was able to read the Stasi report on the incident, it confirmed his belief that this had indeed been a pre-planned and high-level sanctioned ambush operation. In 2011, now a retired major general, he met the driver of the 10-ton truck, who admitted that this was an intended assassination attempt. The driver told him that those involved had received two weeks' extra pay for their efforts that day, and that had they succeeded in killing them, then it would have been six weeks' extra leave and 1,000 Marks. One might see the sense of humour in this exchange until one is reminded that a French mission member was killed in such a Stasi-directed ramming in 1984.

BRIXMIS had many intelligence successes over the years, amassing information about new Soviet and East German equipment, training and tactics, troop movements, and wartime deployment areas. For example, in 1955, BRIXMIS was the first to identify the new T-54 tanks and AK-47 rifles; it also identified surface air-to-air guided missiles in 1962, and the first nuclear weapon storage sites a few years later. While BRIXMIS, like everyone else, was unable to predict when the Cold War would end, the prescience of its intelligence assessments, suggesting that the Soviet threat had been exaggerated, was later proved to be correct. For the Duke of Norfolk, the BRIXMIS legacy was a simple one: "the Cold War ended as a bloodless victory, and the victory was ours."

For the more conventional British Army presence in West Germany, field training exercises, command post exercises, annual firing camps, and low-level unit training were the staple diet of activity outside the barrack gate.

The larger field training exercises like Exercise *Quarter Final* and the many that followed in the twilight years of the Cold War were the highlight of the training year unless a regiment was to train at Suffield, in Canada, where the use of live ammunition, including tank and artillery shells, was allowed across a prairie of some 1,000 square miles. Field training exercises in Germany were planned many months before the armoured vehicles on their transporters rolled out of barracks, to their drop-off points, and into their assembly areas, well camouflaged in woods and forests. There was nothing unpredictable about this; everyone knew when the exercise started and when it ended (normally about three weeks from deployment to final recovery back home), but only a very few knew where they would be going.

The scale of these exercises was impressive, and something that is never likely to be repeated. Christopher Mackarness, on his first exercise in Germany in the 1980s, recalls "the sheer number of armoured vehicles on the final assault", their only limiting factor being the availability of spares and fuel. He also remembers the Mobile Bath Unit on the banks of the River Weser, a facility that all ranks of 4th Armoured Brigade visited before the start of the next phase, and the Army Catering Corps "producing a piping hot meal in hayboxes at about 0300hrs for at least one rifle company in the middle of nowhere", a task that would defeat many civilian catering contractors.

River crossings, reminiscent of scenes from the film *A Bridge Too Far*, were always exciting events to be part of or just to observe from the sidelines; local civilians often gathered to watch armoured vehicles crossing a wide river in rapid defile. A visit to the 'rear area' was more interesting than the term implies: field workshops hidden in thickly wooded forests, with REME fitters working through the night to repair broken vehicles, or vast ordnance parks servicing the vital needs of an armoured division on the move.

The 'recovery' of armoured vehicles at the end of a large exercise also had its moments of excitement and drama. A young captain from The Life Guards recalls the arrival of the Tank Transporter Unit (Royal Corps of Transport) at the end of Exercise *Quarter Final* in October 1982. The vehicles were driven by Polish drivers from the MSO, many of them veterans of the Second World War who had fought both the Russians and the Germans; impressive and tough men, often in their fifties, including former Polish officers who commanded their transporter units with military precision. On this occasion, The Life Guards' regimental tank loading plan had been drawn up in detail in the regimental headquarters, as laid down in the requisite staff table, stipulating distances between vehicles, the number of traffic guards required, estimated 'timing past the post', etc. A nearby crossroads had been selected and the local police had been informed, as the tanks lined up along one of the roads, with civilian cars struggling to get past. Then the Polish officer arrived, and, swiftly assessing the situation, made the bold decision to send the passing civilian cars up the road opposite the tanks, a route that probably led to nowhere. As the early evening skies darkened, the tank transporters, with the MSO drivers at the wheel, started arriving at a perfect interval and a steady speed. All control now rested with the MSO officer, standing like General Patton in the centre of the crossroads, ordering each tank forward with a quick movement of his left forearm to indicate a sharp turn onto the main road, onto to the moving tank transporter ramp as it trailed slowly past without stopping. As a precision performance, conducted with a professional calm and hardly any talking, it was as impressive a sight as any Queen's Birthday Parade on Horse Guards, without the sounds of the massed bands.

While these big set-piece field training exercises were always in the annual training programme, there were others that occurred unexpectedly, at any time of the day or night. *Active Edge* was the code name for testing a unit's mobility to deploy from its barracks, fully equipped and ready for action. It was an appropriate name because, unlike a planned exercise, there was always just a chance that this could be the real thing. *Active Edge* had the habit of being called at the most inconvenient time and was always an extremely effective way of testing professionalism and readiness. Early in 1982, The Life Guards in Detmold were 'crashed-out' at 3am on a Monday morning, and a newly commissioned officer, Stephen Ellis, who had arrived the previous afternoon, soon found himself commanding a Land Rover, with a driver he had never met, conducting a map reading exercise on a local training area he had never visited. At the end of the exercise, at the debriefing in a hidden-away corner of the barracks, the Brigadier made particular mention of this young officer, who had clearly impressed him during the exercise: "Second Lieutenant Ellis – please raise your hand" – but he was nowhere to be found. Very tired from the drive from England the previous day, and still in shock from the friendly practical jokes at dinner that evening, and now this exercise, he had already returned to the only place in barracks that he could find: the officers' mess.

On 27 March 1985, the Colonel of the Welsh Guards, the Prince of Wales, arrived at Campbell Barracks, Hohne, sat down for lunch in the officers' mess, and then, over coffee, initiated a call-out. Soon, the entire battalion was mounted on its tracked armoured personnel carriers and command vehicles, with the Colonel leading his own Company, The Prince of Wales's Company, making its way to the nearest training area, with members of the press trying to keep up behind in an Army truck.

Just after 1st Battalion Grenadier Guards arrived in Münster in January 1986, a bitterly cold month, the commanding officer received an 'Active Edge' call-out to test the married quarters' recall system, a much more complicated process before the days of mobile phones. Wives also needed to know the plan in the event of a real war. As the wife of the Grenadiers' Quartermaster recalls: 'We were told that … we would have to put our pets down or give them away … we could take only one suitcase". Münster was perhaps a better place to be for the wives, because they were within striking distance of the Channel ports by car, but for those families living further east and in Berlin, there would be no escape.

Exercises in Germany certainly had their moments, both the unexpected ones and the planned ones, and the performance of regiments and individual commanders could make or break a career, since these were the activities by which judgements were made. However, the starker realities and uncertainties of soldiering were often taking place elsewhere.

There was only a small BAOR involvement in the Falklands War in 1982, and no major units were deployed from Germany. The Falklands campaign was regarded in those days as an 'out of area' operation, a euphemism that was to completely lose its meaning eight years later when a division and two brigades deployed to the Gulf. Back in 1982, the Falklands seemed a long way away for those serving in BAOR, although the course of the conflict was followed closely; and there were many friends involved, particularly in The Blues and Royals, Scots Guards, and Welsh Guards. News was slow to arrive in those days; there were no live UK television news programmes available to the British community in Germany, so a recording of the previous day's BBC *9 O'Clock News* was flown by air and re-broadcast 24 hours later.

For Major John Kiszely, who served with 2nd Battalion Scots Guards in the Falklands War, returning to Germany later that year as the Brigade Major of 7th Armoured Brigade, the experience of being back in BAOR was "slightly frustrating" because it was going from "doing it for real to going back to something where you're playing at soldiers, to put it unkindly, i.e., training for war". Having fought in a real war, Kiszely was "frustrated with what appeared to be the pettiness of training in Germany, compared with the Falklands, where certain things mattered a great deal and other things didn't matter much — and that wasn't necessarily the order of things in Germany. But you just got on with it."

Northern Ireland had an immediate and sometimes disruptive effect on the steady and ordered life in BAOR. When the Troubles began in

1969, it was soon clear that the four-month roulement commitment of unit tours could only be sustained by Germany-based units taking their turn. By the mid-1970s, the number of troops in Northern Ireland had risen to its highest peak of 21,000, and all major units, including those not normally in the infantry role, were re-trained for deployment in Northern Ireland. The Household Division was fully committed from the outset, and over the years of Op *Banner*, BAOR-based units took their turn to serve in Northern Ireland, many times.

The 2nd Battalion Coldstream Guards arrived in BAOR in 1969, to re-role as a mechanised infantry battalion, a change which required the learning of new trades such as driving and maintenance (most young soldiers in those days did not have civilian driving licences, let alone tracked or heavy goods vehicle licences). The more complicated matter of mechanised infantry tactics could only be learned in Germany. This was all a lengthy process, so when, in 1970, the Battalion was warned for an emergency tour in Belfast, this required an entirely different and demanding training package. Although the tour was only four months in length (later tours were six months), this commitment routinely took a battalion away from its normal training cycle for most of a year, by the time Northern Ireland training, and pre- and post-tour leave were taken into account. The 2nd Battalion had not served in Germany since 1955 and, as this was its first tour in Northern Ireland, the learning curve, in both directions, was a steep one.

It was a similar experience for 1st Battalion Scots Guards, who returned from Belfast in December 1971, only to move to Waterloo Barracks in Münster exactly a year later having been warned for a tour in Northern Ireland in May 1972. In the short time available, the Battalion's members managed some low-level training on their tracked vehicles before moving into 'Tin City' based on the edge of the Sennelager Training Area. By early May, they had arrived in their various bases in Co Armagh and Co Tyrone, just 18 months after their last tour, having spent a year in England, followed by a move, with their families, to Germany. While the absurdities and rigid nature of the Arms Plot are difficult to explain all these years later, the logical alternative being a delay in the move to Germany until *after* the Northern Ireland tour, the risks of a 'knock-on effect' for numerous other units and their families was too difficult to contemplate. For the 38 years of Northern Ireland deployments which ended in 2007, the Household Division quietly and professionally simply got on with the task, whatever the effects on individuals and their families; it was part of the job.

———

There were other routine military tasks in Germany, for example three-day patrols along the Inner German Border that ran through the Harz Mountains where, in the words of one former Coldstream officer, "it was depressing to see what lengths the communists would go to ensure their citizens could not get to the West". Notwithstanding, these were welcome breaks away from barracks, in which the Guardsmen stayed in a local *Gasthaus*, patrolling every day in the shadow of East German border posts, barbed wire, and minefields. It was important to show a NATO presence along this unnatural border that had arbitrarily divided a country, and it was also something of a stark education for soldiers to see this place which, in the words of the regimental history of the Scots Guards, "delineated that most inhuman of all international boundaries".

A more tiresome and less interesting experience, but certainly one of utmost importance where there was no margin for error, was the 'Site Guard' duties conducted at often isolated storage bases hidden away in woods and forests. One of these was a facility close to Münster, a nuclear ammunition storage site, on an area of the map totally blanked out, consisting of a barbed wire compound overlooked by four 'goon towers'. This was a regular duty for the nearby 4th Guards Armoured Brigade, and while it was certainly one of the dullest for those taking part, the task had an operational edge: those on guard carried weapons and live ammunition and needed to be able to deliver a verbal challenge in both English and German.

The possibility of war was always present, however remote the chances, and so it was important to keep focusing on the real threat. Frequent briefings on Soviet tactics and vehicle recognition were required to bring this hidden enemy to life. And all of this required style, confidence, and humour, as demonstrated by a briefing given by the late Peter Owen Edmunds, Welsh Guards, on the new Soviet tank, the T-80, in the early 1980s. Peter had recently returned with his Battalion from the Falklands War and was now serving as the regimental intelligence officer in Hohne, where the Welsh Guards had converted to the mechanised role. Following the briefing, the recently arrived commanding officer launched a volley of questions about the Soviet tank: "How thick is the turret armour? How many rounds of ammunition can it carry? What is its speed across country? What's its fuel capacity?" Peter answered each question confidently and without hesitation, but somehow the audience could sense the unfairness of this inquisition. Then, a Welsh Guardsman with an unmistakable North Wales accent pointed to the photograph of the Russian tank and asked, "Sir, do you know the driver's name?" Without missing a beat, Peter replied "Of course; it's our old friend, Private Popov!" And he was almost certainly right, since he was later selected to serve in BRIXMIS, one of the last Guardsmen to do so before it was disbanded at the end of the Cold War.

In November 1982, the Secretary of State for Defence, John Nott, conducted several visits to regiments in Germany. While visiting the 2nd Battalion Coldstream Guards, based in Fallingbostel, he was invited to fire a Milan simulator by Lieutenant James Bucknall, and "shown the delights of NBC [nuclear, biological and chemical] training" by Major Anthony Biggs. While there, he met the Intelligence Section wearing authentic Russian uniforms, including Captain Simon Holborrow wearing the uniform of a colonel in a motor rifle regiment. When Nott had arrived at the Ministry of Defence in January 1981, he was shocked to learn that BAOR had about one week's stock of ammunition, making it likely, in his words, that, if the Russians did attack, "we could only have fought a conventional war for a few days before we had no choice but to go nuclear", something that he found to be an "utterly shocking state of affairs". It did no harm, therefore, to gently remind the Minister that there was a real enemy on the other side of the Inner German Border, some 50 miles to the east of Fallingbostel.

There were frequent occasions when the Household Division was called upon for its ceremonial skills, and in the days when a Guards battalion served in Berlin, the Queen's Birthday Parade was performed there with all the expected high standards of drill. On 7 July 1977, on the Sennelager Training Area, there was an even bigger event to commemorate: Her Majesty The Queen's Silver Jubilee. 4th Armoured Division was on parade, with 3,000 soldiers, 578 tracked vehicles, and over 450 wheeled vehicles. There were 785 musicians from 24 bands, ten corps of drums, and three pipe bands. Christopher Wolverson, now second-in-command of 1st Battalion Irish Guards, together with the Regimental Sergeant Major and drill sergeants, was responsible for the 27 Standard, Colour, and Guidon Parties, a huge task that, along with other tasks that day, was assigned to the Household Division.

After the parade and march past, the Queen and Duke of Edinburgh, with the President of Germany and his wife, together with all the senior officers, adjourned to luncheon in the officers' mess in Sennelager Camp, where, only a few months earlier, "two enormous cartwheel chandeliers had crashed to the floor, leaving footprints all over the recently decorated walls and ceiling". The Scots and Irish Guards were both in the camp at the time, and soon the two Seconds-in-Command, Robin Buchanan-Dunlop and Christopher Wolverson, found themselves in the line of fire from "an incandescent Brigadier Infantry" but "fortunately the Commanding Officer of the Scots Guards was coming up to Sennelager that afternoon. He took the flak and the matter was resolved ... Never were we so pleased to see Murray Naylor!"

When the Cold War ended in 1990, so too did the stately dance of deterrence that had lasted since the late 1940s. The reunification of Germany, dismantling of the Berlin Wall and the Inner German Border, and the disintegration of the USSR, all followed soon after. With the benefit of hindsight, it seems extraordinary that this all came so unexpectedly and so quickly. In the years preceding this sudden seismic change, only a few observers and journalists dared to suggest that the Cold War's days were numbered. One of them was Bernard Levin in *The Times*, in 1977, in an article entitled 'The fuse of revolution is laid, now only the match is needed'; and when, in 1987, US President Ronald Reagan implored the Soviet leader, Mikhail Gorbachev, to "tear down this wall", he was more criticised for these words than praised. When Major General Robert Corbett became General Officer Commanding British Sector and British Commandant, Berlin, in January 1989, he had 'endless discussions' with his new civil and military staff "about the possibilities of progress in divided Berlin". Whenever he asked, "What chance?", "there was always a shaking of heads together with an occasional concession that the Wall might become more porous – 'permeable' was the expression used." He was always assured that "the situation was essentially set in concrete; there would be 'No change in our lifetime'." And as he wrote in an article published in 2009, "How wrong those words would prove to be."

If no one was contemplating the end of the Cold War in Berlin in early 1989, neither had there been any speculation during the Army Staff College course at Camberley which had ended a month earlier, in December 1988. For the directing staff and students (among them ten Guardsmen), there was no doubt about where the Army's centre of gravity lay: it was in Germany where a large proportion of the Army's forces were based. For many years, the command and staff training at Camberley had been predicated on the threat posed by the 3rd Shock Army based in East Germany, while the study of 'out of area' operations was a neatly self-contained and short module of its own.

One of the big events of the Staff College year was the visit to NATO forces in West Germany and the Berlin Infantry Brigade, the latter being easily the highlight of the entire year. Prior to boarding the Royal Air Force VC10 to fly down the air corridor into West Berlin, in early May 1988, the students visited a static display and tactical demonstration laid on by the British 3rd Armoured Division, displaying their wares at the Sennelager Training Centre. Everything here was tailored to *the war* on the North German Plain, the war for which BAOR had been training since its inception in the early 1950s. Nothing of course was said or known about the *real war* which took place just over two years later, in the winter of 1990/91, for which most of the equipment on display that day was to be packed up and sent to Saudi Arabia.

On that two-day visit in May 1988, on the Sennelager Training Area, Staff College students were given a demonstration of the tactics and equipment of the German 1st Panzer Brigade, a presentation by the staff of Headquarters I British Corps, and an opportunity to see what a British armoured division headquarters, an armoured brigade headquarters, and an armoured company group, looked like in the field, along with all their supporting logistical units. The company group deployed on that occasion was the Queen's Company 1st Battalion Grenadier Guards, with its three platoons of Warrior armoured fighting vehicles, a reconnaissance section of Scimitar armoured cars, anti-tank and mortar sections, and a troop of three Challenger tanks from The Blues and Royals. In support were a Royal Artillery forward observation officer, a Royal Engineer reconnaissance party, an Engineer field section, the A1 Echelon (logistics), and the Royal Electrical and Mechanical Engineers Fitter Section.

For those who had never seen this kind of military hardware, it was an impressive sight. The finale of the two-day programme of events was the tactical demonstration laid on by 4th Armoured Brigade, sadly no longer a Guards formation and now with only one Guards battalion (the Grenadiers) under command. The demonstration began at 3pm with the spectators gathered on stands at the Scharnhorst Bunker Viewing Point, watching the spirited and animated introduction by the brigade commander, a cavalryman, as he described the 'counterstroke' about to take place. Positioned nearly 1 mile to the south-west, the Challenger tanks of 14th/20th Kings Hussars, on the left, and the 17th/21st Lancers, on the right, began to rumble forward, followed by the Warriors of 1st Battalion Grenadier Guards, on the centre line. The sound of the advancing enemy, 2½ miles to the north-east, could only be dimly heard, then to be drowned out by the Challengers and Warriors sweeping past the viewing stands. Soon the dust from the tracked vehicles entirely obscured them behind a mobile smokescreen, by which time the Brigadier had given up all attempts to provide a running commentary. Then they were gone, like the Sovereign's Escort on Horse Guards, to perform a 'counterstroke' into the flank of the oncoming enemy formation, somewhere in the far distance.

Underpinning this demonstration of armoured *élan* was a doctrinal and tactical shift that had begun in the early 1980s when Lieutenant General Sir Nigel Bagnall was commanding I British Corps. Bagnall was an unusual soldier and one of the most gifted thinkers of the post-war generation of Army officers. With his unruly ginger hair, unsoldierly gait, piercing manner, tone-deafness, and dislike of wearing medals, he might have been mistaken for an Oxford history don rather than a former infanteer who had won two Military Crosses in Malaya. Not impressed by NATO's defensive strategy, and more influenced by the Wehrmacht panzer generals who had fought the Red Army on the Eastern Front and by the work of the Soviet Studies Research Centre at Sandhurst, Bagnall set about shaking up the mindset. If NATO was prepared to lure an advancing enemy force into a trap, and on a narrow frontage, then it could attack and destroy it from a flank. It was a more aggressive, dynamic, and exciting strategy than the static tactics of the past.

Charles Guthrie, commanding 4th Armoured Brigade in the early 1980s, who would later go on to command I British Corps and BAOR in the early 1990s, believed that the Bagnall reforms were "just the shake-up BAOR needed". This was a tired institution where there was too much complacency and lethargy, and where the culture of "the 'BAOR warrior' type, who had served in Germany for too long, knew every training area backwards, and had become accustomed to exercises that were predictable and unimaginative". The 'counterstroke' was a special role assigned to 4th Armoured Brigade, "the jewel in the Corps' crown, and made life for us all a lot more worthwhile and enjoyable than that experienced by others in BAOR. We even began to look forward to the ritual dance of BAOR autumn exercises, usually heavily choreographed, where we would execute the counterstroke operation in the glorious landscape of North-Rhein-Westphalia ... We practised and rehearsed until we were close to pitch perfect. The sense of renewal began to spread through the whole of BAOR."

These ideas provided a renewed focus for training in BAOR, and this was helped by new equipment in the shape of the Challenger MK1 main battle tank and the Warrior armoured infantry fighting vehicle introduced into service in the late 1980s.

Back in 1986, 1st Battalion Grenadier Guards was selected to conduct the trials for Warrior, the first new British infantry vehicle to be introduced since the early 1960s. Colonel Jonathan Lloyd, a major at the time, recalls being warned off the previous year that this would be his task to oversee when he returned to the 1st Battalion in Münster, commanding No 2 Company. When he first saw Warrior performing on Salisbury Plain, he realised that this "was altogether a different beast from its aging predecessor, the FV432". For the first time, here was a vehicle with "the power and mobility to make it more than capable of keeping up with the Challenger main battle tank". Equipped with the 30mm Rarden cannon and 7.62 Hughes chain gun, and capable of carrying a crew of ten (which included seven infantrymen), Warrior would "provide the infantry with a capability it had not hitherto possessed". Warrior had been procured specifically to operate in a Cold War scenario on the Central Front, and now for the first time BAOR had a vehicle capable of countering the Soviet BMP armoured infantry fighting vehicle.

There were several challenges to overcome for the Grenadiers, the most significant being the training of gunners. With 18 Warriors in each company and three in battalion headquarters, every commander, including the commanding officer, would need to be trained in new skills and, for these to be taught, there was a requirement for instructors, gunnery simulators, and other aids. Since the establishment of a BAOR-based armoured infantry battalion was now larger than a UK-based battalion, an enhancement, known as the Armoured Infantry Manning Increment (AIMI), to make up the numbers was now required. This led to an element of mixing between Guards regiments, something that was comparatively easy to achieve because of the common values and standards that existed across the Guards.

Once No 2 Company was proficient in all the basic skills of driving and maintenance and gunnery, it was ready to start the trial of the vehicle itself, which included testing its reliability under different conditions and developing tactics that exploited its mobility, firepower, and protection. The contrasts with the FV432 were stark, since the latter was no more than a "battlefield taxi ... which struggled to keep up with the armour it accompanied", while Warrior was a fighting vehicle with all the potential to actually lead an attack, and also to take on enemy vehicles in direct engagements.

When the trial was over, Jonathan Lloyd wrote up a detailed trial report (there were no computers in those days, and it took a typist six weeks to type it up and incorporate the revisions). Although the Grenadiers had identified a few teething problems, for example the reliability of the Hughes chain gun, which had been plagued by stoppages, overall the trial proved beyond doubt that, for the first time, the infantry in BAOR was to be "equipped with a reliable, capable and flexible fighting vehicle". With the success of the trial, the lessons that the Grenadiers learned, and the tactics that they helped to develop, the Warrior was now ready to be rolled out to other infantry battalions in Germany.

Warrior was to have a fine operational history, although it was never employed in Germany other than on exercise. It first saw action in the First Gulf War in 1991, pairing well with Challenger as the 1st Armoured Division swept through the desert in warfighting mode, attacking enemy positions and armoured vehicles. The Balkans was an entirely different scenario, and one for which Warrior had not been designed, and yet it proved its worth in its white United Nations livery: from "ugly duckling" to "handsome swan" as described by Major General Peter Williams, who commanded the 1st Battalion Coldstream Guards in Bosnia in 1993. Although described as a "peacekeeping operation", the situation that the Coldstream found when they arrived was very different, a scenario that "called for a well-armed, well protected, mobile force structure", one that only an armoured infantry battalion with Warrior could provide. Warrior was a mainstay in the Balkans and was later employed in warfighting operations in the Second Gulf War and in Afghanistan.

When the 1st Battalion Scots Guards, serving in Catterick, handed over their Warriors in the summer of 2014, it was the end of a long era that dates back to the Guards Armoured Division in the Second World War. For nearly 70 years, the Foot Guards had served as both mechanised and armoured infantry. However, this time, as Peter Williams acknowledged in an article published in 2014, there was to be no 'end of armour' parade for the Guards, although perhaps there should have been.

The last major field training exercise to take place before the end of the Cold War was Exercise *Iron Hammer*, in November 1988, involving some 25,000 soldiers, 300 tanks, 70 helicopters, and 30 fixed-wing aircraft, together with 6,000 tracked and wheeled vehicles of various sizes. The Blues and Royals in their recently acquired Challengers and 1st Battalion Grenadier Guards in their new Warriors were part of the main exercising troops, and for the Grenadiers this was an early opportunity to practise their Warrior skills. The weather was already cold when the exercise began on 1 November, and by the second week the conditions deteriorated with snow, ice, and temperatures down to -17°C, all made worse by the periods of inactivity that were inevitable on such large-scale manoeuvres.

The exercise was in two parts with a brigade work-up exercise in the first week, in preparation for a divisional-level exercise during the following week. One of the newer features on *Iron Hammer* was the emphasis on avoiding unnecessary damage to the environment, although the YouTube footage of the exercise, easily available some 35 years after the event, gives a different impression. While efforts were being made to reduce the movement of tracked vehicles, with more areas being placed out of bounds, and a new telephone 'hot-line' for complaints from members of the public, this was still a vast exercise on both public and private land, and Challenger tanks, Warriors, and other tracked vehicles can be seen advancing across farmland and crops, turning on roads, churning-up tarmac and kerbstones.

During the second week, progress slowed, with appalling weather conditions and freezing temperatures. Despite these "Siberian blasts", to quote the regimental history, the Grenadiers pushed on with "five defensive positions, stopping the enemy advance, and drawing them into a full scale battle". Soon the exercise was curtailed as the ground began to thaw, the roads turned to slush, and there were more concerns about causing unnecessary damage. Neither the Challengers nor Warriors, in their first and only Cold War large-scale field training exercise together in Germany, were able to show themselves off to their full potential by demonstrating the fast-moving 'counterstroke' finale envisaged in the days when the older armoured vehicles were simply not up to the new more mobile tactical thinking. To quote the Grenadiers' regimental history, there was a feeling that "the name of the last big exercise in BAOR was a poor choice"; a more accurate one would have been 'Rubber Mallet'.

This might have seemed at the time to have been something of a disappointing anti-climax to BAOR's long period of Cold War exercises, but their wider purpose had at least achieved the aim, and there were some unexpected surprises just around the corner. Firstly, deterrence had worked, or at least it was one of the many important strands that had prevented war in Western Europe since 1945 while helping to bring the Cold War to an end in 1990. Secondly, no one could have known then, nor indeed until the early autumn of 1990, that the armoured soldiers and vehicles of BAOR were soon to see action for the first time, in an entirely new theatre of operations.

In Berlin, and throughout the spring and summer of 1989, Robert Corbett began to spend as much time as he could in East Berlin, trying to get a sense "of the true state of affairs beyond the Wall". Here, he formed "some seeds of doubt about the durability of Erich Honecker's grim Communist regime in East Germany" – small indicators that were hardly noticed at the time, but on reflection were all part of a shifting pattern. Borders were opening between Austria and Hungary, and then Hungary opened its border with Czechoslovakia. Once East German refugees began to move through Hungary and into Austria, "the die was cast".

When Mikhail Gorbachev, on a visit to East Berlin for the German Democratic Republic's 40th anniversary celebrations on 7 October 1989, delivered his famous words, "Those who do not learn the lessons of history will be punished by life", for Robert Corbett and his colleagues "Suddenly the penny dropped" ... and a month later, "the Wall broke open with the first mass crossing of East Berliners into the West at Checkpoint Charlie at 2120 hours on 9th November 1989". It was an extraordinary moment for Robert Corbett, who had first come to Berlin as a young Irish Guards subaltern in 1961. Barely a year later, at midnight on 2/3 October 1990, he and his wife "stood beside President von Weizsäcker on the dais at the Reichstag before a crowd of over a million people gathered" as the new reunified Germany was declared.

In the meantime, the unexpected happened, just as the Cold War was ending. In the summer of 1990, Saddam Hussein invaded Kuwait, and the British Army was immediately committed as the junior partner in a US-led operation to deter the Iraqis and then to liberate Kuwait. All the planning assumptions were that this would be a high-intensity war involving armoured formations, and the likelihood that sooner or later Saddam Hussein would resort to the use of chemical weapons, as he had done in previous wars. Four Guards regiments were committed in one way or another to the operation, and most of the forces came from BAOR, where the capability, training, and equipment resided.

The First Gulf War in 1990–91 was a blessing in disguise because it forced the British Army to shake off the last vestiges of Cold War soldiering. However, in other ways it was to be a salutary lesson for the British government and its Army because it took most of the resources of BAOR to deploy a division and two brigades to the Gulf. Years of slow procurement and financial restrictions had affected training and recruitment, rendering BAOR far less able or ready to fight the war for which it had been raised and maintained.

It is now over 30 years since the end of the Cold War, the demise of the USSR, and the expansion of NATO, with many countries of the former Warsaw Pact becoming members of this defensive alliance. The inevitable 'peace dividend' was seized upon by many, including

Britain, as a way of justifying further reductions in defence spending, something that had been declining for many years. Without a credible threat from the Russian Federation, the concept of deterrence soon lost its way, to be overcome by other more immediate demands on the British Army and the Household Division: warfighting in Iraq, NATO-led peace support operation in the Balkans, and a NATO-led operation in Afghanistan.

The story of British troops in Germany, however, goes beyond the end of the Cold War, even if their primary purpose changed. Germany was soon reunified, the Soviet troops had gone home, and there was no longer a role for NATO troops on German soil. Many Germans could see this only too clearly, and while there was some local sadness when garrisons closed and farewell parades were held, and indeed some economic impact (for example on employment and trade), circumstances had changed; the end was inevitable. In the meantime, Germany was to be a reliable base for British units as they continued to be deployed to other theatres, including the Gulf, Northern Ireland, the Balkans, and Afghanistan.

Life in Germany during those last few years of the British presence was to be very different. There was no threat from the East, and many of the places that during the Cold War had been mere names on a military map overlaid with red symbols were now soon to be accessible. Famous towns along the Elbe, like Magdeburg, Wittenberg, Meissen, and Dresden, could be reached by car within just a few hours. No longer was the only land route to Berlin along the narrow corridor from Helmstedt, and there were many more places in Eastern Europe to explore, like Poland and the Czech Republic. For the more adventurous travellers there was much to discover, particularly in the early days when a journey to the old East Germany was a step back in time. A group of young officers from The Life Guards made it to Colditz sometime in 1991, posing in their British Warm greatcoats, with collars upturned, at the railway station from where many prisoners-of-war had marched through the cobbled streets to the castle overlooking the town; not much appeared to have changed since Colditz had been liberated in 1945.

The British Army in Germany continued to be busy in the post-Cold War era, but it was a different experience, as Lieutenant Colonel James Bucknall, commanding 1st Battalion Coldstream Guards, explained in an article published in the *Guards Magazine* in 1998. There was no longer "that single minded focus of the Cold War years"; however, "the demise of one certainty, the Soviet threat, has given rise to a host of uncertainties, particularly in central Europe and the Middle East." At least there were other compensations; for example there was no longer a requirement for some units to be on six-hours' notice to move to defend West Germany, nor were there any restrictions on minimum manning during leave periods. "On the last Friday before Christmas 1997, the Channel Tunnel and the French ports were brought to a standstill by the migration of British servicemen going on leave – unthinkable during the Cold War."

There were considerably fewer British units in Germany by the late 1990s, with only one armoured division still there, although with better equipment than its predecessors. Many barracks and garrisons had been handed back to the Germans and some remained empty and unoccupied. Münster, the old home of 4th Guards Armoured Brigade, had once had eight major units based there; by 1998 there were only two. The training areas so well known to Guardsmen during the Cold War, such as Soltau, had become protected areas of heathland. The huge annual field training exercises had gone, and although the introduction of simulation had improved the quality of training, "the lack of opportunity for field training, particularly at formation level ... resulted in a decline in certain skills which would have been taken for granted in previous years". The best and most realistic training was still available in Canada, and also in Poland on old Soviet training grounds well behind the Iron Curtain, but opportunities like these only came around once every three years.

Thankfully, the Red Army never invaded West Germany, although in late 1997 the Russians did "finally reach Münster" when "they ground to a halt two kilometres [1¼ miles] from Oxford Barracks" where the Coldstream were based, "having run out of petrol". This was the Band of the Russian Airborne Forces, prompting a Coldstream officer to remark that "he has spent 30 years waiting for the Russians" and if he had known "they would run out of fuel before they had even reached us he would have gone home years ago".

The British Army's presence in Germany ended in 2019 (except for a small training team). The troops of BAOR never fought the battle for which they had trained for 45 years, and, perhaps because of this, to quote the historian David French, "historians have nothing dramatic to describe and analyse". However, this is only part of the story. With small and sometimes larger conflicts taking place around the world throughout that long post-war era, at least deterrence in Western Europe really did work. The British Army and the Household Division played their full part, and the much-feared Third World War never happened. The so-called 'balance of terror', which was so reliant on the nuclear deterrent, prevented war in the one place where NATO had invested all its resources. This long period of stability helped the West European nations to create successful economies and high standards of living, based on sound democratic and fiscal principles. This in turn encouraged countries behind the Iron Curtain to aspire to the same, and all of this contributed to the end of the Cold War and to communism in Europe.

Over 30 years on, the old Russian enemy has now re-emerged in another and even more unpredictable form, but this does not alter the past. The Cold War (1946–92), with Britain's largest overseas military commitment since the end of the British Raj in India 1947, may not have earned any battle honours, but it was still a victory.

5

Disengaging from Britain's Far-flung Battle Line

The embers of the old empire. It was our task to let those embers glow over a brighter future for our former colonies and Crown Dependencies. In this, the Household Division did supremely well with tact, diplomacy and great dignity.
MAJOR GENERAL SIR SEBASTIAN ROBERTS

By the end of the 1960s Britain had all but withdrawn from east of Suez. There remained only the garrison in Hong Kong and a Gurkha battalion in Brunei paid for by the Sultan of Brunei. In the Mediterranean, British troops had left Malta and had more or less left Gibraltar's defence to the Royal Gibraltar Regiment. After Cyprus won its independence in 1960, the British presence was just a handful of sovereign base areas in Cyprus. Many Guardsmen wore blue berets to keep the peace between Greek and Turkish Cypriots after independence in 1960. That wonderful Captain's appointment, tied to the Household Division, of Training Officer, Mauritius Defence Force, was lost in 1972.

To the west of the UK, there remained just the outposts of British Honduras/Belize and the Falkland Islands.

HONG KONG

The Queen's Birthday Parade in Hong Kong was always held on 21 April, which was Her Majesty's real birthday as the mid-June heat was considered too ferocious for the Queen's traditional birthday parade. The Battalion wore white uniforms not red tunics. The Irish Guards, posted to the Hong Kong Garrison 1970–72, called it their 'Ice Cream Kit'.

The parade was followed by a march through the streets. Little had changed since the British took possession of Hong Kong in January 1841 at the end of the First Opium War – a war in which the Chinese ceded Hong Kong to the British, who had made huge sums of money selling opium to the Chinese. It was an historic humiliation for the Chinese which they have never quite forgotten.

China had long regarded Hong Kong as Chinese territory, but claimed that it they saw no need for conflict; the historic question of who would own Hong Kong Island would be solved when the time was ripe. China, as with Taiwan today, was always happy to bide its time. The British lease of part of Kowloon and all the new territories was to expire in 1997. China, however, needed Hong Kong as an outlet for trade and as a source for almost half its foreign exchange earnings. China's policy towards Hong Kong was therefore expected to remain benign, while local communists took every opportunity to widen the base of their influence within the colony, preparing for the eventual day that they took over.

The Irish Guards quickly discovered that they had to train for and be proficient in five different types of warfare, the principal one being internal security. The others were limited war, jungle warfare, counter-revolutionary war and civil assistance.

Since the end of the war, Hong Kong had become a hotbed of sedition. The 1956 disturbances were caused by Kuomintang (Chinese Nationalist Party) supporters and then exploited by the secret Triad societies. In the early 1960s, communist-inspired riots had threatened law and order. They were followed by the 1962 mass influx of illegal immigrants from China, and the 1966 riots, which arose from social and economic pressures.

But the Irish Guards were in the safe, albeit slightly jumpy, hands of Lieutenant Colonel Tony Plummer who had been an instructor at the Staff College. His patience tended to run a little short when faced with reports from the Naval Shore Patrol on the exploits of Irish Guardsmen in the Wanchai District, or "exchanging pleasantries" with soldiers from the Black Watch who had come over from Gun Club barracks in Kowloon. Even when playing golf, he kept an immaculately turned-out signaller as his caddy with an A41 radio so he could respond instantly to any 'incident'.

All in all, it was the traditional 'Mick' tour: stepping up to the plate when needed, witness the award of the George Medal to a newly joined ensign, Johnny Gorman, who along with many Irish Guardsmen rescued many survivors after an extraordinary tropical storm had collapsed a block of flats in central Hong Kong; and the great good humour as they embraced all that Hong Kong had to offer in sport, adventure training, and jungle warfare in Malaysia, and all under the watchful eye of the Padre, Father Frank Robson, whose performance in the pirate-themed officers' mess barbecue lives on in the annals of the Regiment.

———

In late 1974, Lieutenant Colonel David Fanshawe, commanding the 2nd Battalion Grenadier Guards, promised his men in Victoria Barracks, Windsor, that their tour to Hong Kong 1975–76 would be "a tour of a lifetime". Colonel David was true to his word. Not all Household Division battalions prospered in Hong Kong, but the Grenadier tour was memorable.

Jock Lloyd-Jones, a subaltern on the tour, remarked:

Yes, it was the tour of a lifetime, first, it was brilliantly led by Colonel David Fanshawe and RSM David Webster. They had both served together in the Guards Independent Parachute Company. Then you had a wonderful group of Grenadier officers who were to make their mark in the Regiment and wider Army: Evelyn Webb-Carter, Sam Coleridge, Conway Seymour, Patrick Holcroft, Hugh Westmacott (sadly, later killed by the IRA while serving in the SAS), Oliver Lindsay, Edward Hudson, Robin Cartwright …

The Sergeants' Mess was no less talented and then we had Dwin Bramall as Commander British Forces (later Chief of the Defence Staff) and the Governor, Sir Murray MacLehose, to whom we provided ADCs [aides-de-camp], who both made it clear from the outset that they expected the highest standards from the Battalion in sport, adventure training, recreation, entertainment and training for whatever was thrown at us … Dwin understood soldiering and that a battalion busy all the time training and drilling would soon melt away in the excessive heat and humidity.

The Grenadiers, like the Irish Guards, were billeted at Stanley Fort on the most southern peninsula of Hong Kong Island. The barracks had been well built before the war on high ground around several playing fields and a barrack square. Spacious white buildings with wide verandas contained the Guardsmen's sleeping quarters, offices, stores, and a few married quarters. Before the surrender of Hong Kong to the Japanese in December 1941, the final stand of British and Canadian troops took place in Stanley Fort.

Major Oliver Lindsay, who was the Battalion's senior major and a former editor of the *Guards Magazine*, wrote an account of the tour in his regimental history, *Once a Grenadier.* One of the striking observations from the tour was the care and attention taken by the Battalion over the wives and families. As Lindsay wrote, "It had always been anticipated that a number of families would have difficulty in settling in Hong Kong because military duties on the border, in Brunei and elsewhere, would lead to excessive separation. The fact that the tour was such a resounding success was in no small part due to the fact that we saw the Battalion as one large family."

Illegal immigration, which took up much of the Battalion's time, followed a similar pattern to the one in Europe today. The police were understrength on the border with China; 'snake head' Chinese patrols from Hong Kong like today's traffickers tried to make money out of the illegal immigrants; many suffered from malnutrition, shock, thirst, and exposure; a few would try to swim across a treacherous sea in unseaworthy boats paddled by ping-pong bats only to drown or be devoured by sharks.

Jock Lloyd-Jones remembered the patrols with mixed feelings:

I always wondered why we had to hand the immigrants back immediately, and I know Colonel David took it up with a government official in Hong Kong. He got a supine response citing overcrowding in Hong Kong and the need to appease China. We all enjoyed the border patrols until some jobs worth in the MOD disbanded the Mule Troops, sure footed animals and carrying everything we needed,

THOSE MUST BE THE GUARDS

like the Chindits in Burma, up precarious and steep tracks to our Observation Posts.

'Zest for life' was Colonel David's philosophy. A simple enough guiding principle which allowed any officer or Guardsman to take his soldiering seriously but also to pursue any activity for which they had a talent. It was a fine Grenadier Battalion and the finest of tours. Thirty-six years later another fine Grenadier Battalion had two outstanding tours. But, as we shall see, in Afghanistan in 2010 and 2012 the circumstances could not have been more different.

THE CYPRUS EMERGENCY, 1974/75

The island of Cyprus became an independent republic in 1960 with Britain retaining control of two Sovereign Base Areas: Akrotiri and Dhekelia. The Turkish invasion of Cyprus in July 1974 put an end to Greek Cypriot ambitions of the Hellenic Republic of Cyprus. The 2nd Battalion Coldstream Guards and the 1st Battalion Welsh Guards deployed to Cyprus as part of the United Nations (UN) peacekeeping force.

The Cyprus Emergency was not unlike the Northern Ireland crisis. The Turkish minority had become increasingly resentful over the treatment they were receiving from the Greek Cypriot majority. Archbishop Makarios had no physical resemblance to the Northern Irish demagogue, Ian Paisley, but possessed the same ability to fire up his own people. There was a State of Emergency from 1955 to 1959. Independence was granted the following year. Cyprus simmered for the next 14 years.

By the time the 2nd Battalion Coldstream Guards deployed to Cyprus in May 1974 under Lieutenant Colonel The Hon Christopher Willoughby, matters were coming to a head. At 5am on 20 July, the Turks invaded Northern Cyprus. At 6am, two Turkish parachute battalions were dropped into the Turkish enclave in the north. Seaborne landings followed. It all looked dramatic on the world's media.

The Battalion was split between two locations: battalion headquarters with two companies and a Royal Armoured Corps parachute squadron was under UN command at Limassol in the south. They wore the UN blue beret. The remainder, under the second-in-command at the UK Sovereign Base area of Dhekalia, were part of Headquarters Near East

Land Forces. They wore their normal khaki beret. There was much fighting in Limassol despite the leaders of both sides having promised that neither would attack the other unless first attacked. The Battalion's vehicles were stationed to remind them of their promise. Once one shot was fired, in this instance by the Greek National Guard, the relative calm unravelled fast. Chaos reigned until the Turkish Cypriot fighters, heavily outnumbered, laid down their arms. Guardsman Lawson was killed when a weapon went off among a pile of impounded arms.

By the end of July, the situation had stabilised. The Turks had made their point and consolidated their advance from the north at Famagusta on their 'Attila Line'. From then the Battalion did what any Household Division Regiment does well: sensitive handling of refugees; swift and efficient administration and allocation of resources, food, and water; and all done with characteristic courtesy, self-discipline, and good humour.

Amusingly, two of the Battalion wives, Mrs Macfarlane, married to Major J.R. Macfarlane, and Mrs Robinson, married to Company Sergeant Major Robinson, who had both arrived before the invasion, set up an impromptu observation post, 'Mrs Squirrel's OP'. It had a panoramic view of everything that was going on – a vital source of intelligence to battalion headquarters. The SAS could not have done a better job.

Later that year the 1st Battalion Welsh Guards deployed, with Lieutenant Colonel (local rank) Charles Guthrie in command of the UK Sovereign Base of Dhekalia with The Prince of Wales Company and Support Company. The rest of the Battalion, under Lieutenant Colonel Peter Williams, were part of the UN Force.

By the autumn, Colonel Charles recalled:

the embers of the summer fighting had more or less died down, the Coldstream and the UN had done a great job, I just found myself holding the hand of the brigade commander who had a tendency to flap, it was his last posting after years hidden away in the MOD. I took the time to meet the Turkish general who had fought with the Turkish Brigade in Korea. He exuded calmness. I remember his words even now: "Even if the Turkish Cypriot Community did not exist,

Turkey would not have left Cyprus to Greece, but we must defend our peoples here against Greek Nationalism." He went on, "Please remember, Colonel, we do not want to fall out with the British. We both suffered at Cape Helles in 1915 where we fought each other to the death."

Colonel Guthrie felt able to reassure the British Forces Brigadier that there was no cause for alarm. Fortunately, if the Brigadier was windy, the General Officer Commanding Near East Land Forces was steady as a lighthouse. General Corran Purdon was an Irish-born Commando who had taken part in the St Nazaire raid where he won the Military Cross. Purdon thought the Coldstream and the Welsh Guards were wonderful. His son, Tim Purdon, joined the Irish Guards and later commanded the Welsh Guards.

The Coldstream had their hands full after the invasion but the Welsh Guards under Colonel Peter Williams, a fine trainer of men, made sure that the Guardsmen made the most of their time in Cyprus: skiing in the Troodos Mountains was particularly popular with the Guardsmen.

The Cyprus embers have not quite died out. On 20 July 2020, President Erdogan of Turkey made an inflammatory speech, calling for "a permanent solution to the island dispute, and equal rights over the island's natural resources".

Cyprus continues to be of strategic importance to the UK. It remains an essential part of any security dynamic in the region affecting NATO. It was a vital staging post in the Iraq and Afghan campaigns, an important RAF base to this day and a wellspring for intelligence gathering in the region. Colonel Simon Soskin, who was the senior major during the Grenadiers tour of Afghanistan in 2007, spoke of its importance as a place for 'decompression' after Op *Herrick* tours. The Irish Guards went on to serve in Cyprus in 2013 as part of Op *Tosca*, the name given to the British contribution to the United Nations Peacekeeping Force in Cyprus (UNFICYP).

THE RHODESIA OPERATION, WINTER AND SPRING 1980

It was very much a Household Division affair, fraught with potential danger and mildly eccentric, elephant

dropping recognition as part of our training, massive
air drops with Durex but no water, and my Irish
blackthorn stick but no weapon.
Major General Sir Sebastian Roberts

The problem of Rhodesia (Zimbabwe), the last British colony in Africa, had plagued successive governments in the 1960s and 1970s. When the Conservatives under Mrs Thatcher were re-elected in 1979, they decided to resolve the growing question of what to do with the 'rebel colony'. They were right to do so. The country had been involved in a bitter civil war for a decade. Over 20,000 people had been killed; the government of Ian Smith, a white supremacist, was illegal – Smith had declared independence from the UK, which had demanded black majority rule; the economy was flagging; the white community had been emigrating at the rate of 1,500 a month; and externally trained guerrillas and outlawed black nationalist parties fought hard to bring the regime down.

The signing of the Lancaster House Agreement on 21 December 1979 effectively ended armed conflict in Rhodesia. It also marked the end of Rhodesia's Unilateral Declaration of Independence (UDI). British colonial authority was to be restored during the transition period during which free elections would take place under British government supervision.

It was against this background that Op *Agila* was launched in late December 1979 under the command of Major General John Acland, a former commanding officer of the 2nd Battalion Scots Guards. His formal title was Commander Commonwealth Monitoring Force and Military Adviser to the Governor of Southern Rhodesia. The governor was Sir Christopher Soames, who had served in the Coldstream Guards and was married to Winston Churchill's daughter, Mary.

General Acland had been a superb commanding officer and was one of those rare officers who was not afraid to speak out if he felt higher command or politicians had got things wrong. On one occasion he received a reprimand from the Army Board after he had written to *The Times* about the possible disbanding of the 2nd Battalion Scots Guards. On presenting himself to the Army Board, he famously asked for a written copy of the reprimand as he wished to frame it and hang it in his downstairs loo. This did his promotion prospects no favours. But he had his supporters who recognised in him the *sangfroid* needed for trying circumstances.

The task for General Acland and the Commonwealth Monitoring Force (comprising Australia, New Zealand, Fiji, Kenya, and the UK) was to provide a framework within which the guerrillas of ZIPRA (under Johsua Nkomo) and ZANLA (led by Robert Mugabe) could be assembled and monitored in line with the Lancaster House ceasefire agreement, signed on 21 December 1979, ending the Rhodesian Bush War. The white Rhodesia Security Force (RSF) had also to be kept firmly in check. It was an essential prerequisite before general elections were held from mid-February to early March. They were to be the first elections for the first parliament of the independent Zimbabwe.

This became a rather in-house affair: the Foreign Secretary (Lord Carrington) and Home Secretary (Willie Whitelaw) were former Guardsmen. Ian Gilmour, a former Grenadier, co-chaired with Carrington the Lancaster House talks. There was a strong Coldstream and Irish Guards presence, with many officers from across the Division, many of whom like Captain Sebastian Roberts, Lieutenant Colonel Willie Rous, Major Andrew Parker Bowles and Major Timothy Purdon went on to distinguished careers. Other British Army regiments played an important role but the Household Division was prominent at all levels of command. As Captain Sebastian Roberts, Irish Guards, remarked:

> Sir Christopher Soames held a dinner party for all Household Division officers at the beginning of the operation. No doubt naysayers would take a pop at the 'Bob's your Uncle' side of things. But it worked. We were all like-minded and got on well at a high political level and on the ground dealing with the rebels and the Rhodesia Security Force. John Acland's No. 2 and operations officer was the outstanding John Learmont, a Gunner officer, later a four-star general, who kept everything on track.

On a sadder note, Lord Richard Cecil, a former Grenadier officer, was shot dead in 1978 while covering the 'Bush War' as a journalist. He was described by Rhodesia's Foreign Minister as "the finest young man I ever knew and all that made Britain great". As to Cecil's character and courage, it was certainly true.

General Acland was later to remark, "it wasn't really a military operation at all ... It required, however, the courage, sense of judgement and degree of self-control on the ground to deal with a hitherto-unexperienced situation in which the use of military force would mean the operation had failed." In that sense the strong Household Division presence, with ten years of hard experience in keeping the peace in Northern Ireland, sat comfortably with the task in hand.

Rhodesia was divided into six operational areas, each area being controlled from a Joint Operation Centre (JOC). The JOCs were subdivided into sub-JOCs, each sub-JOC occupied by a battalion of troops and an equivalent number of policemen. During the ceasefire, the Rhodesian security forces were monitored down to company level, and the Patriotic Front guerrillas in their assembly places. The Coldstream were concerned with Op *Thrasher*, the easternmost operational area, its headquarters in the border town of Umtali. *Thrasher* was commanded by Lieutenant Colonel Willie Rous.

The assembly was to be completed by midnight on 4 January 1980. The number of guerrillas coming in was far larger than expected. It was quite a challenge. Moving guerrillas from rendezvous points (RVs) to assembly areas in yellow Salisbury Corporation buses over roads thought to be mined, in pretty treacherous conditions and across distances difficult to cover in less than 20 hours was to test everyone's courage and good judgement. The guerrillas refused to unload their weapons; their weapon handling was pretty dreadful, causing 12 deaths and 53 seriously injured. At RV 'Foxtrot' 3, run by the Coldstream, 1,000 guerrillas were still to be moved to Assembly Area 'Foxtrot', commanded by Major Tim Purdon, Irish Guards, who was awarded the MBE for his role, and which already contained 6,000 guerrillas, and where the British contingent of Irish Guards backed by the Coldstream was never larger than 50 men.

And then there was the logistical challenge of feeding, watering, and administering 22,000 guerrillas in the assembly areas. The Rhodesians said it was not their problem. British Army quartermasters are adept at begging, borrowing, and commandeering what the Army needs. Eighty tons of beef were brought in from South Africa, tentage from the US, clothing from Hong Kong, underwear from Australia (there were 700 women guerrillas in ZANLA). Civilian water tankers found themselves doing a 200-mile round trip as Royal Engineers fixed up pipelines from lakes. Occasionally things went adrift. Captain Sebastian Roberts recalled the "unforgettable sight of 200 gallons of water exploding after a botched airdrop".

The Guardsmen's humour and ability to make the best of what was thrown at them was never far away. Lance Sergeant Buckley, Irish Guards, who with Captain Roberts and a contingent of Micks was at Assembly Area 'Romeo', remarked on his arrival, "No giraffes, no elephants, no sun, and they call it Africa." Captain Roberts's liaison officer from ZANLA was the splendidly named 'Comrade King N. Kasa' whose first words were, "they want to kill you Comrade Roberts ... they fear for my safety among you white men."

Captain Roberts took all this in his stride and made a point of never carrying a weapon and wearing combat fatigues with desert boots. "We wanted to look as peaceful as possible which was all to the good as I reminded myself that our briefing on arrival in Salisbury (Harare) consisted of a session on elephant dropping recognition and, rather more seriously, de-mining as the place was littered with mines of every description."

Captain Hugo Morgan-Grenville, a Coldstreamer, was responsible for sub-JOC Rusape, a small town bordering the Mozambique border. He described his patch as a "prime tobacco-growing area, fields of tall, golden tobacco plants, gnarled msasa trees, thatched mud huts, cattle rooting in the long grass, brightly clothed Africans working in the fields, the eastern highlands in the distance, snow clad and shimmering in the noon day haze."

He was less sanguine about the prospects for a successful outcome:

There was equal mistrust and suspicion with the guerrillas and the RSF. The RSF knew their day had long gone but were reluctant to relinquish what they thought was rightfully theirs. The rebels for their part were sometimes drunk and high on 'dagga', often too far gone to unload their AK47s. And although we completed the first part of our task, the move to the assembly areas went well, I was concerned about the next phase, the elections, and the growing levels of intimidation.

Morgan-Grenville was right to be concerned. There was no reduction in violence. He was witness to many atrocities; one on a civilian bus killing all passengers was particularly horrific.

But it all came good in the end. Ninety per cent of those eligible voted, the reassuring sight of British policemen and women standing by to see fair play and good order. The result was a victory for Mugabe's ZANU-PF. Joshua Nkomo's Patriotic Front won a fair number of seats. black majority rule was established. The British government's calculated risk paid off. Britain excelled itself at a time when its critics were many and its friends few.

Courage, good judgement, and self-control, qualities that General John Acland had highlighted in his post operation report, were plain to see in the Army's response to what was a complex and sensitive undertaking. And in this, the Household Division had played a significant role. At the end of the Rhodesia operation, Mary Soames gave an address to the assembled former guerrillas. Some feared for her safety. They need not have worried. She was cheered to the echo.

General Acland received a knighthood at the end of the operation. Characteristically, he said he would only accept it on one condition: that all the Commonwealth Monitoring Force received a medal to mark their service.

BELIZE: RISK AND REWARD

Belize, or British Honduras as it was known, had been a British colony since the Anglo-Spanish treaty of 1786. Both Guatemala and Mexico had laid claims to Belize since the early 19th century. In 1948 Guatemala referred to Belize as an integral part of the Guatemalan State. It threatened to invade. In response, the British government established a military presence to deter any prospect of an invasion. Britain's military presence was given the engaging name of the 'Caribbean Battalion'. The Irish Guards served there more than other Household Division battalions as, for political reasons, it was unable to serve in Northern Ireland till the early 1990s.

It was not always quite the plum posting. The threat of a Guatemalan invasion had led to the 2nd Battalion Grenadier Guards' six-week exercise in 1971/72 being extended to a seven-month tour. In 1981, Belize became an independent state within the British Commonwealth. During the Falklands campaign, there was the possibility that Guatemala, conscious of previous slights to its pride, would side with Argentina and seek to invade once again. The scare passed. The British government, however, announced that the Army would remain in Belize "for an appropriate period" to safeguard the country's territorial integrity.

The Irish Guards made the most of their tours in Belize as Vince McEllin, a former Regimental Sergeant Major and late entry commissioned officer, recalled. In true Irish Guards fashion, McEllin remembered only the more 'Mickish' aspects of the Belize tours: the Queen Mother's address to the Battalion on St Patrick's Day 1979 being drowned out by a wayward helicopter pilot who was late in dropping off comfy chairs for the VIP guests; the Major General on a formal visit who complimented the Battalion on the good behaviour of the Guardsmen as they returned through the main barracks gate after a night out in Punta Gora to celebrate the great day. The Major General was none the wiser that the Regimental Sergeant Major had created a temporary gate in the perimeter fence well to the rear of the Major General's quarters.

If the Irish Guards were to encounter little to upset their composure in Belize, the 2nd Battalion Grenadier Guards, five years later, found the political context had changed.

In 1984, Guatemala had internal problems and a failing economy. External aggression was just the sort of smokescreen that Galtieri had attempted in Argentina to win popularity. Guatemala thought it could pull off the same stunt, albeit with greater success than Argentina in its unsuccessful invasion of the Falklands.

The Battalion's mission was to act as a deterrent to aggression from Guatemala. They were there to support the small Belize Defence Force. The US was anxious that the British forces remain in Belize; the Central American states were largely unstable, and there was the continual fear, particularly on the part of the United States, that Belize would become a communist foothold in Central America.

Belize has the second longest barrier reef in the world after Australia's. The Inkerman Company's area of responsibility included the southern half of the reef amid some 300 tropical islands. A section of two non-commissioned officers and six Guardsmen spent a week at a time on the southernmost island of Hunting Caye which was within 35 miles of the coast of both Guatemala and Belize. The reception by the Mayan Indians was always friendly, a refreshing change from Northern Ireland. The young Mayan children, overawed by the white giants, huddled together in timid groups or clutched their mothers' skirts.

As Guardsmen had learned many times before in similar surroundings, the training benefits of jungle patrolling were enormous. Officers and non-commissioned officers discovered what command

1. Lance Corporal James Ashworth, VC. Killed in action on 13 June 2012 in Afghanistan and later awarded a posthumous Victoria Cross for leading his fire team in an attack on an enemy-held compound. (© Regimental Headquarters Grenadier Guards)

2. Academy Sergeant Major Ray Huggins, MBE, at the Royal Military Academy Sandhurst, 1971. (Crown Copyright)

3. Fathers and sons in the Irish Guards, St Patrick's Day, 2008. (© Regimental Headquarters Irish Guards)

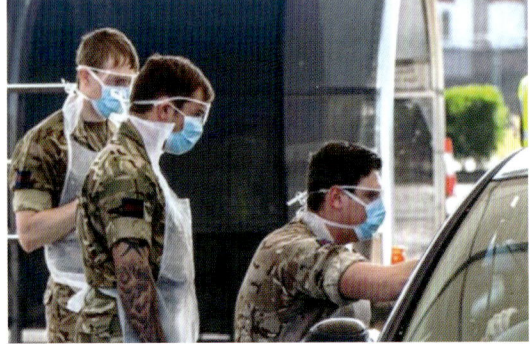

4. Recruits from the Guards Depot firefighting in London, November 1977. (Crown Copyright)

5. Grenadier Guardsmen testing members of the public for Covid-19 in April 2020. (Crown Copyright)

6. 2nd Battalion Grenadier Guards. Captain Charles Woodrow and the Drummers on the streets of Londonderry, 1969. (© Regimental Headquarters Grenadier Guards)

7. 2nd Battalion Coldstream Guards, West Belfast, 1970. Guardsman Seldon and a local resident. (© Regimental Headquarters Coldstream Guards)

8. The Secretary State for Northern Ireland, William Whitelaw, formerly Scots Guards, visiting 2nd Battalion Scots Guards in Londonderry, 12 August 1972. From left to right: Lieutenant Cheape, William Whitelaw, Guardsman Forbes, Guardsman Dukes and Lance Corporal McDonald. (Crown Copyright)

9. A riot squad from The Life Guards facing a mob in East Belfast, 1973. (Crown Copyright)

10. On 14 May 1977, Captain Robert Nairac, on undercover operations in South Armagh, was abducted by the PIRA and later murdered. Robert Nairac was posthumously awarded the George Cross. (© Regimental Headquarters Grenadier Guards)

11. 1st Battalion Coldstream Guards, South Armagh, winter 1982/83. The result of Guardsman Neville's bomb, from which, miraculously, he only suffered a broken kneecap (© Regimental Headquarters Coldstream Guards)

12. Lieutenant Colonel Charles Guthrie, Commanding Officer 1st Battalion Welsh Guards, and the Prime Minister, Margaret Thatcher, South Armagh, Christmas 1979. (Crown Copyright)

13. A patrol of the Queen's Company Grenadier Guards, near Crossmaglen, November 1983. Back left to right: Guardsmen Meak and Rushton. Front left to right: Guardsman Elliott and Lance Sergeant Watson. (© Regimental Headquarters Grenadier Guards)

14. Lieutenant Colonel Tim Spicer, Commanding Officer 1st Battalion Scots Guards, speaking to an RUC policeman in West Belfast, summer 1992. (© Regimental Headquarters Scots Guards)

15. Guardsman Pengelly, Right Flank, 2nd Battalion Scots Guards, training on the *QE2* during the journey to the Falklands. He was later awarded the Military Medal. (© Regimental Headquarters Scots Guards)

16. RFA *Sir Galahad* following the air attack during which 48 crew and soldiers, including 32 Welsh Guardsmen, were killed on 8 June 1982. (Crown Copyright)

17. Marked map for the Battle of Mount Tumbledown, 13–14 June 1982, belonging to Lieutenant Colonel (later Major General) Mike Scott, DSO. (© Regimental Headquarters Scots Guards)

18. A Scorpion of 3 Troop, B Squadron, The Blues and Royals, about to replenish. (Crown Copyright)

19. The Scots Guards under fire in the assembly area prior to the Battle of Mount Tumbledown. (© Regimental Headquarters Scots Guards)

20. Major John Kiszely, MC, commanding Left Flank, 2nd Battalion Scots Guards. (© Regimental Headquarters Scots Guards)

21. Members of 7 Platoon, G Company, 2nd Battalion Scots Guards, on Mount Tumbledown, 14 June 1982. (© Regimental Headquarters Scots Guards)

22. Lieutenant Colonel Johnny Rickett, Commanding Officer 1st Battalion Welsh Guards, and his team on Sapper Hill at the end of the campaign. From left to right: Lieutenant Mark Coreth, The Blues and Royals; Captain Piers Minoprio; Captain Julian Sayers; Lieutenant Colonel Johnny Rickett; and Captain John Henderson. (Johnny Rickett)

23. The Senior Colonel, The Duke of Edinburgh, talking to Regimental Sergeant Major Tony Davies at the Falklands Medal Presentation. To the left is Lieutenant Colonel Johnny Rickett. (Crown Copyright)

24. A luncheon party at Schloss Schenke, on the North German Plain, organised by Brigadier Charles Guthrie during Exercise *Quarter Final*, Sunday 17 October 1982. (Crown Copyright)

25. A new regiment. B and C Squadrons, The Blues and Royals, preparing to move out on exercise in BAOR, 1969. (Crown Copyright)

26. A lucky escape. Captain Peter Williams standing next to his BRIXMIS vehicle which minutes earlier had been rammed deliberately off the road by a Stasi hit team. (Peter Williams)

27. Major General (later Sir) Robert Corbett, General Officer Commanding Berlin, visiting the western side of the Berlin Wall in 1989. (Crown Copyright)

28. Members of the Welsh Guards serving with the Grenadier Guards, Münster, West Germany, 1990. From left to right: Sergeant Davies (39), Guardsman Bayliss, Captain D.R. Evans (87), Captain R.J.D. Parry (81) and Sergeant Barton. (Crown Copyright)

29. The 1st Battalion Scots Guard Battle Group on the prairie at Suffield, Canada, on completion of Exercise *Medicine Man*, May 1990. (Crown Copyright)

30. The Band of The Blues and Royals at the Berlin Tattoo, October 1992. The band is standing in front of the Brandenburg Gate, on the eastern side. During the Cold War, the Berlin Wall ran along the western side of the gate. (Crown Copyright)

31. Ferret Scout Cars of C Squadron, The Blues and Royals, on patrol in Cyprus in early 1973. (Crown Copyright)

32. Guards Independent Parachute Company on Families' Day, Hankley Common, 11 July 1975. From left to right: Lance Corporal Tinsley, Coldstream Guards; Captain Simon Falkner, The Life Guards; Captain Peter Mills, Coldstream Guards; Major Robert Corbett, Irish Guards; Captain Nicholas Emson, MC, Coldstream Guards; Captain Nick Nicholas, Coldstream Guards; and Captain The Hon Richard Bethell, Scots Guards. (Robert Corbett)

33. 2nd Battalion Grenadier Guards dragon boat racing in Hong Kong, 1976. (© Regimental Headquarters Grenadier Guards)

34. Major General (later Sir) John Acland, CBE, being welcomed by Richard Metaure, ZIPRA zonal chief of operations, at Assembly Point 'Romeo' in Rhodesia (now Zimbabwe), 1980. (Crown Copyright)

35. Members of ZANLA at Assembly Point 'Foxtrot' handing in their weapons prior to voting under the watchful eye of Lance Sergeant Cullen, Irish Guards, in Rhodesia (now Zimbabwe), 1980. (Crown Copyright)

36. The scene shortly after the IRA bomb attack on The Queen's Life Guard on 20 July 1982. (PA Images/Alamy Stock Photo)

really meant when alone with five or six Guardsmen far from support or assistance. They developed self-reliance and adaptability and learned the importance of a comrade's support.

The oppressive atmosphere in the jungle was not easy to get accustomed to. Those with vivid imaginations wondered if the rustling amid dense vegetation was an enemy, some wild animal or a slithering snake. One patrol was out during torrential rains. The river started to rise rapidly and the patrol had to evacuate their position very quickly. As they made their escape, they were approached by a huge alligator. They loosed off a burst, but the Armalite rounds were not as heavy as the 7.62 and just bounced off the alligator's thick skin. It was enough to persuade it to find a meal elsewhere.

The Caribbean had its own distinctive challenges. Colonel John was at one stage warned off by Commander Joint Forces Turks and Caicos to arrest the Prime Minister on this idyllic island and colony for drug dealing; Lieutenant Richard Winstanley found himself accompanying the British Ambassador to Haiti, the country of the notorious 'Papa Doc' and the cult of voodoo; an enterprising Guardsman caught an indulgence flight to Miami for $10, went to the local US Army base there, pretended he was a sergeant and lived luxuriously for two weeks for a dollar a day in return for which he regaled his hosts with tales of derring-do.

As one Guardsman said on his return to Chelsea Barracks:

> For me, Belize offered a glimpse into the world of the old empire, where duty called and good men took up the burden of Empire; foot patrols, moving from village to village among people whose prized possession was a football. With bare breasted women and barefoot children, we entered the prehistoric world of wooden huts thatched with palm leaves. It was a far cry from the unyielding gravel of Horse Guards and a rare chance to put the clock back 100 years when a Briton was a Demi-god with his pale face and head held high.

Outdated sentiments today, but for a Guardsman in the early 1980s a world apart. The commanding officer took a more guarded view:

> We are all fitter than on arrival; we have become more self-reliant and we are able to survive and fight in what is a very tough, demanding environment. We have walked hundreds of miles, visited remote

corners of the world, and met some very different people and cultures. Above all, we have earned a high reputation in the local community for being smart, courteous and professional.

A quarter of a century later, officers and Guardsmen were to find themselves in a much more unforgiving environment: Iraq and Afghanistan. Patrick Hennessey, Grenadier Guards, author of *The Junior Officers' Reading Club* based on his experience in Afghanistan, wrote a little irreverently about the generation of BAOR and Northern Ireland. He misread the trials and sacrifice of Northern Ireland but he was right to envy the opportunities for travel, adventure training, and living among friendly cultures.

THE GUARDS INDEPENDENT PARACHUTE COMPANY 1947–75: A VALEDICTION

The Guards Independent Parachute Company, disbanded in 1975, was emblematic of all that is best in the Household Division. It truly was an elite force, combining the best attributes of the Parachute Regiment, 'fast, far and without question', with the self-discipline, personal initiative, and ever-present sense of humour that you find among Guardsmen. It was also a great brotherhood with a special spirit that lives on to this day, not only among its fraternity of veterans, but also within its successor, the Guards Parachute Platoon.

The disbanding of the Company was a great loss to the Army and the Household Division. The Company was never more than 60 strong but its reach and impact was much greater. For those Guardsmen who joined, the Company was a robust channel for those seeking the spirit of adventure and soldiering that would test their resolve. Those privileged to serve in the Company took their soldiering seriously but never themselves. They were far from dull, and if to work hard and play hard has become an overused phrase, it does at least capture the ethos of the Guards Independent Parachute Company. They were always independent of mind and temperament. Many went on to distinguished careers in the Army, and those who felt that soldiering had palled somewhat after their time in the Company went on to make their mark in civilian life.

The Company's provenance, like that of the Parachute Regiment, was rooted in the Household Division. It was General 'Boy' Browning, a Grenadier who had won the Distinguished Service Order aged just 20 in the Great War, who persuaded Churchill to form the airborne forces. 'Boy' Browning commanded the 1st Airborne Division at its formation. It was Browning's remarkable wife, the author Daphne du Maurier, who came up with the idea of the maroon-red beret and the emblem of Pegasus and Bellerophon worn on the shoulder sleeve. The maroon-red beret is now worn by airborne forces in 48 countries.

The Guards Parachute Battalion had been formed in 1946, but in 1948 this became the Guards Independent Parachute Company. The Army Board at the time felt that the reliability and discipline of the Household Division combined with the élan, dash, and astonishing fitness of the 'Red Devils' would be a battle-winning factor. They were to be proven right.

The Company's last years were as exciting and varied as ever. The Company's institutional memory was strong: it never lost sight of the example set by the Company's role in the Borneo Campaign 1963–66 or the legendary Murray de Klee (Scots Guards) jump with his entire stick onto the strongly held El Gamil airfield in the Suez campaign.

The dialogue with Northern Ireland began in early 1970, often undercover, and billeted at the intriguing address of the Red Hart Bottling Factory, Belfast: trialling the new steerable parachute at Boscombe Down, a tactically sound innovation but one that removed the drama of involuntary drop zones on autobahns or turkey farms; high-altitude climbing in the Alps above Zermatt; pathfinder and parachute training in Sharjah for the Company's primary role as pathfinders for 16th Parachute Brigade; exercises in the Mediterranean and Cyprus with Italian and French paratroopers; acting as the eyes and ears of 4th Guards Brigade in BAOR; and, finally, receiving the occasional reminder from senior officers of the need for traditional standards in turnout, in both uniform and plain clothes, including hair and sideburns.

The farewell parade, taken by the Colonel of The Blues and Royals, Field Marshal Sir Gerald Templer, was staged at Pirbright on 24 October, 1975. The last company commander, Major Robert Corbett, the Major General 1991–94, was unable to lead the parade. He had broken his leg on the Company's last hurrah, a drop at dusk in high winds in the French Montaignes Noires. There was a sense of great pride that autumnal day, but also a feeling of unfathomable sadness that comes with the passing of an institution that meant a great deal to the Household Division and to those who served in the Company. A year later to the day, the Company Colour was handed over for safekeeping in the Guards' Chapel in the presence of Sir John Nelson, a much-revered Grenadier, who commanded the 1st Guards Parachute Battalion and was the Major General Commanding the Household Division 1962–66.

The Household Division's Airborne tradition did not die that fateful day. Almost the entire body of the disbanded Company volunteered for G Squadron 22nd Special Air Service Regiment (22 SAS) and achieved a 100 per cent pass rate. The normal pass rate is 5 per cent. In the late 1980s, The Life Guards in the reconnaissance role in the Strategic Reserve were placed in support of 5th Airborne Brigade. It was the brainchild of the then brigade commander, Robert Corbett, and Colonel James Ellery who pioneered the Household Cavalry's parachute role. Many officers in the Household Cavalry, including the current Gold Stick and former Major General Edward Smyth-Osbourne, owed much of their subsequent success to their time in 5th Airborne Brigade. Captain Simon Falkner was the first Life Guards officer to serve in the Company. He was later to command the Household Cavalry Regiment with distinction.

There is a memorial to the Guards Independent Parachute Company at the National Memorial Arboretum in Staffordshire. A substantial sum was raised including generous contributions by the SAS and the Parachute Regiment. There was a huge turnout for the unveiling. The Association, whose President is Major General Sir Robert Corbett, remains extraordinarily robust, only gently fading away as time takes its toll.

THE HOUSEHOLD DIVISION AND SPECIAL FORCES

From the founding of the Special Air Service in the Second World War to the present day, the Household Division has made a significant contribution to the reputation and success of Britain's Special Forces. Remarkably, at the beginning of 2023, the majority of troop commanders in 22 SAS had served in the Household Division.

Such has been the pass rate in what is a formidable test of physical endurance and mental aptitude that the current Major General

Commanding the Household Division has had to concern himself unduly with the officers' careers plot for the five Foot Guard battalions and the Household Cavalry Regiment. Perhaps it was a good problem to have: certainly a source of pride for the Household Division.

Field Marshal Lord Guthrie, who commanded G Squadron 22 SAS before commanding the Welsh Guards, and later was Colonel Commandant of the SAS, wrote of his time in the SAS that "only when you learn to manage yourself can you lead and manage others and for that I remain indebted to the SAS."

It is a sentiment echoed by one of today's SAS troop commanders:

Trooping the Colour on Horse Guards is a lonely place. The eyes of the world are on you. You learn to play up and play the game at Sandhurst and the Platoon Commanders' Course at Brecon, but there's something about ceremonial, its inextricable link to detail with a critical eye, that I return to when faced with a task that might seem overwhelming. In a curious way it calms me and allows me to focus on what really matters.

Special Forces are now a key strategic asset. It is a well-trodden path to the higher reaches of the Army. Former Guardsmen Field Marshal Lord Guthrie, General Sir Michael Rose, General Sir Mark Carleton-Smith and General Sir Roland Walker bear witness to this. If our historic contribution to Special Forces remains, then the Army and the Household Division can only but gain.

The exploits of the Guardsmen who have served in Special Forces remain largely unsung. "Do good by stealth, and blush to find it fame" (Alexander Pope, *An Essay on Man*).

6

Pomp and Circumstance:
Ceremonial and Drill

State events get off to a good start "because visiting Heads of State are always impressed with my Troopers and Guardsmen".
HER MAJESTY QUEEN ELIZABETH II

For the Household Division, state ceremonial and public duties (SCPD) are a fundamental aspect of being Household Troops, underpinning the Household Division's unique responsibilities to guard the Sovereign and the Royal Family as well as undertaking the full range of military tasks.

This dual role is at the core of the Household Division's ethos, supported by all the qualities required to deliver professionalism and excellence, whether on Horse Guards Parade, on a far-flung battlefield, on a United Nations peacekeeping mission in Africa, or conducting Covid-19 lateral flow tests in a community centre in Liverpool. Discipline, leadership, training, and teamwork, in equal measure, are required, regardless of the task in hand.

Ceremonial events are of course particularly special because of the grandeur and excitement that they create, making them compelling to watch and to participate in. However, they also have a greater significance than their component parts. They help to define Britain as a nation with a constitution that has evolved over a millennium. At the centre of this is the Sovereign, the Head of State, in a constitutional monarchy that recognises the primacy of an elected

Parliament, where almost all the real power resides. This separation allows the Sovereign to act as a focus for national identity, unity, and pride, giving the nation a sense of stability and continuity. Ceremonial events, in which the Household Division has a key role to play, are part of the outward and recognisable pageantry that helps to define the character of the nation while also underpinning a long constitutional tradition.

This relationship helps to explain why the image of a Guardsman in red tunic and bearskin is such an iconic one, instantly recognisable around the world as distinctly British. Tourists arriving at London Heathrow Airport see many similar images as they make their way from the aircraft to passport control. They are a welcoming and familiar theme, like the London black taxi, a red double-decker bus, a policeman, a red telephone box, or a yeoman warder from the Tower of London. For some years now, passengers arriving at Heathrow have been met by the reassuring photograph of former Garrison Sergeant Major Billy Mott, Welsh Guards. Although he retired from the Army in 2015, Billy Mott is still on duty at Terminal Five, saluting visitors as they arrive, next to a large 'Welcome' sign. Some 80 million passengers pass through Heathrow every year, so this photograph, even if one cannot quite see Billy's face, will be known to many: a good reminder that they have arrived safely in London.

This visible presence does not end at Heathrow. The Guards are a powerful brand, although shameless product placement is much rarer now than in the past when contractual agreements and copyright were not issues to worry about. "They've got to be great to be GUARDS" was the catch-line for a packet of 20 Guards cigarettes in the early 1970s (price 4/10 shillings, with coupons). "The size, taste, style. The consistently high quality … It can only spell Guards. A big, satisfying born leader of a cigarette." A great slogan that really would not work if the soldier in the background was in a drab camouflaged uniform. Instead, it's the silhouette of an Irish Guards officer clasping the Queen's Colour, and it is instantly recognisable as something with class. The young ensign in the advert was the late Roger Belson, who was not paid for the photo shoot, and later claimed that although he was often seen on billboards around London, it did little for his social life, since no girls ever believed it was him in the picture! The cigarettes remained in production until 1977, with the slogan "You

can count on the Guards ... the best way to get quality and value",
a reassuring message in the era before smoking health warnings and
graphic images became much more prominent on the packet than the
brand itself. It is the ceremonial aspect and the distinctive uniforms
that Guardsmen wear that makes this such a recognisable way of
promoting London tourism and all things British.

There is a close relationship between the ceremonial role for which
the Guards are known around the world and the operational role that
forms the basis of the profession of arms. Although different, they both
rely on the same qualities required for military service. Drill helps to
turn recruits into trained soldiers; it is the point of departure for the
training that follows.

Drill is based on a series of prescribed movements, and for soldiers
to perform these, both individually and collectively, they have to be
rehearsed and practised. This requires discipline, self-control, and the
ability to respond instantly and without question to words of command.
Drill develops a sense of teamwork which can help soldiers overcome
the physical and psychological challenges they face in moments of fear
and uncertainty; these can occur most obviously on a battlefield, and
also during a ceremonial event, or even on the drill square. There is
nothing new about this; to quote Vegetius, writing in AD 378, "troops
who march in an irregular and disorderly manner are always in great
danger of being defeated".

Ceremonial events are choreographed, everything is rehearsed, and
nothing is left to chance. They are planned with all the precision of
any military operation, and it is no coincidence that they are also
called 'operations'. They share many similarities, from basic skills and
procedures, discipline, and leadership at all levels, to the manner in
which they are planned and delivered.

For the individual Guardsman who strives to be the best in all
that he does, it is the attention to detail in the preparation of his
personal kit, getting on parade in good order, and being ready and
prepared for what follows, that contributes to the success of the day.
As in all operations, the actions of one person can often have an
effect on the outcome, successful or otherwise. For those in overall
command of a ceremonial event, from the Major General, Brigade
Major, and Garrison Sergeant Major, responsible for its shape and
form, to the Guardsmen, of all ranks, on the parade itself. Planning

and preparation, the dissemination of clear orders to all involved (at every level), thorough training and rehearsals, discipline and precision in execution, and teamwork; these are all key to the success of any ceremonial event.

Her Majesty Queen Elizabeth II died at Balmoral Castle on Thursday 8 September 2022, the longest-serving monarch in Britain's history. A remarkable reign, during which the Queen gave Britain and the Commonwealth a wonderfully assured sense of continuity, helping to sustain the country through sad, happy and challenging times. While we all knew that the Queen's life was drawing to a close on that afternoon, the announcement at 6.30pm came as a profound shock. Nothing would be quite the same again, and so the manner in which a nation said farewell to a much-loved monarch over the next ten days was vitally important. The dignity and sense of service with which the Queen had lived her life needed to be reflected by the events and military parades that would take place across Britain, leading up to the State Funeral. In all of this, the Household Division played a central role.

Operation *London Bridge*, the plan for Queen Elizabeth's funeral, had been in existence for decades, with its many pages, diagrams, annexes, appendices and details of various 'courses of action' dependent upon many factors that could not be predicted; for example, the time and place of the Queen's death. Thousands of people, including members of the Household Division, many of whom were now well into their retirement or no longer alive, had played their part in drafting, revising and updating the plan. On the afternoon of 8 September, it became increasingly clear that Operation *London Bridge* was about to begin for real. It was the responsibility of the Duke of Norfolk, the Earl Marshal, closely supported by the Household Division, to deliver the plan that had evolved over so many years.

Everyone remembers that afternoon on 8 September very clearly. The Brigade Major, Lieutenant Colonel James Shaw, was in his office when he received a call from the Garrison Sergeant Major at 12.20pm to ask a simple question: "Is everything quiet in the headquarters?" Warrant Officer Class One 'Vern' Stokes had been attending a routine meeting that day with the BBC, ITV and Sky, and so was well placed to pick up the fragments of news that were about to be broadcast around the world. James Shaw knew instantly why this rather odd question was being asked, and Major General (now Sir) Christopher Ghika, also remembers a similar conversation with the Garrison Sergeant Major. By 2pm that afternoon, the first informal meeting at Horse Guards had begun, an opportunity to review the plan for *London Bridge*, just in case.

At 7pm, following the announcement of Queen Elizabeth's death, the second of many meetings of the London District Core Group was convened. There was now a clear sense of immediacy. *London Bridge* was no longer just a plan; the operation began formally the following day, known as D-Day, leading to D+10, Monday 19 September, the day of Queen Elizabeth's State Funeral. For many involved, the real days of the week became meaningless; it was only the 'D' Days that mattered, and the many events and rehearsals that would take place during this period.

The first of these, on D-Day, was the Death Gun Salute – 96 rounds marking Her Majesty's 96 years – fired in Hyde Park by the King's Troop Royal Horse Artillery at 1pm. Then, on D+1, the Proclamation at St James's Palace during which the State Trumpeters of the Household Cavalry blew the fanfare while 7 Company Coldstream Guards provided the Guard of Honour. For the State Trumpeters it had been a particularly hectic 24 hours; they had just landed in Canada on the day of the Queen's death, to be recalled home without leaving the airport. The Proclamation was also a surreal moment, since it was the first time that many of those there and watching on television heard the words 'God Save the King', spoken by Garter King of Arms, David White.

Over the next ten days, the Household Division was closely involved in all the events that took place as the nation said farewell to the Queen. For the four days prior to the State Funeral, the Queen's coffin lay in state in Westminster Hall, and it was the Household Division, with over 300 officers, both regulars and reservists, who mounted a constant vigil.

Many former Guardsmen took part in the events of that period as members of The King's Body Guard for Scotland, The King's Body Guard of the Yeomen of the Guard, Pall Bearers, and in other roles, including commentating live on television. One of the Gentlemen at Arms, Brigadier James Stopford, a retired Irish Guardsman, was in Corfu at his daughter's wedding on the day the Queen died. As he recalled in a later article, receiving the message "You are commanded to return immediately to the United Kingdom to attend to your duties for Her Late Majesty's Funeral ..." was not something that the 'father of the bride' expects to receive on his mobile phone while making his speech. And yet there was no alternative, and he would not have wished it any other way, since it was an honour to be part of such a momentous occasion. "We raised our glasses to the Bride and Groom, closely followed by The Late Queen and His Majesty" and in the morning, James Stopford was on his way home to take up his duties "honouring our Queen".

The 'mission statement' for the military aspects of Queen Elizabeth's State Funeral was probably the most extraordinary that any Guardsman had seen in his lifetime: deliver in procession the Coffin bearing Her Majesty Queen Elizabeth II from the Palace of Westminster to Westminster Abbey for the State Funeral Service and from Westminster Abbey to Wellington Arch for the onward journey to Windsor. A seemingly straightforward task, and yet its enormity only struck home when the Brigade Major displayed these words on a screen in a packed Guards' Chapel for the 'procession brief' that took place six days before the event itself. For James Shaw, this "mission we had been set was the most important of our military careers and perhaps the greatest duty of our lives".

The Guards' Chapel briefing in which all of this detail was covered was followed immediately by a recce, conducted in busy streets where it was almost impossible to keep everyone's attention amongst the distractions and noise. Partly because of this, the overnight rehearsal that followed two days later did not go entirely to plan. In the darkness, a marshal responsible for the Massed Bands could not find the correct 'chalk mark' to position his group, because a familiar bus stop had been removed in preparation for the funeral. The Pipes and Drums were slow to start and the procession stepped off on the wrong foot. The Gentlemen at Arms could not find their correct route from New Palace Yard and exited via a turnstile, not an elegant sight. The rehearsal, to quote the Garrison Sergeant Major, had been a "comedy of errors" and in retrospect had been held too early in the busy schedule of activities. But then, rehearsals are where mistakes are intended to be made, mistakes that were not to be repeated on the day.

The bearer party had a very special role to perform, and it was one in which there was absolutely no margin for mistakes at all. The Queen's Company, Grenadier Guards, were deployed in Iraq on Operation *Shader* when the Queen died, and there was never any doubt that it would be the Guardsmen of this company that would bear the Queen's coffin on its last journey. Most of these young men had never met a member of the Royal Family when they gathered in Buckingham Palace on D+6, the day when the Queen's coffin was to be moved to Westminster Hall for the Lying-in-State. A few days earlier, the Garrison Sergeant Major had met the bearer party for the first time during one of their many rehearsals. Recalling his wedding many years' earlier, when he was 18, he sometimes looks at the photograph and wonders why he had all that hair, and "an awful long moustache". So, he said to these Guardsmen, "if you carry Her Majesty's coffin, and in 20 years of age, when it comes to having your own children and your own grandchildren, you'll regret that your hair was too long and you never combed it". He told them to get a haircut and every time he saw them thereafter, he told them to get their combs out. Good advice indeed.

For those who watched the State Funeral on 19 September, the sombre music from the massed bands, the slow marching of Guardsmen with their weapons reversed, the carrying of the Queen's coffin by the young Grenadier Guardsmen, the graceful manner in which the State Gun Carriage rolled steadily, drawn by naval ratings, without any stop-starts, everything seemed flawless. However, there had been many challenges to overcome during that exceptionally short period, and nothing could be left to chance. Although the plan had existed for many years, the service personnel involved had little time for rehearsal; indeed, on D-Day few knew what they would be doing during the following ten days. Also, while the Household Division was providing many of the key personnel, there were many other individuals and organisations, including the Royal Navy and Royal Air Force, that would be involved. Everyone needed to be briefed. And most importantly, at the centre of all the planning and the events during this period was the King and the Royal Family, mourning their loss while also providing solace to a grieving nation.

The Household Division fulfilled its last and solemn duty to its Colonel-in-Chief just below the altar in St George's Chapel, Windsor, during the Committal Service on the afternoon of 19 September, when the Camp Colour of the Queen's Company was handed to the King and laid on the Queen's coffin. A few days' earlier, the Garrison Sergeant Major was asked by a *Daily Express* reporter where he would be sitting during the service, and he explained that his duties ended formally once the Queen's coffin entered the west door. Fortunately, the Earl Marshal spotted the article and made sure that there was a seat reserved, as it was entirely appropriate that 'Vern' Stokes should be there since he had played a vital role in every single event in London and Windsor during the previous ten days. He was, in his own words, "the chief adviser to everybody, because everyone from the King, right down to the junior Guardsman, and junior Naval Rating, at some point, had a briefing from me, telling them exactly what they had to do."

———

On 26 April 2023, the Guards' Chapel, just a few hundred yards from Buckingham Palace and the Mall, was packed, with 700 people attending, every seat taken, and only standing room at the rear. This was not to be a religious service, although the first to speak by way of welcome was the Senior Chaplain, the Reverand Deiniol Morgan. The gathering was for the Headquarters London District briefing on all the processional aspects of His Majesty The King's Coronation, to be held ten days later, on Saturday 6 May. The Coronation itself had been in the planning for the past six months, and unlike Queen Elizabeth's funeral on 19 September 2022, these plans were new; they had not been the subject of a detailed instruction developed over many years.

Major General Christopher Ghika, in command of the parade, and responsible for ceremonial planning and execution for the Coronation, gave the introductory address. Ten per cent of those military personnel who would take part in the actual parade, he said, from all the Armed Services, were in the Guards' Chapel that morning and "the success of the Coronation itself depends upon those of you sitting here today, so do not let the Sun go down without understanding your role".

There was much to achieve in that short period. Although all of the detailed planning had already taken place, and many smaller rehearsals would continue until the day itself, this was the moment when all the strands were to be drawn together. There was to be a full rehearsal at RAF Odiham in Hampshire (some 40 miles south-west of London) on 30 April, followed by another full rehearsal in London over the night of 2/3 May. With a total of 10,007 ceremonial and support troops taking part in the Coronation, including representatives from 40 Commonwealth nations, this was a huge undertaking, just as complex as any military operation could be, with no margins for error, and all taking place over a matter of hours. To quote Lieutenant Colonel James Shaw, the Brigade Major: "six months in the planning; six hours in the delivery".

The main brief on 26 April was conducted by Garrison Sergeant Major Andrew 'Vern' Stokes with the detail set against a tight timeline and eight separate phases. This was a plan that would be 'delivered' by the Household Division, with Guardsmen taking key roles in every aspect and at every turn of the procession. However, there were many other organisations and people involved in the Coronation itself. Integral to the success of the entire day was the close co-operation of the Royal Mews, who would provide all the carriages, horses, and cars for the Royal Family; Network Rail, responsible for bringing Service personnel into London by train to Waterloo Station; Westminster Council, in charge of preparing the routes to and from Westminster Abbey; and the Metropolitan Police, responsible for the huge task of securing the processional area and controlling the many thousands of spectators.

Crucial to the success of the day was also that this important state event, the Coronation of a new sovereign, could be seen by the nation on television and, indeed by anyone around the world who wished to watch. The three main UK broadcasters, BBC, ITV, and Sky, played an important role in this respect and had representatives at the briefing on 26 April, including expert commentators, who were all former Guardsmen. With many camera positions along the route and in the Abbey itself, together with reporters on the ground and anchors in the temporary studios, this was an operation for the broadcasters as well, with plenty of practice required.

The long television lens would be ever-present, during the overnight rehearsal (a useful debriefing tool for Headquarters London District) and on the day of the Coronation itself. On several occasions, during the briefing on 26 April, and again during the debriefing following the rehearsals, the Garrison Sergeant Major reminded everyone that they would be 'on camera' and essentially in the 'public domain'. Since they could not always be aware of this, it was best to assume that they could be seen from the moment they stepped off the early train from Farnborough or Aldershot until safely on their home journey in the afternoon. This point was made clear, and with a touch of humour, during the debrief on the afternoon of 3 May following the overnight rehearsal, a huge conference call conducted across the internet. In response to a question from a Foot Guard commanding officer about whether the Guardsmen could carry their bearskins while traversing the slippery marble concourse of Waterloo Station, the Garrison Sergeant Major paused for just a short moment as he glanced across the table towards the Major General. "No Sir," came the reply. "You and your Guardsmen will be in the public domain as soon as they step onto the platform ... the Guards wore their bearskins at Balaklava, so they will wear them at Waterloo Station too." It was a logic with which no one could argue.

When the 90-minute briefing on 26 April came to end, delivered with no notes and with the aid of some animated maps and slides, the Garrison Sergeant Major's final words were "Ladies and Gentlemen: that is the scheme of a manoeuvre", to which the audience responded with a spontaneous round of applause. It was an impressive briefing, given by someone who had spent many weeks thinking about every aspect of the plan, and how the success of the day could be assured. The assembled company was now ready for the reconnaissance of the entire route, to include Waterloo Station, Buckingham Palace, The Mall, Whitehall, Westminster Abbey, and back. This all focused on the underlying aim of the military contribution to the big event on 6 May. To quote the Garrison Sergeant Major: "to make this the best possible day for The King and Queen ... a Coronation which will be excellent."

There are 'no hiding places' during a ceremonial event, to quote 'Vern' Stokes. Everyone has their place in a procession, and everyone needs to know what is expected of them, all the time. Even in the early stages of rehearsals, the "drill square can be a really lonely place", with all eyes on the drill instructors who must have the confidence to anticipate things going wrong and take swift action. This is one of the reasons why the Household Division has "such great non-commissioned officers and warrant officers". They have the ability and confidence to stand out in front of a squad or a parade, with the "conviction, courage, discipline, and confidence" to do the right thing at the right time. When something does go wrong, it is the swift and assured action that avoids disaster, and it is often the experienced drill instructors who will be the first to spot those moments.

This highlights the most significant differences between operations on the battlefield and those ceremonial events conducted most frequently in London, but also elsewhere. The famous Clausewitz observation that "no plan survives contact with the enemy" simply does not work for a ceremonial event; firstly, for the obvious reason that there are no real enemies on these occasions; and secondly because there are few margins for error. The manner in which a ceremonial event is conducted, in the full view of spectators and television cameras, is the standard by which it is judged. For this reason, again to quote the Garrison Sergeant Major, ceremonial events are "no-fail operations". They do not just happen, even if they might appear to work like clockwork and in an unchanging way. Every event is unique.

Rehearsals are the key to success and the ability to record and review them has developed considerably over the last 50 years. For the Queen's Birthday Parade in 1974, the Staff Captain at Headquarters London District used a video tape recorder to catch unsuspecting Guardsmen on film during the Guard Mounting and the rehearsals for the event, while the Brigade Major, mounted on his charger, took notes on a pocket recorder. By 2019, with sophisticated digital equipment now available, it was possible to record every part of a rehearsal and make these recordings available on the screens in each of the coaches so that the Guardsmen could watch themselves as they travelled back home. Allowing soldiers to see their mistakes so soon after the rehearsal has proved to be an effective way of helping them to learn lessons quickly, while everything is fresh in the mind.

Watching a great ceremonial event, or being part of it, whether it is a happy or sombre occasion, is a unifying experience: everyone is there for the same reason. Those who stood in the long queue for the Lying-in-State of Queen Elizabeth on 19 September 2022, or on the route of the funeral procession, will attest to that; the normal British reticence to talk to strangers is somehow absorbed into the wider significance of the event. There were many occasions during Queen Elizabeth's long reign, from the beginning to the end, when this was the case: the Coronation in 1953, the annual Queen's Birthday Parade, the Jubilee celebrations (Silver, Golden, Diamond, and Platinum), and the royal weddings and funerals.

To take the example of just one of Queen Elizabeth's four Jubilees, the Silver Jubilee in 1977 comprised a special series of state events and certainly the biggest since the Coronation in 1953. In all other respects, 1977 was a year during which nothing dramatic seemed to be happening on the world stage or, indeed, at home. James Callaghan's minority government clung to power with the help of the Liberal Party, industrial strikes continued intermittently, Red Rum won the Grand National for the third time, British Airways began its regular Concorde service from London to New York, and at the other end of the travelling experience, Freddie Laker started Skytrain with a £59 single fare from London to New York. In contrast, the Queen had possibly the busiest year of her long reign, conducting six jubilee tours in the UK and Northern Ireland, and travelling some 56,000 miles to visit Commonwealth countries.

On the evening of Monday 6 June 1977, the Queen lit a bonfire beacon at Windsor which started a chain of beacons across the country. The following day, the Queen travelled in the Gold State Coach to St Paul's Cathedral for a Service of Thanksgiving. For the parade itself, the Household Cavalry provided four escorts, a staircase lining party on the steps of St Paul's Cathedral and state trumpeters on duty inside. The Queen's Company 1st Battalion Grenadier Guards mounted a Guard of Honour, and Foot Guards lined the Mall, with each Regimental Lieutenant Colonel commanding a sector of the route to St Paul's. Some 500 million people from around the world watched on television; the Queen made several appearances on the balcony of Buckingham Palace, and there were street and village parties across the country, with 4,000 held in London.

It was also a busy summer for the Household Division. The Household Cavalry provided mounted escorts in London, Edinburgh, Cardiff and, for the first time ever, in Glasgow. The regimental bands conducted a Beating Retreat on Horse Guards over three nights with, for the first time, a floodlit performance on the final evening. A few days later, there was a Royal River Pageant and Firework Display, followed by the massed bands playing on the forecourt of Buckingham Palace from 10pm until midnight. Another Beating Retreat took place two weeks later, in the garden of Buckingham Palace, when the Queen held a dinner for the Heads of State of the European Economic Community. The finale came at the end of June, when a Military Musical Pageant was held at Wembley Stadium, with over 2,000 musicians from the three Armed Services and led by the Mounted Bands of the Household Cavalry.

There are also the more private events that are an expression of the close relationship between the Sovereign and the Household Division. The presentation of new Standards to the Household Cavalry or

Colours to the Foot Guards regiment are always by invitation only. They are family occasions at which serving Guardsmen are on parade, watched by their families and by former members of the Regiment. To take just one of many examples, since these are always regular events: in 1988, the Presentation of New Colours to the 1st Battalion Irish Guards by Her Majesty The Queen took place on a gloriously sunny May morning, in the Gardens of Buckingham Palace. Many families were there, and the parade was followed by lunch in the various messes; an immensely happy occasion for everyone. A month later, the new Colour was trooped on the Queen's Birthday Parade for the first time. The Micks rose to the occasion, giving a splendid performance despite the challenges involved in mastering the British Army's new SA80 rifle, which was making its first appearance on the Queen's Birthday Parade.

There is never a day in the year when a Guardsman is not seen publicly somewhere in London. Tourists are naturally drawn to the Changing the Guard ceremony at Buckingham Palace and The King's Life Guard at Horse Guards because these are so obviously part of Britain's national heritage and seeing them is part of the experience of visiting London. And for many who live in London or visit from elsewhere across the country, the presence of the Guards on ceremonial occasions or guarding royal palaces is a reassuring sight, because of the continuity this provides. It is also the daily routine of duties which provides a continuing professional focus since the novelty of guarding buildings can soon wear off.

Back in 1988, when WO1 'Vern' Stokes joined the Army, the pool of ceremonial troops was much greater than it was to become post the *Options for Change* reductions in the early 1990s. In those days, Vern Stokes recalls, "You had about 3,500 soldiers to do the duties, so they didn't come around very often", perhaps "once a week or fortnight, maybe". Now, over 30 years later, with fewer Guardsmen available to mount daily guards, the length of each guard duty has been extended so that at least Guardsmen are not constantly going on and off guard. The much smaller size of today's British Army has placed additional demands on Guardsmen, for example, the agility required to jump from the 'green' Army to ceremonial duty on the 'blue line'. The years when Guardsmen spent months exclusively on ceremonial duties have now gone, and the time available to switch from one role to another has been much reduced.

Given the link between ceremonial and the British constitution, the most important annual event of all is the State Opening of Parliament. Traditionally, this is a grand occasion, in which the Sovereign is escorted from Buckingham Palace to the Palace of Westminster by the Household Cavalry and given a Guard of Honour on arrival at the Sovereign's Entrance by the Foot Guards. Once inside, the Sovereign is led up a flight of stairs lined by Household Cavalrymen, dismounted but dressed in their full ceremonial state uniform (helmet, cuirasses, sword, boots), to the robing room. Then, wearing the Imperial State Crown and the Robe of State, the Sovereign leads the procession to the chamber of the House of Lords.

In the meantime, Black Rod, a senior House of Lords official, is sent to summon Members of Parliament from the Commons chamber, only to be rebuffed by a slammed door, a firm yet symbolic act demonstrating to everyone, including the Sovereign, that the Commons is independent from the Monarchy. Having made their point, the Members of Parliament then follow Black Rod to the House of Lords, where the Sovereign delivers a speech drafted by the government of the day, setting out its policies and proposed legislation for the new parliamentary session.

The State Opening of Parliament is not the most spectacular ceremonial event in the year, because the most important parts of the day, the whole purpose of the occasion, happen not on the Mall or on Horse Guards, but inside the Palace of Westminster. This is also demonstrated by the fact that, in the later years of Queen Elizabeth's reign, the procession from Buckingham Palace became a low-key one, by car, and not by horse-drawn carriage with mounted escorts and street-lining.

None of this, however, changes the constitutional importance of the event, nor the special role that the Household Division plays in protecting the Sovereign, along with the Instruments of State. In a symbolic way, the Guards are there for one specific purpose: to 'guard' their Head of State and Colonel-in-Chief. Without the Sovereign or the Sovereign's representative at the State Opening of Parliament, there would really be no meaningful role for the Guards at all. Parliament has its own security and ceremonial staff; the Guards are there for their Head of State, the Sovereign, not Parliament.

Sometimes it takes a foreign visitor to fully understand the symbolism of such an event. In a sermon delivered by Lord Waldegrave of North Hill, Provost of Eton College, just a few days after the death of Queen Elizabeth II on 8 September 2022, he recounted an occasion in the early 1990s when, as Minister of State in the Foreign Office, he had the honour to receive the first Foreign Minister of a free, non-communist Poland:

> It was the day of the opening of Parliament. We held our talks, while outside there was the noise of the preparation of the great procession when the monarch, escorted by the Household Cavalry, travels in the royal coach from Buckingham Palace to Parliament. There were [Guards] bands playing, commands shouted, the clash of arms coming to the present. It became clear to me that my Polish colleague wanted to watch the parade rather than to talk to me. So we put our papers aside and stood by the window and watched. He turned to me, this hero of anti-communist resistance, who had helped free his country and said: "Minister, what we are watching matters. The communists robbed us of our rituals." He was right.

The most high-profile annual ceremonial event is the Sovereign's Birthday Parade, Trooping the Colour, which has become the nearest that Britain has to a national day of celebration. The Queen's Birthday Parade took place in every year of Queen Elizabeth's reign, except for 1955, when there was a national rail strike, and has always provided a wonderful spectacle, not just for the soldiers on parade, but for those watching from the stands. However, in a more personal way, it has always been the Household Division's special birthday gift on the occasion of the Sovereign's official birthday, an expression of loyalty and respect for their Colonel-in-Chief. On Saturday 17 June 2023 was the first King's Birthday Parade of a new reign, a demonstration of both continuity and renewal.

For many years now, the Birthday Parade has taken place on a Saturday, except in 2022, the year of the Queen's Platinum Jubilee, when it was on Thursday 2 June, the first day of a five-day period of celebration. This was also the only occasion in Queen Elizabeth's 70-year reign when she did not take the salute on Horse Guards, although she did join other members of the Royal Family on the balcony of Buckingham Palace at the end of the parade just before the traditional Flypast by the Royal Air Force.

Her Majesty Queen's Elizabeth's presence on the Birthday Parade has provided the longest period of continuity of all. As Princess Elizabeth, she first appeared on the parade in 1947, and took the salute in 1951, deputising for King George VI. The Queen always rode until, in 1986, her horse, Burmese (presented to her by the Royal Canadian Mounted Police), was retired at the age of 24 following 18 years' service on the Birthday Parade. Rather than train another horse for this role, the Queen decided that in future she would ride in an open carriage and take the salute from a dais.

The Birthday Parade itself has evolved in shape and design, although most of the major changes took place many years ago, all designed to make the event more of a spectacle, an opportunity for the Sovereign to be seen by the public. For example, in 1914 it was King George V who decided that he would ride down the Mall at the head of his Guards, a tradition that has continued to this day. In 1950, King George VI decided that the Household Cavalry should have a role on the Birthday Parade itself rather than merely escorting the Sovereign to Horse Guards and then returning to barracks.

Major General Evelyn Webb-Carter, during his tenure commanding the Household Division in the late 1990s, made a proposal to Prince Philip, the Senior Colonel, that the King's Troop Royal Horse Artillery should be included in the Birthday Parade. The idea came originally from General Sir Michael Gow, a Scots Guardsman who had studied the history of the parade in some detail and written several books on the subject. The idea was always likely to gain favour with the Queen, not least because of her special interest in horses and the fact that she had decreed that the name of the King's Troop should remain unchanged in honour of her father, George VI. However, some work was required on the details and mechanics, and in due course an audience with the Queen was arranged during which Evelyn Webb-Carter explained "the proposed new format of the parade ... on a large piece of paper". And since there was no table, he was soon on his hands and knees "in front of my Sovereign ... a surreal experience which she found amusing".

The inclusion of the King's Troop on the Birthday Parade has now become an accepted part of the parade, adding to the splendour of the event. There have been other smaller changes over the years, much less discernible to anyone but an expert observer. Prince Philip, the Duke of Edinburgh, once referred to "the basic simplicity of the sequence of the event and the curiously intimate nature of the whole thing ... The Birthday Parade has always been a typically British mixture of impeccable ceremonial with a very human and personal purpose." And there was always one person who knew more about the parade than anyone else, never failing to spot the occasional flaw or minor change from the norm: the Queen.

In 2020 and 2021, during the Covid-19 pandemic, when it was not possible for the Queen's Birthday Parade to take place in the normal way on Horse Guards Parade and in the presence of many thousands of spectators, a smaller parade was held at Windsor Castle. The Queen and a few members of the Household were present; there were no spectators. The parade went ahead because it was the Queen's Birthday Parade; it was for the Queen.

State Visits have always been important, playing a vital role in strengthening and maintaining Britain's relationships with countries around the world. During Her Majesty Queen Elizabeth's 70-year reign, she hosted 116 State Visits with the majority of these, 94, taking place during the period 1969–2019, with often two and sometimes three in the course of a single year. The Household Division always has a key role to play in all the ceremonial aspects of these occasions.

For many years, visiting Heads of State would arrive at Gatwick Airport for a three-day visit, to be met by a member of the Royal Family and taken on the Royal Train to Victoria Station, where they would be formally welcomed by the Queen and the Duke of Edinburgh. The visitor, accompanied by the Queen, would then travel in a state carriage (usually the 1902 State Landau), down the Mall to Buckingham Palace, escorted by the Household Cavalry with street liners provided by the Foot Guards, and Union flags and the flags of the visiting country adorning the flag-poles along the way. Guards of Honour were normally provided by a Foot Guard battalion at Horse

Guards and Buckingham Palace, and various mounted escorts were provided during the short visit.

Occasionally, as Lieutenant Colonel Sir John Johnston GCVO, MC, a former Grenadier and Comptroller in the Lord Chamberlain's Office in the 1980s, recalled in an article in 1998, "the suggested visitor ... seemed to be rather a surprise choice, for example President Mobutu of Zaire in 1973 and President Ceausescu of Romania in 1978". The latter was "convinced his rooms at Buckingham Palace were bugged and he used to hold meetings with his entourage outside on the terrace".

State ceremonial is about continuity; its purpose does not, and cannot, change. Major General Sir Simon Cooper, a former Major General Commanding the Household Division, who was later to serve as Master of the Household, once remarked that the mode or method by which the Guards protected their Sovereign and Head of State was less important than the duty itself. Motorcycle escorts and soldiers dressed in camouflage would certainly lack some of the grandeur and panache for which the Household Division is known, but it would not change the fundamental covenant by which these duties are conducted. However, while uniforms designed for another era of warfare may seem an anachronism, they are an important part of the spectacle.

It was not until some years after the Second World War, at Princess Elizabeth's wedding in 1947, that the Guards returned to wearing ceremonial dress on state occasions. During the Second World War, the Household Cavalry often escorted members of the Royal Family with their Daimler armoured cars (the same fighting vehicles that would lead the Guards Armoured Division from Normandy to Germany), while a group of Coldstream Guardsmen, known as the Coats Mission, were charged with providing close armed protection to the Royal Family. When the Royal Family (the King, the Queen, and the two Princesses) left London, they were escorted by the Coats Mission. Their mission, during a period when there was a real threat of an enemy invasion, was unequivocal: to guard the Royal Family to the last man and the last round.

On Saturday 13 June 1981, as the Royal Procession on the Mall approached the Horse Guards approach road, just prior to the formal beginning of the Queen's Birthday Parade, a 17-year-old teenager fired six blanks in quick succession at the Queen, riding side-saddle on Burmese. As the shots rang out, the horses of the Sovereign's Escort lurched forward while the escort commander, Major Anthony de

Ritter, rallied the escort with his sword and advanced to protect the Queen. The teenager was quickly apprehended by two Guardsmen on street lining duties and then quietly led away by the police. He was later charged under the 1842 Treason Act with wilfully discharging a gun "at or near Her Majesty The Queen ... with the intent to alarm or distress Her Majesty". The fact that Marcus Sarjeant was firing blanks could not have been known to those closest to the Queen that day, nor indeed to the Queen herself, who was momentarily startled by the shots, as was Burmese, but soon regained her composure. In later sentencing Sarjeant to five years' imprisonment, the Lord Chief Justice, Lord Lane, was clear on the gravity of the crime: "I have little doubt that if you had been able to obtain a live gun ... you would have tried to murder Her Majesty".

The Metropolitan Police has the primary responsibility for providing protection to the Royal Family, government ministers, and visiting Heads of State, a role that has been in place for many years. While police officers often function in the background, sometimes in plain clothes, the role played by the Household Division, principally on state occasions, and at royal palaces such as Buckingham Palace, St James's Palace, and Windsor Castle, is much more public and overt. Their physical presence is always impressive.

Conducting state ceremonial and public duties is not without risk to those taking part; indeed ceremonial troops are an obvious and vulnerable target for terrorist attacks because of the public nature of their duties; they do not sit behind barriers or fences. On 10 October 1981, a terrorist attack took place outside Chelsea Barracks, when the Provisional IRA used a remotely controlled nail bomb hidden in a nearby laundry van to blow up a bus carrying 23 Irish Guardsmen. Two civilians were killed, and 40 people injured, some of them seriously, including 22 of the soldiers on the bus. Two further buses, each full of Irish Guardsmen, were travelling just a few minutes behind, and it is likely that these were the main target. Had the bomb been detonated just a few minutes later, there would have been many more fatalities and injuries sustained.

The most high-profile and tragic of the terrorist attacks on Household Troops on duty in London took place on Tuesday 20 July 1982, just after 10.40am, as The Queen's Life Guard, provided by The Blues and Royals, was making its way along the South Carriage Drive towards

Hyde Park Corner, *en route* to Horse Guards for the 11am Changing of the Guard. An improvised explosive device (IED), with 25 pounds of commercial explosives, and packed with 4- and 6-inch nails, concealed in a car parked on the road, was triggered remotely as the centre of The Queen's Life Guard drew parallel. Less than two hours later, there was a second explosion, in Regent's Park, killing six soldiers of the Royal Green Jackets Band and injuring 24, including spectators.

The effect of the Hyde Park bomb on both the soldiers and horses was devastating. Lieutenant Anthony Daly, the Captain of The Queen's Life Guard and on his first guard, Staff Quartermaster Corporal Roy Bright, carrying the Standard, Lance Corporal Jeffrey Young, and Trooper Simon Tipper were killed. Three other soldiers were seriously injured and a further three spent time in hospital. Those who were killed and most seriously wounded had been closest to the bomb when it was ignited. There were also a number of lucky escapes among the soldiers, and there can be no doubt that their helmets, thick uniforms, cuirasses, gauntlets, and jack boots helped to minimise some of the injuries.

The horses, however, had even less protection and were a more vulnerable target. Seven died at the scene and many of the remainder received shocking injuries caused by the blast and penetrating nails that had packed the bomb itself. Many years later, in 2019, the families of those killed brought an action in the High Court against one of the convicted members of the IRA responsible for the bomb. Simon Utley, a former Trooper, who was just 18 years at the time of the bomb, gave evidence at the hearing. As the Press Association reported at the time, Simon Utley's "voice wavered with emotion" as he described these terrible events:

> I was riding along; it was my first guard so I was excited ... I remember I was talking to the guy to my left, just asking about what I would be doing later on ... and then the bomb went off ... It was a noise that I can't describe, but it was a painful noise because it took my eardrum out. Then I was aware of the heat and at that point my horse just took off into Hyde Park. I couldn't stop it, it just galloped off with me on it. It took me a fair way into the park before I managed to stop it.

He saw the gaping hole on the left-hand side of his horse, "the size of a dustbin lid", and tragically the horse had to be put down because of the extent of his injuries. Utley described looking back towards the scene of the explosion: "I turned round and all I could see was black smoke just billowing", and later, when he removed his uniform, he found a nail embedded in his cuirasse.

Sefton was the most severely injured of the horses to survive on that fateful day in July 1982, with a severed jugular vein, wounded left eye, and 34 wounds over his body. He was also one of the more experienced horses on parade that day. Aged 18, he had hunted and taken part in show-jumping competitions and point-to-points in Germany, had been part of the Household Cavalry Quadrille and had appeared at the Royal Tournament. When the bomb went off, he was steadfast and calm. He later endured some eight hours of surgery, and not long after was retired to an equine rest home in Buckinghamshire. His extraordinary bravery caught the imagination of the public; he received many hundreds of cards and letters, and books were written about him. Sefton lived until 1993 when sadly, at the age of 30, he was put down because he was by now incurably lame, a direct consequence of the injuries sustained in 1982.

Two members of the PIRA were charged with the murder of the four soldiers who were killed in this cowardly attack. One of them served 12 years before being released under the terms of the Good Friday Agreement; his conviction was later quashed. The trial against the other collapsed on a legal technicality.

***

Music plays a vital part in all ceremonial events; indeed it would be difficult to envisage how such occasions could be possible without the sound of music and the steady drumbeat that helps soldiers to march in step. Military music has a long tradition dating back to the battlefield itself with origins that are similar to drill. It provides a rallying call; it can lift the spirits and raise the morale of soldiers when they need encouragement. For a ceremonial parade, music provides the accompaniment that lifts the event to an almost celestial plane, for both those watching and those taking part.

For many years, an effective system that could coordinate the music and the sound of the bass drummers across an entire parade and beyond the line of sight had been deemed impossible. While technically it might be feasible for everyone to step off together, keeping the time from thereon had never been tried successfully. The Garrison Sergeant

Major, 'Vern' Stokes, recalls that he had "watched the RAF Regiment perform their bespoke drill routines using discreet headphones that played a tempo click-track" and began to wonder whether such a system would work for the Coronation on 6 May 2023. Not everyone agreed but it was certainly worth a determined effort. If it did work, not only would the entire procession, all eight contingents, step off at precisely the same moment, they would have a coordinated beat with which to keep the step. Also, something that had never been achieved before: each of the eight bands would simultaneously play the same music, generating a powerful and harmonious sound along the full length of the procession.

As Colour Sergeant Neil Brocklehurst, the Senior Timebeater for the Household Division Massed Bands, explained in an article later published in the *Guards Magazine*, "coordinating a procession of this size would clearly not be an easy task ... various experiments followed" and "it was decided to use a click track to sync all bass drummers, with Drum Majors, Directors of Music and other percussion players at a pre-determined tempo of a stately 108 beats per minute". The earphones themselves were specially moulded with noise cancelling since the click through normal headphones would not be heard because of the sound of the drums.

The click track was first tested with four bass drummers at each corner of the square at Wellington Barracks to see if they could all step off at the same time. More tests followed, and the system was then tested along the entire route of the coronation procession during the overnight rehearsal, with multiple bands playing the same music while the bass drummers kept to the perfectly coordinated drum beat. Neil Brocklehurst had an important task on the day itself: "my job was to make sure I came in exactly when the click started and to keep with it all the way from Westminster Abbey to Buckingham Palace, cutting off each march in the correct place, so the music worked to the pacing." It all worked perfectly.

The Guards' close and special relationship to His Majesty King Charles III was most obviously demonstrated during the Coronation of the King and Queen on 6 May 2023. During the procession from Buckingham Palace to Westminster Abbey, the King's carriage was accompanied by a Sovereign's Escort of the Household Cavalry, commanded by Lieutenant Colonel Tom Armitage. As the King's carriage emerged from the archway at Buckingham Palace on to the forecourt, a Tri-Service Guard of Honour, led by the Guardsmen of No 7 Company Coldstream Guards and commanded by its company commander, Major Andrew Dickinson, was formed up ready to present arms as the carriage passed on its way to the Abbey. The route down the Mall and Whitehall was lined by members of the Armed Forces; however, it was the Guardsmen, with their distinctive red tunics and black bearskins, that so prominently caught the eye of the television lens.

At the Abbey, an hour before the King's arrival, five members of the King's Company, the same Guardsmen who had served Queen Elizabeth as part of the Queen's Company, stood ready in Westminster Abbey just below where the Coronation would take place. These Guardsmen (the Captain, Major Johnny Hathaway-White; the Ensign, Second Lieutenant Rupert Elmhirst; the Company Sergeant Major, Company Sergeant Major Dean Jones; and two escorts, Sergeant Kane Ellis and Sergeant Matthew Hadfield), took their places on either side of the aisle. They would remain there, hardly moving, except to salute and pay their respects to members of the Royal Family as they made their way to their seats. They were in position for the next three hours and 13 minutes, later described by Johnny Hathaway-White as "a long, but immensely proud stand indeed".

The King's procession of 137 people arrived just before 11am, with each one processing in order of precedence, followed by courtiers carrying the State Crowns. Then the Queen, recently appointed as Colonel of the Grenadier Guards, arrived, and she was clearly delighted to see her saluting Grenadiers, glancing and smiling broadly as she made her way to her seat. Closely behind was the King, and as he passed the Grenadiers, the Ensign slowly lowered the Company Colour in a salute. For those five Grenadiers in the Abbey that day, it had been a huge privilege to be so close to the Coronation itself, bearing witness to the crowning of their Company Commander.

Outside the Abbey, at the end of the Coronation service, the Household Division was again centre stage for the procession back to Buckingham Palace, with the King and Queen, resplendent and crowned, now travelling in the Gold State Coach. This was not a hastily assembled group of soldiers merely waiting outside for the King to appear (as it might have been centuries ago). The procession, a mile long, had formed up during the service and now stretched along Whitehall and into the Mall with, at its front, the Brigade Major, Lieutenant Colonel James Shaw, mounted on his horse, poised to move off. When the order came, it was from the Chief Marshal, Colonel Piers Ashfield, positioned outside the Abbey: a simple 'Walk–March' over the radio to earphones along the procession, together with a raising of his baton to indicate to the mounted troops of the King's Escort that they were to start moving forward. The Gold State Coach, with divisions of the Household Cavalry front and rear, together with 1,000 Guardsmen, began its slow and triumphal procession back to Buckingham Palace, accompanied by music from eight bands, mostly out of sight from each other but perfectly synchronised. For James Shaw, with nearly half a mile of clear road in front of him, the huge King's Standard flying above Buckingham Palace, and tens of thousands of people cheering on either side, it was a moment he will never forget, although it was not an entirely relaxing one; it was only when he arrived safely at the Palace, still on his horse, that he could begin to enjoy this really extraordinary experience.

The penultimate part of the Coronation came as a surprise to even the most seasoned of observers. Great ceremonial events normally conclude with the procession down the Mall and a Royal Salute, followed a little later by the appearance of the Royal Family on the balcony of Buckingham Palace, a tradition that Queen Victoria began in 1851. On this occasion, however, there was an additional event, the 'garden moment' as described by Major General Christopher Ghika. It was the idea of the Garrison Sergeant Major that there should be a final Royal Salute in the garden of Buckingham Palace, followed by a 'Three Cheers for Their Majesties': a personal tribute from the 4,200 troops who had taken part in the procession, an opportunity to see and pay respects to the newly crowned King and Queen. Although this event would be well covered by the television cameras, it was also a more intimate occasion. There would be no cheering crowds: just the King and Queen and several thousand soldiers, sailors, and aviators.

There was nothing in the drill book that provided a neat template for moving this number of troops through a very narrow gate and into the garden without creating a ripple effect on the procession itself and, most importantly, the Gold State Coach, all 4 tons of it. One afternoon some months earlier, the Garrison Sergeant Major, together with the Guardsmen of No 7 Company Coldstream Guards, had devised a plan to reduce the columns of marching personnel in order to pass through the gate without causing any change of step or tempo down the line. As the procession approached, its frontage narrowed, and this new drill manoeuvre was executed without a flaw.

The 'garden moment' was the only part of the Coronation that had not been rehearsed in the garden itself, because the lawn needed to be preserved for the Coronation Garden Party that was to take place a few days before the big event. On the day itself, Colonel Tom Bonas, a Welsh Guardsman about to retire following 53 years' service, was ready at the entrance to the Bow Room, to pass the message to Lieutenant Colonel James Coleby, Coldstream Guards, and the parade commander, that the King and Queen were about to step out on to the garden veranda. Fortunately, the rain lifted for just ten minutes as the parade came to attention and the Royal Salute was given. Then, moments later, came the order from James Coleby to 'Ground Arms', followed by the order given by the Garrison Sergeant Major to 'Remove Headdress', and then 'Three Cheers for Their Majesties'. Bearskins and assorted headdress from the three Armed Service and Commonwealth representatives rose in unison into the air, as each cheer reverberated and became louder than the last one. None of the photographs or television footage can do justice to what it was like to be there that afternoon and to take part in this extraordinary event. All of those on parade had been up since three in the morning, everyone was tired and wet from the intermittent rain, and yet the excitement of the day had sustained them throughout, and on their march back to Waterloo Station and the train journey home.

State events like a royal funeral or a coronation do not happen that often. For many of the Guardsmen on these two great occasions, in September 2022 and May 2023, this will have been a once-in-a-lifetime experience. However, most of the other events in the canon of state ceremonial and public duties happen every year, and some, like the King's Life Guard and the King's Guard, are regular events; they happen every week. They are a fundamental part of the Household Division's special role and its close relationship with the Sovereign and the Royal Family.

7

Cold War, Hot War and *Options for Change,* 1990–92

At the moment of going to press (15th January 1991) some 32% of the Household Division are either deployed, warned for deployment, or in support of the forces in the Gulf. Every Regiment is represented to a greater degree (most of The Life Guards, 1st Battalion Grenadier Guards, 1st Battalion Coldstream Guards, 1st Battalion Scots Guards, and the Scots Guards Band), or to a lesser degree, as detachments or individuals
THE GUARDS MAGAZINE WINTER 1990/91 EDITION

The end of the Cold War in late 1989 came suddenly and unexpectedly, and few had predicted the speed and intensity with which these momentous events were to unfold. One journalist who did was Bernard Levin, in his regular column in *The Times*, writing in August 1977 that the end of the Soviet Union was "inevitable, and ... it may come much sooner than anyone would now dare to hope". He even offered, for "neatness' sake", a precise date, 14 July 1989, and was only wrong by a few months. However, predictions only make sense after the event, and in 1977 few would have taken serious notice of Levin's eloquent words. For the Armed Forces, including the British Army of the Rhine and the Household Division units serving there, it was business as usual, with only one potential enemy of any size to worry about: the Group of Soviet Forces in Germany.

There had been encouraging political developments in Eastern Europe during the late 1980s, notably the rise of Solidarity in Poland. Speculation about the future of the Warsaw Pact was still not making headlines, although Donald Trelford, editor of the *Observer*, returning home from Moscow in March 1989, was convinced that the Soviet Union was heading for imminent collapse. When the end, or the beginning of the end, did come later that year, it was dramatic and exciting. The fall of the Berlin Wall on 9 November 1989 was a hugely symbolic moment in history, signifying so much that could never be the same again, closing an era that had lasted since the end of the Second World War in 1945.

A month later, in December 1989, at the Malta Summit, the leaders of the two superpowers, President George H.W. Bush and President Mikhail Gorbachev, effectively declared the end of the Cold War. The collective policy of deterrence, underpinned by the nuclear guarantee and the deployment of NATO troops in Europe, had worked, despite conflicting pressures. Throughout the 1970s, 1980s, and 1990s, the British Armed Forces had suffered defence cuts, and while Britain had always met its NATO obligations, the state of its military capabilities was being stretched. While a high priority had always been given to procuring the best equipment to meet the Soviet threat, its reliability and sustainability, particularly of the armoured vehicle fleets upon which BAOR depended, had been undermined. Training had suffered, with measures such as 'track mileage' designed to limit the use of armoured vehicles. Notwithstanding, the British Army had been equipped and trained for high-intensity warfare, a policy that would serve it well in the challenges to come later in 1990 and beyond.

As the sledgehammers were swinging along the Berlin Wall, with East Germans flowing freely across the Inner German Border and Hungarians arriving in Austria, The Life Guards in Combermere Barracks, Windsor were preparing to move to West Germany. For some, particularly the returning 'Cold War Warriors', there were some moments of introspection. Since the early 1970s, the two Household Cavalry regiments had enjoyed a five-year rotation between the popular garrison towns of Windsor and Detmold, but this time it was different. They would not be returning to Detmold, with its cobbled streets and solidly built *Wehrmacht* barracks, but would be heading to Sennelager, a large garrison town and a prefabricated military base of little charm. More importantly, and from a professional perspective, what was to be the future of soldiering in Germany? There were 55,000 troops facing a border that no longer existed, and an enemy that would soon be on its way home.

1st Battalion Scots Guards, based in Hohne in West Germany, had completed a four-month operational tour in Northern Ireland in October 1989 and, as Christmas approached, were looking forward to a major battle group exercise in Canada in the spring, followed by conversion onto the Warrior infantry fighting vehicle, equipped with its turret-mounted 30mm automatic cannon and 7.62mm chain gun, with a crew of three and capable of carrying seven infantrymen in the back compartment.

The 1st Battalion Coldstream Guards were now about to start their last year of public duties in Wellington Barracks while contemplating their move to West Germany in December 1990. However, little did they know that their tour in Münster was to be delayed by a further year while, in the meantime, they would be going somewhere entirely unexpected. Likewise, the 1st Battalion Grenadier Guards were beginning to prepare for life back in London, at Wellington Barracks. Perhaps this was a good time to be leaving BAOR but their scheduled move did not take place as planned; and the Grenadiers were also to be surprised by where they did go later in 1990.

As Christmas 1989 approached, The Life Guards began to hand over their light armoured reconnaissance CVR(T) vehicles and their 'out of area' role to the advance party of The Blues and Royals. Once in Germany they continued their conversion onto the British Army's main battle tank, Challenger. This big 70-ton beast, clad in its 'Chobham' (composite ceramic) armour, with its 120mm gun and thermal gun sight, was an impressive and modern vehicle. But what was its utility now, and how did the professional demands of armoured soldiering compare with the more varied skills required of an armoured reconnaissance regiment based in the UK with opportunities to deploy worldwide? In contrast, heavy armoured vehicles, both the Challenger and the Warrior, were cumbersome, difficult to move very far, and designed for an all-out war in northern Europe that now seemed inconceivable. These were the latest variants of several generations of military vehicles and equipment built for one specific purpose; no one had ever envisaged seriously that they would be deployed beyond the North German Plain.

In January 1990, 1st Battalion Irish Guards began their move from Chelsea Barracks to Berlin and were there by the end of the month. Berlin had just seen momentous changes with the fall of the Wall and German reunification on the agenda; however, legally and technically, its military occupation by the four powers (US, USSR, UK, and France) was to continue for another ten months. For the Irish Guards it was a case of getting "to grips with the cosmopolitan metropolis" while training in the role assigned to infantry battalions in Berlin: fighting in built up areas. For the Micks, like other NATO units serving in West Germany, life went on as normal for the time being, in the knowledge that these roles would inevitably end soon.

When wars end, there is usually a call for defence cuts, and this time the phrase 'peace dividend' was being used across NATO to describe the expected savings. Field Marshal Guthrie recalls a comment made to him around this time by John Keegan, the distinguished historian who had taught many generations of officer cadets at Sandhurst and was now the defence editor of the *Daily Telegraph*: "Charles, you will do well to remember the opportunity costs of defence. If there is a peace dividend, it will not be reinvested in defence"; and he was right.

Options for Change, the British government's white paper outlining its proposals to reduce the size of the UK Armed Forces, was published in July 1990, just as the agreement between East and West Germany to establish monetary, economic, and social union was coming into effect. It seemed a good time for some radical thinking, and with reassuring caveats about balancing forces against threats and the ability to "build back up our forces ... should international circumstances ever require us to do so", the British government set out its proposals: "a structure for our regular forces appropriate to the new security situation and meeting our essential peacetime operational needs". The main impact for the British Army was a reduction in its presence in Germany by around 50 per cent, from four armoured divisions to two.

Regimental amalgamations and disbandments were now firmly on the agenda, leading to speculation about who would catch the selector's eye. The other imponderable to feed the rumour mill was the Arms Plot, the detailed plan by which units moved between the UK, West

Germany, and elsewhere. Never simple in design or execution, this was a huge process, requiring re-training for new roles and equipment, while acknowledging the impact on people, including service families, wives' careers, children's schools, etc. Not surprisingly, these upheavals were now being scrutinised more closely by the Ministry of Defence: could their cost be justified, and what benefits did they accrue? For many years, throughout the steady drawdown from colonial outposts and during the long British military presence in West Germany, the Army had always favoured this concept of moving units periodically, particularly combat units, from one station to another. The Arms Plot and the concept of 'accompanied service' for families ('following the flag') was more than just a mechanism. It was an entire way of life that was to take the next 15 years to unravel, against a backdrop of economic and social change, the removal of overseas 'resident' stations in West Germany and Hong Kong, and further defence cuts. The process of moving from a deployed army to an expeditionary one presented many challenges for the Army, including the Household Division.

The debate on all these big issues moved up a gear in 1990. The Army had seen a fair share of reductions over the years, but since the downsizing in the aftermath of the Second World War, the Household Division had remained relatively untouched. But now there was a greater sense of vulnerability. With three Guards units based in West Germany and one in Berlin, some changes were inevitable, perhaps even a loss of 'cap badges'. Speculation at regimental level and in the press was to become a frequent and ongoing topic.

On a wider stage, the challenge for the 14 NATO member states was to make sense of the dramatic events in Europe: the reunification of Germany and the disintegration of the Warsaw Pact. For NATO troops based in West Germany, there was some temporary respite, since the Germans were keen to see a continued presence on their soil for the time being. But with monetary pressures at home, it was easier to address the issue of defence savings rather than to answer the difficult question: what kind of military forces will be needed in a world of unforeseen threats?

With much to be thinking about, life in BAOR continued as before, with the normal round of exercises, trade training, site guards, visits, sport, and adventure training. The Life Guards were settling in to their new posting while completing their conversion onto Challenger, and it was much the same for the 1st Battalion Grenadier Guards, now beginning to re-focus from armoured infantry tactics to preparing for a return to public duties, home service uniform, and drill. For 1st Battalion Scots Guards, the highlight was to be Exercise *Medicine Man*, at the British Army Training Unit Suffield (BATUS) in Alberta. Always a memorable exercise because it was the closest training to real war, this one remained in the Battalion's memory for other reasons as well, "not least the constant maintenance of vehicles and the massive logistical problems the RAF had in moving [personnel] and freight to and from Canada".

The only difference to this routine was that BAOR was no longer training for *the* war, the war that now seemed inconceivable, but for *a* war against an unidentified and unknown enemy. In some respects, it was a refreshing and liberating moment, but this rather surreal period only lasted for a few months before something entirely unexpected happened. Against all the odds, the probability of armoured warfare, in an unfamiliar theatre of operations, was back on the agenda; and this time it was for real.

In the early hours of 2 August 1990, Iraq invaded the small state of Kuwait. The operation was led by the Iraqi Republican Guard and supported by air attacks and heliborne landings, and within a few hours Kuwait City was occupied, the international airport seized, and key government buildings and installations captured. The Kuwaitis put up a determined defence, but with the complete element of surprise and no international intervention or threat of involvement, the outcome was inevitable. Iraq now declared that "we will turn Kuwait into a graveyard to anyone who tries to commit aggression or is moved by the lust of invasion", and soon there were more Iraqi units taking up positions along the border facing Saudi Arabia.

War was not new to Iraq, nor to Saddam Hussein who, in 1980, had led his country into a ghastly and inconclusive conflict with Iran lasting eight years. By the end, Iraq was in an economic mess and owing huge international debts, but with a large army and air force and an extensive military arsenal, including chemical and biological weapons. With the Iran–Iraq War over, Saddam turned his wrath on Kuwait, levelling numerous accusations about stealing oil and violating OPEC oil quotas, while gathering his troops along the Kuwaiti border. The general international view was that this was mere posturing, and so there were no real attempts to deter Iraq before it was too late.

A day after the invasion, the UN Security Council passed a resolution demanding that the Iraqis withdraw all forces from Kuwait. For a moment it seemed that they might comply, but there was now a new and more worrying threat: to Saudi Arabia, a country that could easily have been overrun had the Iraqis kept going. Soon there was another twist to the crisis, when it was revealed that the Iraqis were rounding up Western civilians in Kuwait and moving them to Baghdad, holding them as 'human shields'.

More UN resolutions followed, applying trade sanctions, backed up by a naval blockade. Many doubted that this would solve the crisis, but even more important was the need to deter Iraq from attacking Saudi Arabia, since an invasion would have had serious consequences. Over half the world's oil supplies were there, and if Saddam had invaded, then shifting him would have been more difficult, perhaps even impossible. Margaret Thatcher, visiting the US in early August, was quick to give President Bush her candid views about what needed to be done. The early military response from the US and Britain was to increase naval forces in the area and deploy fighter aircraft. Four days after the invasion, elements of the 82nd US Airborne Division began to arrive to occupy defensive positions around the port of Al Jubail, thus drawing President Bush's 'line in the sand' aimed at deterring further Iraqi aggression. International support steadily grew, with many of the Arab nations determined that Saddam's forces in Kuwait should, if necessary, be removed by force.

Op *Granby*, the British military response to the crisis, was to become the British Armed Forces' largest deployment since the end of the Second World War, and all the Household Division units were to be represented. By February 1991, one Household Cavalry regiment and three Foot Guard battalions had deployed, but not in the conventional and organised way that units normally go to war. When the official 'order of battle' (orbat) of the 1st Armoured Division was published, just prior to the offensive, only the name of 1st Battalion Coldstream Guards appeared on the main list, responsible for prisoner-of-war handling. However, most of The Life Guards, 1st Battalion Grenadier Guards, and 1st Battalion Scots Guards were also there, along with individual reinforcements from The Blues and Royals, Welsh Guards, and Irish Guards. Staff officers representing all the regiments of the Household Division were in theatre, including officers of the deployed units, and a lieutenant colonel of The Blues and Royals who played an invaluable role in US Central Command (CENTCOM) Headquarters, in the 'innermost sanctum' of General Norman Schwarzkopf's planning staff in Riyadh, Saudi Arabia.

The crisis in the Gulf had come at a difficult time for the British government since it now had to plan for a possible war while also delivering the promised post-Cold War 'peace dividend'. Initially, ministers and civil servants in London seized on the 'defensive' nature of the deployment, determined that their response would be tailored to this role rather than a possible warfighting mission to liberate Kuwait. As Lieutenant General Sir Peter de la Billière, the British joint commander in the Gulf, later wrote: "the Government was anxious ... not to be dragged into a conflict which would demand an ever-increasing commitment of men and resources". The 'numbers game' dominated the debate, with Whitehall always seeking a lower deployed number of troops than the Army believed necessary. Some of Whitehall's caution during the early days was reasonable; however, as the defensive posture shifted to the likelihood of warfighting, there "appeared to be continual hold-ups caused by questioning of the reinforcements" considered necessary for such a mission. Ministers and their civil servants imposed tight controls; everything had to be justified, leading to protracted decision-making.

An important early decision was to have a profound effect on how the British Army went to war in 1990; indeed, it was the cause of much of the confusion and disquiet in Germany and elsewhere. As part of the mobilisation plans for BAOR, in place for many years and frequently practised, units would be brought up to their war establishment by reservists, called up by legislation. However, mostly for political reasons, the government chose not to pursue this route, except in the case of some medical and other specialist trades. As a result, decisions about deployments affected not just those units selected, but also those required to help with additional numbers. The steady routine of BAOR soldiering, bound by the 'forecast of events', planned exercises, adventure training, and block leave periods, finally died in that first week in August 1990, never to return. From then on, rumour was rife, and no one knew what to expect next.

The Life Guards had been on leave when the Iraqis invaded Kuwait in early August. A week or so later, during their command meeting on return to work, the commanding officer recounted a conversation with another Guardsman who worked in Military Operations in London. Some of those present laughed quietly or perhaps a little nervously as they were told of a proposal to re-form the 4th Guards Armoured Brigade and despatch it along the Berlin–Baghdad railway. It was no doubt a joke but struck a chord. How would the British Army go to war, and who would be chosen?

A few weeks later, on 15 September 1990, Tom King, Secretary of State for Defence, announced that 7th Armoured Brigade, based in Soltau, was to deploy to Saudi Arabia to form part of a US-led defensive operation to deter the Iraqis from venturing across the border. It had been an eagerly awaited decision, with ramifications for those units selected and those that were not. For The Life Guards, these orders arrived by helicopter, in a sealed and embargoed letter, to be read out to the Regiment by the commanding officer. Within the detailed instructions was the disappointing decision that The Life Guards were not deploying, while many of their Challenger tanks would be going, with other units.

A happier outcome for one Life Guards officer, Captain Edward Smyth-Osbourne, was an offer, enthusiastically sought by him, of the post of 'battle captain' in one of the squadrons of the Royal Scots Dragoon Guards. In the days before his departure, he regaled his squadron leader with stories of his father, whose artillery regiment was mobilised in 1939. Mobilisations, it seems, rarely go entirely to plan: when the quartermaster's staff opened the mobilisation boxes on arrival in France in the early autumn of 1939, they found obsolete horse harnesses from a different era; no one had checked the kit for years. In 1990, the story was different, because most of the equipment came not from a 'war reserve' but from other units, while Edward, following a farewell dinner in the officers' mess, set off to join his new unit with a copy of Fitzroy Maclean's *Eastern Approaches* tucked in his rucksack.

1st Battalion Grenadier Guards, in Münster, serving with 4th Armoured Brigade, had already begun its move to Wellington Barracks, with the pre-advance party back in London and families packing up and preparing their married quarters for handover. Lieutenant Colonel Robert Cartwright, who had just assumed command, was expecting just a short time here before bringing his Battalion back home. But by the time he arrived, all had changed. With the decision to deploy 7th Armoured Brigade, the Grenadiers were now to provide Warriors and 85 Guardsmen to the 1st Battalion The Staffordshire Regiment, together with 25 Guardsmen as Battle Casualty Replacements. It was a disappointing outcome, borne stoically and professionally in all respects. As Robert Cartwright was later to explain, the decision to exclude them had nothing to do with the impending move to London; it was that 4th Armoured Brigade had not been selected to deploy. As the 'pioneers of Warrior', the Grenadiers had more experience of this vehicle and the new armoured infantry tactics than any other unit in Germany, and furthermore, they were at the peak of their training, and their equipment and vehicles were also at an extremely high standard of maintenance, having been prepared and inspected, ready for handover.

For 7th Armoured Brigade to have all that it needed to go to war, it was now necessary to draw on the entire resources of BAOR, and few if any units were left untouched. The Scots Guards, recently returned from their exercise in Canada, and now in the middle of their conversion onto Warrior, soon found themselves helping to train the infantry of 7th Armoured Brigade while also handing over their own vehicles to deploying units. For all those affected in this way, it was a difficult call, particularly for the crews who had worked tirelessly on maintaining their vehicles.

On 7 November, the Scots Guards were warned for a possible future deployment to Saudi Arabia to relieve one of the armoured infantry battalions already committed. This warning order, which came just a few days after the Scots Guards Band had arrived in the Gulf as part of 33 Field Hospital, was an acknowledgement that Op *Granby* might become a protracted campaign, hence the need for unit rotations, or perhaps even reinforcements. Although the warning order was vague on detail, there was now at least a chance that if the Scots Guards did deploy, it would be as an armoured infantry battalion.

1st Battalion Irish Guards, serving in Berlin, were to be relatively untouched by *Granby*, although they were later to make important contributions, by providing teams to help train Battle Casualty Replacements in Germany, by filling important gaps left by deploying troops, and by despatching a 'handful of Micks' who were to serve with other units in the Gulf.

The challenge for all units in Germany was to maintain morale during this period of uncertainty, and particularly in the units that had lost personnel and equipment. For example, it was difficult to reconcile the fact that many units had now been rendered both non-deployable and non-operational, and even before any fighting had taken place. During this period, a squadron leader in The Life Guards recalls a chance conversation with a soldier from another regiment, in an autobahn service station:

"How is Granby affecting your regiment?" he asked. "We are losing most of our tanks."

"You think you have problems, sir! Not only have they taken some of our tracked vehicles and engines, our wheeled vehicles have also gone – we are grounded."

As the days and weeks went by, the demands became more desperate, with some vehicles being dismembered to provide spare parts bound for the Gulf: not an orderly process. The urgency of the situation, determined in part by the lead times for getting everything into theatre, gave way to wire-cutters rather than screwdrivers.

For the first time in its history, BAOR was preparing to deploy an armoured brigade, with additional logistic units, to a new theatre and region, thousands of miles from home. To quote the Chief of Staff of 7th Armoured Brigade:

No Staff College exercise author could have written such a fanciful scenario. Your Brigade has been stationed in Northern Germany for 40 years, training and operating within the tactically cosy matrix of the General Defence Plan. During the next 26 days your establishment is to treble in size. You are to move your strategically immobile main battle tanks to Saudi Arabia in order to counter Iraqi aggression. You will be operating under the tactical control of the United States Marine Corps. Oh, and by the way, the first ships leave in 14 days' time.

'Rumour control' was generating some alarming scenarios. Pundits and armchair generals made gloomy predictions about how a campaign might unfold, with high casualties, falling public opinion at home, and no easy way out once the troops were in the Gulf. Others predicted ecological disaster, including the deliberate destruction of the oilfields, while lurking in the background was the spectre of Iraq's biological and chemical weapons and even the possibility of a secret nuclear capability. There was also a concern among some senior British officers in Germany that the essentially defensive NATO doctrine and training would create special challenges if and when the US-led Coalition went on to the offensive. Iraqi positions along the border were laced with obstacles and minefields, and Saddam would probably use chemical weapons early if attacked. On the political level, there was also concern about maintaining the international Coalition, and the possible role of Israel if attacked by Iraq.

Then there was the alarming thought that if the Coalition went to war to liberate Kuwait, where would the additional forces and equipment be found, given the manner in which the British Army of the Rhine had been stripped bare to send one brigade to the Gulf? Robert Cartwright recalls a I British Corps Study Day, hosted by the corps commander, Lieutenant General Sir Charles Guthrie, at which General Sir John Chapple, the Chief of the General Staff, was the senior guest. "Why has it been necessary to decimate I British Corps to furnish a brigade?" asked one of those present, to which the Chief of the General Staff replied, "The sky is black with chickens coming home to roost." It was a damning indictment of the defence cuts of preceding years, a reminder that field commanders are so often constrained by past decisions.

With 7th Armoured Brigade now forming up in Saudi Arabia and beginning its training in the desert, General Sir Peter de la Billière, in his headquarters in Riyadh, was considering the Brigade's future role. If, as seemed increasingly likely, the Coalition went onto the offensive, the plan was that the US Marine Corps, with 7th Armoured Brigade under command, would attack Kuwait from the southern axis, close to the sea. However, the secret plan that General Schwarzkopf was now working on was to use the US Marines as a diversion, with the main attack into Kuwait taking the form of a massive, armoured left-hook, swinging in from the west and through the Iraqi desert.

The option to leave 7th Armoured Brigade with the US Marines was not one that General de la Billière favoured. Firstly, the ground south of Kuwait, on the eastern littoral, facing the heaviest Iraqi defences, was "not at all suitable for the far-ranging, fire-and-manoeuvre tactics" for which the British Army had trained, while the open ground further west was ideal and also had the advantage of being on the Coalition main axis. Secondly, there was the difficult subject of casualties. The US Marines had a fearsome reputation, and were also prepared to take casualties, predicted to be as high as 17 per cent, in order to get to Kuwait first. If 7th Armoured Brigade remained here, then this percentage might lead to some 1,700 British dead, a figure that de la Billière believed both unacceptable and out of proportion to the overall national effort. Supporting the main attack from the west seemed a better option, but to do this, the British would need to commit more troops and logistical support.

After some debate, the decision was taken in London and announced on 22 November to send the 1st Armoured Division, commanded by Major General Rupert Smith, with 4th Armoured Brigade, a sizeable artillery group, a reconnaissance regiment, an engineer regiment, an air corps regiment, and more logistical units. The Division was to be operational by the end of January 1991 while, in the meantime, 7th Armoured Brigade continued to train with the US Marines, a useful strand of the deception plan to persuade the Iraqis that the main attack would come from the south.

Now that 4th Armoured Brigade was off to the Gulf, the Grenadiers' problem was that they were no longer able to deploy as a cohesive battle group because they had lost so many Guardsmen and vehicles. Robert Cartwright accepted this reality; however, he was equally clear that "as far as possible, if the Battalion was to be asked for more manpower, we must not be sent piecemeal, but as formed sub-units". He told the Commander 4th Armoured Brigade, Brigadier Christopher Hammerbeck, that he could provide two companies, and then warned off battalion headquarters to convene a bidding conference the following day, chaired by him. The aim was to form two strong armoured infantry companies based on the Queen's Company, destined for the 1st Battalion Royal Scots, and No 2 Company, for 3rd Battalion The Royal Regiment of Fusiliers. Major Grant Baker, the Captain of the Queen's Company, and Major Andrew Ford, commanding No 2 Company, were asked in turn to select from the available pool of manpower, and two new companies, each with a strength of 148, were formed by virtually disbanding the remaining Grenadier companies. This proved to be a pragmatic approach in challenging circumstances, making best use of the situation and ensuring that Grenadiers would at least deploy together. It was equally challenging times for the families, since no firm decision had been taken about when the Grenadiers would be moving back to Wellington Barracks. This uncertainty, in Robert Cartwright's words, engendered an element of "high farce" with "the clean ovens ready for handover ... not [being] used again because the wives bought microwaves instead".

By the time the decision to send more troops to the Gulf was made in late November, The Life Guards, with B and C Squadrons, had embarked on a planned deployment to Canada, on Exercise *Medicine Man*, in Alberta. A huge area of open prairie, seven times larger than Salisbury Plain, ideal for live-firing tactical exercises, this was the most realistic and challenging training available. In some respects, it was probably the best place to be, a clear focus for the next month, an opportunity to train hard and prepare for a possible future deployment, while being away from the relentless rumour mill. But there were drawbacks: a six-week deployment away from Germany and the tiresome requirement for the tank crews to convert onto the older Chieftain tanks still being used at BATUS. It was a strange turn of events that led to the obvious joke about the availability of tanks in Germany; might these old Chieftain tanks, inherently unreliable, also be needed in the Gulf?

The Scots Guards had been hoping for a battalion deployment; however, on 22 November they were ordered to provide a large platoon, totalling 45, of Battle Casualty Replacements; to be followed ten days later with another warning order, placing the entire Battalion on seven days' notice to assume responsibility for providing all the 1st Division's infantry Battle Casualty Replacements. It was a sobering moment, since once committed to the Gulf, the Scots Guards would be providing individual reinforcements to wherever they were needed, across the entire 1st Division. There can be few tasks less palatable than this one, but at least they would have a role, although there was little detail on how this would all work.

As Christmas 1990 and the deployment of 4th Armoured Brigade approached, the debate about numbers continued. Everything was being scrutinised by Whitehall, where there were suspicions that the Army was slipping more troops into theatre without proper political clearance. For example, the Queen's Own Highlanders' advance party arrived in Saudi Arabia on 11 December, with an expected battalion deployment to follow. Their arrival coincided with a ministerial visit and within a few days they were on their way back to Germany, the deployment having been cancelled as 'off orbat'. Now, with no prospect of deploying, the Jocks proceeded on leave to Scotland and elsewhere. Just before midnight on New Year's Eve, the commanding officer received a call from a Ministry of Defence duty officer asking, "When can your battalion deploy to the Gulf?", to which he responded, "You must be joking, do you know what time it is?" But it wasn't a joke; the following morning the Queen's Own Highlanders were placed on seven days' notice to move to the Gulf, and were soon back there, to find that most of their equipment had now been reallocated to other units.

Robert Cartwright described the atmosphere over Christmas as "surreal", with the Grenadiers split between Münster and the Gulf. For The Life Guards, back from Canada, and with A Squadron already detached to the 14th/20th King's Hussars, and with no tanks in the barracks, there was little to do except to keep up their training and wait for the next warning order. Just before Christmas, A Squadron returned from a week's leave and, on Boxing Day, its advance party departed for the Gulf. The previous few months had been a difficult one for the Squadron: on two occasions, the tank crews had brought their tanks to the highest of standards, only to watch them being handed over to other regiments. They seemed to have missed out on everything, including the chance to go to Canada. But now they were finally on their way, having only just handed over their second fleet of tanks a few weeks earlier. It was an almost inexplicable turn of events, but at least The Life Guards were now committed to Op *Granby* with one fully formed sub-unit. Within a few days A Squadron were in Blackadder Camp, Al Jubail, taking over their third fleet of tanks in three months and preparing for an intensive period of desert training.

1st Battalion Coldstream Guards, still in Wellington Barracks and wondering when they would be going to Germany to take over from the Grenadiers, were not expecting any surprises when they started their Christmas leave, prompting the Commanding Officer, Lieutenant Colonel Iain McNeil, to say: "They won't need us in the Gulf. If they do, I'll eat my hat." The Battalion was "operationally in limbo" to quote McNeil. Warrior training on external courses had been completed, the families were ready for the move to Münster, now delayed. So, with nothing else in the diary, the Commanding Officer wrote to the Sultan of Brunei (an honorary Coldstreamer) to see if he would send planes to fly the Battalion to Brunei for training. "Unsurprisingly," he heard nothing "other than the irritated MOD system that didn't like spontaneous action!"

All changed on the evening of 29 December, when the picquet officer telephoned the second-in-command, Major Hugh Boscawen, to tell him that a conference would be taking place at Horse Guards the following morning, a Sunday, at 10am. The Coldstream Guards were to deploy to the Gulf with 520 men, but there were no details of the mission, no order to deploy, and no direction to recall personnel from leave. Fortunately, the *Daily Mirror* ran the story and all ranks responded with enthusiasm as the Guardsmen, including those posted on courses and some who had left the Army, returned swiftly to barracks while the Commanding Officer conducted a quick recce in the Gulf.

The task for the Coldstream emerged early in the New Year, a surprising one although as important as any other. Iain McNeil, with the rank of acting full colonel, was given the task of forming the Prisoner of War Guard Force (PWGF), with the Coldstream and two infantry battalions (Royal Highland Fusiliers and King's Own Border Regiment), together with several hundred other attachments (including Royal Engineers and Royal Army Medical Corps). The size of this hybrid organisation, very different from the accepted template for operations in Europe, acknowledged the possibility of large numbers of Iraqi prisoners (their morale was known to be low), and the fact that a pared-down 1st Armoured Division, with reduced rear area support and strung out over extended distances, would not be able to cope with enemy prisoners and its long lines of communication. This grouping was to be the size of an infantry brigade capable of conducting other tasks, to include clearing the battlefield following the armoured advance, and even the possibility that these troops might be needed to re-take Kuwait City. The Battalion was on its way to Saudi Arabia by the third week in January.

Back home and among the journalists in the Gulf, the future of some of the deployed regiments following more *Options for Change* announcements prompted further speculation. Occasionally there was an element of humour, for example, a letter by Lord Kingsale in the *Daily Telegraph* on 22 December. Could the need for defence cuts and "Mr Major's stated ideal of a classless society in which excellence and elitism could have no place" be served by reducing the four battalions of Grenadiers and Coldstream into "one regiment of two battalions, to be known as the English Guards? There need be no objection to each of the new battalions retaining some idiosyncrasies and customs of their parent regiments, though maybe the red and white plumes should be combined into an attractive shade of pink and worn on the centre front of the bearskin." And who would be the ideal choice as Colonel-in-Chief? Ignoring that Her Majesty The Queen held that appointment for all Guards regiments, the author offered his own nominee: "Miss Barbara Cartland".

Two days later, Robert Fox, reporting for the *Daily Telegraph* from the Gulf, added a more serious edge to the speculation with an article entitled 'Grenadiers face cost cut battle'. The brunt of the proposed cuts, he said, would be taken by the infantry, with famous regiments like the Grenadiers and the Black Watch being reduced to company-sized units and distributed around larger battalion or brigade groups. He used the Queen's Company as an example, basing his prediction on the hybrid way in which the deployed 1st Armoured Division had been assembled. It was a clever piece of journalism but not one that soldiers needed to read just as they were going to war.

The build-up continued in the New Year as more troops arrived in the Gulf. On 15 January 1991, the Scots Guards handed over the last of their Warriors as their advance party flew to Al Jubail where, on arrival, the commanding officer, Lieutenant Colonel John Cargill, was told to take charge of Blackadder Camp and "to sort out the BCR system". The camp had been named after Captain Edmund Blackadder, the anti-hero star of the BBC *Blackadder* comedy series, and perhaps only the British would have seen the funny side of the association. It had become a grim and scruffy place that also needed to be sorted out, a task that the Quartermaster, Major Ron Clemison, and the Regimental Sergeant Major, Warrant Officer (Class One) Ray Walker, immediately took on. To quote the regimental history, "RSM Walker remembers 'being absolutely appalled' by what he found, but, having taken a series of decisions that probably only a Household Division Sergeant Major could have taken and in doing so, in the words of the *British Army Review*, 'made himself the most unpopular man in Al Jubail', order slowly emerged from the chaos that had greeted the advance party." By the time the remainder of the Battalion arrived two weeks later, "Blackadder Camp had been brought firmly under Scots Guards command and a system for registering, organizing and training BCRs was beginning to take shape."

With the Scots Guards now complete in the Gulf, the Commanding Officer was warned that his three armoured infantry companies would be moving forward to join the Armoured Delivery Group under the command of the Queen's Own Highlanders, now back in theatre following their return in the New Year. Again, it was a rather unsatisfactory command arrangement, with Battalion headquarters remaining in Blackadder Camp to oversee the Battle Casualty Replacement training programme. The Commanding Officer sought permission to be allowed forward to join the remainder of the Battalion, but it was not to be.

The remainder of The Life Guards, commanded by Lieutenant Colonel Anthony de Ritter, were deployed on 17 January as Battle Casualty Replacements, however, not as a formed regimental unit. B and C Squadrons, and later a re-constituted D Squadron, were attached to the Armoured Delivery Group, commanded by Lieutenant Colonel Seymour Monroe, Queen's Own Highlanders, while regimental headquarters would remain separate, poised to

38. Her Majesty Queen Elizabeth riding Burmese on the Queen's Birthday Parade on Saturday 15 June 1985. (Crown Copyright)

37. The officers and seniors of the Queen's Company at Windsor Castle on 19 April 1983. Back row, from left to right: Warrant Officer II (CSM) David Ling, Lieutenant Greville Bibby, Lieutenant David George, Lieutenant Lord Michael Cecil, Colour Sergeant Stephen Dehnel. Front row, from left to right: Major Evelyn Webb-Carter, HM The Queen, HRH The Duke of Edinburgh, Captain John Wills. (Crown Copyright)

39. Her Majesty Queen Elizabeth accompanied by the President of Poland, Lech Wałęsa, arriving at Home Park, Windsor, during the State Visit on 23 April 1991. (Crown Copyright)

40. The Queen's Birthday Parade, Windsor Castle, Saturday 13 June 2020. The Colour of 1st Battalion Welsh Guards is being trooped. On the dais, Her Majesty Queen Elizabeth is flanked by, on the left, Lieutenant Colonel Michael Vernon, Comptroller of the Lord Chamberlain's Office, and, on the right, Admiral Sir Tony Johnstone-Burt, Master of the Household, and, further right, Lieutenant Colonel Nana Kofi Twumasi-Ankrah, Her Majesty The Queen's Equerry. (Crown Copyright)

41. The funeral of HRH The Duke of Edinburgh at Windsor Castle, 17 April 2021. (Crown Copyright)

42. Meeting of the London District Core Group to discuss Operation *London Bridge*, held on the day of Her Majesty Queen Elizabeth's death, 8 September 2022. (Crown Copyright)

43. The Garrison Sergeant Major marching in front of His Majesty King Charles III and other members of the Royal Family, as they follow the procession of the State Gun Carriage to Westminster Abbey on the day of Her Majesty Queen Elizabeth II's State Funeral, Monday 19 September 2022. (Crown Copyright)

44. The bearer party from the Queen's Company, 1st Battalion Grenadier Guards, carry the coffin of Her Majesty Queen Elizabeth up the staircase of St George's Chapel, Windsor, 19 September 2022. (Crown Copyright)

45. Moments before His Majesty The King stepped onto the terrace of Buckingham Palace for the 'Three Cheers for The King'. (Crown Copyright)

46. Company Commander's Memoranda in the desert, 1st Battalion Grenadier Guards, on Op *Granby*. (© Regimental Headquarters Grenadier Guards)

47. The Life Guards Command Team on Op *Granby*, 1991. From left to right: Captain Chris Slater (Quartermaster), Warrant Officer Tony Belza (Regimental Corporal Major), Lieutenant Colonel Anthony de Ritter (Commanding Officer), Captain Hugh Robertson (Adjutant), Captain Nick Garrett (Ops Officer) and Second Lieutenant Martin Rees-Davies. (Crown Copyright)

48. Company Sergeant Major Ric Howick and Lance Corporal 'Lennie' Lenthall, 1st Battalion Coldstream Guards, with Iraqi prisoners of war. (© Regimental Headquarters Coldstream Guards)

49. C Company, 1st Battalion Scots Guards, in Assembly Area RAY prior to the beginning of the land offensive during Op *Granby*. (© Regimental Headquarters Scots Guards)

50. General Norman Schwarzkopf, Commander US Central Command and Coalition Commander during the First Gulf War, inspecting a guard of honour provided by 1st Battalion Coldstream Guards in June 1991. On the left is Major Peter Hicks. (Crown Copyright)

51. Lieutenant Colonel (later Major General) Peter Williams, commanding 1st Battalion Coldstream Guards, briefing visitors on Op *Grapple* 3 in 1994. (Peter Williams)

52. Lieutenant General (later General) Sir Michael Rose, DSO, while commanding the United Nations Protection Force in Bosnia and Herzegovina, 1995. (Crown Copyright)

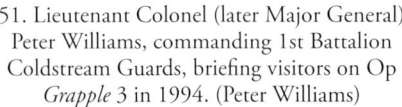

53. A Scimitar of 1 Troop, B Squadron, The Life Guards, at Rama Lake, Prozor, Central Bosnia and Herzegovina, in 1995. (Crown Copyright)

54. Battalion Headquarters Irish Guards, Pristina, Kosovo, on the first day of the operation in 1999. From left to right: Major Mark Grayson, Major Michael Moriarty, Captain (later Major General Sir) Christopher Ghika and Captain (later Colonel) Peter MacMullen. (Christopher Ghika)

55. Commanding Officer's Orders, 1st Battalion Irish Guards, Kosovo, 1999. In the centre: Major Michael Moriarty. On the right: Lieutenant Colonel (later Major General Sir) William (Bill) Cubitt. (Christopher Ghika)

56. Alexander Barracks, Pirbright, 1968. The interior of one of the new barrack rooms. A new concept was used in the design: six beds in each of the four sections, with a large clear space in the centre for group activities. (Crown Copyright)

57. Her Majesty The Queen speaking to Trooper Moore, The Blues and Royals, during her visit to the Guards Depot on 22 June 1970. (Crown Copyright)

58. Regimental Sergeant Major John Holbrook (the 'Blade') speaking at the pace stick luncheon held at the Guards Depot Sergeants' Mess in 1971. On the left are Colonel John Swinton and Academy Sergeant Major Ray Huggins. (Crown Copyright)

59. Junior Drill Sergeant Ferguson, Irish Guards, with Major General Sir George Burns and Captain The Hon Tom Clifford at the Juniors Passing Out Parade, Guards Depot, 1975. (Crown Copyright)

60. Now there are five. The sons of Sergeant McEwan, formerly Scots Guards, marching on the square at the Guards Depot with their father, 1978. (Crown Copyright)

61. Major General (later Sir) Simon Cooper (The Major General) talking to Junior Guardsman Dolan during his visit to the Guards Depot in 1990. (Crown Copyright)

62. Lieutenant Colonel Charles Bremner, Welsh Guards, presenting a medal to the boxer Frank Bruno, who had just completed the Depot Assault Course with 'Ed the Duck'. (Crown Copyright)

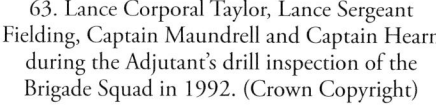

63. Lance Corporal Taylor, Lance Sergeant Fielding, Captain Maundrell and Captain Hearn during the Adjutant's drill inspection of the Brigade Squad in 1992. (Crown Copyright)

64. Where it all began: the Manhattan skyline following the terrorist attacks on 11 September 2001. (Hiro Oshima/WireImage via Getty Images)

65. A Warrior fighting vehicle and an Irish Guardsman cover British combat engineers extinguishing an oil fire outside Basra, April 2003. (WO2 Giles Penfound/Crown Copyright 2020)

66. Shia militia fighters, the Jaysh al-Mahdi Army, in Najaf (north-east of Basra) in 2004. (SAEED KHAN/AFP via Getty Images)

67. Chaos in Basra in 2005: a reckoning for the British Army. A burning Warrior fighting vehicle near the Al Jameat police station. (Atef Hassan/Reuters)

68. Mortar Platoon, 1st Battalion Grenadier Guards, on Op *Herrick* 6. (© Regimental Headquarters Grenadier Guards)

69. Captain Piers Ashfield, Grenadier Guards, as part of the Brigade Reconnaissance Force, 2007. Captain Ashfield was later to be awarded the DSO on Op *Herrick* 16. (Piers Ashfield)

70. Grenadier Guardsmen of the Brigade Reconnaissance Force in contact with the enemy on Op *Herrick* 6, 2007. (Piers Ashfield)

71. Household Division commanding officers on a reconnaissance in Helmand Province, Op *Herrick* 10, 2009. From left to right: Lieutenant Colonel (later Lieutenant General Sir) Roly Walker, Grenadier Guards; Lieutenant Colonel Rupert Thorneloe, Welsh Guards (killed in action, 1 July 2009); Lieutenant Colonel Toby Gray, Coldstream Guards; and Lieutenant Colonel Harry Fullerton, The Life Guards, commanding the Household Cavalry Regiment. (Andrew Speed)

72. Welsh Guardsmen disembark from a Chinook helicopter in Helmand Province, May 2009, during Op *Herrick* 10. (Cpl Rupert Frere RLC/Crown Copyright 2020)

73. Lieutenant Barney Campbell, The Blues and Royals, beside his Scimitar after a lucky escape from an IED strike, south of Musa Qal'ah, with members of his troop from C Squadron, the Household Cavalry Regiment: Lance Corporal Duncan Chalklin, The Life Guards; Trooper David Wilcox, The Blues and Royals; and Sergeant Adam Stores, Royal Electrical and Mechanical Engineers. (Barney Campbell)

74. The Quartermasters and Regimental Corporal/Sergeant of the Household Division on Op *Herrick* 11, November 2009. From left to right: Major Anthony 'Tadge' Tate, The Life Guards; Warrant Officer Class 2 W. Brown, The Blues and Royals (Household Cavalry Regiment); Major M. Gaunt and WO2 S. Monro (Grenadier Guards); Captain K.T. Fox and WO2 S. McMichael (Irish Guards); Major A.P. Jasinski and WO2 M. Quinton (Coldstream Guards). (Crown Copyright)

75. Piper Fraser Edwards takes a smoke break. A Battle Casualty Replacement, this was the young soldier's first day in the field. (Max Benitz)

76. The Duke of Cambridge, Colonel of the Irish Guards, talking to Guardsman Kason Lynch of the Mortar Platoon at Camp Bastion, 2010. (© Regimental Headquarters Irish Guards)

77. The Commanding Officer's O Group at Forward Operating Base Price. 1st Battalion Irish Guards on Op *Herrick* 13, 2010. From left to right: Lieutenant Colonel (later Major General Sir) Christopher Ghika, Major Mickey Stewart, Captain Ed Paul, Major (later Major General) Al Turner, Major Matt Collins (later killed in action) and Captain Hugh Dickinson. Major Collins was killed in action in Afghanistan, together with Lance Sergeant Mark Burgan (also Irish Guards), on 23 March 2011. (Christopher Ghika)

78. A Scots Guards officer advises an Afghan Army officer in Gereshk, October 2010, at the end of Op *Herrick* 12. (Cpl Mark Webster/Crown Copyright 2020)

79. Guardsmen of 1st Battalion Scots Guards fixing bayonets before entering Popolzai. From left to right: Guardsman Ryan Gowans, Lieutenant Charlie Pearson and Guardsman Steven Fuller. (Max Benitz)

80. Lieutenant Douglas Dalzell, MC, killed in action in Afghanistan on 18 February 2010. (With the kind permission of the Dalzell family)

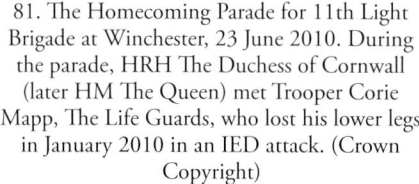

81. The Homecoming Parade for 11th Light Brigade at Winchester, 23 June 2010. During the parade, HRH The Duchess of Cornwall (later HM The Queen) met Trooper Corie Mapp, The Life Guards, who lost his lower legs in January 2010 in an IED attack. (Crown Copyright)

deploy if required at the front. Again, it was a rather odd decision since, with the exception of A Squadron, under command of the 1st Battalion Royal Scots, the remainder of the Regiment had now deployed.

By early February, some 500 Grenadiers were in theatre, serving in 14 different units. While this was a new experience for many, particularly the young Guardsmen, they were getting on with the job with determination and pride in their own regiment. General de la Billière visited the Staffordshire Regiment over Christmas, and was impressed with the Grenadier platoon, later recalling a non-commissioned officer telling him that "far from settling for a second-class job, they were doing things the Brigade of Guards' way, which naturally was better than the Staffords' way and in fact they were showing the Staffords how to carry on!"

Around that time and for a while after Christmas, General de la Billière was in correspondence with Major General Simon Cooper, General Officer Commanding London District and the Major General Commanding the Household Division, about the latter's request that Guardsmen attached to other units should be allowed "to wear brigade insignia, either in the form of cap badges or as red-and-blue arm-bands". De la Billière, however, had little sympathy "for the Household Division's obsession with sartorial detail", pointing out in one of his replies that "the core of cohesion in battle has always lain in group loyalty at brigade and battalion level", and that the problem of regimental identity was being "quietly resolved without recourse to formal and distracting action at a time when there are more pressing issues to be getting on with". The exchange continued into the New Year with the arrival of a fourth letter from Simon Cooper, by which time, "in the run-up to war", de la Billière "did not feel inclined to devote much time to the subject".

Looking back, this does seem to be something of a storm in a teacup, a real fuss about nothing. The request that Guardsmen be allowed to display a small token of their regimental identity was entirely reasonable at the time, particularly given the untidy and ragged way that the deployment had taken place. Indeed, it was soon to become normal practice across the Army, a small concession that recognised the value of the regimental system while accepting that sending troops to war only as formed units was probably a thing of the past.

One common experience for all soldiers, regardless of their role or unit in the Gulf, was the conditions, together with the deprivations and challenges of being in an operational theatre. The heat, some 30°C, was just one factor, but there were others. The desert is generally flat: the tactics required for desert warfare were to be very different from those in Europe, and sand is ubiquitous; it gets everywhere. Although Al Jubail, the staging post for all, was some 120 miles from the Kuwaiti border, and even further from Iraq, the threat of attacks from Scud missiles was a real one. Although these Soviet-era missiles were relatively basic in design, they had the capacity to carry any number of unpleasant payloads, including chemical and biological weapons.

For this and other reasons, an emphasis was placed on nuclear, biological, and chemical (NBC) training for which the British troops were better placed than the Americans, since they were all equipped with NBC suits and masks. The decision was taken to protect the troops with a range of medical countermeasures which, in addition to the normal inoculations for overseas deployments, included a combination of pills to block nerve gas agents, together with vaccinations to protect against anthrax and plague. One young Territorial Army officer attached to The Life Guards who, all these years on, can't quite understand why he was allowed to deploy to the Gulf with only a few weeks' training, still has his inoculations record showing "3 x Cholera, 2 x Anthrax, 2 x Pertussis and Plague; all received between Jan and Feb 91". The whole issue was sensitive and veiled in secrecy at the time. The press was discouraged from discussing the topic, and the decision to start the inoculations, which were voluntary, was delayed in the hope they would not be necessary. In the years that followed and to this day, the subject of 'Gulf War Syndrome' has never entirely gone away, despite the inconclusive evidence about the potential danger of this concoction of drugs.

Satellite navigation was in its relative infancy back in 1990, the equipment was sparse, and it was not as user-friendly as it was to later become, since it was reliant on satellites that were not always in alignment. However, it was available, and particularly useful in the featureless desert, where it could get armoured formations travelling in the right direction in all conditions, and at night. In a presentation after the war, Brigadier Patrick Cordingley, commanding 7th Armoured

Brigade, in describing the impact of satellite navigation, said that "for the first time in the history of the British Army we were likely to know where we were when we fought a battle", a comment for which he was not thanked by the veterans of former wars!

By mid-January 1991 over 95 per cent of the 1st Armoured Division had deployed to the Gulf. 7th Armoured Brigade, with 85 Grenadier Guardsmen attached to the Staffordshire Regiment, had been training hard since their arrival in October and were now well prepared, having completed a progressive series of demanding exercises. By contrast, 4th Armoured Brigade, with A Squadron The Life Guards, the Queen's Company, and No 2 Company Grenadier Guards under command, was a composite brigade consisting of several major units that had not previously trained together, and time was now short. January was therefore an intensive period of training, during which 7th Armoured Brigade continued to hone its skills while 4th Armoured Brigade pulled itself together, compressing all its training into just a few weeks. Battle drills, well suited to desert conditions, became the only practical option given the time available.

The US-led air campaign began on the night of 16/17 January, with a phased plan which started with the suppression of the Iraqi air defences, a strategic bombing offensive against Iraqi command and control assets and its nuclear, biological, and chemicals plants, and then finally the bombing of key logistical supply lines and front-line Iraqi troops. As the Coalition troops trained in the desert and waited patiently along the border, this last phase of the air campaign was an obvious morale booster, since its aim was to reduce the Iraqi Army's effectiveness and will to fight. The campaign was conducted with an unprecedented level of precision and accuracy, for example a Tomahawk cruise missile, described by John Simpson of the BBC, seen travelling down a street in Baghdad, below the level of the rooftops. At the other end of the spectrum, B-52 strategic bombers, dating back to the early 1950s, delivered a huge weight of bombs onto forward Iraqi troop positions in Kuwait. Another less conventional bomb was the 7-ton 'Daisy Cutter', delivered from the back of a C130 Hercules, a weapon system developed during the Vietnam War for clearing helicopter landing sites, and now deployed to attack Iraqi defensive positions.

There remained a hope during this period that a combination of the Coalition air campaign and the possibility of a last-minute diplomatic breakthrough might just avert the need for a land offensive to liberate Kuwait. But any hope that air power alone could finish this war proved to be forlorn. As the weeks of intensive training went by, with the heat in the desert rising and the fear that Ramadan might disrupt the timetable, the real fear was that Saddam would stage a partial withdrawal which might weaken the resolve of the Gulf states to see the mission through.

In those last few weeks before the land offensive, the three Household Division commanding officers in the Gulf but not in command of their own soldiers (Anthony de Ritter, Robert Cartwright, and John Cargill), made all efforts to get forward to their deployed sub-units, to wish them well, and to give them upbeat news from the rear parties and families back in Germany. This often entailed many hours of driving along the very busy main supply route north-west from Al Jubail up to the forward assembly areas. Regiments are closely knit organisations, and everyone wanted to hear about what was going on elsewhere since there was no simple way of knowing.

On 18 February, Seymour Monroe, commanding the Armoured Delivery Group, gave his orders to his assembled sub-unit commanders from The Life Guards, the Scots Guards, and others. The role of the Armoured Delivery Group was to bring together the majority of the Battle Casualty Replacements and reserves in theatre, including vehicles and equipment from the War Maintenance Reserve. The plan was that the Armoured Delivery Group would move behind the two brigades, ready to reconstitute either of them following any losses in action. The Challenger tanks were to move on tank transporters, the wheeled flat-bed trucks that had been a familiar feature back in Germany during the Cold War. During the short period available for training in this entirely ad hoc organisation, the Armoured Delivery Group developed a series of drills and orders of march which included anti-ambush drills in the event of being attacked by the enemy. Tactical drills such as these had never been used back in the BAOR days since the idea of deploying wheeled tank transporters so far forward had never been envisaged. As the author of an article on the 'Highland

Deliverers' commented after the war, "the vision of main battle tanks firing their main armaments from the back of a transporter before 'hopping off' to engage an enemy was best left as an act of necessity rather than practicality."

Although the Armoured Delivery Group was only called upon twice to provide replacements during the land offensive, it did have its moments of uncertainty and excitement. Major Giles Stibbe, commanding C Squadron The Life Guards, recalls, in the middle of one of those nights, hearing several loud explosions that:

> sounded to me as I quickly gained consciousness like a fusillade of Scuds landing very close by, [and] thoughts raced through my mind: "Nine seconds to put my gas mask on. Have my soldiers remembered their well-practised drills?" Anyway, having put my gas mask on, I popped my head out into the night. To my eternal relief what I thought had been NBC chemicals splashing down on our bivouac tent turned out to be rain, and the explosions were those of thunderclaps!

On Friday 22 February 1991, President Bush, on behalf of the Coalition, issued a final ultimatum to Saddam: if Iraq did not start withdrawing from Kuwait within 24 hours, to be clear of Kuwait City within 48 hours, and out of the country within seven days, then the next phase of the Coalition operation would begin.

It was a clear and uncompromising ultimatum, much easier for Saddam to ignore in the hope that his reputation as a great Arab leader and survivor would prevail. For the Coalition, this was the moment of 'no return': a huge and powerful international military force, well supported by politicians at home, was now ready along the southern border, like a coiled spring. The task of getting them there, veiled in secrecy, had been a remarkable achievement, involving a deception plan to fool the Iraqis into thinking the attack would come from the south-east.

Everyone was apprehensive, given some of the predictions, but there was also a real desire to get the job done and to go home. Some of the British troops, notably 7th Armoured Brigade and the Grenadier Guardsmen attached to the Staffordshire Regiment, had been in the Gulf now for four months, and they were keen to move to the next stage.

The ground war, Op *Desert Sword*, began in the early hours of 24 February 1991. On the eastern flank, in an operation designed as a diversion, 1st and 2nd US Marine Divisions broke through the minefields along the Kuwaiti border, exactly where the Iraqis expected the main attack to come. The battle unfolded swiftly, the Iraqis fought for a matter of minutes before they were ready to surrender, and soon the US Marines had taken some 3,000 prisoners. This was not, it seemed, an army prepared to stand and fight as Saddam had predicted. By early evening, the Coalition was within 20 miles of Kuwait City. For the US Marines, also worried about defence cuts back home, this was just the result they needed for their long-term survival.

On the western flank, in the wide expanses of the desert, VII US Corps, with the 1st Armoured Division under command, and reinforced by French forces to the west, was poised to start the advance on the evening of that first day, with the mission to cut the main route from Basra to Baghdad. Now, however, General Schwarzkopf took the decision to bring the whole operation forward by 15 hours, thus reducing the planned artillery preparatory mission from two hours to just 30 minutes. What followed was one of the most remarkable phases of this short war. With just six hours' notice to move, an armoured corps similar in size to a Second World War army group crossed its Line of Departure, on its new schedule.

The scale of this Coalition attack was impressive, an orchestrated operation which involved many nations contributing in different ways; however, it was the US forces that provided the essential framework and firepower. The airborne attack by the 101st Assault Division (the Screaming Eagles) was a case in point, a bold mission to establish a forward operating base, FOB Cobra, deep inside Iraq, a huge and impressive undertaking. Despite a delayed start, within a matter of hours, some 2,000 personnel, 50 Humvee vehicles, plus artillery and fuel, were secure 50 miles beyond the Saudi–Iraqi border.

A news blackout had been imposed prior to the attack on 24 February; however, by the afternoon General Schwarzkopf called a quick press conference. He was in an upbeat mood as he described the dramatic successes so early in the operation: low Coalition casualties, over 5,500 Iraqi prisoners so far, and Coalition forces well set to envelope the enemy entirely. When asked what his strategy was going to be, he replied that his forces would be "going around, over, through, on top, underneath and in any other way" to liberate Kuwait. However, he was less specific about his designs on Saddam's 'elite' Republican Guard, north of the Kuwaiti border.

The 1st Armoured Division's mission was to "defeat the Iraqi tactical reserves in order to protect VII US Corps' right flank", allowing the Corps to focus on Republican Guard divisions in the far north-east. In giving his orders on G-Day, 24 February, the General Officer Commanding, Major General Rupert Smith, was clear that the plan would evolve as the intelligence picture became clearer; despite good aerial imagery of some of the enemy positions, there was always the possibility that the Iraqis might start moving around, in which case the Division needed to be ready to attack them wherever they threatened VII US Corps' flank.

Once 1st Armoured Division had conducted their passage of lines through the US forces to their front and the breached minefields (both operations in themselves), the two brigades would be deployed sequentially against groupings of enemy positions and vehicles, with the aim of destroying them rather than capturing ground. In the meantime, the British artillery, supported by a US National Guard Multi-Launch Rocket System (MRLS) brigade that had only just arrived in theatre, would concentrate on the enemy's depth positions, allowing the Challengers and Warriors to use their superior firepower on each of their objectives. The GOC's rallying call was a stirring one: "Gentlemen. This rugby game is the hardest one we have ever played. When we leave the breach, the ball comes out of the ruck and the try line is the Euphrates!" Keeping the Division's resources balanced would require some deft work, akin to a boxer, striking with one brigade while preparing the other for the next attack. The lengthening of the lines of communication as the advance continued was a challenge.

The first big event for VII US Corps was the breaching of the Iraqi defences along the border with Saudi Arabia. Always regarded as one of the most crucial and risky parts of the plan, it all proved to be much easier than anyone could have expected. The task was given to the 1st US Mechanized Infantry Division (the Big Red One), and in just over an hour, 16 safe lanes had been opened, allowing US cavalry units to push through ahead of the main armoured units. For the 1st Armoured Division, this early success was to determine their order of march through the obstacles. Had the breach operation faltered, the infantry-heavy 4th Armoured Brigade would have led, but given the way the battle was unfolding, 7th Armoured Brigade was given the task.

Brigadier Cordingley recalls the sense of anticipation as his troops prepared themselves: "It was cold, it was wet, and it was overcast and we were wearing NBC suits and quite expecting the enemy to use chemical weapons against us. We didn't know what state the enemy artillery was in or indeed quite where the Republican Guard was. And despite the fact that we knew the enemy morale was low, it was for nearly all of us, a first and therefore a concerning time."

In the early hours of 25 February, the reconnaissance vehicles of 16th/5th The Queen's Royal Lancers rolled through the well-marked safe lanes to establish their forward screen. They were followed at around midday, on a dull and grey day, with strong winds blowing the heavy grains of sand across the desert, by the tanks of the Queen's Royal Irish Hussars, *en route* to their first objective, COPPER.

Captain David Russell-Parsons, Grenadier Guards, serving with the Staffordshire Regiment as second-in-command, B Company, recalls this "formidable arrowhead", with many tanks on a 10-mile frontage. "I felt we were unstoppable as we progressed at about 25km [15½ miles] per hour and the US A-10s continued to fly very low, very fast past us." Early the next morning, he heard the "awesome thunderous roar as our MRLS and artillery opened up again. The ground trembled and the air cracked before we heard massive explosions on the objective and saw great arcs of white light." With the objective at COPPER abandoned by the enemy, B Company's first proper action was now on to PLATINUM, where:

all our aggression focused on a static defended position and a solitary truck trying to get through us. It was destroyed by a Milan missile. Sergeant Harding with his Grenadier section dismounted to pick up the pieces. An unknown number of enemy were killed as the Company cleared the position with grenades. Numerous PoWs were taken. One Warrior later had a miraculous escape when it survived a direct hit from a Challenger main armament round at less than 500m [c.550 yards]. I saw evidence of an Iraqi officer who had been shot by his own men – a single entry and exit point, lying face down in the sand, very dead. We did not linger.

Guardsman Darren Chant, Grenadier Guards, a Warrior gunner with C Company Staffordshire Regiment (who became Regimental Sergeant Major of the 1st Battalion and was killed in Afghanistan in November 2009), recalled:

> My vehicle commander, a corporal in The Duke of Edinburgh's Royal Regiment, fired over the heads of the surrendering Iraqis. We were told to debus and get them. The enemy position was a maze of bunkers, buildings, and vehicles. Suddenly the Iraqis fired an RPG-7 rocket which passed through Private Moult before hitting my Warrior. I saw my trousers were alight and that the vehicle commander was on fire and unconscious. I knocked him hard to bring him round. The whole Warrior was in flames until I got a fire extinguisher to put them out. I felt desperately that I must find my steel helmet. The face of the dead Private Moult was perfect, but he had lost the side of his body, and both his arms had blown off. The lads on each side of him were in shock.

4th Armoured Brigade was soon on the move heading to its first objective, BRONZE, with No 2 Company Grenadier Guards, attached to the Fusiliers, approaching the safe lanes through the breach at around 3pm on 25 February. Lieutenant Colonel Andrew Larpent, the Fusiliers' commanding officer, was there to wish them good luck, receiving "an immaculate salute" from the Grenadier vehicle commanders as they passed his Warrior. As the vehicles continued down the lanes, they saw the first evidence of the enemy: destroyed vehicles and positions were everywhere, as "US Servicemen standing on the side of the lane attempting to trade their personal equipment for British items" including the much sought-after British respirator.

As the weather deteriorated during the afternoon, the Queen's Company prepared for their move at 7.30pm on Monday 25 February, by which time it was raining heavily, and visibility was much reduced. In front of them were 7th Armoured Brigade's logistic vehicles trying to push forward. The GPS equipment was becoming unreliable, the company liaison officer's Spartan broke down yet again, and then, at 11pm the tanks of the 14th/20th King's Hussars reported enemy vehicles and opened fire. An hour later, and the Queen's Company was ordered to clear the position. The Iraqis were not up for fighting, and so the aim now was to avoid unnecessary casualties, on both sides. Illuminated by the Warriors' headlights, and before their surrender was accepted, the Iraqis were ordered to strip half-naked, to avoid concealed booby-traps. Eighty prisoners were then marched off to the rear. In a quieter moment earlier in the campaign, the Captain, Major Grant Baker, had written a 'bluey', in pencil, to the Company Commander, Her Majesty The Queen. He "received a reply from the Private Secretary saying how much The Queen had appreciated being kept up to date and wishing us luck!"

Meanwhile, back home, the news blackout had placed a temporary halt on detailed reports from the front. In a letter to the *Financial Times* on 25 February, General Sir Michael Gow wrote that he was not going to "pontificate on the Gulf war for TV" as "so many retired military men" seemed to be doing. He had seen these same armchair generals "'in action' during the Falklands operation and thought them as dangerous then as I do now. I know no more than I hear from the media; if I were more knowledgeable, I would not admit it." He recounted a recent telephone conversation with a journalist asking why some Scots Guardsmen had not been allowed to deploy. Gow had no idea, suggesting that perhaps they were too tall to be fitted with 'noddy suits', a line that led to the next question: "Do the Scots Guards have bigger men than any other regiment? ... You were a Scots Guardsman, weren't you? How tall are you?" Six feet 4 inches came back the answer, as Gow added that there were some even taller. It was all rather light-hearted as the journalist suggested that officers have to pay for their own combat uniforms, prompting Gow to observe in his letter that perhaps "Guards officers in particular are all so wealthy that they get their steel helmets specially made by one of the better-known London hatters". He concluded his letter by saying that he might "appear on the television as a part of a subtle disinformation strategy, or is that what my fellow retired generals are doing already?" Signed "Sir MICHAEL GOW (General, definitely retired) Edinburgh". None of the Scots Guardsmen would have seen that letter as they sat waiting to be committed as Battle Casualty Replacements, but they would have no doubt chuckled had they done so.

Following up behind 4th Armoured Brigade, Major Hugh Boscawen, second-in-command of the Coldstream Guards as part of the PWGF, was able to clearly observe to his front what appeared to be a large naval convoy displaying its navigational lights: 7th Armoured Brigade's green lights to the north and 4th Armoured Brigade's red lights to the south. It was, he said "a very exciting sight".

The next 4th Armoured Brigade objective was now ahead. The first phase was for the Royal Scots, with A Squadron The Life Guards under command, to attack infantry positions, followed by an attack on to two tank battalions to the south by the 14th/20th King's Hussars, with the Queen's Company.

The Life Guards, in their Challengers out in front of the Royal Scots, scanned the horizon through their thermal sights for enemy positions and vehicles. And then, across their front, appeared a column of tanks, thought to be T-62s on the move, at a range of some 2,700 yards. The contact was immediately reported on the battle group radio-net. The commanding officer urged the Squadron to engage the tanks and push on. But could these really be Iraqi tanks, given that most of the enemy equipment had been dug in and reluctant to move anywhere? Major James Hewitt, commanding A Squadron, now sought confirmation that these were indeed enemy. He was quickly told that there were no friendly forces to his front; the Squadron was to engage, and what a target it appeared to be: 14 or so main battle tanks, silhouetted against the dark sky. Hewitt was still not happy, and neither were his vehicle commanders. 4th Armoured Brigade should be consulted before he was prepared to order his tanks to open fire. The minutes were ticking by, and the consternation in the battle group headquarters was palpable; why were The Life Guards not engaging the enemy to the front and pushing on? The Royal Scots infantrymen, just like the Grenadiers, had been cooped up in their Warriors for hours now; they craved action.

Headquarters 4th Armoured Brigade was now asked the question, more than once. Were there any friendly forces on the move in front of the Royal Scots Battle Group? First the answer came back in the negative, but still, things did not seem right. Hewitt held his nerve; he wanted clear verification before he was prepared to give the order. Again, more exasperation from above: why the delay? Barely a minute or so of feverish checking, it probably seemed much longer, as these dark shadowy images crept across the desert. Then there was a scream of recognition down the radio that normally only occurs on a training range back home when someone or something has wandered into the danger-zone. "Stop"... "Still" ... "Unload" – whatever it was. These were not Iraqi tanks in the far distance, it was an entire squadron of the 14th/20th King's Hussars regrouping from one battle group to another, for the next attack.

It was an extraordinary moment, since the outcome might have been tragically very different. Clearly, the tank crews had been doubtful about what they were seeing through their thermal sights, given the extreme distance; however, they had been cleared from above to engage their targets, and Hewitt was under considerable pressure to get on with the battle. It takes a certain kind of moral courage to hold back as he did that day, and he was right to do so. Fourteen Challenger tanks firing at 14 Challenger tanks, a horrifying thought.

1st Armoured Division's battle was going well and much faster than expected, but the picture was still unclear. While most of the Iraqis were keen to surrender, with many of their vehicles abandoned, there were still pockets of resistance, and the overall intelligence assessment was unknown. Where, for example was the Republican Guard? Could Saddam be planning a concerted counter-attack? It seemed inconceivable that this vast army, in well-prepared defensive positions, was making no real attempt to fight. For most of the soldiers of the two British brigades, travelling closed down in their armoured vehicles, it was impossible to know what lay out there, across this vast and flat landscape.

Major Andrew Ford, commanding No 2 Company Grenadier Guards, recalls that the whole area of one of the objectives "consisted of dug-outs, trench systems and artillery pieces and an enemy that could not surrender fast enough, although this was not immediately obvious ... we collected about 150 prisoners, many of whom were severely wounded. The Guardsmen displayed a typically generous attitude and distributed carefully conserved chocolate to the captured Iraqis."

What was happening on the ground needed to be witnessed first-hand. In the darkness and confusion, soldiers in their Warriors could only assume the worst whenever an objective was approached; constraint and discipline were required at all levels. Everybody was now getting tired, and nobody had slept much for over two days beyond the occasional few minutes of snatched rest. Second Lieutenant Charlie

White-Thomson of the Queen's Company devised a simple way of doing just that: "the trick for five minutes sleep was to light a cigarette, rest your head against the sights, and when it burnt you, you woke up – five minutes kip and no more."

The challenge was to keep moving forward, as fast and as cautiously as possible, ready to fight if necessary. As well as destroyed Iraqi vehicles, there were also small groups of soldiers gathered in the desert keen to surrender, although this was not always apparent to tank crews observing through thermal sights; groups of men at a distance can look just like a vehicle. In one attack, The Life Guards reported infantry running around on their right flank; to some it looked as if they were advancing and then they appeared to take up firing positions. One commander reported a camouflage net, opening up with searching fire from his turret-mounted machine gun, only to discover that it was a tight group of infantry standing close together in the desert. Soon it was apparent that the Iraqis were trying to surrender, with some flags seen in the trenches, and then more soldiers running in the open and even some climbing onto the tanks. These moments had a profound effect on the tank crews; they had no desire whatsoever to kill Iraqi soldiers who might be trying to surrender.

More attacks followed, and with each enemy objective came another formal assault combining armour and armoured infantry. Occasionally there was some minimal resistance, but generally the Iraqis were only too eager to surrender. Many had been in the desert for months, having experienced a sustained air offensive and now this ground attack, preceded by artillery and rocket attack. Captain Greville Bibby, serving with the Queen's Company, had earlier encountered a Sandhurst-trained Iraqi captain: "He was terribly nice and very relieved that we had appeared. He said he would have deserted months before if he had had a white flag. His senior officers had gone off to an orders group and never returned: that's why he knew the Coalition forces must be close by."

One of the concerns during the build-up to the ground offensive was the risk of fratricide ('friendly fire' or 'blue on blue') and given the size of and diversity of this multi-national Coalition, each with its own equipment and procedures, there was a simple answer: vehicles reverted to displaying fluorescent recognition panels on their upper surfaces to protect against air attack and inverted black Vs on the sides of their turrets, sometimes accompanied by national flags and regimental pennants.

Despite these precautions, there were at least four cases of 'friendly fire' in 1st Armoured Division, the most serious being the incident on 26 February when US Air Force A-10s mistakenly attacked two Warriors of the 3rd Battalion Royal Regiment of Fusiliers, in which nine soldiers were killed and 11 injured. Andrew Ford recalled passing the burning vehicles and seeing them being evacuated. As the Grenadiers' regimental history observes, "the Grenadiers were not unduly shaken by the Fusiliers' casualties for it seemed that the war had just begun", assuming sadly that "many more fatal casualties were still expected". Following this tragic incident, 7 Platoon Scots Guards, commanded by Second Lieutenant Lincoln Jopp, was despatched forward to join the Fusiliers Battle Group, the only group of Battle Casualty Replacements to be employed at the front.

The considerable number of Iraqi prisoners of war had vindicated the need for a special prisoner of war handling organisation. Not only was there a legal obligation to do this, but also other important reasons, since the fair and firm treatment of prisoners is the hallmark of any decent and well-trained army, a point that General de la Billière impressed on the Coldstream when they arrived back in January. The PWGF formed up with its three battalions, under the command of Colonel Iain McNeil at Maryhill Camp (named after the barracks in Glasgow), where it continued to train for the task.

On 22 February the PWGF moved into the Forward Assembly Area immediately behind the leading elements of 1st Armoured Division, close to the Iraqi border. The sky, recalled Colonel McNeil, was "an apocalyptic black, set against terrain that was flat without any relief of any kind from horizon to horizon, [and] set an atmosphere of impending doom ... It was testimony to discipline and good junior leadership that everyone remained very steady."

The Orders Group that followed on 24 February took place in a sandstorm, as the wind whipped across the coarse-grained desert. Colonel McNeil later recalled: "After years of BAOR play-acting, this was the real thing. Too much to say – too little? Lives depended on one getting it right ... Orders were crisp, business-like and positive. But as I looked round these men, whom I genuinely liked, I wondered how many I would see again ... We all wore Arab head-dress, wrapped around the head, face and nose, so it was hardly a conventional sight."

The plan had been for the PWGF, together with the 6,000 vehicles of the divisional logistical tail, led by the Coldstream, to begin their move some two days later, but with the operation moving so fast, all the timings had been moved forward by a day. No one had envisaged just how quickly the Iraqi defences would be overrun and how willing the enemy would be to surrender at the earliest opportunity.

It was a strange and bewildering landscape, with bogged down or destroyed vehicles and enemy trenches, some containing the bodies of dead Iraqis. There were also other dangers lurking in the desert: Major Jonathan Bourne-May's Land Rover drove over an anti-personnel mine, blowing the tyres off the trailer, with the shrapnel just missing Company Sergeant Major Howick.

The task of the PWGF evolved as the advance continued. Essentially the aim was to get forward, by wheeled vehicles or sometimes helicopters, to collect prisoners, thus relieving the forward troops from this responsibility, and then move them back into the various holding areas created in the desert. Iain McNeil recalls that one problem they did not have was logistics: the Americans sent so many helicopters to collect prisoners that he "was told to stop offloading PW to the Americans as it seemed to illustrate that we (the UK) had taken none!" Only a very few Iraqi officers were among the prisoners (most had just slipped away), and occasionally there were ex-Sandhurst graduates now reunited with their colour sergeant instructors.

The task was like many in war, and not one that is often rehearsed in peace. Finding Iraqi soldiers was never easy; they were rarely where they were reported to be, and often groups just appeared unexpectedly, and while they were often eager to surrender, this was not always the case and could never be assumed. For example, on one occasion, No 2 Company encountered at least six groups of Iraqis who had not surrendered, and some of them opened fire.

There were many thousands of Iraqis out there, mostly frightened, soaking wet, and hungry, and often abandoned by their officers. Guardsmen often took responsibility for guarding many more prisoners than seemed possible. Lance Corporal 'Lennie' Lenthall, with his small section, was seen by a Coldstream officer "with a large number of prisoners ... teaching a huge phalanx of Iraqis foot drill to keep them warm." "What's my name?" he was heard to say, with "hundreds of Iraqis" shouting back "Lennie!"

There were many similar stories, and if an army can be judged by the way it treats the enemy when it surrenders, then the Coldstream Guards had certainly fulfilled their task effectively and with compassion and decency. Despite the uncertainties, considerable dangers and difficulties, the Battalion had "nonetheless managed to find, guard, feed and transport some 7,300 prisoners, perhaps 2,000 of whom it took itself". Soldiers do not go to war to guard prisoners, but in this case the Coldstream did as they were expected, and they did it well.

The Scots Guards were tasked to provide Battle Casualty Replacements but only a small number were actually called upon to go forward to join the troops in the front line. In the event, there were other tasks to perform after the ceasefire was called, and some of them unenviable. For example, beginning the task of "clearing up the desert, which was littered with abandoned equipment and vehicles", was not without risk. Battalion headquarters was also given the task of processing the huge number of Battle Casualty Replacements, not just Scots Guardsmen, who had arrived in Al Jubail in the weeks prior to the ground offensive. One of the many lessons of *Granby*, something that concerned ministers, civil servants, and the chain of command at the time, was that no one had a real overall grip of the numbers of British service personnel in theatre. Orderly Room Colour Sergeant Cerson played a useful role in this respect by creating a "computer-based 'tally' system ensuring that those claiming to be Battle Casualty Replacements but who had not seen fit to register as such on arrival in theatre did not receive the same priority for return as the genuine article".

Late on the last full day of the ground offensive, 27 February, 1st Armoured Division was given one last mission: "to attack east to cut from Kuwait City to prevent the Iraqi Army from retreating north". 7th Armoured Brigade was given the task and given that a ceasefire was due to take place the following morning, time was short. By 7.25am, just 30 minutes before the ceasefire took place, British forces were astride the main road from Kuwait to Basra. During the previous 66 hours, the 1st Armoured Division had advanced some 180 miles, destroyed almost three Iraqi divisions, and taken over 7,000 prisoners, including several senior commanders.

Once into Kuwait City, Iain McNeil recalls the place being "entirely deserted but extensively looted" and it was on the northern approaches that he "saw the most ghastly sight. The A10s had caught the retreating Iraqis and the road was about a foot thick in emulsified human fat being bulldozed away ... with lots of burnt out vehicles with black corpses sticking out with their flesh pulled back as if they were smiling; white teeth against charcoaled flesh. It was a scene from Hell ... the scene will never leave me."

The land offensive had lasted just a few days, and following the early successes and the acceleration of the plan, the end was inevitable. However, few commentators had dared to predict such a swift victory, and many chose to focus on the gloomiest of possible outcomes. Some of the Western journalists who found themselves, not at the front, but living in hotels in Jeddah, were rather surprised and perhaps even disappointed that it was all over so quickly. One journalist back home who never had any serious doubts that the Coalition would prevail, and do so convincingly, was John Keegan. As he wrote in *The Spectator* shortly after the war was over, "On one side stood a country of 18 million Third World people without a defence industry and with an armoury of second-hand Soviet equipment which could not be replaced if lost in combat. On the other side stood three of the strongest states in the First World with a combined population of 350 million, which are respectively the first, third, and fourth international suppliers of military equipment."

However, none of this explains what it must have been like to be part of this crusade to liberate Kuwait. Soldiers train for war, and in this case they had plenty of time to take counsel of their fears. But fortunately the overall strategy designed by General Norman Schwarzkopf had worked spectacularly well, ably supported by the 1st Armoured Division and the other members of the international Coalition. The air campaign was conducted with a level of precision never seen before, and the ground offensive was on a grand scale, employing all the principles of manoeuvre warfare that came as an antidote to all those years of

Cold War soldiering. Perhaps this would be the shape of future warfare: decisive and swift, with minimal casualties?

The ceasefire on 28 February 1991 came earlier than expected, but the moment was deemed to be the right one. The Iraqis had withdrawn from Kuwait, albeit having caused much wanton destruction and damage in this small state. Perhaps too much of their army, particularly most of the Republican Guard, had escaped, but any notion that the war could have continued was never seriously considered. The aim had been achieved and the Coalition would not have accepted the widening of the mandate to include a march on Baghdad and any suggestion of 'regime change'. There had been some hope that Saddam Hussein would soon be toppled by his own people, but that did not happen and, 12 years later, another US-led Coalition was back for a second Gulf War, a conflict in which the Household Division would play a full and reoccurring role that would endure for much longer than the first.

When the Prime Minister, John Major, visited the British troops shortly after the end of the war, as they sat in their concentration areas in the desert, on the outskirts of Kuwait, he promised that they would be home quickly, and he was true to his word. The Scots Guards, the victim of circumstance in a most unfortunate way, re-formed as a battalion on 12 March and flew back to Germany a week later. The Grenadiers were all back by early April and soon everyone was away on leave. On 14 May, a 'Re-formation Parade' took place, at which the commanding officer used some unfamiliar and new words of command – "The Battalion will Re-form in five Companies and the Light Aid Detachment ... Re-form." The Life Guards were all back in Sennelager in May, following a month's leave. For a while, there were no tanks to work on, but gradually these reappeared in various states of repair, and were painstakingly put back together. For the Coldstream Guards, it was a return to London and public duties until, on 31 August, the Battalion conducted its final Queen's Guard, with the Commanding Officer and Adjutant acting as the Captain and Subaltern. Thereafter, the move to Oxford Barracks, Münster began, overshadowed by uncertainties about how long the Battalion would actually be in Germany. Sometime before the move, in the weeks following the return from the Gulf, Ian McNeil addressed his Battalion and was a little perplexed when everyone stood their ground and did not fall out as expected. At that point, the quartermaster, Major David Yorke, stepped forward and reminded the commanding officer of his words back in December 1990 when he had declared that he would eat his hat if the Battalion was sent to the Gulf. A hat was now produced, made of meringue, and it was duly eaten!

For the Household Division, Op *Granby* had been a strange and not an entirely satisfactory experience given the way in which units were committed to the Gulf. There was a feeling at the time that the "senior Army lobby" didn't like the Household Division much and were keen to "put us in our place". Whether this is true or not, there can be no doubt that those Guardsmen who served in the Gulf, sometimes spread to the four winds, did so in the highest traditions of their regiments. While the tried and tested method of committing troops to war had been overlooked, it was the regimental system itself which managed to sustain everyone, wherever they served. The Grenadiers who fought alongside the Staffordshire Regiment did so with pride, never forgetting that they were Guardsmen. Equally, those Grenadiers who served with other regiments respected their ways and traditions, and maintained their friendships developed in adversity. For example, after the war, the Grenadiers presented the Fusiliers with a silver statuette to be presented annually by their commanding officer to the best non-commissioned officer in his Battalion.

Op *Granby* stands almost alone in the annals of recent history as a major campaign that appeared to have a sudden beginning and a relatively early end, with everyone back home within six months. The deployment of a substantial armoured formation over a distance of some 8,000 miles to fight an entirely new enemy in a desert environment in which the British Army had not operated on this scale since 1943 was indeed a remarkable achievement on every level. If this was an exercise to flush out the cobwebs of the last 45 years of soldiering on the North German Plain, then it had achieved its aim.

Retrospectively, some might claim that the First Gulf War was not a real war for the US-led Coalition, because the enemy failed to fight except on a few sporadic occasions. However, this overlooks the reality. An officer trying to catch a few moments of sleep before the ground offensive began on 24 February was reminded of the words of a soldier from another war in an earlier century: "between the physical fear of going forward and the moral fear of turning back, there is a predicament of exceptional awkwardness from which a hidden hole in the ground would be a wonderfully welcome outlet." All those fears and uncertainties were there during the build-up, and continued until the war was over, and were made easier to bear by good leadership, individual and collective pride, determination, and courage, both moral and physical, all qualities that abound in the Household Division.

When it was all over, there was a hope that somehow this entirely unexpected operation would influence the *Options for Change* debate and the future size of the Armed Forces; but these hopes were in vain. As a brigadier on a visit from London to Kuwait in March 1991, just after the ceasefire, was heard to say as he toured the units, still sitting in the desert, "the war may be over here, but it's just starting back home in Whitehall".

The *Options for Change* proposals took some time to emerge and were the subject of much discussion and lobbying at different levels. For the Household Division, the big changes were soon in the open, and the Major General (Major General Robert Corbett) set these out in the Autumn 1991 edition of the *Guards Magazine*, while acknowledging the lack of detail and uncertainties that remained.

The two regiments of the Household Cavalry, The Life Guards and The Blues and Royals, were to form a 'Union', maintaining their individual cap badges and regimental traditions; however, there were questions and concerns yet to be answered. How, for example, would the special requirements of the Household Cavalry Mounted Regiment be met from a much smaller pool of Household Cavalrymen, and what guarantees would there be for balanced careers in the future? The Union was to take place in Windsor in 1992, when The Life Guards returned from Germany, with the Household Cavalry Regiment forming up with two squadrons of each regiment, and a mixed command and support element.

There was, of course, a good historical precedent here, since two composite Household Cavalry regiments had been formed during the Second World War, and very quickly the individual squadrons became fully mixed down to individual vehicle crews. Essentially, this was how it would work a second time around; however, this was not a view shared by everyone in 1992. As the first commanding officer, Lieutenant Colonel Simon Falkner, explained to the Colonels of the two regiments, as diplomatically as he could, a "regiment is a regiment", and all promotions and appointments must be based on the principle of the 'best man for the job' and their suitability rather than rigidly applying the cap-badge rule. It did not take long for this principle to take effect, and it would not have worked any other way.

The impact of the *Options for Change* proposals for the Foot Guards when the Major General's article was published in September 1991 was less clear, although the big decisions had by now been made. The 2nd Battalions of the Grenadiers, Coldstream, and Scots Guards would go into suspended animation over a 15-month period beginning in June 1993; however, it was much more difficult to predict the implications for individuals and the effect that these changes would have on the five battalions that would now constitute the Brigade of Guards. The scale of public duties would probably change, for example, with a reduction to six Guards on the Queen's Birthday Parade. Another critical factor for the Major General was full participation in the Emergency Operational Plot, since any loss of this would affect the 'operational edge' that was so fundamental to soldiering in the Household Division.

In his article in the *Guards Magazine*, the Major General identified the "most worrying of all the changes as that affecting the Army's Training Organisation and the Guards Depot in particular". The proposals again lacked some detail; however, all the implications were that, in future, recruits would be trained at geographically based training centres rather than by their parent regiments. If implemented, this approach would mean that, for the first time, future Guardsmen would be trained by the Army and not by Guardsmen. "They would therefore, from the outset, have no comprehension of our standards or our way of life."

Two wars were over, a Cold War that had lasted over 45 years, and a Hot War that appeared to have been concluded in barely six months. Uncertainties about the future were perhaps closer to home as the Household Division prepared for a reduction in its size and possible role and the unsettling news that there would be voluntary and perhaps compulsory redundancies among individuals. All of this was to come to pass: the Household Division became smaller, there were redundancies, and the Guards Depot, despite the efforts to save it, closed its gates in April 1993 for the last time.

The *Options for Change* decisions announced in 1991 appear not to have been influenced much by wider strategic issues, let alone any predictions about world events that were to follow over the next 30 years (Balkans, the Second Iraq War, Afghanistan, etc.). Like the rest of the Army, the Household Division took a share of the unwelcome reductions as part of the government's 'peace dividend'; however, it fared better than many of the fine regiments with which Guardsmen had served during the First Gulf War, and with whom they had developed close ties of mutual respect. Within the next few years, most of the regimental names listed on 1st Armoured Division's 'orbat' published on the eve of war in February 1990 had ceased to exist. They had all been amalgamated or disbanded, while the Household Division has endured in all respects except its size and numbers.

8

The Guards Depot: *Septem juncta in uno*

The only place in the world that looks like a prison, treats you like a criminal, and yet you spend the rest of your life telling everyone how much you enjoyed it!
MAJOR PETER LEWIS, MBE, GRENADIER GUARDS

When the British government published its *Options for Change* defence review in 1990, there were some unpalatable decisions affecting the Household Division: the merging of the two Household Cavalry regiments and reducing the Foot Guards by three battalions. However, the hardest decision to accept, and identified at the time by the Major General Commanding the Household Division (Robert Corbett) as "the most worrying of all", was the one that changed the way that Guardsmen were to be trained in the future. If recruits for the seven regiments were no longer to be trained by Guardsmen at the Guards Depot, then how would they learn about the Household Division, its high standards and unique role, both on operations at home and overseas, and on grand ceremonial events watched by millions around the world?

The Guards Depot played a central role for the Household Division for over 160 years. The first was established in 1832 at Warley Barracks (previously the depot for the Honourable East India Company), and remained there, except for a short stay in St John's Wood, until it moved to a new barracks at Caterham in 1877. The Guards Depot was at Caterham throughout the Boer War and the First and Second World

Wars, and remained there until 1960 when it moved finally to Pirbright. Adult Recruits and Junior Guardsmen received all of their training at the Guards Depot until April 1993, when it closed, to re-open as the Army Training Regiment (Pirbright), responsible for training a much wider group of recruits from across the Army.

In 1969, coincidentally the year at which this book begins its story, the Guards Depot moved into Alexander Barracks, Pirbright, a custom-built camp that had cost £2.3 million and taken three years to complete. The barracks were named after Harold Alexander, Field Marshal the Earl Alexander of Tunis, who had joined the Irish Guards in 1911, served in the First World War, and become a senior Allied commander in the Second World War, Minister of Defence in the 1950s, and Colonel of the Irish Guards: the most distinguished Guardsman of his generation.

Planning for the new barracks had begun some nine years earlier and it was to be built on the site of the old 'C' Lines, while the Depot continued to occupy the adjacent 'D' Lines. The contractors took over the site in April 1966, demolishing nearly 150 buildings and replacing them with 33 new ones. The barracks began to be occupied from mid-1968, with the main move in the summer of 1969 coinciding with the unexpected death of Harold Alexander on 16 June 1969, aged 77.

With its new brick buildings and modern accommodation blocks, Alexander Barracks was a considerable improvement on the old wooden huts that it replaced. The old 'D' Lines, however, now renamed Brunswick Lines (although for many it will always be 'D' Lines), survives to this day, and was often used by the Guards Depot to accommodate courses such as the Brigade Squad (the potential officers' course) and as an overflow for recruits when numbers were higher than normal. 'D' Lines remains an evocation of another era, and the buildings themselves have now been identified as 'heritage assets': examples of early and mid-20th-century military structures that will hopefully be preserved for posterity. Remembered by many who spent time there, 'D' Lines also remains the home of the Household Division and Parachute Regiment Centralised Courses.

These old 'spider' buildings conjure an image of a bygone age, and remarkably, the old Sandes Soldiers' Home, a good place for 'tea and wads', is still there on the Brunswick Road, just below 'D' Lines. These wooden single-storey barrack rooms were traditional in style, with large open dormitories in which each recruit had his own 'bed-space' consisting of a standard metal framed bed with a thin mattress, a wooden or metal locker, and a side table. In their time, not a bad place to be, particularly for recruits born and raised in inner-city slums or the ugly high-rise flats that replaced them.

In contrast, the recruit accommodation blocks in the new Alexander Barracks were mostly two-storey brick buildings, designed in the 'Modern Movement' style. The old barrack room, where the instructor could stand at one end and see every recruit's bed-space, had been replaced by something that looked just a little more like home. The beds were more generous in their dimension, now with wooden headboards. There were fitted cupboards, and each bed-space had slightly more privacy as they were no longer arranged in straight lines like the old barrack blocks. The windows were larger, there was now central heating, and the washrooms were under the same roof, not in a separate building.

Alexander Barracks also had a new indoor swimming pool, a rarity in those days, even in the most exclusive of educational establishments. The pool was there primarily to teach young recruits to swim but was also a recreational facility for the staff and their families. There was an indoor gym and a new junior ranks' mess, which included a shop, games rooms, a well-stocked bar for those who were allowed to drink alcohol, and colour television sets.

Colour television was a real innovation in 1969, something that few soldiers would have seen before arriving at the Depot, since they were expensive (around £2,000 in today's prices) and only 200,000 sets were in use across Britain at the time. Colour television broadcasting was launched on BBC2 in 1967, with the remaining two channels, BBC1 and ITV, going live in mid-November 1969, just a few months after the move into Alexander Barracks was completed. For the Guards Depot to have colour television in 1969 was something of a luxury, although, with their often hectic and busy days, the recruits would have had little time to sit around and watch it.

Three new churches had been built in Alexander Barracks, reflecting the diversity of religious affiliations across the Household Division: All Saints' Church (Church of England), St Edward's Church (Roman Catholic), and St Columba's Church (Church of Scotland). Each with their own Padre, they had been separately consecrated with services of dedication. The Depot became a wonderful place to celebrate the various regimental Saints' Days, namely, St David (Welsh Guards), St Patrick (Irish Guards), and St Andrew (Scots Guards).

The new square was soon settling down on its foundations, receiving the regular pounding of studded ammunition boots; together with the echo of the bass drum reverberating off the drill sheds, a noise that could often be heard across the camp and as far as the nearby village of Brookwood. There was never a shortage of drill squares at the Guards Depot. The old square at 'D' Lines remained and continues to be used to this day, along with the main square at Alexander Barracks.

The new Alexander Barracks was entirely modern, and with better facilities than many other camps of that era (complete barrack rebuilds were a rarity then as they are now). There were new classrooms (particularly important for the Junior soldiers who attended educational lessons), the cookhouse, a new headquarters building overlooking the main square, the quartermaster's department, a NAAFI shop, the guardroom, the officers' and sergeants' messes, a telephone exchange, and all the infrastructure required for a depot designed to train young soldiers. New married quarters were also built, just a few minutes' walk from the centre of the camp. The barracks was like a school campus; everyone lived close to where they worked, and during 'term' time the working day was never a neat 'nine-to-five' existence. This was a busy and absorbing place, full of activity, with the sounds of marching soldiers, the loud voices of drill instructors, the crack of small-arms fire on the ranges, the drummer's beat, and even the more melodious notes drifting from the Junior Musicians' Wing at the end of the main square.

A short ceremony was held in the early autumn of 1969, at which the Countess Alexander of Tunis unveiled a plaque bearing the words "This plaque was unveiled by the Countess Alexander of Tunis on 25 September 1969, to mark the opening of the barracks named in memory of Field-Marshal The Earl Alexander of Tunis, K.G., Colonel, Irish Guards." After the ceremony, Lady Alexander toured the barracks, concluding with a visit to the cookhouse where the Junior Guardsmen and Recruits were having their lunch. Lady Alexander was then entertained in the officers' mess; a happy occasion marred only by the absence of the barracks' namesake.

The Guards Depot was to remain essentially the same for the next 25 years, and unlike some of the other barracks constructed in the 1960s and 1970s, notably in nearby Deepcut and Aldershot, it had a cohesive feel about it: a perfect place to train young soldiers. Well laid-out and landscaped, the barracks is surrounded by trees and heathland, one of the benefits of being close to small-arms ranges and the safety areas beyond. Leaving aside the noise of gunfire during working hours, rather like being 'behind the lines' during the First World War, at other times this was a tranquil and quiet place. The local towns, Camberley and Woking, are a few miles away, with the centre of London only an hour's drive, and yet Alexander Barracks has a semi-rural, village-like setting. The training facilities, including ranges, are a short distance away and easily reached on foot, and the cookhouse is just a short walk from the accommodation. The sporting facilities, the running track and playing fields, are in sight of the main square and, certainly back in 1969, were probably as good as those in many private schools.

Almost every Guardsman who joined the Army before 1993 has spent time at Pirbright, and many of them would return there on courses or on the training staff. Most officers, although a few missed this memorable experience, had their first exposure to the Army at Pirbright, on the Brigade Squad, an eight-week basic recruit course that imbued them with the culture and standards of the Guards while also preparing them for officer selection at the Regular Commissions Board, followed by officer training at the Royal Military Academy Sandhurst.

The Brigade Squad holds a special place in the memories of those who attended this course, including the candidates who never made it to a Guards regiment or, indeed, to Sandhurst. These young men, the majority of whom were already blessed with the advantages and privileges of a private education, would arrive at Brookwood Station not quite knowing what to expect, and they were rarely if ever disappointed.

From the moment the tailgate of the 3-ton truck was thrown open with a shuddering clang by a smart lance sergeant in No 2 Dress, followed by a firm instruction to 'get in the back' with their luggage and without the aid of a stepladder, these young men, indeed every recruit that arrived at Pirbright, began to have an inkling of what might be in store for them. And however much they prepared themselves by having the shortest haircut, their attempts were never acceptable. An early visit to the barber was mandatory and all part of the initiation process, along with the constant floor polishing ('bumpering') that kept the recruits occupied while waiting for their relatively short and sharp time in the barber's chair. The standing joke was always the same: "How would you like your hair today?" There was always a collective laugh from the assembled company when the answer came back: "Perhaps just a little off the top, and please, not too much off the sides", an instruction that was always ignored. "Something for the weekend, Sir?" as the next victim took their place in the chair.

Many Brigade Squad recruits will remember similar stories from different eras. For those in doubt, watch the first ten minutes or so of *They Were Not Divided*, a film made in 1950 about the Guards Armoured Division during the Second World War, and directed by Terence Young, a wartime Irish Guards officer who went on to direct three of the early James Bond movies. The film opens with a young gentleman recruit asking for directions to the Guards Depot in Caterham. Very soon, he is subjected to the haircut scene, and is then seen on the square with other bewildered recruits, being drilled by real Guardsmen, including the legendary Regimental Sergeant Major 'Tibby' Brittain, the "loudest voice in Britain". The film is over 70 years old, and yet there are some things that really do not change.

The Brigade Squad recruits were never allowed to forget their lowly status at Pirbright, and while there they would not receive any of the privileges of being an officer cadet. No one called them 'Sir', they would be frequently shouted at by their instructors, mealtimes lasted a matter of a few minutes by the time they reached the end of a long queue in the cookhouse, and they would be expected to march or run everywhere. Regular physical training was demanding; 'Heartbreak Hill', which formed part of the obstacle course through the woods, was an experience that few could ever forget. Alan Clark, the Conservative politician, described the physical "brutalisation" of the Brigade Squad, similar to the "intellectual brutalism" of his old school, Eton, an experience "probably worse than you will get anywhere outside a Victorian prison". Clark overstates his case, perhaps partly because his time in the Army was extremely short and he was never commissioned.

Attendance at the Brigade Squad was a badge of honour. Every year, in the *Guards Magazine*, there are short reports recording anniversary lunches or dinners. In the accompanying photograph (there is always a photo) nearly all the original recruits are there if they are still alive, along with their former platoon commander or sergeant, and also the recruits who attended the course and never made it to Sandhurst. As one of these recalled at a 21st anniversary dinner in 2009, "for those of us that did not join the Army, it does not matter how bad work gets, all we have to do is look back and realise that it could not be as bad as Brigade Squad and it makes you laugh."

For another of these reunions, in 2018 (40 years on), the author observes that while 'Brigade Squad 20' did not produce any high-ranking officers, in all other respects they were a successful and "eclectic bunch: a Master of Foxhounds, a Member of Parliament, a world renowned sculptor, the current President of the Countryside Landowners Association, together with successful landowners, Christian leaders" and a host of other business and creative people, including in the fields of "gaming, radio, television, and not to mention Hollywood".

The Brigade Squad did have its detractors, particularly among some of the senior Guardsmen who had served in the Second World War, who suspected that the motives of the course were questionable. Was it giving these young men an unfair advantage at the Regular Commissions Board? Was it not better to allow this Army selection process to make a judgement about a candidate's suitability than to providing 'private-tutoring'? Or was it, in Alan Clark's words, a "brutalising" experience that was "quite rightly ... worse than that to which the ranks are subjected"?

The Brigade Squad was a combination of all these motivations. Other parts of the Army ran their own short courses to prepare their chosen candidates for Sandhurst, and there was some envy elsewhere about the results the Brigade Squad achieved. More importantly, the principle of starting at the very bottom and being expected to master the basics of soldiering faster than an ordinary recruit was not only a character-building experience, but one that would pay dividends when a young officer finally met his young Guardsmen on joining his regiment. He could look them in the eye with some confidence and mutual respect because he had been through an even tougher initiation than they had.

However, there is another important aspect about Brigade Squad that should be acknowledged. This generation of potential officers had spent time away from home at boarding schools, unlike the young recruits for whom Pirbright must have been a considerable shock to the system since for many of them this was likely to be their first experience of living away from their families.

Lieutenant Colonel Charles Bremner, Commandant of the Guards Depot in the early 1990s, spent a great deal of time keeping an eye on Brigade Squad training and taking an interest in those on the course. As he says, this was an ideal opportunity for the candidates and the Guards to have a long look at each other and to form a view about their compatibility. There were often surprises along the way; those expected to do well did not always flourish, and there were those who soon concluded that the Army was just not for them: no harm done, a character-building experience, and something to remember in years to come.

The Brigade Squad often attracted the interest of senior officers and, indeed 'senior parents' who would be quickly on the phone to the Commandant if there were questions about how their sons were faring. Charles Bremner remembers receiving a call from the Commander-in-Chief Land Command (not a Guardsman) to pass on a complaint from some friends who were concerned that their son had asked them for £60 as his contribution to the Squad's present to their Platoon Sergeant at the end of the course. Excessive 'present-giving', a mark of genuine gratitude, was also a feature at Sandhurst, a phenomenon that was not encouraged by the senior hierarchy.

There was another important dimension which applied equally to everyone, regardless of background or rank, who spent time at the Guards Depot. The teenagers and young men who stepped off the train at Brookwood Station, whether they were public school boys or young teenagers from an inner-city housing estate, were entering an institution that was somehow separate from the rest of the Army, because all the staff, with just a few exceptions, were Guardsmen. From the moment these young recruits were formed up into squads, and before they had even been issued with their uniforms, the message was the same. And it was a message that never changed. In a scene in *They Were Not Divided*, a Guards drill instructor, a real one, not an actor, roars across the drill square: "You are not in the Army now, you are in the Brigade of Guards."

Everything taught at Pirbright was designed to demonstrate that the Guards were firmly at the top of the tree, better than the rest of the Army, demanding the highest standards of excellence in everything. Turnout was to be immaculate, and attention to detail in all things, big or small, was a guiding principle. '*Be the Best*' has for many years an Army recruiting catchphrase, but for the Household Division it has always meant more than that, and for each Guardsman it is about being the best that you can be, striving for excellence in all that you do, on operations, the drill square, and everywhere else.

Commandants invariably emphasised these sentiments in their introductory addresses to recruits when they arrived at the Depot. As Charles Bremner recalls, he would often open his talk by saying "Well done for choosing the Household Division. It is the Household Division that sets the standard, and what we are doing today, the rest of the Army will be doing tomorrow."

These young men, who often knew nothing of the wider Army, were easily convinced that the Guards were simply better than the rest. "If you want to go and join the fish and chip mob," the Coldstream Platoon Sergeant on the 1974 Brigade Squad was prone to say, on almost a daily basis, "then go now, the door is over there. Pack your bags and get away."

For everyone, time at the Guards Depot, along with the friendships made there, transcended the singular experience of serving with one regiment. It was here that they had the opportunity to spend time in the place that gave real meaning to the Household Division's motto: '*Septem juncta in uno*'. The Guards Depot was hugely important; it was the one place where Guardsmen of all ranks could meet people from other regiments and make friends. It meant that wherever they were, serving away from their own regiments, they would find someone that they knew from their time at Pirbright.

The Guards Depot was a natural focus for all those who served in the Household Division, a familiar place that provided an important continuity for over 30 years, a period that was to see great turbulence and change, both in the Army and beyond. In this sense, it was like a good school, adapting gradually to the outside world, while maintaining all its familiar characteristics and standards; those who returned there on courses or later postings were rarely disappointed or surprised by what they found at the Depot. To quote Lieutenant Colonel Malcolm Ross, writing in 1983 when he was the Commandant: "Popular opinion would have it that nothing at the Guards Depot ever changes, and, as always, popular opinion is right."

Everyone, particularly young officers and recruits, was required to have an understanding for the distinct traditions of each of the seven regiments and was frequently tested on 'regimental intelligence'. For the subalterns serving at Pirbright, a formal test was normally conducted by the Brigade Major prior to lunch as part of the Major General's Inspection, and while this was intended to be a serious event, it often generated humour. There was always at least one hapless lieutenant who had chosen an evening in London rather than some last-minute revision, generating a fair amount of amusement for the onlookers. To quote Captain Barry Gubbins, recalling the halcyon days of the early 1970s, "The fact that no one had the faintest idea who the Gold Stick or the Silver Stick were, or what they did, or looked like, didn't matter a jot. You just had to know his name and try and keep a straight face." On another occasion, this time in the early 1980s, the Brigade Major was confidently informed by a subaltern that the 'Serrafile Captain' was a spare officer in London responsible for kits and capes, clearly not the right answer.

The unique traditions and delightful variances between Guards regiments were important to know, and they somehow had more meaning in a place where *all* of these differences (minor when compared to the similarities) were respected. For example: that Troopers and non-commissioned officers of The Blues and Royals saluted when not wearing headdress, a custom dating back to 1760 when, in the midst of a battle, the Marquess of Granby saluted having lost both his hat and his wig. Or the language – for example, Grenadiers never answer a question with the words "No, Sir" or "Yes, Sir"; it is simply "Sir", intoned in an appropriate way to the answer. 'Commanding Officer's Orders' are known in some Guards regiments as 'Memoranda', and procedures during these formal occasions also vary. For example, in some regiments, the soldier asks for 'leave to carry on' while in others he asks for 'permission'. There are also differences on the drill square, for example the style and technique adopted when officers 'patrol' before falling in.

These important minutiae of regimental life would go unnoticed in a battalion where everyone is used to them, but they took on a greater meaning for those serving at the Guards Depot because they subtly demonstrated the differences between regiments, and of course the pride and unity (seven joined in one) that this afforded to all. Lieutenant Colonel Simon Soskin, a Grenadier, was one of the last generation of platoon commanders to serve at the Guards Depot and continued to serve there after the transition to the Army Training Regiment. He recalls that before the changeover, the young subalterns had fun on Adjutant's Memoranda (as the Grenadiers call it) by marching into the office "in the wrong order ... creating as much chaos as possible as we all had different speeds and turning traditions."

Attending courses at the Guards Depot was important for any Guardsman with ambition, as was a posting on the staff there, although perhaps less so for officers. For a non-commissioned officer, as Charles Bremner recalls, "to be an instructor at the Guards Depot was a career step", and without that under one's belt, it was very difficult to progress beyond junior rank. The key to this was attendance at the Guards Depot Instructors' Course, "really quite a difficult course" and more demanding than some of the similar courses open to the rest of the Army. Successful completion gave non-commissioned officers a real edge and a sense of confidence because it required the very highest standards. For example, no one who aspired to be an instructor at Sandhurst, teaching officer cadets, could hope to get there without successfully completing a cadre course at Pirbright.

Throughout its long existence, the priority for the Guards Depot was to train young men for the seven regiments of the Household Division, and this was the place where it all started, for officers and recruits. The special challenge at Pirbright was the two distinct paces of life. One was for the Junior Troopers and Guardsmen who arrived aged 16 and spent a year at the Depot, with more time for sport, education, adventure training, hobbies, and leave. And the other pace of life was for the recruits, who arrived aged 17 or older, for a shorter and much more intensive 15–20 week course (the exact duration of the recruit course varied over time), in which they learnt drill, became proficient with a rifle and other small arms, and acquired a basic understanding of tactics and fieldcraft. For the Brigade Squad, everything was literally at double-time.

For those recruits arriving at the Depot, only a very few would have marched in a 'squad' before unless they had spent time in a combined cadet force (a feature of some private schools) or a local Army cadet force, and most of them would never have handled weapons, carried them while marching, or fired a live shot on a range. There was of course much more in store during their training, such as obstacle courses, bayonet drill, and 'battle inoculation': advancing towards the 'enemy' with rapid automatic machine-gun fire passing above their heads; a terrifying experience. All of this they had to achieve, along with everything needed to become a trained soldier, ready to be posted to their battalion on public duties or operations.

One of the special rituals at the Depot was the Pay-Parade, in an era where most soldiers were 'cash paid'. Normally during term-time these payments were restricted to small amounts of pocket money to ensure that the recruits' savings were not frittered away, since all the essentials (food and accommodation) had been deducted at source. The balance was given to them just before they proceeded on leave, at the Pay-Parade. On the appointed day, the paymaster and his staff would hand over the cash, often many thousands of pounds, to the young platoon commander charged with paying each trainee. The trainees would line up and be marched-in. Stepping sharply forward to the 6-foot table once they were at the head of the queue, their cash would then be counted out by the officer, watched by witnesses and the recipient. In most cases, it was then: "Pay present and correct Sir", salute, smart turn to the right, and away on leave. Occasionally an eager-eyed witness would spot more than one note being accidentally handed out (they were often crisp and new), and even more occasionally the trainee would ask for a recount as was his right. Invariably, the really nervous moment came when the last trainee arrived to collect his cash. Would the officer have the right amount, or was it to be a case of "Would you accept a cheque?"

The music at the Guards Depot was special, and it was at the Junior Musicians' Wing that young musicians, aged 15–17, began their training to become military bandsmen. The Wing was opened at Pirbright in July 1962, and soon 50 Junior Musicians had enrolled, receiving their initial training before going on to the Royal Military School of Music at Kneller Hall, Twickenham. Most of the music teachers who taught at Pirbright were civilians, and some combined their time there with teaching at other prestigious music schools, like Kneller Hall and the Royal Academy of Music.

From Band Boy to Director of Music was a well-trodden path, and although not every young musician began their career at Pirbright, it was the Household Division upon which the most talented and ambitious musicians set their sights. To take just one example: Lieutenant Colonel Douglas Pope, who was largely responsible for creating the Junior Musicians' Wing at Pirbright in the early 1960s, joined the Army in 1918 as a Band Boy and was later bandmaster of several regimental bands. In June 1944 he became Director of Music of the Band of the Coldstream Guards, in the immediate aftermath of a terrible tragedy: the V2 rocket attack at the Guards' Chapel, which killed 121, including the Director of Music and five musicians.

Douglas Pope ended his regular service as Senior Director of Music of the Household Division, before moving to Pirbright in 1963 as a retired officer running the Junior Musicians' Wing, which he combined with being Professor of Music at Kneller Hall. The Wing thrived under his leadership, and it was soon over-subscribed, with a long waiting list of aspiring young musicians. He retired in 1970, to be followed at the Junior Musicians' Wing by the next generation of former Guards Directors of Music.

One of Douglas Pope's young trainees was Fred Harman, who arrived at Pirbright in the mid-1960s, joined the Band of The Life Guards in 1967 as a percussionist, and later became Band Corporal Major at the age of 29. During his service, Fred played with his band in many concerts at home and around the world, taking part in television and radio concerts, and recording sessions. Like many other Guards musicians, he also performed with civilian orchestras, including at the Royal Opera House, Covent Garden. On leaving the Army in 1989, he joined British Airways, becoming the Bandmaster of the British Airways Band in 2001. Fred Harman is just one example of many talented young men, and latterly women, who have joined the Household Division as musicians, following interesting careers both in and beyond the Army.

In 1969, the BBC broadcast a television programme in its *Omnibus* documentary series entitled *Makers of the Queen's Music*, which shows young military musicians as they begin their careers at the Guards Depot. The programme, still available to watch on the BBC's online archive, is very different in style to the 'fly on the wall' genre of a later era, with a very uncomplicated 'look at life' format. Young musicians are shown learning the piano, string, and percussion instruments from their much older teachers, mostly pensioners with a wealth of musical knowledge to impart. What shines through, all these years on, is that these young students come over as well educated, rather more so than the average recruit.

Lieutenant Colonel Pope explains in the programme what it was that the Guards were seeking in their young musicians. They mostly arrived at the Depot being able to play at least one instrument, perhaps a recorder, and would leave being able to play competently on two instruments. As another distinguished Guards Director of Music, Major (later Lieutenant Colonel) Rodney Bashford, observes later in the programme, the Army never aspired to recruit the most naturally talented musicians of the day, those who had a glittering career ahead in the more commercial world. But these young soldiers were fine musicians nonetheless, and some did, in due course, hit the big time in civilian life.

The curriculum for these young musicians was varied. For example, Junior Household Cavalrymen spent time in the riding school at Pirbright, and, of course, everyone was taught drill, the most basic of all military skills. "Use your heel as your drum – you're all musicians," shouts the Guards drill instructor, neatly underlining the essential link between military music and ceremonial; it's the sound of the drum that acts as a perfect metronome on the drill square and for marching down the Mall. During their time at Pirbright, the Junior Musicians would often play for a passing-out parade, or in the officers' and sergeants' mess for a dinner night, or for a Sunday church parade. Like all Junior Guardsmen at Pirbright, they had their own rank structure, progressing from Junior Bandsman to Junior Bandmaster.

After the closure of the Guards Depot, the Junior Musicians' Wing broadened its scope to include musicians bound for other parts of the Army, including the Royal Artillery and Royal Engineers. This path into the Army for young musicians still exists, via the Army Foundation College at Harrogate to the Royal Military School of Music, now based at HMS *Nelson* in Portsmouth following the closure of Kneller Hall in 2021. The Junior Musicians' Wing at Pirbright was a wonderful place while it lasted, but like so many aspects of Army training, the Guards have now had to integrate more with the wider Army.

The Guards Depot went through some considerable changes in the early 1970s, due to the generally more consistent and higher Junior recruiting levels, set against a declining number of Adult Recruits. For example, during 1968, 751 recruits joined their battalions from the Guards Depot, a drop of some 20 per cent from the previous year. In the early summer of 1970, a new intake into the Junior Guardsmen's Company brought the number of Juniors in training at Pirbright to nearly 750. In December 1971, 800 Juniors took part in the Junior Guardsmen Company's passing-out parade.

In the autumn of 1973, the Major General (James Bowes-Lyon) decided that the Depot would be reorganised, acknowledging these recent recruiting trends. The individual regimental recruit companies were to be replaced by one large recruit company, the Caterham Company, while the Junior Guardsmen Company was to be disbanded and re-formed with junior companies for each of the Household Division regiments (The Life Guards and The Blues and Royals in a Household Cavalry squadron, together with five companies for the Grenadier, Coldstream, Scots, Irish, and Welsh Guards).

The Junior Guardsmen's Wing had been a great success over the previous 16 years and, by the time of its disbandment, some 1,000 Juniors a year were passing out of the Depot to join their regiments and battalions. However, as a single grouping at the Depot, the Wing had now become too unwieldy to administer: individual companies sometimes numbered 400 in size, with platoons of 150. Over the years, the Wing had developed a magnificent *esprit de corps*, often excelled in Army sports, and was turning out excellent young Guardsmen, many of whom would rise through the ranks of their future regiments. To quote the Commandant at the time of this big reorganisation, Lieutenant Colonel Iain Ferguson, "it was terrible to even contemplate breaking up something so ... successful, but the Juniors had the numbers, the Juniors had the future and it was the Juniors who could now preserve the Regimental Squadron and Regimental Companies of the Guards Depot." The numbers of trainees at the Depot in the autumn of 1973, and once the reorganisation was complete, speak for themselves: the total number of recruits in the Caterham Company was 186, while the number of Juniors (divided among the six regimental companies) was over three times greater, at 604.

The key to the Guards Depot's success as a training establishment was the quality of its staff. To become an instructor at Pirbright required an extremely high standard in leadership, drill, skill-at-arms, and infantry tactics, and regiments only selected their most promising candidates. It was a demanding course; the average pass rate was 40 per cent, with the drill phase accounting for most of the failures. To quote Iain Ferguson, writing in 1974: "No risks can be taken when selecting instructors for we depend upon them not only for achieving the standards of the Household Division but also for low wastage rates for those in training. Their influence upon Juniors and Recruits is immense and ... the personal example they set ... is so important to the successful future of the Household Division."

'Wastage rates', a rather clumsy term that remains an accepted one across the Army, has always been an important and complex issue, referring to the number of trainees who, for various reasons, never make it to their passing-out parade. Sometimes this was due to injury, illness, or simply because individuals were unable to cope with the demands of being a Guardsman. However, there were other times when 'wastage' really could be avoided, particularly in the early days of training when both Juniors and Adult Recruits had the right to leave without any recourse. Being young and often immature, they could leave for the wrong reasons. Following a bad day, recruits could just walk out of camp and go home, often to everyone's disappointment, including their own. Maintaining morale and, most importantly, keeping the trainees occupied with interesting, worthwhile and challenging activities, was always important, and was essentially down to the quality and commitment of the non-commissioned officer instructors.

One of the factors that affected wastage rates was the policy introduced in the early 1970s to send Adult Recruits off on leave until the next platoon formed up, designed to avoid them becoming bored while waiting to get started. However, there was a downside: when a recruit was sent home on a lengthy leave, there was often the inclination for him not to return. In the summer of 1976, the Guards Depot conducted an experiment that reduced this figure. Rather than allowing recruits to drift off home, before they had been properly assimilated into the Army, they were sent to Devon for adventure training and to the West Coast of Scotland for navigation training, first-aid and survival skills. This latter period culminated with an imaginative air crash rescue exercise, with pieces of wreckage borrowed from local airports scattered across the snow-clad hills, and members of the staff pretending to be casualties.

Supervision was the key to many of the challenges that faced the Guards Depot during the post-1970 era. A key appointment at Pirbright, and not a role that existed anywhere else across Army training establishments, was the 'Trained Soldier'. Each of the Caterham Company platoons, where the pace of life was high, had a 'Trained Soldier' who lived in the platoon accommodation, helping the recruits to find their feet in their new environment, by showing them how to clean their kit and to be punctual and properly turned out for parade and for all the many daily activities. The 'Trained Soldier' also had another vital role; he was always around in the evenings and at weekends, providing the type of supervision that was so important to the care and wellbeing of young soldiers. Those Guardsmen filling these posts had to be of the right calibre, having demonstrated experience in their regiments and the potential for promotion. In recognition of this, in the mid-1970s the Major General decreed that a 'Trained Soldier' who had successfully taken a platoon from its arrival at the Depot to its passing-out parade would be promoted to Lance Corporal. Thus the term became 'Barrack Room Instructor', acknowledging their status.

The Guards Depot became one of the most popular destinations for senior visitors over the years; easily accessible from London and the perfect place to showcase the Army at its best. Almost every year a member of the Royal Family came down to the Guards Depot, for example, the Duke of Edinburgh, the Prince of Wales, and the Duke of Kent, often in their capacity as Royal Colonels. The 1970s and 1980s was also the twilight era for the distinguished wartime Guardsmen who had all achieved high command. To name just a few: Major General Sir Allan Adair, a Grenadier who had commanded the Guards Armoured Division, Major General Lord Michael Fitzalan-Howard, a Scot Guardsman who later became Colonel of The Life Guards, Major General Sir George Burns, who had commanded the 3rd Battalion Coldstream Guards during the Second World War, and General Sir Basil Eugster, who fought with the Irish Guards at Narvik in Norway as a young officer in 1940 and went on to command UK Land Forces and be Colonel of his Regiment. The Depot was also a regular destination for the Major General, both for his annual formal inspection and as the inspecting officer for passing-out parades.

George Burns, known as 'Uncle George', was a legendary Guardsman who had a magnetic charm and was genuinely loved by all. For him, there could be nothing better than spending a day with the Coldstream Guards or visiting the recruits at the Guards Depot. Always slightly dishevelled looking, with liberal deposits of cigarette ash on his uniforms, his catchphrase was "Anyone got a light?" Professor Sir Michael Howard, who was a young officer in Burns's battalion in Italy during the war, recalled, in 2018, just what an electric effect a visit from the Commanding Officer had on the Guardsmen:

> Following a particularly nasty 'stonk' [a Second World War expression for artillery fire], a very heavy stonk indeed, we were just pulling ourselves up when George Burns appeared, pipe in one hand, walking stick in the other, beaming at us. And from the moment he appeared, everything seemed to be alright. It was astonishing what that man did ... it made me realise what Clausewitz said was absolutely right. What really matters in an army is morale and moral strength and fibre. Once George appeared, everything was ok.

George Burns was dined out at the Guards Depot on the very last day of his service in 1962; as the clock chimed midnight and the port glasses were raised, George Burns became a civilian. Although, happily as Colonel of his Regiment, he had many active days ahead. There is a wonderful photograph of him in the Spring 1988 edition of the *Guards Magazine*, visiting the Depot to open the Burns Room. Everyone is laughing and smiling, as 'Uncle George' stands with the Commandant, looking down on a group of happy recruits, each with a can of beer.

Brigadier (late Lieutenant General Sir) William Rous, a Coldstreamer, always known informally as 'Willie', who later became Colonel of the Regiment, was a wonderfully charismatic speaker. Willie Rous took the salute at the passing-out parade of Marne and Loos Intakes in June 1985 (one of the many parades from that era recorded on video and now available to watch on YouTube). Commanded by Major Nigel Hadden-Paton, The Blues and Royals (mounted on his charger), with the Band, Pipes and Drums of the Irish Guards, and several thousand spectators, including Chelsea Pensioners in their scarlet uniforms, by any standards, this parade looks impressive. The sound of rifle fire from the nearby range can be heard as the Guardsmen form up to march on parade. The officers 'patrol' up and down the drill square as everyone waits for the inspecting officer. The band plays throughout, saving the regimental marches for the final march-past. And then Willie Rous, without any notes, addresses the Guardsmen on the parade, commending them for their performance, congratulating them on their achievements, and thanking the families for their support. There is a wonderful happy and carnival atmosphere about the event, like a village fete for a very large family. And that is how many who passed out at Pirbright remember the Guards Depot, a place they will never forget.

One of the more flamboyant senior visitors at the Depot was Lord Mountbatten, Colonel of The Life Guards. He had an engaging and rather regal style, arriving for visits having been reminded by his temporary aide-de-camp of the names of those he would meet, and in what order as he emerged from his Austin Princess staff car. He always liked to lace his conversation with references to the Royal Family: "As I was saying to the Queen just the other day," or 'I must talk to the Colonel-in-Chief about those potholes on Horse Guards Parade." Like most of his generation he was an inspiring speaker at passing-out parades, impressing the young soldiers and the proud parents in the stands. His particular trick at the end of the parade, perhaps designed to challenge the drill sergeants, was to order the assembled company to "break ranks" and gather round. Like a scene from *In Which We Serve* (a wartime film loosely based on his time as a naval captain), he would stand among the Junior Guardsmen as he delivered his speech. He did this on the passing-out parade in December 1973, with 1,000 Junior Guardsmen on the square. Despite these huge numbers, and in true naval form, Colonel Dickie's order to "break ranks", although unrehearsed, was completed without chaos.

Lord Mountbatten's last visit to the Depot was in June 1979. After the parade he was escorted to the junior ranks' club, where, in frock coat, and trailing his sword and scabbard, he gingerly, and with great charm, negotiated his way around spilt beer mugs and overflowing ashtrays, to meet the elated, and sometimes worse-for-wear parents, step-parents, and grandparents, and of course, the new 'trained soldiers'. Two months later Lord Mountbatten was dead: blown up by the PIRA with members of his family in a fishing boat moored just outside the harbour at Mullaghmore, County Sligo.

Numerous government ministers visited the Guards Depot over the years, including Lord Balniel, in September 1971, and Lord Carrington, in July 1973, both former Grenadier Guardsmen. The Depot, in Charles Bremner's words, "was very much on the visitors' list". Members of the Army Board and the various Arms' Directors (Armoured Corps, Infantry, etc.) would come down to Pirbright, and this was a regular occurrence in the early 1990s following the publication of *Options for Change*. As Charles Bremner recalls:

> And almost without exception, during our conversations walking around the Depot, or in the letters that followed the visit, these visitors would say to me "this is a centre of excellence, something you can be very proud of, and you can be absolutely assured that the Guards Depot will be protected under *Options for Change*." And the person who was most definite about that was the Adjutant General, General Sir David Ramsbotham, who was absolutely unequivocal about it. Why would we ever consider closing the Guards Depot?

Despite all of this, the decision was indeed taken, and perhaps in a wider context this was inevitable at the time, given all the changes taking place elsewhere in the aftermath of the Cold War: decisions that were predicated by financial savings.

Her Majesty Queen Elizabeth II visited the Guards Depot for the first time in June 1970. She was escorted around the barracks by the Commandant, Lieutenant Colonel John Ghika, meeting both Junior Guardsmen and Adult Recruits, and watching them taking part in trade training lessons. In the junior ranks' club, the Junior Corps of Drums played a slow march written especially to mark the occasion, and then the Queen spent over an hour with some 150 members of staff and their wives, and trainees, talking individually to almost everyone present. After lunch in the officers' mess, a group photograph was taken, particularly notable because it was an occasion that embraces several generations. The Queen, as Princess Elizabeth, had become Colonel of the Grenadier Guards in April 1942; and all the quartermasters in the photograph had seen active service in the Second World War, with at least two having been awarded the Military Medal. One of those who met the Queen that day was Lieutenant Colonel Douglas Pope, just before his final retirement following 52 years' service. As the Queen left the Depot, she was cheered as her car drove slowly down Brunswick Road, to return in 1993 for her very last visit to the old Depot before it became an Army Training Regiment.

The Guards Depot was an enjoyable and challenging place to serve as an officer or non-commissioned officer. As a training establishment, it had routine; everything was programmed by the Training Wing, to maximise the facilities and get everyone through to their passing-out parades, and there was always scope for the platoon staff to design interesting exercises for their trainees. There was a demonstrable result at the end of each training intake: a passing-out parade for trained Guardsmen, in which a senior officer took the salute, with proud parents watching from the stands. For the troop and platoon staffs, it was immensely satisfying to see these young men leaving the Depot as trained soldiers ready to serve with their regiments.

There was plenty of time, particularly for the Junior Guardsmen, for sport, and not just field games and cross-country running but tennis, sailing, and other pursuits. Adventure training was also a high priority, particularly for the Junior Troopers and Guardsmen, either at the Guards Adventure Training Wing at Fremington on the North Devon Coast, or at Tregantle Fort, on the South Coast, just west of Plymouth. The fort had been built in the early 1860s, as a response to the great French invasion scares. It was a maze of casements and barrack accommodation, overlooking the beach, and was a wonderful place for a two-week camp in early September, often coming just after the summer leave period. Everything was on the doorstep for these teenagers and their instructors: water-skiing, sailing, pony trekking, fishing, cliff walks, pot-holing, canoe surfing, rock-climbing, and visits to Royal Naval ships in the nearby naval dockyard. For many, it really did seem like an extension of the summer holidays, which for the Juniors were similar in length to school holidays.

The Depot had its share of characters and eccentrics, and there is simply not room here to record the many amusing stories and events that took place over the years at Pirbright. One of the most fondly remembered of all officers at the Guards Depot was the late Captain Michael Boyle, Irish Guards, known to his friends as 'Docker' after a particularly ostentatious and rich industrialist to whom he actually bore no resemblance at all, except that they were both rich and loved cars and boats.

'Docker' Boyle's final posting in the Army before he retired in 1966 was at the Guards Depot, where he was the Training Major. 'Docker' would normally motor down from London in his chauffeur-driven Rolls Royce, informing the adjutant by radio telephone if, for some reason, traffic on the A30 might delay his arrival. On one occasion, he was indeed late, this time for a meeting with a visiting US general who had come to look at the ranges. As the Rolls Royce drew up and halted outside the headquarters, 'Docker' emerged in his greatcoat, to be smartly saluted by the Company Sergeant Major, and then by the bemused US general.

Lieutenant Robert Law, Scots Guards, served at the Guards Depot in the late 1970s, and as his obituary records, was "consistently in trouble with authority". When he found his application to ride in a military point-to-point race at Tweseldown had been denied by the course authorities, he was determined to take part. Positioning himself on his horse *O'Flaherty*, he hid in the woods by the starting post, dressed in puttees, buckskin breeches, tweed coat, cap and pipe. He fell at the first fence and was soon posted to Australia!

Sometime during the summer of 1979, Lieutenant Tim Bendix, a Coldstreamer, and an able mechanic, found an old Ferret Scout Car on the ranges at Pirbright that had now been retired from active service to become a 'hard target' for anti-tank firing. A quick 'indent' to the quartermaster for the requisite missing parts, and the vehicle was a runner again, proving very useful for firefighting duties when there was a heath fire on the ranges. But soon, the authorities spotted the FSC and it was returned to the range for target practice.

Household Cavalry officers, to the amusement of their Foot Guard colleagues, were sometimes required to 'top up' their infantry skills, and this happened on at least one occasion in the early 1980s when two young officers were despatched to the Guards Depot Battle Camp on the Thetford Training Area (now a small modern housing estate). No one had forewarned the Officer Commanding, Captain Anthony Biggs, Coldstream Guards, of their arrival, and so they were told by him, firmly and in no uncertain terms, to make themselves scarce and not get in the way of the serious business of training Guardsmen. They duly obliged, enjoying a few days of gentle walking on the training area, afternoon visits to the Odeon in Bury St Edmunds, and the local pub just a few minutes' walk from the camp.

In late 1982, as the regimental notes in the Winter edition of the *Guards Magazine* record in an amusing and light-hearted tone, there were some musical chairs taking place at the top. A new Commandant (Malcolm Ross) had just arrived, the Adjutant (Sebastian Roberts, almost certainly the author of the magazine update), had been short-toured for another posting, two company commanders had departed, and the second-in-command, Major Philip Wright, had just resigned from the Army to take up a new appointment as Deputy Serjeant-at-Arms at the House of Commons. To make matters worse, this all happened in the midst of a visit from the Inspectorate of Establishments, who were determined to make as many staff savings as possible. All of this was followed a short while later by a farewell party for Philip Wright in the officers' mess. It would be fair to say that this party, which involved the hiring of a stripper and the intake of much alcohol, would probably not pass muster today, and in any event, memories of that evening all those years ago probably differ. The same Guards Depot report recorded a rather less-informed description of the evening: Philip Wright "left us after a dinner party memorable for its extreme decorum, so in keeping with his reign as President of the Mess Committee".

There are many more stories, and a few that are no doubt apocryphal or of dubious provenance. Humour abounded at the Guards Depot, as it should in any institution, and while not all the memories of the place are happy ones, it's the fun and laughter that endures. 'Play hard, work hard' was the adage, and there was more tolerance at the Depot than some realised. On one occasion, a Household Cavalry officer, clearly the worse for wear from the night before, was found asleep on a sofa by the Commandant, Lieutenant Colonel David Lewis, a Welsh Guardsman. The rude and startled response from the young officer when he was awoken by a gentle prod was handled with considerable restraint; David Lewis somehow knew that the outburst had been unintentional.

There were many commandants at the Guards Depot, all Guardsmen hewn of the same overriding philosophy and understanding of the place, and how important it was for the Household Division. David Lewis became Commandant in 1977 and, to quote his obituary:

> it was one of the happiest periods of his life because it brought him in contact with all seven regiments of the Household Division and played to his great strength in getting the best out of people. Everyone who served with him during this time felt they were the better person for the experience. He also knew the importance of having fun in the otherwise serious business of soldiering. The Guards Depot fancy dress balls became the stuff of legend with his Dame Edna Everidge impersonations being the evening's highlight.

One young Household Cavalry officer remembers a subalterns' dinner party, given by David and Sue Lewis in January 1979 in their Army quarter. It was a riotous evening full of laughter, left-over joke Christmas presents, and party hats, and the fact that it was the commandant's party made it all the more fun, and surprising. At one point in the evening, Lewis returned from the kitchen, with a deadpan expression and adorned with a knitted 'willey warmer' attached to the outside of his trousers.

The All Arms Drill Wing, separate but under command of the Guards Depot, remained at Pirbright after the closing of the Depot until it moved to Catterick in 2006 to form part of the Army School of Ceremonial. The Drill Wing has had a long and proud history, and to this day it has the closest of links with the Household Division even if it is no longer technically under command. Formed in 1947 at Caterham, it moved to Pirbright in 1960, running drill courses for both the Regular and Territorial Army and for overseas students. Most of the Regimental Sergeant Majors across the Army attended the 'Guards Instructor Course' at the Drill Wing, and for any Guardsman who aspired to promotion beyond sergeant, it was an important course.

In the years that followed the closing of the Guards Depot, the All Arms Drill Wing frequently sent teams overseas to help other armies with their drill. For example, in 2004, it ran a course in the Maldives,

Sri Lanka, and Mauritius. In the Maldives, there were two challenges for the instructors: firstly, the humidity which left them soaking wet for most of the day; and secondly, the hotel, full of honeymoon couples not accustomed to seeing "a couple of hairy Guardsmen cutting about the place"! The Military Academy at Diyatalawa in the central highlands of Sri Lanka was a stark contrast for Regimental Sergeant Major Evans, Welsh Guards, and Colour Sergeant Stevens, Grenadier Guards. The civil war which had begun in 1983 was still not over, funding for the academy was limited, and morale was low: the standard punishment for cadets was to cut the grass with a scythe in full marching order and helmet. The aim of the visit from the All Arms Drill Wing was to help build a foundation upon which to develop a sense of discipline amongst the cadets, all non-commissioned officers who had fought in the civil war. Despite the language barrier, and with the use of a few pictures and sign language, the two Guards drill instructors achieved their aim. Another demonstration of just how military drill can develop *esprit de corps*.

When the announcement came that the Depot was indeed closing in 1993, despite all the assurances that it would survive, the news came as both a shock and a surprise. It did seem inexplicable to those who had trained or served there, and as Charles Bremner explained, it was not as if there were obvious savings to be made by closing the Guards Depot. The huge material investment in the camp was retained, but its focus as a centre of excellence for the training of Guardsmen was removed. Nobody, it seemed, really benefited from the loss of the Guards Depot.

On 5 March 1993, the final three platoons of Junior Guardsmen in Pirbright Company passed out, joined by the Adult Recruits of Waterloo Platoon of Caterham Company. It was a grand parade, with the salute taken by Major General Michael Rose, Coldstream Guards. It marked the completion of the first phase of basic training for these Junior Guardsmen before joining the Guards Training Company, which formed up at Pirbright before moving to Catterick in September 1993. In the days of the Guards Depot, these young Guardsmen would have completed all their training at Pirbright, prior to being posted to their battalions. Now, their training would be conducted at establishments no longer commanded and administered by the Household Division.

Another passing-out parade at the Depot followed a week later, while, in the meantime, the Commandant, Lieutenant Colonel Shane Alabaster, visited the Guards Adventure Training Wing at Fremington Camp on the North Devon Coast for the last time before the change of command to Headquarters Foot Guards. The much lauded Household Division and Parachute Regiment Centralised Courses Wing also changed command in March 1993 but thankfully was able to continue to provide excellent training courses, as it still does.

On 17 March 1993, the Irish Guards celebrated St Patrick's Day at the Depot, with Queen Elizabeth The Queen Mother handing out the Shamrock in the traditional way. Two days later, Her Majesty Queen Elizabeth II visited the Depot for the final time, spending several hours walking around the camp, meeting staff and their families, and trainees. The Queen ended her visit by walking along Adair Walk, named after the distinguished Grenadier Major General Sir Allan Adair, talking to Guards Depot families and children from the local schools, before departing for Windsor.

The final passing-out parade at the Guards Depot took place on 26 March 1993, when the Major General (Robert Corbett) took the salute for Aisne Platoon, the last platoon to pass out directly to their battalions. The Commandant held his last parade at the Guards Depot on 27 March 1993, followed by a march through the camp and around the married quarters, accompanied by the Band of the Grenadier Guards. Five days later, on 1 April 1993, the Army Training Regiment (Pirbright) formed up, with Guards Company under command. In the early days Pirbright did not seem to change much, except for the arrival of recruits and staff from other parts of the Army. The key posts in the new regiment continued for a while to be held by Guardsmen, and the high standards of the old Depot were maintained, often to the envy of the newcomers.

The closing of the Guards Depot and other regimental training depots also saw the end of Junior Entry. In a period when the Army was getting smaller, coinciding with concerns about the ethics of recruiting 'under-age soldiers', it probably seemed sensible to restrict Junior Entry to the more technical trades rather than to include the combat arms. The sadness for the Army was that recruiting statistics for

Juniors, particularly at the Guards Depot, had always been consistently higher than for the older Adult Recruits, arguably a more difficult group to persuade. Thankfully, the Army re-introduced Junior Entry for the Infantry and Royal Armoured Corps, including the Household Division, in 1998, when the Army Foundation College in Harrogate opened its doors, offering a 49-week course along similar lines to the courses run so successfully for many years at the Guards Depot.

Following the Guards Depot's closure in 1993, and to the relief of many, Guardsmen would indeed continue to be trained by Guardsmen, at Pirbright for the first ten weeks, at Catterick for their 13-week Combat Infantry Course, and then later entirely at Catterick with the Guards Training Company. This has proved a considerable success, and on a smaller scale, the Company has managed to keep the spirit of the Depot alive.

One part of the old Depot that still thrives and remains where it has always been is the Household Division and Parachute Regiment Centralised Courses Wing in Brunswick Lines. It is also no coincidence that this small unit, the envy of many across the Army, is run by the Household Division and the Parachute Regiment, consisting of staff from both of these parts of the Army and from the Royal Marines. All of its courses have one of two purposes: to train, test, and qualify soldiers in a specific skill, such as a sniper qualification; or to prepare them for external courses run elsewhere in the Army.

The single most important course that the Household Division and Parachute Regiment Centralised Courses Wing runs, as it has done for many years at Pirbright, is the four-week Junior Non-Commissioned Officer Cadre, in which a Guardsman or Paratrooper has the chance to demonstrate leadership potential in order to gain the all-important first promotion to lance corporal. This has always been a huge leap for a young soldier; Field Marshal Sir William Robertson, who began his career as a Trooper in the 16th Lancers in 1877, and became the Colonel of the Royal Horse Guards in 1928, regarded promotion to lance corporal as a greater achievement than acquiring a field marshal's baton many years later.

Army training has gone through a transition over the last 20 years or so and is being much better resourced now than it was in the period following the closure of the Guards Depot in 1993. An Army-wide spotlight illuminated many of the weaknesses and failings in the later

1990s and early 2000s, principally caused by a failure in some parts of the Army to invest in the right number and calibre of people charged with training young men and women. The deaths of four recruits at Deepcut, another training camp only a mile from Alexander Barracks, raised the profile of the problem, which was fundamentally about supervision and the lack of trained staff.

Although the Guards Depot had its fair share of problems over the years (it was not immune to accusations of bullying), these were considerably less serious than elsewhere for one simple and overriding reason: this was a place that was inextricably linked with the part of the Army that it served, the Household Division. Many officers and a larger proportion of non-commissioned officers aspired to serve at Pirbright, training the next generation of Guardsmen, and for the latter it was often the route to advancement. They wanted to be there, and for those who did well at the Guards Depot, there were more opportunities elsewhere. Somehow, the seven regiments always found the right people to send to the Guards Depot, even if they had to bear gaps in their own ranks to achieve this.

The Guards Depot continues to be missed by those who served there. It was truly a place where Guardsmen from all corners of the Household Division could meet, serve together, and make friends. However, the Guards are hugely adaptive, and despite all the challenges of the 1990s and beyond, a demanding period of high tempo operations and commitments, the ethos of the Depot has somehow endured and perhaps even strengthened in different ways. Guardsmen of all ranks frequently serve with Guards regiments other than their own. The young recruits at Catterick are trained by Guardsmen, and long may this continue.

Alexander Barracks still retains something of the spirit of the Guards, and many traces of those days of the Guards Depot remain. Adair Walk is still there, as is the original Caterham Stone, the Weather Vane, and the plaque marking the opening of Alexander Barracks in 1969. The 'Sand Hill', 'Heartbreak Hill', and the 'Sisters', all special features of the obstacle course, are also remembered, perhaps less fondly, but they are there, all the same.

There are still a few Guardsmen at Alexander Barracks, now serving at the Army Training Regiment, Pirbright, doing similar jobs that they might have done during the good old Guards Depot days. The

Household Division and Parachute Regiment Centralised Courses Wing is there, a centre of excellence demanding the highest of standards.

Finally, and thankfully, Guardsmen are always returning to Pirbright to make sure that the drill square gets the regular pounding of studded drill-boots that it was built to absorb back in 1969. Every year, rehearsals for state events take place here, most notably in 2021 for Prince Philip's funeral, in 2022 for Queen Elizabeth's funeral, and in 2023 for King Charles III's Coronation. It is to Pirbright, the spiritual home of the Household Division, that Guardsmen return every year, to practise and practise. Because that's what Guardsmen do.

9

The Household Division in the Balkans, 1993–2007

I ordered my old Regiment, the Coldstream, to break through the Serb control point. The Serbs held their fire. Such was our fearsome reputation for returning fire among the warring parties, we were known by the title of 'Shootbat' rather than the UN title of 'Britbat'. The Times *demanded that politicians match the more robust military approach.*

GENERAL SIR MICHAEL ROSE, *FIGHTING FOR PEACE*

The Balkan Wars were a series of separate but related ethnic conflicts, wars of independence and insurgencies resulting from the breakup of Yugoslavia from 1991 to 2007. Civil wars strike deepest of all into the behaviour of people. The Balkans erupted into civil war with the collapse of the Republic of Yugoslavia in the early 1990s.

Like all civil wars, the savagery between the warring parties was indescribable. For the Guardsmen who served in the Balkans during the civil war, even though there was a justifiable sense of pride in trying to establish peace, the experience would see many shaken by what they had to witness. The Balkans conflict was to leave an indelible mark, an enduring reminder to Guardsmen of the worst of human behaviour. They were peacekeepers doing an impossible job, and in the absence of any agreement in the West of what to do, peace became an illusion.

For any Household Division commanding officer charged with the task of taking his Battalion or Regiment to the Balkans, the challenge to explain why they were there, and what had provoked the latest bout of internecine bloodletting, was formidable.

The collapse into civil war of the former Socialist Federal Republic of Yugoslavia in late 1991/92 resulted from the absence of a controlling power or 'strongman' to keep a tight grip on the complex web of ethnic and religious groups. That 'strongman' had been President Tito of Yugoslavia who died in 1980, aged 87. During his presidency, Tito had suppressed all ethnic and religious tensions by ensuring that no one group was in the ascendant and that everyone had a crack of the whip in positions of power or influence.

Tito would stand for no external pressure, famously writing to Stalin, who was always looking to extend Soviet influence, "Stop sending people to kill me. We've already captured and executed five of your assassins. If you don't stop, I'll send one to Moscow, and I won't have to send a second."

Without Tito's iron grip at the helm, few of his fellow countrymen or Western observers had confidence in how the region would govern itself. They were right to worry.

Yugoslavia comprised six constituent republics: Slovenia, Croatia, Serbia, Macedonia, Montenegro, and Bosnia-Herzegovina (Bosnia to the British military veteran). There were two autonomous provinces: Kosovo, with a significant Albanian and Muslim population, a region which was to exercise the minds of the Irish Guards later on in the conflict; and Vojvodina in the north with a significant Hungarian minority.

The religious map of the Balkans was a kaleidoscope of Sunni Muslims and Christians of differing hues. It was a tinderbox and Tito's death had lit the fuse, at first a slow burning fire, then with the fall of communism in 1989 impossible to contain.

War between these irreconcilable factions was therefore only a matter of time. It did not help that European sympathies also ran along ancient alliances. Most European countries had a dog in the fight. Germany, with its large and influential Catholic population, inclined towards Slovenia and Croatia; for historical reasons, France, Britain, and Russia were more sympathetic to the cause of Serbia.

Unfortunately, 'the common European home' after communism's collapse was to prove to be a myth. Aggressive nationalism rose again.

The West was gripped by war in the Gulf after Iraq invaded Kuwait. A squabble in the Balkans seemed trivial against the tensions in the Middle East with its implications for Western economies. The European Union (EU) was also trying to adjust to the reunification of Germany. Russia was fast becoming a mess as the Soviet Union unravelled. First, Slovenia won its independence in 1991. This was followed by the Croatian War of Independence which began when Serbs in Croatia who were opposed to Croatian independence announced their secession from Croatia. In 1992, a further conflict engulfed Bosnia and Herzegovina as it also declared independence from what was left of Yugoslavia. The war was a conflict between the Bosnian Muslims (Sunni Muslims) who wanted to preserve the territorial integrity of the newly independent Republic of Bosnia and Herzegovina, the self-proclaimed Bosnian Serb state and the self-proclaimed Croat Bosnia. Violence between the various warring parties became unspeakable.

It was against this tangled and blood-soaked background that the regiments of the Household Division deployed to the Balkans from 1994 to 2007.

In November 1991, a United Nations (UN) Security Council Resolution paved the way for peacekeeping operations. The hastily formed UN Protection Force (UNPROFOR) drew heavily on regiments based in Germany. The first Household Division involvement was the husband-and-wife regimental medical officers from the Household Cavalry and 2nd Battalion Coldstream Guards in support of the Royal Army Medical Corps in Croatia and Bosnia. This was purely a humanitarian support operation, Op *Hamden*. But there was pitifully little semblance to humanity as ethnic cleansing took on its own horrifying momentum.

The United Nations had to rise to the appalling levels of violence. Op *Grapple* was the title given to UK operations in support of the UN peacekeeping missions in the former Yugoslavia. This included the deployment of British Forces in Bosnia and Croatia from October 1992 until December 1995 as part of the UNPROFOR. This saw the deployment to Bosnia of the first British battalion (BRITBAT) Warrior-equipped armoured infantry battle group, 1st Battalion The Cheshire

Regiment, with a medium reconnaissance squadron from the Light Dragoons who were to witness the Ahmići massacre of 120 Bosnian Muslims by the Croatians. The world at last began to sit up.

It was against this backdrop of violence and deprivation, where thousands died and around half the population found itself displaced, that 1st Battalion Coldstream Guards deployed to central Bosnia – Op *Grapple* 3 – from their base in Münster, Germany in November 1993 under Lieutenant Colonel Peter Williams.

The timing was fortuitous. A couple of months after the Battalion arrived, Lieutenant General Sir Michael Rose, a former Coldstream and SAS officer, was appointed as the UN Commander in Bosnia. There was a renewed sense of optimism that the darkest days of the conflict would recede as Rose was determined to shake up UNPROFOR's way of operating and use the Coldstream Warrior armoured vehicles to demonstrate his willingness to use force. Rose ordered the Coldstream to break through a Bosnian Serb checkpoint obstructing the only usable road for delivering aid to the besieged city of Sarajevo, home to largely Bosnian Muslims.

The Warrior was a formidable deterrent to any hostile action. Fittingly, it was the 1st Battalion Grenadier Guards under the command of Lieutenant Colonel Evelyn Webb-Carter and later Lieutenant Colonel Euan Houston, who had trialled the Warrior as part of 4th Armoured Brigade in BAOR in 1988.

Lieutenant Colonel Peter Williams was cut against the grain of Guards officers at that time. He had read history at Magdalene College, Cambridge, and had carved out a career as a qualified intelligence officer and Russian interpreter working for BRIXMIS in East Germany in the 1980s. His innate understanding of Balkan history, of the mentality of Soviet-style Yugoslav commanders, and of how events had come to such a vicious pass allowed him to take a rational but hard-headed approach to his battle group's mission.

Colonel Peter recalled, "The apparently simple UNPROFOR mission was to support the humanitarian relief efforts of the UN High Commissioner for Refugees (UNHCR). But we soon found ourselves in the midst of a complex and heavily armed conflict. There was only the one main supply route, Route Diamond, and despite difficult weather conditions we managed to get a considerable tonnage, some 25,000 tonnes, of aid to those in need."

Much credit for this success was down to No 1 Company under the leadership of Major Andrew Johnston. No 1 Company sat in Gornji Vakuf astride Route Diamond on the fault line between Muslims and Croats. The town had been levelled to rubble. The company was under constant mortar and rocket attack, yet it still managed to provide shelter and food to convoys marooned in the town if things got really bad.

The relief operation was not without its mishaps, but for Guardsmen familiar with Northern Ireland's lawlessness, if not the savagery of the Balkans, the business of the day was well within their stride. The mission played to the Coldstreamers' strengths: good discipline, exemplary restraint, and controlled aggression if the situation demanded it.

An example of this robust attitude occurred on 17 April 1994. The Coldstream carried out a fighting withdrawal from a front-line UN observation post in Sarajevo by members of the reconnaissance platoon in Scimitar vehicles led by Lance Sergeants Minshall and Waterhouse. This thwarted Bosnian Serb plans to seize six Coldstreamers to be used as political hostages. A fierce firefight ensued, which Waterhouse repelled with consummate courage and speed of reaction. It was as a result of this contact that Lance Sergeant Darren Waterhouse was awarded the Military Cross; his was only the second such award to a junior non-commissioned officer after the revision of the gallantry awards introduced by Prime Minister John Major allowing all ranks to win the award of the Military Cross, if so merited, rather than just officers.

As Colonel Peter announced to his men at the start of the tour, "I expect every one of us to behave like Yeomen of England, we have left 381 wives back in Germany and if you discredit yourselves or the Regiment, I will not fine you or punish you but you will be sent straight back to Germany." The Guardsmen took his words to heart. Over a six-month tour, in trying circumstances, only one man was returned to Germany for disciplinary reasons.

Colonel Peter was often reminded of the differences and similarities between soldiering in Northern Ireland and the Balkans. On one occasion, he stopped at a Coldstream mortar platoon checkpoint in Bosnia one winter's day in early 1994. It was raining steadily and it was bitterly cold. "It's not too bad here, is it, Guardsman Armstrong? Certainly better than East Tyrone." The Battalion had served there a year earlier.

"Actually, Sir," Armstrong replied, "I'd rather be in Northern Ireland because there I could understand the abuse that I received on checkpoint duty from the locals. Here it seems a bit less menacing, but I can't understand what the desperate locals are so angry about. I can't even hand out sweets to the children in case it encourages them to rush out in the path of oncoming vehicles, hoping for sweets or something. To be honest, Sir, I'd rather be back in Dungannon."

In that sense, and given the Guardsman's frank appraisal, if Northern Ireland was a 'section commanders' war' with relentless patrolling to keep the PIRA off balance, Bosnia was very much an 'officers' war'. The commanding officer, company and platoon commanders, and the network of liaison officers were invariably engaged in negotiations with local warlords, mayors, priests, NGOs, and UN agencies to win consent to deliver much needed humanitarian aid.

The Battalion was based in Vitez, some 50 miles north-west of Sarajevo, at the heart of the action as the Bosniak Army of the Republic of Bosnia-Herzegovina sought to crush the Bosnian Croat enclave around the town. Despite this, the Battalion did its best to entertain the local community and give them some respite from the hellish conditions.

The Corps of Drums performed at numerous events; parties were organised for children including a TV show run by the Adjutant, Captain 'Magoo' Giles. The experience stood him in good stead. An eclectic officer, 'Magoo', who was asked on an Army staff course whether he wanted to be a clown or a staff officer, later became the founder and much respected principal of Knightsbridge Preparatory School. As Lieutenant General Sir James Bucknall, Colonel of the Coldstream Guards, once remarked, "The Household Division is much the richer for the breadth of interest and broad mosaic of its officers, we never look for the generic in our recruiting."

Central Bosnia deteriorated seriously in late January 1994. The free passage of humanitarian and UNPROFOR vehicles was hard graft. Just a fifth of the projected aid tonnage was getting through to local municipalities. General Rose's arrival had, however, begun to make an impact. Not only was he a fine soldier, unafraid to tread where many senior officers would be so, he was politically astute and quite happy to stand up to Serbian tough customers, many of whom were later to be indicted as war criminals: Milošević, Karadžić, and Mladić.

The winter of 1993–94 was the darkest period for central Bosnia and the Coldstreamers had to witness its grimmest moments. On the morning of 5 February 1994, a 120mm mortar bomb exploded in the Markale market square in Sarajevo, the Bosnian capital, killing 68 and wounding 144. Tragedy and suffering at last galvanised the international community into action. The US, a hitherto reluctant observer of the Balkans vortex, swung NATO ministers into line, demanding that the Serbs withdraw all their heavy artillery.

Rose worked hard to establish a peace accord between the Sarajevo government, who supported the Bosnian Muslims, and the Bosnian Croats, which came into effect on 25 February. The week before, Major Bill Cubitt, commanding No 2 Company Coldstream Guards, had led the first British company into Sarajevo. Sarajevo, defended by Bosnians of various ethnicities, religions, and loyalties, had been under siege for two years by the Bosnian Serbs whose objective all along had been a Greater Serbia. Cubitt's task was to collect Serb heavy weaponry, which had at last been brought to heel by the threat of NATO air strikes.

The operation was a success. Cubitt was to write:

Despite some difficult incidents with resentful Serb troops – they were after all an unbeaten army – firm action on our behalf but with no heavy handedness and a good dose of Guards courtesy and charm bore fruit. All heavy Serb weapons were under UNPROFOR control to satisfy the NATO ultimatum. Ironically, at a low level, the Serbs frequently expressed their liking for the British as a result of our help to the Yugoslav partisans in fighting the Nazis in the Second World War.

As always in the Balkans, there was unfinished business. The Bosnian Muslim and Croat defenders in Maglaj were still subject to heavy Serb artillery. Aid was still not getting through. On 20 March, a combination of No 3 Company under Major The Hon Richard Margesson, the SAS, high-level political pressure and the Light Dragoon Guards, saw the first aid convoy getting through to Maglaj. It might have been the liberation of Paris or Brussels in 1944: Margesson and No 3 Company were treated as the heroes of Maglaj.

On 20 March 1994, thousands of spectators gathered in the Sarajevo football stadium to watch a football match between an UNPROFOR team and Sarajevo. The Coldstream Regimental Band, resplendent in red tunics and bearskins, marched on to the applause of all those present and to international acclaim. Operational professionalism and ceremonial excellence had once again worked its magic.

General Rose said, "We see here today yet another small step towards normality in this beautiful land. This is an irreversible process because people have had enough of the senseless killing and destruction." The Serb artillery was trained on the stadium but the Serbs were wise enough just to witness a remarkable event.

The Coldstream Op *Grapple* tour was an experience that few of the 800 Guardsmen, 53 Foot Guards officers, and one Blues and Royals officer would ever forget. Once again, it bore testament to the principle of impartiality and admirable restraint which has always been a hallmark of the Household Division.

Statistics rarely speak for themselves but it is a matter of record that the Battalion had more than 200 contacts, returning fire in 70 with over 4,000 rounds to suppress the hostile fire directed at them by snipers from all the warring factions. The Coldstream's Battle Group had also moved over 25,000 tons of aid.

The Op *Grapple* 3 Honours and Awards List was to see 13 members of the Battle Group being given awards for bravery or valuable service in addition to Lance Sergeant D. Waterhouse's Military Cross.

Captain R.W. Yorke won the Queen's Gallantry Medal for his tireless efforts as a liaison officer, which included managing the exchange across active front lines of the bodies of 171 Bosnian, Serb, and Croat soldiers and civilians. Also on the list was Major M.G. Tucker, the Battalion's Royal Australian Regiment exchange officer, who was awarded a Member of the British Empire award for his Herculean efforts as the Battle Group's operations officer.

But if it was an experience that few would forget, it was also a time that took its toll on the mental wellbeing of officers and Guardsmen alike. Senseless savagery, particularly of the innocent who had lived for years in relative harmony, was hard to witness and bear. Colonel Peter felt that, subsequently, between 5 per cent and 10 per cent of his officers and non-commissioned members of the Battle Group suffered from stress-related, PTSD-type conditions.

Lieutenant Colonel Bill Rollo, commanding the Household Cavalry Regiment, had deployed to central Bosnia in the autumn of 1994 as part of Op *Grapple* 5 to be greeted with, if not quite open arms, a strong sense of approval from the local population at the sight of the blue-red-blue cap badge. The Coldstream had been remembered with affection and respect. Rollo was amused that one local had referred to the Coldstream as a cavalry regiment. He wondered if this was a reference to the Warrior armoured infantry fighting vehicle but was told it was their Coldstream hospitality, talent for throwing a good party and natural élan.

The Household Cavalry, similar to the Coldstream, were charged with keeping the peace in central Bosnia and ensuring aid convoys were getting through to those communities most in need. Rollo recalled the mission statement given to him: "To ensure all inhabitants of Bosnia are able to live in relative peace and prevent the Bosniaks and Croats fighting each other again."

Rollo immediately picked up on the ambiguity of the phrase in 'relative peace'. He summed up, "The fight was at least three-sided: Croats were siding with the Serbs against the Bosniaks and other Croats were lined up with the Bosniaks against the Serbs. Confusing to say the least, but we had to live with ambiguity and, as the Serbs continued to shell Bosniak towns and villages, it was clear that the Croats were waiting in the wings to see who would prevail."

Rollo went on:

It was most of the time, one step forward and near enough two steps back. I also had to manage a pretty fractured deployment with A and B Squadrons as BRITBAT 1 attached to the Royal Highland Fusiliers in Western Bosnia, and the rest of the Regiment in BRITCAV-BAT – how the British Army loves throwing acronyms at a problem – sorting out the tangled affairs in Maglaj. As one Trooper remarked to me, "Why are we providing humanitarian relief in a town which is still able to sell kiwi fruit?"

The British Army, with its Northern Ireland experience as an important backdrop, was by now pretty adaptable to whatever was thrown at it. Rollo was reminded of this as he observed soldiers being billeted in a disused abattoir, chilly at the best of times, bone cold in the depths of a

Balkan winter. It was not unlike the experience of soldiers in the depths of a bleak Northern Ireland winter.

The Household Cavalry dealt with any number of disparate tasks but all geared essentially to building trust and getting the warring communities back to normality: patrols with medical aid; emergency shelter to shell-damaged houses; escorting UN aid convoys to warehouses while avoiding snipers, all amidst shelling and the sheer madness of a world gone wrong.

But the old Household Division tradition of finding humour in adversity and professionalism in execution saw the Household Cavalry complete a successful tour. Colonel Bill was later to command 4th Armoured Brigade in Kosovo and would point to his experience in central Bosnia as "cold comfort" as he wrestled with much the same challenges as a brigade commander. "Working with other nations was the fun part of things for every rank, we had fond memories of the Royal Canadian Dragoons, even our Russian Civil Affairs officer, Baktiyar Tukhamedov, known to us all as 'Mr Red October'. For myself, I learnt the invaluable lesson of the challenges of building multi-national alliances. It was to stand me in good stead when we entered Kosovo four years later as part of the NATO-led Kosovo Force (KFOR)."

The Bosnian War eventually drew to a close. The international community, at last with US heft behind it, had had enough. The suffering of all the inhabitants came to a halt. The presidents of Serbia, Croatia, and Bosnia signed the Dayton Accords Agreement on 21 November 1995. The settlement at least brought the fighting to an end but was full of anomalies. The Bosnian question, particularly its economic development and the co-operation between the Serb, Croat, and Bosnian communities, remained unsolved. The Household Division was to hold the line, somewhere in the Balkans, for another decade.

Context matters if you examine the success or otherwise of operational tours. UNPROFOR in the Balkans attracted a good deal of criticism, little of which was justified. General Rose, a former Coldstreamer, who saw at first hand the challenges faced by the 1st Battalion under Colonel

Peter Williams, was under no illusions as to the scale of the task that peacekeepers had to face:

> In 1994, all the necessary conditions for an end to the war were not yet in place. Most of the population was still heavily dependent on UN aid for its survival. Peacekeepers were extremely vulnerable to being taken hostage. It wasn't until mid-1995 that the political climate changed in which military force at a strategic level had some purpose. The Americans finally accepted that a 'just' political settlement was not obtainable and that concessions would have to be made to the Bosnian Serbs. NATO was still trapped in the logic of the Cold War. If NATO had deployed to Bosnia in 1992 rather than 1995, things might have been very different.

Rose felt that the greatest weakness of the UN mission in Bosnia was the failure to win the information battle. Rose was so concerned about the importance of public relations that he brought in Tim Spicer, who had recently commanded 1st Battalion Scots Guards in Belfast, to handle PR. Spicer's experience in managing PR in Belfast was to stand him in good stead. In chaos and confusion, the influence of the media on a peacekeeping mission was critical. The Coldstream Battle Group, like UNPROFOR as a whole, had to live and operate under that challenge. Rose also had two Coldstream aide-de-camps in his headquarters, such were the demands on his time and presence.

The greatest PR disaster for UNPROFOR during its mission was the United Nations Safe Area policy. It gave the impression that the territory and populations of the safe areas would be guaranteed by the UN. The massacre at Srebrenica in July 1995 proved otherwise. The wishy-washy wording by the UN about 'deterring' and not 'defending' or 'protecting' made the policy of safe areas unworkable. The 1st Battalion Coldstream Guards had therefore to operate under an ambiguous mandate backed by barely adequate resources, though the Warrior armoured infantry fighting vehicle was a powerful deterrent.

For this critical time during the Balkans conflict, the final word must go to General Rose, who left Bosnia in January 1995: "I recall the beauty of the countryside and the welcome of ordinary people, but most of all I remember the heroism, humour and courage of the thousands of young men and women of UNPROFOR who came from all over the world and risked their lives so willingly that others might live."

———

Five months after the Dayton Accords and the framework for peace in Bosnia-Herzegovina had been signed in Dayton, Ohio, on 21 November 1995 and formally signed in Paris on 14 December that year, the newly formed Kosovo Liberation Army murdered three Serbs who were enjoying a quiet drink in a café in western Kosovo. The Kosovo Albanians had seen that their Serb oppressors had been brought to heel in Croatia and Bosnia with NATO's help. Bosnia had also received $5 billion in aid. Albania had received nothing at all, and the Serbs under Milošević continued to deny them rights in a regime of unrelenting repression.

True to form, the international community turned a blind eye to the murders, hoping the whole thing would quietly go away. The West had become tired of the Balkans. Albania began to descend into chaos. To add to the turmoil, Serbia's tiny sister Republic, Montenegro, turned against Milošević. The death toll began to mount.

That winter, UNPROFOR had handed over the peacekeeping mission to NATO's Implementation Force (IFOR). That lasted a year before it became the Stabilisation Force (SFOR). There was a strong Household Division presence at a senior level. Major General Evelyn Webb-Carter, Grenadier Guards, was the Commander of Multi-National Division (South-West) for SFOR in Bosnia in 1996; Major General John Kiszely, Scots Guards, took over from him as well as assuming command of Britain's 1st Armoured Division; he then handed over to Major General Reddy Watt, Welsh Guards, in 1998.

The EU and the US began to see that a full-blown war was about to break out in Kosovo, where the ethnicity was 95 per cent Albanian. A war in Kosovo was likely to draw in Macedonia, which had a large Albanian minority. If Kosovo won its independence, then Macedonia might be drawn into the idea of a Greater Albania. And if that happened, Greece, which insisted Macedonia was part of Greece – a belief going back to Alexander the Great – would join in the fight. The complexity of it all. The curse of Balkan history.

Milošević, the ruthless leader of the Serbs, refused to accept a NATO peacekeeping force, Kosovo Force (KFOR), to guarantee autonomy for the Kosovars. If NATO backed down on this guarantee, its word would stand for nothing. The massacre of Kosovo Albanian farmers in January 1999 steeled NATO to the task. Milošević continued to play for time. NATO started bombing the Serbs on 24 March. Bombing was a statement of intent but in itself did little except unite Serbs around Milošević, who knew only too well that ground troops in a peacekeeping role were paper tigers. The inadvertent bombing of the Chinese embassy, killing three diplomats, did little to steady NATO's nerves.

Milošević's bluff was called as it became clear that by late May NATO was ready for a ground invasion with combat-ready troops. KFOR now had real teeth. In June, KFOR, based on the Allied Rapid Reaction Force (ARRC) and commanded by General Sir Mike Jackson, entered Kosovo to bring matters to a close. The high-readiness battle group, the Irish Guards, which had been training in central Macedonia since February was off the leash.

On 12 June 1999, 1st Battalion Irish Guards entered Kosovo in one of the largest armoured operations in Europe since the Second World War. The Micks were under the command of Lieutenant Colonel Bill Cubitt, a former Coldstreamer who had served in the Balkans half a dozen years before as a company commander with his own Battalion. Colonel Bill, quietly spoken, calm, and a clear thinker, was the perfect complement to the effervescent Micks. He was later to become the Major General during the worst days of the Afghanistan campaign. Colonel Bill took to the Micks immediately: "I was impressed by their special character, the sense of family which you see throughout the Household Division but seemed of a nature of its own in the Micks, the atmosphere, the humour, their belief that they were different. And on their day, they really were."

Colonel Bill was also proof that transferring from one regiment of the Household Division to command another was no hindrance. The Household Division ethos was a constant, it was just the nuances in provenance and character that a newcomer had to get to grips with. As a distinguished Household Division four-star general was later to remark, "It takes a Coldstreamer to smooth out the rough edges of the Micks' administration."

The Irish Guards had the key roles of securing the Kosovan capital, Pristina, and the northern town of Podujevo, which had suffered badly at the hands of the Serbs. The name of Pristina will echo throughout history because of the almost tragicomic events surrounding the events of that early June.

In the early hours of 11 June, Russian troops in a deft sleight of hand occupied Pristina's airport. General Sir Mike Jackson, the redoubtable KFOR commander, was ordered to take them on. Jackson dismissed the order – "I am not going to start World War III on your say-so" – a remark he addressed to Wesley Clark, the US Supreme Allied Commander in Europe. The Russians calmed down. They had made their point that they should be consulted about things that directly or indirectly affected their sphere of influence or historical ties.

Colonel Bill and the Irish Guards could only look on with an anxious but wry smile, their temperament more than equal to the task. The Micks supplied the Russian troops with water while No 1 Company under Major Edward Melotte raced forward to liberate Podujevo amid great Albanian jubilation. Serb troops remained surly and prone to individual acts of violence. Guardsman Bradford received a Joint Commander's Commendation for shielding a helpless Albanian child from an angry Serb soldier.

The Irish Guards Battle Group were the first NATO soldiers to enter Pristina. Like the Coldstream experience in Maglaj, the local community was overjoyed, garlanding the Guardsmen with flowers. Battle group headquarters was run ragged as the Micks were the only organised force in Pristina, the fire, ambulance, gas, electricity, and police services having long given up the fight. As Cubitt wrote, "It was time for initiative, resource and humour, something the Micks are never short of. I remember Sergeant Meadows disarming an excitable Albanian poised to attack Serbs with a hand grenade saying to me with an insouciant shrug, 'I saw he had a hand grenade and had removed the pin. Knowing this to be an unsafe condition, I placed my hand over the grenade lever and moved him to a safe area.'

There remained, however, some 18,000 Serbs in the Battalion's Tactical Area of Responsibility. There was deep hatred of the Serbs. The Albanians had suffered badly at their hands. Houses destroyed; atrocities committed. It was ever thus in the Balkans cauldron. As Cubitt wrote in a post tour report:

The hardest part of the tour was simply keeping the lid on inter-ethnic violence while coercing both sides to sit down and talk about the future and intractable issues. The UN administration did not arrive until late Summer so it was at least a useful experience for platoon and company commanders who became quasi district commissioners. The combination of boldness and preparedness to talk to the warring parties and police paid dividends.

July and August 1999 were tense and murderous. Fourteen Serbs were murdered while harvesting, Serb towns were mortared, and their monuments bombed. One monument damaged by the Kosovo Liberation Army was a memorial to the 1389 Battle of Kosovo. Once again, Guardsmen saw at first hand that the Balkans was a part of the world where memories last forever and vengeance is never sated. The Battle Group's operational focus switched to protecting the Serbs. Irish Guardsmen were to remember the long vigils in 14th-century Serb Orthodox churches. They took to the job with equanimity, remembering perhaps the devastating effect of religious differences on communities in their native Ireland.

As autumn came, the Irish Guards Battle Group handed over their Tactical Area of Responsibility to two Scandinavian battalions with reassuring names: the Norwegian Telemark Battalion and the Swedish Rapid Reaction Battalion. When they had time to reflect on what had been an intense few months, most Guardsmen would point to working so closely with many different nationalities and regiments as the most rewarding part of their time in Kosovo: Lord Strathcona's Horse; a Canadian reconnaissance regiment, the 14th Canadian Hussars; Finns, Czechs, the Italian Carabinieri, a Russian field hospital ...

There had also been time to embrace the richness of other national cultures. The Russian Army Chorus and Dance Ensemble's performance was memorable. The Irish Guards Regimental Band, deployed in its medical role, nevertheless found time to provide musical evenings to the applause of local people and other nations' troops.

The Irish Guards had had an outstanding tour. Major General Reddy Watt, a former Welsh Guards officer and subsequent Major General Commanding the Household Division (and four-star general), was full of praise for the way the Irish Guards had conducted themselves:

I was then commanding 1st Armoured Division which deployed to Bosnia as Headquarters Multi-National Division (South-West).

I visited the Micks in the field commanded by Lieutenant Colonel Bill Cubitt and 4th Armoured Brigade commanded by Brigadier Bill Rollo. They were both experienced Balkans hands. The Irish Guards were quite excellent. They never looked back as their tours in Iraq and Afghanistan were to prove.

———

The 12th of March 2003 gave just a hint of spring at the end of an unusually bitter winter. Serbia's Prime Minister, Zoran Djindić, who had replaced Slobodan Milošević, was shot dead as he stepped from his car towards the Serbian government building in Belgrade's centre. It was a defining moment. His assassination had serious consequences for economic and social progress in Serbia, and more critically in the region as a whole.

Household Division regiments were to carry out operational tours in Kosovo and Bosnia under the umbrella of the NATO-led Stabilisation Force (SFOR) until the spring of 2005. NATO's campaign in the spring and summer of 1999 might have stopped Milošević in his tracks but left many unanswered questions. NATO's overwhelming power held the line that year but the great powers, particularly the US, did not want to use their political and economic resources to deal with Serbia and the larger Balkan protectorate of Bosnia-Herzegovina. No one seem prepared to invest heavily into the region.

Organised crime found fertile ground and became the most serious threat to the region's stability. Only one country, Croatia, had emerged from the wars in the 1990s with the semblance of a future. Croatia was to join the EU in July 2013, its economy driven by a flourishing tourism industry. Every other country in the Balkans remains to this day an 'EU candidate country'. Corruption, crime, and crippled economies suggest they will be 'candidates' for some time. In that vacuum, long-lasting peace in the Balkans remains a pipe dream.

Milošević, president of the Federal Republic of Yugoslavia, fell from power in 2000 and was carted off to the International Criminal Tribunal in the Hague to be tried for war crimes. The indicted war criminals, the Bosnian Serb duo Radovan Karadžić and General Ratko Mladić, were shortly to follow.

Meanwhile the British Army, along with many other NATO troops, continued to carry out the heavy lifting in the region. As one former UN Secretary-General famously put it, "Peacekeeping is not a job for soldiers, but only soldiers can do it."

The Welsh Guards' first operational deployment outside Northern Ireland and the Falklands campaign began in March 2002. It was called Op *Palatine*, an oblique reference to the Palatine Hill in Rome, the epicentre of the Roman Empire. Ironically, the Battalion deployed to the epicentre of Bosnia, the city of Banja Luka. It was predominantly Serb. Once again, its mission was to 'secure a peaceful Bosnia'.

The Welsh Guards tour followed a predictable pattern: the search for weapons, a huge haul of 1,000 rifles and pistols, 165,000 rounds of ammunition and 22 mortars; and a hearts and minds campaign to support the civilian population on their road to normalisation. This rather amusingly included a donation of £3,000 from Eton College to re-equip a school (the commanding officer, Lieutenant Colonel Robert Talbot Rice, was an old Etonian); anti-smuggling operations which exposed the limitations of the Battalion's policing role; and the highlight of any Household Division tour, and never to be underestimated in its effect on goodwill, a performance by the Regimental Band to a sell-out audience in the historic Banja Luka castle.

The evening's highlight was the Welsh Guards Choir whose stirring rendition of 'God Bless The Prince of Wales' and 'Cwm Rhondda' brought not only the locals to their feet, but also the Battalion. A Welsh Guardsman's emotions are never far from the surface and this is part of the Regiment's innate strength, as well as its weakness if channelled in the wrong direction.

For a year or so there was a peace of sorts in Kosovo, but in March 2004 things turned for the worse after reports that Serbs had drowned three young Albanian children. The Queen's Company 1st Battalion Grenadier Guards under the Captain, Major Carew Hatherley, and the Second Captain, Piers Ashfield, all part of the UK's Spearhead Battle Group, was rushed to Kosovo Polje, 'The Field of Blackbirds', where the Irish Guards had been billeted five years before. It was a testament to the Grenadiers' readiness that Hatherley got the Queen's Company, some of whom were on Windsor Guard, on the plane to Pristina, kitted and armed, within four hours. The operations, which ran from 18 March to

21 April 2004, were given the names Op *Mercian* and Op *Puma*. The Queen's Company arrived in the nick of time.

What confronted the younger Guardsmen, many of whom had never been outside the UK, was the sheer savagery of the Balkans. Serbs burnt alive in drainage ditches outside their homes, Serb schools, homes and hospitals razed to the ground, it was quite a baptism of fire. Many of the other KFOR troops had failed to respond, afraid to stir up trouble for themselves and exacerbate the tension. Major Hatherley appeared on Kosovan national television and broadcast a clear message: 'no-go areas' for KFOR troops were to cease immediately and the rule of law would be enforced with actions proportional and responsive to each event, from truncheons to tear gas to live bullets.

Commendable restraint, which had so characterised the Household Division in Northern Ireland, had now become part of the Grenadiers' collective unconscious. Old Grenadier hands knew what to do and other KFOR troops from different nationalities took note. Whatever stereotypical views they had of the eccentricities of the British soldier; they were quickly dispelled. They saw that steadfastness, good discipline, and a robust but controlled response had a quick and profound effect on ethnic violence.

The Grenadiers enjoyed the hospitality of other nations. They even persuaded the Finnish contingent to lend them their comfortable tents, designed for a Finnish winter, and to sweat off a fortnight's worth of dirt and detritus in their pristine saunas. The Grenadiers were marginally disappointed to witness the Finns' 'vegetarian' days in their cookhouse. After all their exertions, this was short commons for the strapping men of the Queen's Company.

In the House of Lords debate in the spring of 2004, the Grenadiers were praised for the speed of their deployment. Lord Astor of Hever remarked that "the importance of the quick and robust deployment in Kosovo should not be underestimated. We cannot afford further bloodshed and instability in the Balkans."

There remained unfinished business. Ten years after the war, Bosnia remained traumatised. Crime and corruption were rife. There were major obstacles to EU accession. Warfighting, deterrence, and humanitarian assistance would remain at the heart of NATO's operations. The region was as close to failure as to success. The smell of violence still lingered in the air. Economic growth was low or non-existent, criminal gangs linked to politicians and institutions were pervasive. The public was distrustful. The Grenadiers commanded by Lieutenant Colonel David Russell-Parsons deployed on Op *Oculus* and Op *Althea* from 28 September 2004 to 28 March 2005.

The size of the NATO Implementation Force (IFOR) fell from 60,000 after the Dayton Peace Agreement in December 1995 to 32,000 at the transition to the Stabilisation Force (SFOR). By January 2003 this had decreased to 12,000. In December 2004, the EU had taken over the 'peace mission', a deadline which meant the Grenadiers, who had deployed as a Battalion in September 2004, commanded by Lieutenant Colonel David Russell-Parsons, served under both a NATO and an EU banner.

Russell-Parsons remarked, "The Battalion was motivated by the prospect of six months away from Victoria Barracks. The mission was reasonably straightforward as, unlike Kosovo, there was little potential of the warring factions returning to conflict. But it was our first time in the Balkans as a Battalion, it was winter in a large area of responsibility. The Battalion needed to demonstrate presence, discipline and energy to provide deterrence."

As Russell-Parsons was also to comment presciently, "It was very apparent that Dayton was a ceasefire agreement and not an arrangement for permanent stability."

As the only multi-national battle group in the NATO-led Stabilisation Force (SFOR) in the north-west (NATO divided Bosnia into three regions), the Grenadiers had a Dutch rifle company and a Bulgarian platoon under command. The role given to the Grenadiers by the brigade commander of Multi-National Task Force (North-West) was couched in predictably dry military language: "to conduct recce, manoeuvre and information operations across the Area of Operations". The reality was somewhat different. The Battalion was there to provide a robust military presence and to aid the capture of war criminals. This was a sensitive and challenging task and, once again, played to the Battalion's flexibility and dependable junior leadership and initiative.

The Battalion's main operating base at Banja Luka was the core of all the Multi-National Task Force (North-West) intelligence, logistics and administration. The Italian Carabinieri, the Romanian aviation assets, the Canadian liaison and observation teams, Czechs, Austrians, New Zealanders, and Dutch all came to recognise, in the words of one Carabinieri Colonel, "*La disciplina non detta e calma efficienza delle Guardie Britanniche*" (the unspoken discipline and calm efficiency of the Guards).

In late January 2005, the temperature was -21°C. The country came to a halt and only the few BV 206 Winter tracked vehicles had any chance of getting through to the remote communities. It was just as well. Major Ben Hancock, one of the Battalion's company commanders, recalled: "There were not many people to whom we talked who said the war was over. They told us only that the war had been stopped by NATO. Therein lay a subtle difference."

Something which did make a marked difference, however, was the introduction of the liaison and observation teams. It was a concept not unlike the building of watchtowers in Northern Ireland, the use of which did so much to improve security in South Armagh's murderous bandit country. Teams of eight to ten soldiers served as the eyes and ears on the ground, a matrix of contacts embedded with the local community. Major Carew Hatherley, now the Battalion's Senior Major (second-in-command) said: "It was one of the best things I saw in the Balkans and I suspect one of the reasons why operations have been relatively successful."

The liaison and observation team commander in Bosanka Gradiska, a Serbian enclave and site of one of the notorious Ustaše camps in the Second World War, was Captain Simon Gordon Lennox: "Organised crime and smuggling were the main focus. The local hood, shaved head, thick set, blinged up, perennial dark glasses, and straight out of Central Casting with his gangster's moll at his side, would frequently invite us for a free night in his nightclub, offering to look after our Browning 9mm pistols with only the very best 'Slivo' to drink. We never took up the offer."

The poignant reflections of Major Ben Hancock convey something of the region's more harrowing challenges: "We had several war graves commission sites in my AO [area of operations]. We drove up to a scene straight out of Hamlet. The smell engulfed your senses. It was wretchedly intoxicating. I went forward to greet the international community who were pulling small bones of children out of the ground. An experience I will never forget."

The different approach taken by the other multi-national battalions was also an experience which Hancock took to heart:

> I think the biggest challenge we faced was our Grenadier approach versus the approach taken by the other multi-nationals. Their approach was too touchy-feely for our liking. They felt that they were there purely to make friends, civil-military co-operation, handing out sweets, delivering the latest newsletters to the civilian population. This may have helped the transition from SFOR to EUFOR [European Union Force] but I question their deterrent value.

This approach by other multi-national troops was surprising given the experience of Srebrenica where a Dutch battalion allowed 8,000 unarmed Muslim men and boys to be murdered, a sickening stain on the conscience of the international community and the UN; it is hard not to sympathise with Hancock's views.

Lieutenant Colonel Russell-Parsons summarised his Battalion's tour:

> The basic skills were search and surveillance but in the latter stages of the Battalion's tour the focus was on fighting organised crime, fuel smuggling and illegal logging. Our large and experienced intelligence cell could not make up for the lack of national assets and intelligence from Sarajevo HQ. The endemic gun culture and unstable ordnance and ammunition all over the region meant we did not have operational flexibility. We needed bomb disposal and Royal Engineer expertise. And the numerous low level guards we were asked to provide was not the best use of well-trained, search-aware, public-order capable soldiers. Still it gave us an excellent foundation for the operational challenges in Iraq less than 12 months later.

On 28 March 2007, Adam Ingram, the Labour Minister of State for the Armed Forces, awarded the Balkans campaign medal to the Welsh Guards at a parade in Wellington Barracks. He simply remarked that the parade "marks the end of the era".

The Welsh Guards, commanded by Lieutenant Colonel Richard Stanford, had deployed in late autumn of 2006 to carry out reconstruction work in the Balkans under the command of EUFOR. It was a largely uneventful tour though rewarding enough as it allowed the Battalion to work alongside a detachment from Chile and a Dutch company, the "Princess Irene Guards", who had fought alongside the Welsh Guards in 1944–45.

No 2 Company under Major Rupert Pim was under NATO command in Kosovo as the Force Surveillance Company with a Swedish platoon attached. Like the Grenadiers, they were kept busy tracking down criminals and war criminals. The Balkans conflict had, for the time being, come to an end. A 15-year commitment by the British Army had cost 55 lives, but probably a great deal more in the minds and mental wellbeing of soldiers who had often witnessed unspeakable savagery.

Ingram insisted at the medals parade that "this is not a cut and run job but a job well done". He knew then that another era was about to begin: an era that was to test the British Army's courage and resilience to its limit, and which was to cost a great deal more lives. It was a period which Ingram's immediate boss at the Ministry of Defence, John Reid, famously said "would probably last for three years without a shot being fired."

The challenges and demands that the Household Division faced in the Balkans seemed exceptional at the time. But there was very little combat in either Bosnia or Kosovo. Household Division regiments that entered Iraq and Afghanistan could look back on almost a quarter of a century of successes from Northern Ireland, Zimbabwe, the Falklands campaign, Op *Desert Storm*, and the Balkans conflict. A degree of overconfidence crept in.

When the Household Division in Iraq and Afghanistan found itself fighting against enemies who rejected Western values and were prepared to stand, fight and die, the shock to the Household Division and Army as a whole was profound. And it was also the first time that public opinion was not wholly with them.

How the Household Division learned and adapted to a new reality owed a great deal to battlefield discipline, the foundations of which lay in its mastery of ceremonial.

The turn of the 21st century had begun in the Balkans with what seemed a simple mandate for the Balkan countries: defeat corruption and organised crime and enter the EU. Bulgaria, Romania, and Croatia passed the test and joined the EU as well as NATO. The other players in the murderous theatre of the Balkan vortex, Albania, Serbia, Montenegro, Kosovo, Bosnia and Herzegovina, North Macedonia, remain EU candidate countries.

The Balkans remains unfinished business. It will come as no surprise if a regiment from the Household Division once again finds itself holding the line in a region weighed down by its history.

10

Iraq and Afghanistan, 2003–21: A Strategic and Political Failure?

It became pretty clear that the Army in Iraq and Afghanistan was over committed. There was confusion over effort.
LIEUTENANT GENERAL SIR BILL ROLLO, GENERAL
OFFICER COMMANDING MULTI-NATIONAL DIVISION
(SOUTH-EAST) IRAQ

It was a slate-grey day at RAF Lyneham and damp underfoot from the previous night's rain. The Major General Commanding the Household Division, Bill Cubitt, was attending the repatriation of the body of Guardsman Neil 'Tony' Downes, Grenadier Guards. Guardsman Downes had died of his injuries sustained in an explosion in Helmand Province, Afghanistan on 9 June. It was General Bill's first repatriation since he had taken up the post as the Major General earlier that month. He was to be present at many more repatriations, not only to receive back members of the Household Division killed in action, but also as the Chief of the General Staff's representative. The Household Division was the only formation in the British Army whose fallen were received back by 'their General'.

There was a break in the clouds and some ten miles away General Bill could see the C-17 and its slow descent towards the runaway. He glanced at the family of Guardsman Downes and the bearer party chosen from Downes' Regimental friends. General Bill could not help but feel a strong sense of pride and sadness in equal measure. A senior Royal Air Force officer was later to remark to General Bill, "The Guards do this the best."

Iraq and Afghanistan have been the defining experience of the Household Division this century. It took part in seven operational tours of Iraq (Op *Telic*) and 24 operational tours of Afghanistan (Op *Herrick*). The Roll of Honour records the names of 46 Guardsmen killed in action in Afghanistan alone. But that stark statistic, grim as it is, does not bear witness to the countless others who suffered life-changing and life-long injuries. Few who served in Iraq and Afghanistan were to escape its emotional impact. Afghanistan, in particular, was a ferocious campaign.

The campaigns in Iraq and Afghanistan were in stark contrast to the British Army's experience in Northern Ireland, the Falklands and the Balkans. It would be unjust to say that complacency had set in. But after its successes there the Army felt at ease with itself, particularly in the higher levels of command. And that was to prove an uncomfortable feeling as it found itself facing an enemy who saw death through a different prism. As Corporal of Horse Michael 'Mick' Flynn CGC, MC from The Blues and Royals remarked after a failed operation in 2006 to relieve the garrison at Musa Qal'ah, "That's the thing about the Taliban – they stand and fight, they just don't know when to give up."

This was a sentiment and a predicament shared by Regimental Sergeant Major D. Bailey of the 1st Battalion Grenadier Guards. In 2010, Bailey was a platoon sergeant on Op *Herrick* 11. As he looked back on that time, he remarked, "It was a profound cultural change in the face of terrorism of a different nature from NI. We really had to switch on. The IRA would shoot and scoot, the lot we were up against would stand and fight."

The bleak conclusion is that the Taliban were not defeated. They overcame the Afghan government, the US and its allies where the British contribution was second only to the US. A senior British officer remarked at the fall of Kabul in August 2021 that "The British Army was never beaten tactically", to which the Taliban response was simply, "That is not relevant". The Army may not have been defeated in Iraq and Afghanistan but no one emerged with much credit except the soldiers who fought bravely in often desperate circumstances.

Against this salutary background, the Army and the Household Division in particular can draw comfort from the way they conducted themselves in a brutal and unforgiving environment which placed great physical and mental strain on soldiers and their officers.

Lieutenant Colonel Roly Walker, who commanded the Grenadiers on Op *Herrick* 11, was later to praise the Household Division's 'courageous restraint' in Afghanistan. The term 'courageous restraint' was the name given to the change of strategy in Afghanistan in 2009 by US General Stanley McChrystal, who was Commander US and ISAF (International Security Assistance Force) in Afghanistan. Nevertheless, it was a strategy that played to the Household Division's innate strengths and battlefield discipline.

One hundred and seven operational honours and awards bear witness to the Household Division's courage and resilience in Afghanistan alone. This does not account for the awards given to those Household Division officers and soldiers who served with Special Forces whose exploits remain hidden. 'Courageous restraint' does seem, in hindsight, a fair observation as later chapters will reveal, particularly when overwhelming firepower was available and scant regard was given by some Army units to collateral damage.

An enormous amount has now been written about Iraq and Afghanistan. The indescribable horrors of the Great War were expressed through poetry. The truth was too unpalatable through any other medium. Articles in the *Guards Magazine* and regimental journals such as 'Grenadier Guards, An Account of Operations 1996–2015', or the Coldstream's '10 Years in Afghanistan' are factual and accurate reflections of what took place.

Many interviews have taken place and most face to face. This is less true of other chapters but memories of Iraq and Afghanistan remain remarkably fresh. They are footprints in the sand that will never wash away.

The chapters covering Iraq and Afghanistan are seamless in the sense that the two campaigns were indivisible. The two campaigns had a cause-and-effect relationship. But they do not pretend to cover all the Household Division's operational tours in Iraq and Afghanistan. Some, like Op *Telic* 1, the invasion of Iraq in March 2003, and Op *Herrick* 10,

11, 12, and 13, including Op *Panther's Claw* in 2009, witnessed some of the bloodiest fighting and are covered in greater detail than others. Not that any Guardsman serving on Op *Herrick* 6 or Op *Herrick* 18 would have noted any difference in the need for professionalism. It was always a relentless campaign against a resolute enemy.

No one who was alive and old enough on 11 September 2001 will ever forget the haunting images of the two Al Qaeda hijacked Boeing 767s smashing into the twin towers in New York's Lower Manhattan from a clear blue sky within minutes of each other.

It was the greatest strategic shock to the US since the 'Day of Infamy' in December 1941 when the Japanese struck Pearl Harbor. Unlike the twin towers attack, Pearl Harbor led to a clarity of thinking between the Western leaders, notably Roosevelt and Churchill. After 9/11, no one seemed to be able to think straight. In that sense, 9/11 was a more profound strategic shock.

Major General Reddy Watt, who was at the time commanding the Household Division, heard the news driving back from Colchester where he had been visiting the Guards Parachute Platoon attached to 3 Para. He knew things would change, but if he had been told then that a decade later Household Division regiments would have completed 22 operational tours of Iraq and Afghanistan, he would have been more than taken aback.

Churchill once wrote, "Study history, study history, in history lies all the secrets of Statecraft." Churchill was right. We had been in Afghanistan before. The British Army had been involved in Afghanistan three times in the 19th and 20th centuries, and on each occasion, the Army came away the lesser for it, and often badly bloodied.

After the 9/11 attacks, the US launched a remarkably swift and effective campaign between October and December 2001 which removed the Taliban at a stroke. It was an audacious operation in which the British government and the Armed Forces and intelligence services played no small part. What was missing, however, was a resolute follow-up. And this failure was to cost the West dearly. The US policy was determined to have a 'light footprint'.

But Afghanistan was no place for a light footprint. Taliban and Al Qaeda fighters were allowed to spirit away into Pakistan. A strong force of US Rangers or Marines would have sealed off the escape routes from the mountainous Tora Bora region into Pakistan, but this was turned down by the US Secretary of State for Defence, Donald Rumsfeld. Bin Laden was allowed to escape. The Taliban bided their time aided by sympathisers in Pakistan. They were to return with a vengeance in 2006.

British troops returned to Afghanistan in December 2001. This was a result of the Bonn Agreement to send a UN-mandated force, the International Security Assistance Force (ISAF), to maintain security in Kabul. Prime Minister Blair jumped at the chance and sent 16th Air Assault Brigade commanded by Brigadier Barney White-Spunner, The Blues and Royals, with a number of Household Division officers on his staff. They restored order to Kabul, Afghanistan's capital, and shored up the new government headed by President Hamid Karzai. But the US and the UK soon had little appetite for ISAF expansion in Afghanistan. Eyes had turned towards Iraq and the Weapons of Mass Destruction (WMD). The false mirage of WMD was to prove a reckoning for the British Army and lesson in the dangers of political vacillation.

Op *Cobra* II was the name US commanders gave the operation to depose Saddam Hussein's regime in Iraq. The attack was launched on 19 March 2003. Just a few hours before the attack, US Central Command received a letter from the British contingent earmarked for the invasion that London was unsure if the invasion was legal. The government bowed to US pressure.

At the last moment, the UK government committed British troops, the headquarters of 1st Armoured Division and three brigades: 3 Commando Brigade, 7th Armoured Brigade, including armoured infantry companies from the Irish Guards, and 16th Air Assault Brigade which had the Household Cavalry Regiment under command. Op *Telic* was the codename under which all the UK's military operations were conducted from the invasion's outset until the withdrawal of the last remaining British Forces in May 2011.

The legacy of Iraq was mixed and salutary, but what is certain is that every regiment in the Household Division played a full part in a complex and politically controversial campaign. There was an undeniable naivety in the British Army about what would happen next after the warfighting phase had come to an end. But that was hardly the

Army's fault. The campaign was poorly conceived from the beginning and the follow-up by the politicians even more of a mess. *The Times* newspaper did not pull its punches in a Leader article on 20 March, 2023 – the Iraq War's 20th anniversary: "The Iraq war was a disaster for Iraq, the Middle East and the world. Its consequences reverberate still."

For the Household Division, however, Op *Telic* was to provide vital lessons in all arms co-operation, an experience which was to stand every Household Division regiment in good stead when faced with the greater trials of Afghanistan.

By early 2003, the invasion of Iraq was imminent. Personnel and *matériel* were moved to the Gulf much more quickly than in the First Gulf War. The eventual British ground contribution was around 30,000 troops: 1st Armoured Division comprising 7th Armoured Brigade, 16th Air Assault Brigade and 3 Commando Brigade. The Irish Guards were part of 7th Armoured Brigade and D Squadron The Household Cavalry Regiment in 16th Air Assault Brigade. Troops were moved to their assembly areas in northern Kuwait, a flat landscape of greyish desert. There was a sense of urgency to get started. To delay until the fierce summer heat was to court trouble.

The 1st Battalion Irish Guards and D Squadron The Household Cavalry Regiment fought from the outset. The invasion of Iraq began on 23 March 2003. Their training in Kuwait had been exemplary and for the first time most of the officers, Guardsmen and Troopers became confident working with engineers, artillery, air power, logistics, everything that made up an integrated battle group.

Audrey Gillan was a journalist from the *Guardian* attached to D Squadron The Household Cavalry Regiment on the invasion of Iraq in late March 2003. She had expected to be sent to other regiments in 16th Air Assault Brigade but not, as she wrote, "to the oldest and most traditional Regiment in the British Army." She was quickly put at her ease when she met Major Richard Taylor, The Life Guards, who commanded D Squadron. Taylor said, "We live together, sleep, and do everything any person has to do on operations together, do you think you can handle it?"

Corporal of Horse Mick Flynn was equally down to earth in his advice, "Ma'am you need to scale down your kit." Gillan was always conscious of what she called her "admin vortex".

Audrey Gillan's articles in the *Guardian* were frank and striking in their honesty but full of admiration for the way D Squadron conducted itself and the respect and courtesy with which she was treated. "Don't worry, I'll never, ever leave you," remarked the commander of her Spartan vehicle 33a. Two members of the Parachute Regiment who tried to take compromising photographs of Gillan were given short shrift by Household Cavalry Troopers.

The invasion of Iraq which began on 20 March 2003 was initially, like that of Afghanistan in 2001, a triumph. Major Taylor said, "At the end of the fighting we were euphoric, we had fulfilled the doctrinal dream of reconnaissance deep strike. We also assumed the 'what next' was in the capable hands of our politicians and diplomats, we were a little wide-eyed I suppose."

The Household Cavalry's performance in Iraq and later in Afghanistan was a testament to the link between mounted ceremonial duties, equitation training, and battlefield discipline. Major Richard Taylor, who commanded D Squadron on Op *Telic* 1 and won the Distinguished Service Order for his leadership, and Colonel Harry Fullerton and Colonel Jim Eyre, who commanded the Household Cavalry in Afghanistan, were as one:

> Most Household Cavalry soldiers start their careers at mounted duty in London, its hard graft teaching them the link between personal and battlefield discipline, how to practice, rehearse and execute drills, the bond between horse and soldier, it's an outstanding apprenticeship which stands them in good stead when they convert to Armoured Reconnaissance. The army knew all this in 19th century soldiering but it's only The Household Cavalry and Royal Horse Artillery who carry on this invaluable tradition. Part of our collective or institutional memory if you like.

Major Richard Taylor went on, "I also felt it helped with the concept of 'Mission Command', the decentralisation of orders to exploit individual initiative, flexibility and judgement. At one stage, D Squadron had a frontage of 45km [28 miles] and we were 70km [43½ miles] from the forward edge of the main battle group. Mutual trust is at the heart of that."

D Squadron's performance on Op *Telic* 1 bore this out. The atmosphere in D Squadron attached to the 1st Battalion The Parachute Regiment Battle Group was electric. Their task was deep strike reconnaissance for 16th Air Assault Brigade. The Brigade's task was to interdict Highway 6, Basra to Baghdad along the Shatt-al-Arab river at the confluence of the great rivers of Tigris and Euphrates. Its more exotic name was the Garden of Eden. Denying Iraqi control of the Rumailah oilfields was a secondary but important objective. Such was their rate of advance that the media thought they were just north of Basra at the airport. D Squadron did three years' UK track mileage in the blink of an eye.

It was exhilarating stuff but courage and tragedy sat side by side. D Squadron lost three soldiers through a blue-on-blue (friendly fire) incident killing Lance Corporal of Horse Matty Hull, and an accident when a CVR(T) overturned in a ditch killing Lieutenant Alexander Tweedie and Lance Corporal Karl Shearer.

Corporal of Horse Mick Flynn was awarded the Conspicuous Gallantry Cross for fighting while outgunned and outnumbered by Iraqi tanks when helping the wounded to safety after the blue-on-blue incident. Trooper Chris Finney was awarded the George Cross for his bravery and for his devotion to his colleagues in the same action.

Lance Corporal of Horse Jonathan Woodgate, just 19, who was the vehicle driver, also displayed great composure. His driver's hatch was jammed as he struggled to free himself, as the Scimitar had been opened up like a tin can by the American A-10 tank-busting aircraft. He was to serve again on Op *Herrick* 4. He was killed in action by an insurgent grenade in March 2010 on Op *Herrick* 11. Ironically, he was on foot patrol.

D Squadron of just 105 men won more medals than any other unit in the British Army of comparable size who fought in Iraq. The Household Cavalry, like their colleagues in the Falklands campaign, were never ones to put forward their claims. It is not the Household Division way. But the evidence of their professionalism was only too clear to see. And it was to be repeated with interest in the Afghanistan campaign.

Major Richard Taylor, despite the losses from friendly fire and the vehicle accident, remarked on leaving Iraq, "I am convinced that the Iraqi people face a better future now than they did when we first deployed." This was not naivety on his behalf, merely optimism born out of what had been a successful operation.

The Irish Guards had made their name in Kosovo in 1999 under Lieutenant Colonel Bill Cubitt. Their exemplary record continued under Lieutenant Colonel James Stopford who handed over command to Lieutenant Colonel Charlie Knaggs on the cusp of the Iraq War and the Battle of Basra.

The Battalion's role, as part of 7th Armoured Brigade, was to support the Scots Dragoon Guards, and the Black Watch Battle Groups. No 2 Company under Ben Farrell, equipped with the Warrior armoured vehicle, soon found themselves in the thick of it. Their role was to deny the enemy the chance to reinforce Basra, 7th Armoured Brigade's objective, from the north. They came under harassing fire from an Iraqi bunker on their eastern flank. A successful assault by Second Lieutenant The Hon Tom Orde-Powlett and Sergeant Perry saw off the threat. It was the Micks at their best. Orde-Powlett was awarded the Military Cross.

Any number of actions and skirmishes took place as well as coordinated attacks into Basra to seize and hold key ground. Nothing was as it seemed, the enemy often invisible springing from nowhere in civilian clothes with bravery bordering on madness. One Fedayeen played dead, then leapt up hurtling grenades only to be 'neutralised' by a high-explosive round from a Challenger 2 tank.

One Fedayeen fighter, however, got through, killing Lance Corporal Malone and Piper Muzvuru. Brigadier Bill Cubitt attended the funeral of Lance Corporal Malone in Dublin in late April. He was later to write, "The funeral, attended by 1500, gave tacit recognition to Irishmen serving now and earlier in the British Army. His [Malone's] death and turnout demonstrated to his family and friends the romance of the Regiment."

On 7 April, Basra fell to British Forces. Major Farrell witnessed the joy on the children's faces. "It was just a matter of unweaving Saddam's intricate web," he was later to write. But it wasn't long before the web became infinitely more complex and one which the British Army found far from easy to unravel.

———

The campaign had been an undeniable success. But no one had thought through what was to happen next. War turned into an insurgency and, inevitably, with so many warring parties of varying ethnicities and religions, this soon became a civil war. The optimism from the first Iraqi elections in 2005 was short-lived. The US-led Coalition was unable to suppress the sectarian conflict between the Shia and Sunni. The Coalition's transition strategy, 'As the Iraqis stand up, we will stand down', did not stand up to serious scrutiny.

Op *Telic* 5 saw 1st Battalion Welsh Guards deployed from November 2004 to the end of April 2005. 1st Battalion Scots Guards also deployed. Both were under the command of 4th Armoured Brigade whose history was so closely linked to the Household Division. 1st Battalion Coldstream Guards, under 12th Mechanised Brigade, were deployed on Op *Telic* 6 from end of April 2005 to end of October 2005. 1st Battalion Grenadier Guards, under 20th Armoured Brigade, deployed on Op *Telic* 8 from May 2006 to November 2006. Once again, there was a strong Household Division presence at a senior level: the Deputy Commanding General Multi-National Force, Iraq was Lieutenant General John Kiszely, formerly Scots Guards; the General Officer Commanding Multi-National Division (South-East) was Major General Bill Rollo, formerly the Household Cavalry Regiment.

General Bill Rollo, who was General Officer Commanding Multi-National Division (South-East), summed up the situation in Iraq from 2005 onwards:

> The position in Basra became steadily more difficult from 2005 onwards as force levels were reduced in favour of Afghanistan despite declining security across the whole of Southern Iraq. There was a significant Household Division presence at every level from Baghdad to Basra. The UK Special Forces contribution was well regarded by the US but that was about it as the unsatisfactory nature of the campaign became more apparent.

The campaign was becoming increasingly unpopular in the UK. The British government agreed in January 2006 that Iraq was the top priority, but then it announced plans to increase the UK's role in Afghanistan.

The Army was now involved in two wars.

The Welsh Guards arrived in Iraq in early 2005 in Maysan Province, north of Basra, at the height of Iraq's descent into chaos. President Bush's statement on 1 May 2003 on board the USS *Abraham Lincoln*, "Mission Accomplished", could not have been further from the truth.

The US had made a number of strategic, operational, and tactical errors after the fall of Saddam. The most significant of these was the disbanding of the Iraqi Army and the hollowing-out of those institutions which could help the country get back on its feet. The West forgot the lessons from the aftermath of the Second World War where it learned to hold its nose and use mid-level former Nazis to assist in Germany's reconstruction.

The fall of Saddam had created a vacuum and strengthened Shia militias, Sunni insurgents, and Al Qaeda in Iraq. Photographs of US mistreatment of prisoners in Abu Ghraib inflicted a near-fatal blow to the perception of the legitimacy of the US presence.

The Shia militia group, the Jaysh al-Mahdi Army, was particularly deadly. It was a major destabilising force in Iraq. The Princess of Wales's Royal Regiment Battle Group who handed over to the Welsh Guards had fired more ammunition in six months crushing Jaysh al-Mahdi Army-inspired uprisings than the whole of 1st Armoured Division in the warfighting phase.

Lieutenant Colonel Ben Bathurst, commanding the Welsh Guards, took a calm and level-headed approach to the situation in which his Battalion found itself. He saw that, with the Jaysh al-Mahdi Army on the back foot though still capable of great brutality, a change of approach was possible. The Battalion helped to ensure that the democratic and provincial elections were held without fear or favour in January 2005.

More importantly, Colonel Ben played to the strengths of Welsh Guardsmen and their natural humour and good nature to reinvigorate reconstruction projects. Some 19,000 reconstruction jobs were created by the end of the tour. He also recognised that a more positive, conciliatory approach should not be mistaken for weakness. The Battalion kept the pressure up on the insurgents. Based in Camp Abu Naji, and reinforced by Left and Right Flank of the Scots Guards, they numbered over 1,000 men.

The murder of six Royal Military Policemen in late June 2003 was uppermost in Colonel Ben's mind. It had horrified the nation and the Army. The Jaysh al-Mahdi Army had to be crushed or a least rendered toothless. But an assault on the town would invite bloodshed and a loss of initiative. Bathurst decided on a more reasoned approach. His strategy involved a handful of carrots and the suggestion of overwhelming force.

The carrots took the form of reconstruction projects, generators and water purifying units in the smaller towns around Majar al-Kabir.

The local sheikhs took notice and demanded the same support for the town. The Welsh Guards delivered what was needed, backed up in plain sight by four Challenger 2 tanks, 48 Warrior armoured vehicles, mortars, and three helicopters overhead. The town ceased to be a no-go area.

It had been a successful tour. Once again, a Guards battalion proved that a strategy of firmness couched with gentleness and courtesy to the local community was the right approach. And the fact that it did so against a backdrop of growing public dismay back in the UK and a murderous Sunni–Shia civil war was testament to the Household Division's adaptability, born out of both ceremonial and operational excellence.

After the successful invasion of 2003, Britain had offered to take responsibility for Basra city and the four southern provinces. This had included Maysan where the Welsh Guards distinguished itself in 2005. But it had become apparent for some time that there was inadequate British strategic leadership of post-conflict operations. The teaching of counter-insurgency operations at the Staff College had been stopped in the late 1990s in favour of peace support operations.

At a resource level, the Ministry of Defence were unable to deploy enough armoured vehicles with adequate protection against IEDs until the Mastiff vehicle entered service in 2006.

At a human level, the abuse of detainees and the killing of one, Baha Mousa, by the Queen's Lancashire Regiment, was a self-inflicted wound on British legitimacy.

"Well, it was pretty clear to me that we had a strategy that involved extraction rather than achieving mission success. It was, in a sense an exit strategy rather than a winning strategy. And a decision had now been taken to open up a second front in Afghanistan before the situation in Iraq was satisfactorily resolved." These words by Major General Richard Shirreff, the British overall commander of Multi-National Division (South-East) in Iraq in 2006, formed the rather bleak backdrop in which the Grenadier Guards found themselves on Op *Telic* 8 from May to October 2006.

The announcement that they were going to Iraq was met, however, with overwhelming enthusiasm by the Grenadiers. There was some disquiet over their role as Rear Operations Battle Group. This was not the first, or last time, that a Guards Battalion fell into the playbook of senior commanders whose memories of Sandhurst, pageantry, Trooping the Colour and immaculate colour sergeants, led them to believe that Guardsmen were the lesser soldiers for it. Rear ops, manning detention facilities, or providing operational mentoring and liaison teams – known as 'OMLTs' – were, they thought, the Guards' obvious role.

They were to be proven wrong in both Iraq and Afghanistan. Certainly by 2009, the Household Division had built up a good deal of experience at every level. The performance of Household Division battalions during the critical and bloody period of 2009–12 was exemplary. Commanding officers were of a high calibre, tempered by their experience as platoon and company commanders in the early 2000s. The same was true of the senior non-commissioned officers.

As a result, the Battalion's deployment under Lieutenant Colonel David Russell-Parsons involved a myriad of disparate tasks across the US Army's Central Zone which included Baghdad: the protection of Shaibah airfield in Basra; a Baghdad Escort and Protection Force; badly needed reinforcements for Basra; the mentoring of Iraqi Army units; protecting logistics convoys; and supporting the Queen's Royal Hussars Battle Group in Maysan Province. Colonel David remarked, "We were very conscious that Basra was key. It required significant reinforcements. It needed the four extra very large companies we could provide as well as the Battalion command functions and logistics. We were ready to show our mettle, but we were spread too far and wide." There were in effect just 200 soldiers on the ground in Basra, a city of 1.3 million. In West Belfast in the 1970s, there had been a full brigade.

There was some frustration. Apart from the protection of Shaibah airfield at Basra, the Queen's Company, under the Second Captain, Simon-Gordon Lennox, had the task of Baghdad Escort and Protection, extended to protection of the senior military representative in Baghdad, providing a one-star 'taxi' service to visiting UK dignitaries (any number wanting to be seen doing their "bit") as well as a Quick Reaction Force.

The Inkerman Company, under Major Sebastian Wade, fared no better. They were tasked with the Divisional Temporary Detention Facility at Shaibah Logistic Base. This attracted a memorable altercation at the House of Commons Defence Committee where the Chairman said, "The idea that it should be the Grenadier Guards looking after these detainees as opposed to the Military Provost Staff does not answer my question as to who is coping with the levels of violence."

But amongst these somewhat monotonous tasks, there were enough incidents of extreme danger. One such attack was the sustained mortar attack on Camp Abu Naji in July 2006. Fourteen 120mm rounds landed in as many minutes. One Grenadier was severely wounded. Four Guardsmen in 50°C heat rescued their colleague despite another barrage of mortar bombs. The four Guardsmen all received Commendations. What was tragic, however, was that two of those brave Guardsmen, Guardsmen Probyn and Greenhalgh, were later killed in action in Afghanistan on Op *Herrick* 6 and Op *Herrick* 11.

Battalion Headquarters and Support Company returned to the UK in August 2006 to begin training for Op *Herrick* 6. The Queen's Company and Inkerman Company remained in Iraq until September.

In an effort to reclaim Basra from militia control, 1,000 soldiers from 3rd UK Division under Major General Richard Shirreff with 2,300 Iraqi Army troops took part in Op *Sinbad* from late September 2006 to early 2007. It had some local success but the operation was insufficiently resourced. There were just not enough British troops and Iraqi troops did not want to be seen working too closely with the Army for fear of militia reprisals. By late 2007, Basra Palace had effectively been ceded to the Iraqis as had Shat al Arab earlier that year. The British Army had more or less lost control of Basra.

Op *Zenith* became the Army's new plan for the predicament of Basra. The intention was to reduce British forces to a presence at the airport. The Army needed the troops in Afghanistan. It was against this background that the Irish Guards found themselves on Op *Telic* 10 from June 2007 to December 2007 under 1st Mechanised Brigade. With Basra no longer in the Army's control, the Irish Guards tour, through no fault of their own, began in absolute disarray. In essence, they were to become a Security Force Assistance Battalion. There was no proper base, no operations room, no clearly defined task.

The two halves of the Irish Guards tour in 2007 under 1st Mechanised Brigade could not therefore have been more stark. They arrived under the command of Lieutenant Colonel Michael O'Dwyer amidst a cycle of violence and constant battle in downtown Basra. Two squadrons from the Household Cavalry Regiment also deployed on the tour. The Battalion was split up to support the Contingency Operating Base and one of the manoeuvre battle groups, 4th Battalion The Rifles, commanded by Lieutenant Colonel Patrick Sanders, a former Chief of the General Staff. One of the sub-units allocated to 4th Battalion The Rifles which performed with great gallantry was No 1 Company, commanded by Major Fabian Roberts.

The levels of violence took their toll. The summer of 2007 had seen the highest levels of casualties from enemy action during the entire Iraq campaign. Three soldiers from the Royal Engineers attached to the Battalion lost their lives to roadside bombs. Towards the end of the first half of the tour, Lance Sergeant Casey and Lance Corporal Redpath were killed after their vehicle was struck by an IED. After the most moving of repatriation ceremonies, conducted by the Battalion's outstanding Padre, Father Nick Gosnell, the Battalion picked themselves up, determined to press on.

At the beginning of September 2007, the Brigade had handed back Basra Palace to the Iraqis and reached a controversial accommodation with the militia. This at least broke the level of violence. All this, however, was to consolidate the Shia militia takeover of the city. It was a moral and military failure for the Army from which, in the eyes of the US, the Army never quite recovered. The Irish Guards' focus had become the mentoring and training of the Iraqi Army. It was quite a climb down for the Army but the new Prime Minister, Gordon Brown, wanted to end the Army's presence by December 2008.

No 2 Company, under Major Christopher Ghika, who had joined the Company in Baghdad where it spent close to four months located in the International Zone (the 'Green Zone'), demonstrated the typical flexibility required of the Battalion during Op *Telic* 10: it provided protection to the Baghdad Support Unit; force protection to logistic convoys running the gauntlet on Route Irish from the Green Zone to the airport while wearing Osprey body-armour in 45°C heat; vehicle close protection to the endless stream of VIP visitors; and the provision of attachments to the American training teams in Baghdad. At least, off duty, they could take advantage of Uncle Sam's facilities, never knowingly understocked, and equipped with a sizeable swimming pool where the surreal sound of detonating car bombs sharpened the senses.

In April 2008, Lieutenant Colonel Ben Farrell took over as commanding officer, with the Battalion assuming the role of the UK's high readiness reserve battalion. A year later, it would, once again, demonstrate the link between ceremonial excellence and operational effectiveness. The summer of 2009 would see the Battalion being Presented with New Colours and the Troop of the New Colours on the Queen's Birthday Parade, prior to an exercise in Kenya and the frisson of a tour in Afghanistan.

All was not quite over, however, in Basra. There was still a determination to clear Basra of the militias. The operation, beginning on the morning of 25 March 2008, was called *Charge of the Knights*, more commonly known as the Battle of Basra. It took place during Op *Telic* 11. 1st Battalion Scots Guards deployed on Op *Telic* 11 under 4th Mechanised Brigade, which in turn came under the command of the General Officer Commanding Multi-National Division (South-East), Barney White-Spunner, an experienced Household Cavalry officer. Its principal role in Iraq was to guard the 16-mile perimeter fence at the Contingency Operating Base at Basra now under Iraqi control since the much-discredited accommodation brokered between the Jaysh al-Mahdi Army, the principal Shia militant group, and Multi-National Division (South-East). As Colonel Swinton, commanding the Battalion, remarked, "It all feels uncomfortable as we learn our new place, yet we are still attacked at every opportunity." Guardsman G. Boyd was a little more sanguine: "things didn't go quite to plan as things developed in MND(SE) [Multi-National Division South-East], a lot of indirect fire attacks as we carried out our tasks, mainly security for reconstruction."

The operation gave rise to bitter Iraqi accusations that the Army was not up to it. Senior British officers were on leave and despite aggressive and courageous raids by the Warrior armoured vehicles of the Scots Guards into Basra in support of the Iraqis, the British military reputation with the US and Iraqis was, once again, seriously dented.

It would be fair to say that by the end of Op *Telic* 10 the British Army had lost its way in Iraq and were marginalised. Colonel Jeremy Bagshaw, Coldstream Guards, a highly capable and experienced officer who retired in 2023 as Chief of Staff, London District, and was second-in-command to the Irish Guards on *Telic* 10, saw the tour as the low point in an otherwise fulfilling career: "As an Army that prided itself on counter-insurgency operations, I felt we had lost our way; adherence to our own principles of counter-insurgency were seemingly a victim of strategic overstretch which had left the operation with neither the resource nor will to win."

Op *Telic* finally ended in April 2009 with Op *Telic* 12. Many serving and retired British officers consider the failure of British military strategy in Iraq to be a national disgrace. Between 2003 and 2009, the British government failed to produce an integrated political and military strategy for southern Iraq.

This lack of direction had a serious impact on the other major focus of the British Army's operations, as a campaign study of Op *Herrick* published in 2013 said: "There was a poor strategic intelligence picture of Afghanistan at the outset. There was too much wasted effort in Iraq and too little attention had been paid to the growing Taliban threat whilst Op *Telic* in Iraq continued in parallel. We did not know enough about the Taliban."

If there was anything positive to be drawn from the Army's experience in Iraq, it was that the Army finally learnt to adapt to a new reality of fighting against a determined insurgency. The performance of the Household Division in Afghanistan, particularly during the critical years 2009–12, was courageous and admirable.

11

Afghanistan: Operation *Herrick*, 2006–14

*There was individual heroism of course but what we did over there
was to be utterly professional rather than perform than heroic deeds.
Many of our operations were anti-climactic because the insurgents
were not prepared to fight. You see the real skill was to outwit and
outmanoeuvre the Taliban so they can't fight. We conducted ourselves
with 'Courageous restraint'.*

LIEUTENANT GENERAL SIR ROLY WALKER

Given the US and its allies' desire to keep troop presence in Afghanistan
to a 'light footprint', the Taliban infiltrated back into Afghanistan
from 2003. They exploited widespread Afghan government corruption
and the continuing presence of infidels on Muslim soil. The Taliban
benefited from the relative security of their base areas in Pakistan and
their influence in rural Afghanistan increased. By the end of 2005, the
security situation in Afghanistan was no longer containable.

The Household Division was engaged in 24 operational tours of
Afghanistan from April 2006 to October 2013. All the tours were
significant for those who took part in them but not every one of the
24 tours has been covered. It was D Squadron The Household Cavalry
Regiment who were the first element of the Household Division to be
deployed under 16th Air Assault Brigade on Op *Herrick* 4 from April
to September 2006. The 1st Battalion Grenadier Guards deployed on
Op *Herrick* 6 under 12th Mechanised Brigade from April to October
2007. The early years of Op *Herrick* from April 2004 saw the Army

bogged down in a war of attrition against the Taliban. The fight against the Taliban was at its fiercest between 2009 and 2012, though the 2006 fighting in northern Helmand was certainly intense. Every Regiment in the Household Division was deployed from 2009 to 2012, often fighting side by side. The experience gained in earlier tours was invaluable, and by 2012/13 the Household Division's reputation had never stood higher. The 1st Battalion Coldstream Guards completed the last Op *Herrick* tour in August 2014.

By the end of 2005, NATO had taken over the security leadership in northern and western Afghanistan. In the spring of 2006, the British government agreed to assume responsibility for Helmand Province in Afghanistan's south. Not everyone was convinced. "We may be fighting the wrong war in the wrong country," remarked Richard Holbrooke, the US Special Representative for Afghanistan and Pakistan, to Sherard Cowper-Coles, the British Ambassador to Afghanistan in Kabul.

The British government decided that the British-led NATO Allied Rapid Reaction Corps (ARRC) would deploy to Kabul to take command over the International Security Assistance Force (ISAF). Prime Minister Tony Blair and the Chiefs of Staff were keen to play a leading role. The Iraq War had lost legitimacy with the public and the media in the UK. The government was convinced that Afghanistan could be portrayed as a legitimate, 'just war'.

The then Chief of the General Staff, General Sir Richard Dannatt, whose favourite expression was "The Army is running hot", was only too keen to get the Army involved. Iraq had been a failure at a strategic and operational level; the prisoner abuse had damaged the Army's reputation; and Dannatt was well aware of the opportunity costs to the Army's budget and operational effectiveness if it wavered.

The Afghanistan campaign began in a wave of optimism and political naivety. John Reid, Labour's former Defence Secretary, said in April 2006, "We would be perfectly happy to leave Afghanistan in three years and without one shot being fired because our job is to protect the people of Afghanistan, to reconstruct their economy and democracy."

It was a statement of breathtaking ignorance. Worse still, it demonstrated a cultural misunderstanding and failure to learn from history. To the Afghan mind, the return of the British Army was just one in a long series of misjudgements and an invitation to repeat history not as farce as Karl Marx famously said but once again as tragedy. Place names like Lashkar Gar, Sangin, Musa Qal'ah, Kajaki Dam, Garmsir, the Helmand River and Camp Bastion soon became part of the public's consciousness.

The British Army quickly got bogged down in Helmand. Command and control was complicated to say the least. For example, the Commander of 16th Air Assault Brigade, Brigadier Ed Butler, on Op *Herrick* 4, was under command of a Dutch one-star but was answerable to the UK joint headquarters at Northwood, and yet the British effort in Helmand, 'Task Force Helmand', was commanded by Colonel Charlie Knaggs, Irish Guards, from outside the Brigade based in Kabul. It was unforgivably muddled thinking in the higher echelons of the Army who have never been held to account. When the situation started to unravel, 16th Air Assault Brigade staff started to report on what was going on behind the back of Colonel Charlie Knaggs. It was a troubling self-inflicted wound when clarity of command and control was paramount.

Butler, controversially, decided that his Brigade should be spread out in company- and platoon-sized bases. It was a strategy doomed to failure with the size of available forces, and in an area covering close to 23,000 square miles, three times the size of Wales in that time-honoured and over-used analogy. Butler's 16th Air Assault Brigade claimed, with some justification, that the 2006 fighting was the most intense the British Army had experienced since the Korean War. It was vulnerable to Taliban attack and was only able to defeat the insurgents by heavy use of mortars, attack helicopters, attack aircraft and artillery. Troop movement, resupply, and casualty evacuation depended on six Chinook helicopters.

Inevitably, to repel relentless Taliban attacks with what forces they had, 16th Air Assault Brigade had to rely on bombing from the air, or heavy artillery. There was a good deal of collateral damage – that dry euphemism designed to insulate feelings of outrage – but which means the inadvertent killing of civilians and the destruction of homes and livelihoods. This played with interest into the hands of the Taliban recruiting machine.

The Taliban in Helmand proved themselves to be brave and disciplined fighters, often suicidally so. They displayed battlefield learning and adaptability. Western technology more than met its match as the Taliban found countermeasures in merely observing nature. NATO used unmanned drones to pinpoint the insurgents, but the Taliban could watch a 'muster' of crows that circle around soldiers looking for food scraps. By covering themselves in a blanket on a warm rock, the Taliban could evade thermal imaging.

The Grenadiers deployed on Op *Herrick* VI from April 2007 to October 2007. They were the first Foot Guards Battalion to deploy to Afghanistan. Under the command of Lieutenant Colonel Carew Hatherley, they were one of three infantry battalions under 12th Mechanised Brigade. The Grenadiers were tasked in the role in which they had some experience from Iraq, and in which they were regarded as a safe pair of hands. But it was not the role they coveted, that of a ground holding battle group. In the eyes of some, the role of OMLTs, and of training and partnering the Afghan National Army (ANA) was second tier, though events were to prove it was arguably more challenging than that of a ground holding battle group. There was not a single working day where the Grenadiers did not have at least one serious contact with the enemy.

Operation, mentoring, and liaison team commanders needed a high level of skill in the art of persuasion and negotiation and the nuances of counter-insurgency – attributes that had been allowed to lie fallow since the Troubles in Northern Ireland. The Grenadiers provided six operation, mentoring, and liaison teams comprising 231 officers and Guardsmen; the rest of the Battalion were in a support role to the ground holding battle groups of 1st Battalion The Royal Anglian Regiment, 1st Battalion The Royal Welsh, and the Worcester and Sherwood Foresters Regiment. Operating in Land Rover 4x4 vehicles with little land mine protection, they were highly vulnerable. This was in stark contrast to the Danish Brigade, who deployed Leopard tanks to reinforce their Battalion attached to 12th Mechanised Brigade.

12th Mechanised Brigade had little regard for the ANA, regarding them as more of a liability. However, the ANA may have looked like a rabble, often high on drugs with a penchant for pretty well everything. But they were fearless with an ear for trouble and an eye for the out of place. If you took into account the gulf in culture, something which took everyone a long time to grasp in Afghanistan, then the criticism was mislaid and certainly unfair.

The cultural misunderstanding which overshadowed the Army's operations was entrenched at a political level. Few politicians understood that whoever controlled the opium poppy controlled southern Afghanistan. It was a lesson quickly learnt by the Soviets in their defeat by the Mujahedeen in the 1970s. The US and Britain fell into the same world of murky compromise as it sought to wean the Afghan economy off the cultivation, processing, and distribution of opium products. Hare-brained schemes like growing tomatoes were suggested as a viable alternative.

Opium might have been a threat to Afghan security but it was not the greatest threat. That was the Taliban. Counter-narcotics was a contradictory objective and effectively turned the farmer into an insurgent as their historical and lucrative livelihood was threatened. It all played perfectly to Taliban propaganda and made the Grenadiers' primary role, mentoring the ANA, that much more difficult as the ANA's 'hearts and minds' were torn between their people's livelihoods and working with the British Army.

Whatever misgivings the Grenadiers had about their role on Op *Herrick* 6, a combination of selfless acts of valour, their cultural intelligence, and their ability to work around the ANA's limitations allowed them to play a full part in 12th Brigade's operations. Two operations in particular stand out: Op *Silicon* and holding operations in the Upper Gereshk Valley during the spring and early summer of 2007.

Op *Silicon*'s objective was to clear the Taliban from Gereshk, Helmand's economic hub. The Queen's Company fought with distinction and won the praise of the Royal Anglian and Light Dragoons Battle Groups. The courage of their Afghan colleagues did much to change the perception of the ANA and enhance the influence of the Afghan government.

The operation ended with the construction of three patrol bases to hold ground, one of which, Patrol Base South, was commanded by Lieutenant Patrick Hennessey. Patrick Hennessey's book *The Junior Officers' Reading Club* captures the task and atmosphere well: "The structure that rises out of nowhere in the next 36 hours as the Engineers work away is incredible, the Engineers fill lightweight steel-cage boxes with rubble and hardcore for instant blast-proof protection.

Patrol Base South was ours to defend, commanding awesome views over the Green Zone."

The holding operations were not without incident and a sorrowful reminder of the vagaries of fate. On 1 July, an Afghan male suicide bomber launched himself at two Grenadier reconnaissance and close fire support vehicles as they left Patrol Base South. Four non-commissioned officers of the Queen's Company were badly injured. Warrant Officer (Class Two) Edgell and Lance Corporal Mizon drove their wounded comrades for 3½ miles to Forward Operating Base Price. Lance Corporal Mizon had one hand on the wheel and one on the neck artery of Lance Sergeant Shadrake, who survived.

A video was also made by Vaughan Smith, a former Grenadier, which was shown on *Newsnight*, introduced by Jeremy Paxman in September 2007. It shows the Grenadiers – the Company is not named – clearing the Upper Sangin Valley north-east of Gereshk. The canopy of the five senses under which the Grenadiers had to operate is vividly portrayed: the patrols through dense, head-high fields; the days under sweltering sun; Afghan village compounds with walls 12–15 feet high but thick enough to be bearable in the heat; the endless buzzing of the ANA radios like cicadas; baying donkeys and the smell of Qormah, the spicy onion stew, and unwashed bodies; the thud of distant airstrikes and the boom of mortars. And then, of course, the sixth sense borne from experience, not explicable in terms of normal perception, of impending danger.

The Grenadiers provided a number of officers, warrant officers, and non-commissioned officers for the Brigade Reconnaissance Force, commanded by Captain Piers Ashfield. This was a highly trained force operating in Land Rovers fitted with heavy machine guns. They used their mobility to insert forces behind 'Taliban lines' to disrupt their tactic of attacking rifle companies who had, by default, become static as they defended district centres. They were often head to toe with the Taliban. A 'day in the life' contact report read: "At 0700 we entered the Green Zone to conduct a Vehicle Check Point on the canal running NE from the Y junction. We immediately became involved in a Troops in Contact with the Taliban for two and a half hours. Jusyalay dated 28th May: Ammunition expended – 8000 × 7.62 link, 600 × 5.56 link; 66 × 51mm high explosive; 23 × 51mm SMK; 600 × GMG; 4 × ILAW;

1100 × .50 Cal; 2 × Javelin; 4 × Red Phos; 25 × UGL; 700 × 5.56mm ball; One HE grenade."

A comment after the contact from a Grenadier was, "Being so close to death, it was the ultimate affirmation of being alive."

Lieutenant Colonel Carew Hatherley, the Grenadiers' Commanding Officer, in his final reflections was to say, "Afghanistan was a markedly different type of tour to the ones we had done in the previous 20 years. I remain intensely proud of the young Guardsmen, dropped into extraordinary circumstances and yet I saw them regularly perform outstandingly."

There was, however, a sting in the tail of his valedictory comments: "We have had success in Helmand and the Army is getting better, but it's tactics without grand strategy and without a political approach. It is suppressing locally and temporarily the symptoms of the disease. It is not curing the disease."

There was consolation for all the Grenadiers after the immediate end of the tour, and that was the period of 'decompression' in Cyprus. Major Simon Soskin, who was the Battalion's Senior Major on Op *Herrick* 6, spoke of its positive effect on all ranks: "We had a great reunion with everyone, RAF included, who served with and supported us on the tour. I remember some of the staff running the decompression period trying to create a bit of friction between the officers and men. The Guardsmen were having none of it."

By the end of Op *Herrick* 6, 12th Mechanised Brigade, which had taken over from 16th Air Assault Brigade and to which the Grenadiers were attached, had fired 2,474,560 bullets and called in 599 airstrikes and 334 artillery fire missions. The tragedy was that the Grenadiers lost five Guardsmen killed in action. Many more sustained life-changing injuries.

The Honours and Awards List for Op *Herrick* 6 was the usual 'Pick n Mix'. What stood out were the names that were not on it from the Grenadiers tour. One award did stand out, however, and that was the Military Cross awarded to the Captain of the Queen's Company, Major Martin David. The award of medals was an issue of great sensitivity. The Military Cross, one of the most emblematic of awards, had become open to all ranks from 1993. This was the right decision but it probably meant that a number of platoon commanders who displayed exemplary gallantry during active service were awarded a Mention in Dispatches instead. Five Guardsmen also were Mentioned in Dispatches.

The Afghans named a mosque after Carew Hatherley. Perhaps there was no greater accolade than that. A short time after the tour, he retired from the Army and settled in New Zealand. His legacy to the Regiment was assured; his legacy to the ANA was equally certain as their inclusion in operations now became a matter of course.

———

From late 2007 to March 2009, the Army was becoming increasingly stretched in Helmand Province. Right Flank of 1st Battalion Scots Guards took part in Op *Herrick* 7 from August 2007 to March 2008. The remainder of the Battalion under Lieutenant Colonel William Swinton, the son of the former Major General Sir John Swinton, was still deployed in the other theatre of war, Iraq, on Op *Telic* 11.

Right Flank, under the inspiring leadership of Major Chris Bell, was deployed as part of 52nd Infantry Brigade, on Op *Herrick* 7, along with 1st Battalion Coldstream Guards and C and D Squadrons of the Household Cavalry Regiment. In the words of Lieutenant Colonel Edward Smyth-Osbourne (Household Cavalry Regiment), "variety is the spice of life but we all had the knotty problem of Musa Qal'ah".

The Battle of Musa Qal'ah was a British-led military action in Helmand Province launched by the ANA. It followed nearly nine months of Taliban occupation of the town, the largest town the insurgents controlled at the time. There had been a controversial withdrawal in 2006 after the failed 'platoon house' strategy implemented on Op *Herrick* 4 met with unexpectedly fierce resistance from the Taliban and local tribesmen. Late in 2006, Musa Qal'ah was ceded to tribal elders under an agreement with the Taliban. The Taliban reneged on the agreement.

Every cap badge of the Household Division was represented in Helmand at the time and played a significant role in the successful assault of Musa Qal'ah in December 2007. Reflecting on the battle to capture Musa Qal'ah, Colonel Smyth-Osbourne said, "Little did I expect to see the sight of an armoured flank guard by C Squadron Household Cavalry Regiment as an armoured infantry company with Right Flank Scots Guards advance in perfect order only dismounting in close country to swat off Taliban RPG [rocket-propelled grenade] teams."

Success at Musa Qal'ah was short-lived. It was the age-old problem of holding ground with too few troops and too little resource. Brigadier

Andrew Mackay, Commander Task Force Helmand, was full of praise for the Household Cavalry Regiment and Right Flank, and put his head above the parapet declaring that "influence and non-kinetic operations had been overlooked for too long." He went on to say, "The MOD was institutionally incapable of keeping pace with rapid change and associated willingness to adapt."

In October 2008, 400 Taliban fighters attacked Lashkar Gar, Helmand's provincial capital. It was a measure of their growing confidence and battlefield discipline. The Army began to realise there was more Taliban presence in Helmand than they had initially thought. Lashkar Gar was a close-run affair with staff officers scrambling from their desks to defend brigade headquarters. Once again, Harrier Jets, Apache helicopters, and artillery saw off the insurgents but at a price in civilian casualties. The Army's decision to stay put in static patrol bases gave the Taliban free rein to plant IEDs in significant numbers. By early 2009, two-thirds of British casualties were caused by IEDs. For vehicle crews of the Household Cavalry and Household Division infantry platoons, the IED threat was ever present. It required courage and leadership of a high order from young officers and non-commissioned officers to keep their men under command alert and resilient under great psychological stress.

The heavy fighting and ever-increasing casualties had become a strategic shock to the British government, the Army, and the public. What really made Whitehall nervous was that in the first 20 days of July 2009, 20 British service personnel were killed in action. And yet, despite this, the Prime Minister, Gordon Brown, his hands still all over the Treasury, was reluctant to give the Army the helicopters it needed for operations and logistical resupply. In 2009, British battalions had far less support than their forebears had received in South Armagh's 'bandit country' 40 years before.

———

It was against this unnerving background that the British Army launched a major offensive, Op *Panther's Claw*, to secure the ground between Helmand's two most important towns, Lashkar Gar and Gereshk. Op *Panther's Claw* took place in late June 2009 during Op *Herrick* 10, a tour commanded by Brigadier Tim Radford and 19th Light Brigade. It was a tour which bore witness to both awful tragedy and conspicuous courage by many regiments. The 2nd Battalion The Rifles lost 30 men with 75 severely wounded. The 1st Battalion Welsh Guards was to have the desperate misfortune of losing Guardsmen and officers at every level of rank. The years 2009 and 2010 were to prove to be a defining period in the whole Afghanistan campaign and saw the full-scale involvement of every Household Division regiment.

For some time, the British Army had realised that its strategy was flawed for the level of force committed. The idea of platoon and forward operating bases scattered around Helmand Province was not working. For some commentators, they were an unconscious throwback to Rorke's Drift and the Battle of Arnhem, 'stand and fight despite the odds', which had become part of the Army's institutional memory. The Army's presence was also too kinetic, a response to the ever-present danger of 'platoon houses' being overrun, which would be an unthinkable loss and a huge fillip to Taliban propaganda.

The rotation to Op *Herrick* 10 coincided with the arrival of General Stanley McChrystal, a US general, described by the US Defence Secretary, Robert Gates, as "perhaps the finest warrior and leader of men in combat I ever met." It was praise echoed by Major Toby Till, commanding No 1 Company 1st Battalion Coldstream Guards in 2009, who met McChrystal and remarked, "McChrystal possessed an emotional intelligence rarely seen in British generals, his willingness to give soldiers a hug and show a genuine understanding of the threat we faced was inspirational."

Steeped in counter-insurgency, McChrystal re-calibrated the thinking. It was long overdue. "We are fighting for the population and that involves protecting them from the enemy and the unintended consequences of our operations." It was McChrystal who summed up his approach as 'courageous restraint'. It was a phrase whose sentiment echoed with the Household Division, whose soldiers had shown themselves during the Troubles and the Balkans to be disciplined, willing to use force, but conspicuous in their ability to win local support.

The Welsh Guards had deployed to Afghanistan in April 2009 under the leadership of Lieutenant Colonel Rupert Thorneloe. Colonel Rupert was an officer of great promise. By common consent, the highest reaches of the Army were within his grasp. Colonel Rupert had trained the Battalion well, though he had inherited a battalion which had been under the consummate leadership of Lieutenant Colonel Richard Stanford, later to become a major general.

The Welsh Guards were in the thick of it from the outset. There is an account of the Welsh Guards on Op *Herrick* 10 in Toby Harnden's book *Dead Men Risen*, relentless in its detail and, on occasion, questionable in its accuracy. But it does at least convey the visceral nature of the tour.

The Battalion had been tasked as Battle Group Centre South, its area of operations stretching from Camp Bastion to the north-west to Gereshk in the east, and Lashkar Gar in the south, where 19th Light Brigade Headquarters were based. Major Henry Bettinson, who commanded No 2 Company, described the area as "predominantly a flat area of the Green Zone, interspersed with canals, irrigation ditches, tree lines, fields of poppy and wheat, lone compounds, compound clusters and small villages". This was typical perhaps of Helmand Province, but the menace lay in the fact that it gave the Taliban clear lines of fire into ISAF locations and excellent cover in which to move about.

Within a month of its deployment, the Battalion had lost Lance Sergeant Toby Fasfous killed by an IED and Lieutenant Mark Evison, who was hit by gunfire and was later to die from his wounds. Lieutenant Evison's mother, Margaret, wrote an account of his death, *Death of a Soldier*. Charles Moore, the celebrated journalist and former editor of the *Daily Telegraph*, described this account as a "remarkable work: moving from the personal to the wider picture, it addresses some important national issues."

The personal picture touches upon the lack of resources that the British Army had to endure. The wider picture looks at how wounded veterans were treated. Lieutenant Evison died at Selly Oak in Birmingham. Margaret Evison described the suffocating, in her opinion, hand of the Ministry of Defence in handling coroners' inquests and the way they responded to the families of soldiers killed in action that was less than sure footed. But the real value of the book lies in Margaret's description of the raw grief she suffered as a parent. The sentiments she expressed are universal and would be echoed by every family who had lost a loved one in the campaign:

> Early mornings were nearly always difficult. But at any time I could find myself in surprising situations moist-eyed and feeling out of control. The Army returned a parcel I had sent Mark before he died,

which he had not received. In it was the packet of Bird's custard, one of his childhood loves, and my letter chatting about the happy minutiae of daily life in the time before he had died. That was where I wanted to be, and I cried and I cried.

Lieutenant Colonel Rupert Thorneloe was troubled by the concept of operations in Op *Panther's Claw*. In essence, this was a cordon and search operation intended to isolate the target area and capture or kill armed insurgents. He was not alone in his misgivings. The mismatch between helicopter demand and their availability meant that resupply would have to be by road. This was both perilous and slow. All resupply in South Armagh 40 years previously had been by helicopter. There was pitifully little surveillance covering the compounds serving as the Welsh Guards' forward operating bases. The Taliban had an easy job of planting IEDs at night.

The first phase of the operation, to get the cordon in place, began in the early hours of 19 June. A US Marines task force of 4,000 deployed west of the Helmand river to cover Lashkar Gar from diversionary Taliban attacks. The Welsh Guards were tasked with securing Route Cornwall which ran alongside the Shamalan Canal to the east. Later that day, Major Sean Birchall was killed after his armoured vehicle hit an IED on the track.

It quickly became clear that Route Cornwall was too narrow to allow the advance to continue unimpeded. Colonel Rupert was only too aware that momentum, that all important factor in combat, was in danger of being lost. On 1 July, Colonel Rupert made his way to the front in a resupply column but was hit by an IED and died instantly.

Colonel Rupert's death was a profound shock to the Battalion. Major Guy Stone, commanding No 3 Company, remembered the day not only for its raw sadness but for the response of two of his Guardsmen. One, a senior non-commissioned officer, wanted to get out of No 3 Company's base and "do some serious damage to the Taliban"; another, an 18-year-old Guardsman, said, "it's very sad, Sir, but no different from a Guardsman being killed."

Colonel Rupert was the most senior officer to be killed in action in Afghanistan. News of his death further frayed nerves in Westminster desperate for success before the forthcoming election and to avoid the awkward political consequences of Gordon Brown's reluctance to resource the campaign. Colonel Rupert was replaced by Major Charles Antelme, who was serving in London as a staff officer but who had won the Distinguished Service Order in Iraq. On 5 July, Lance Corporal Duane Elson was killed by an IED on foot patrol.

Twenty-three soldiers were killed in action on Op *Panther's Claw*, which ended on 31 July. The operation was a tactical success in driving out the Taliban and giving hope that Lashkar Gar and Gereshk could be joined up. But as the Taliban leadership were wont to say, "tactical successes are irrelevant". At an operational and strategic level its outcome was questionable. The Taliban knew they would be able to re-infiltrate once the operation ended.

'Hot stabilisation' was the term given to the Army's follow-up to Op *Panther's Claw*. The phrase sounded full of positive intent with the promise of development projects that the Taliban's presence had prevented. But Colonel Rupert, always troubled by the concept of operations, particularly the holding of ground, was posthumously proven right. This was to be the responsibility of the ANA. They were not up to it. Op *Panther's Claw* for all its valour and commitment showed that, once again, the Afghanistan campaign needed a rethink.

The campaign's strategy changed decidedly. The Army had tried to apply McChrystal's new approach of 'courageous restraint' but had been constrained by a lack of infantry, armoured vehicles, helicopters, and airborne surveillance. The ever-increasing number of Taliban IEDs and consequently heavy British casualties further unnerved Gordon Brown's government. The emphasis switched to training the ANA and getting them to take the lead, with October 2014 set as the date for withdrawal from Afghanistan. But first, there was unfinished business. In November 2009, Major General Nick Carter, later to be Chief of the Defence Staff when Afghanistan fell to the Taliban in 2021 took over command of Regional Command South. General McChrystal gave him command of Op *Moshtarak* in February 2010 to clear the Taliban from Marjah District, a major insurgent stronghold. It was a politically led effort in full partnership with the ANA. The Grenadiers, the Coldstream, and A Squadron The Household Cavalry were at the heart of this operation.

The photograph of four Household Division commanding officers, three of whom were on a reconnaissance before Op *Herrick* 11, is a poignant reminder of the Household Division's contribution to what was arguably the most intense period of the Afghanistan campaign. Op *Moshtarak*, or the Battle of Marjah, dominated Op *Herrick* 11. It was an ISAF offensive to take back control of the town of Marjah in Helmand Province. It involved a combined total of 15,000 Afghan, US, British, Canadian and Danish troops, and was the largest joint operation of the conflict to date. It was the most significant initiative of the revised strategy to train the ANA to take the lead, and expand the British Army's footprint in central Helmand.

Op *Herrick* 11, from November 2009 to April 2010, was under the command of Headquarters 11th Light Brigade. Apart from A, B, and C Squadrons of the Household Cavalry, the principal ground holding battle groups were 1st Battalion Grenadier Guards, 1st Battalion Coldstream Guards, 3rd Battalion The Rifles, and 1st Battalion The Royal Welsh. Brigadier James Cowan, a former Black Watch commanding officer, was the Brigade commander.

Prime Minister Gordon Brown and his successor, David Cameron, now knew only too well that Afghanistan was, like the war in Iraq, becoming deeply unpopular. It was the same unforced errors: the poor care and support for wounded soldiers on their return and their families; the lethargic provision of adequately protected vehicles and lack of helicopters. All this was at odds with public sentiment badly shaken by media images of repatriation ceremonies and amputees.

Op *Moshtarak*'s aim was to clear the Taliban from the district of Marjah, a major stronghold. *Moshtarak* means 'together' in Dari, Afghanistan's *lingua franca*, and involved the US Marine task force in Marjah, south of Nad-e-Ali, and Task Force Helmand (TFH) to the north of Nad-e-Ali.

Marjah had fallen to the Taliban in 2008. ISAF lacked the necessary forces to clear and hold the district. As long as it remained in Taliban hands it remained a potent threat to the security of Helmand. The plan to clear Marjah had two important characteristics. First, there was a leaflet drop to say that, this time, NATO troops would stay; and secondly, in accordance with the doctrine of 'courageous restraint', there would be a marked reduction in the use of artillery and air strikes. These strikes were down by 60 per cent and the use of smoke shells up by 70 per cent.

Tactical surprise was achieved with a night air assault with 60 blacked-out helicopters leapfrogging the main Taliban defences.

The Grenadier Guards Battle Group had deployed to Nad-e-Ali in October 2009, some four months before the launch of Op *Moshtarak*. As the commanding officer, Lieutenant Colonel Roly Walker, wrote at the time, "We would be in the eye of the storm to regain the initiative from the Taliban in Helmand. Nad-e-Ali was the most strategic piece of ground for the insurgents, a heady cocktail of enemy fighters, narcotics traffickers, Taliban senior leadership and mid-level commanders."

Colonel Roly was under no illusions. "We had to live in a world where you were being spied upon the whole time, you never knew who was talking to who and the Afghans are very adept at working out which side they need to be on. To them it's not duplicity, it's a way of survival. It was crucial for me to understand why the insurgents held sway in some areas and what we could do to help resolve the problems in the villages."

The Grenadier Guards Account of Operations 1996–2015, Section 6, Op *Herrick* 11, is a testament to the importance of thorough planning. Colonel Roly, a former Irish Guards officer, had the imagination of the Micks and the Special Forces and an unerring ability to think laterally to assess where the Taliban's vulnerabilities lay: "they were vulnerable on their logistic resupply, casevac – brave as lions but they wouldn't fight if you prevented them from removing their dead or wounded – and they would also fight shy if their lines of communication were threatened."

This was classic counter-insurgency warfare, something the British Army had pretty well forgotten once the Troubles in Northern Ireland had come to an end. But despite all the thoroughness in planning, the astute cultural awareness, the careful intelligence assessment, tragedy was never far away. Less than a month into the tour, the Grenadiers lost the much-respected Regimental Sergeant Major, Darren 'Daz' Chant, and four others, two Grenadiers and two Royal Military Police with six Grenadiers wounded.

The murders took place on Tuesday, 3 November 2009 at the small Patrol Base known as Blue 25. Led by the Grenadiers' Regimental Sergeant Major, a 16-strong unit had been detached to Blue 25 in a last-chance bid to shore up relations between the local population and the local Afghan police. The police were inept and corrupt. There was every chance that locals would turn to the Taliban to uphold law and order. In pretty short order, the Grenadiers under the Regimental Sergeant Major's leadership had turned the whole thing around. To the locals, 'Mr Daz' as they called him, was a hero; and to the local police, many of whom were riven with corruption, he had given them their pride back.

Sometime after lunch that day, an Afghan policeman, Gulbuddin, without warning opened fire with his machine gun. As the Grenadier radio operator was to say, "It was like being hit with a sledgehammer. One second everything was normal, the next utter chaos and death – it was that quick."

It was a shocking blow to the Grenadiers. The Welsh Guards had lost their commanding officer and now the Grenadiers had lost their Regimental Sergeant Major. In their own way, both were giants of men. As the news broke, many newspapers in the UK began to question the whole nature of British involvement in Afghanistan.

It was a formidable test of regimental resilience but Colonel Roly Walker saw that positive change and action was the only response. The UK sponsored and trained Civil Order Police, which had a proper structure and operated like a battalion, to replace the district police, who were riven with corruption.

The Battle of Crossing Point One, a few days later, began in tragic circumstances when a popular Guardsman, Jamie Janes, and his section were attached to an Irish Guards multiple of 16 men (the Micks were attached to the Grenadiers as much-needed reinforcements). Guardsman Janes was caught in an IED blast and had minutes left to live. As the patrol set about the casevac, they soon came under Taliban rocket and machine-gun attack. As Guardsman Robert Ashley said, "We were almost completely surrounded, it was the most fierce battle I've been in." The Grenadiers and Micks fought their way back to their base at Patrol Base Wahid, some 1¼ miles to their south-west.

"It was like Zulu. The Taliban just kept coming and coming. It was suicidal. The more they sent, the more we killed," recalled Sergeant Dean Bailey, 5 Platoon Sergeant, No 2 Company Grenadier Guards Battle Group.

Morale had been understandably low after the murder of Darren Chant. The Taliban were gloating, claiming that Gulbuddin was one of theirs, a spy who joined the Afghan police with the sole aim of killing British soldiers. In Luy Mandah, north of Nad-e-Ali, No 2 Company struck back with an ambush which, as Colonel Roly had correctly observed, would exploit the Taliban's tactics of attacking the casualty evacuation chain. The Battle of Crossing Point, no panacea for the loss of the Grenadiers' Regimental Sergeant Major, at least helped boost morale.

It was now clear that the best way to ambush the Taliban was to set up a fake IED strike. This required planning and courage of the highest order. Using excellent field discipline, they moved into a compound and established a fire base overlooking the main road known as Route Jupiter. A fake IED strike was triggered and the Taliban took the bait. By the end of the ambush, ten Taliban were dead, cut down by machine-gun and sniper fire. Lieutenant Shephard, 5 Platoon commander, was awarded the Military Cross; he was later to say, "The biggest factor in our success was the standards of our Guardsmen and senior non-commissioned officers, all level-headed, I could not be in better hands surrounded by these individuals."

The murders at Blue 25 had been avenged, though no Guardsmen would have seen it as such. Perhaps, just a quiet pride they had done their duty.

Colonel Roly was later to mirror the compliments paid to the Household Cavalry by 3 Commando Brigade during the Falklands campaign, some three decades earlier:

> In the right hands, the Scimitar vehicle was marvellous. Towards the end of the tour we inherited A Squadron of the Household Cavalry who were in the East but allowed us to push out to Marjah. They did exactly what we asked of them to secure the route from Lashkar Gar at the key T-junction which divided the principal route to Nad-e-Ali and south to Marjah. They also had to prove a potential cross-country route towards Marjah and see what the Taliban were up to in the Bolan Desert. We had to shape the battlefield for Op *Moshtarak* and with Captain Jim Young, our recce platoon commander whose mission was simply to find, fix and destroy the enemy, the Household Cavalry proved themselves to be outstanding in conducting pre-emptive and overwatch operations, sometimes and rather precariously acting as 'tethered goats' to draw the Taliban in.

D-Day for Op *Moshtarak* took place on 13 February, towards the end of the Grenadiers tour. By then the Grenadiers, battle hardened and at the peak of their professionalism, played a full part in the retaking of their objective, Marjah. Colonel Roly remarked that at the end of the operation, the brigade commander, James Cowan, wanted the Grenadiers to push further south to link up with the US Marines. It was a measure of Colonel Roly's standing that he was able to tell the Brigadier that there was a danger of British forces over-reaching themselves and that it was a task best left to their successors on Op *Herrick* 12.

The operation itself was anti-climactic. But this is a testament to the thoroughness in the operation's planning. The Taliban were disorientated, and though they would stand and fight they would only do so if they had a reasonable chance of success. As Colonel Roly said, "At battlegroup level, the real skill was to outwit and outmanoeuvre the enemy which meant there was rarely any fighting."

The Inkerman Company, as part of the Grenadier Guards Battle Group on Op *Herrick* 11, was tasked to hold the town of Chah-e-Anjir under the command of Major Edward Boanas, Irish Guards. It was an eclectic mix of Grenadiers, Guardsmen from other Household Division battalions, and officers and non-commissioned officers from various infantry regiments and the Royal Artillery and Royal Engineers. In that sense, it was a true all arms group. The Company took over from The Prince of Wales's Company, commanded by Major Giles Harris, who was awarded the Distinguished Service Order for his leadership on Op *Herrick* 10.

The human picture inside Chah-e-Anjir was complex but no more so than any other town in Helmand Province. Historical and tribal loyalties coupled with Taliban intimidation, endemic unemployment, police venality, and a poppy crop that far outweighed any other source of income, shaped the background in which the Inkerman Company had to operate. The tour followed the classic counter-insurgency philosophy of securing the population: 'winning them over' was too ambitious in such a complex culture, but partnering the Afghan institutions and outwitting and defeating the insurgents gave the local population confidence in the ISAF coalition.

One operation stands out: Christmas 2009. This was no game of football between two opposing sides like Christmas 1914, but a company deliberate attack, Op *Tor SHPA'H*, to seize and clear a junction to open an important route. Either side, the dirt tracks north and south of the canal were threaded with IEDs. With the attack planned for midnight, the Company's preparations took on a rather surreal feel, including visits from the UK Ambassador, the Brigade and Deputy Commander ISAF and the head of the provincial reconstruction team. Visits by VIPs and senior officers may have been a distraction in the campaign but, to the astute commander, they were a welcome opportunity to influence people in a position to do something concrete.

The operation was a complete success and gave the Inkerman Company the confidence drawn from the 'friction of battle' to prepare for Op *Moshtarak* six weeks later. The friction of battle builds experience and battlefield discipline, and the ability to sense where things are not quite right, the terrain not as it should be, the local population acting not as they normally do. It is that crucial sense of intuition that prevents injury and death.

Op *Moshtarak*, on the face of things straightforward in its objectives, was complex in its detail. Inkerman Company was instructed to be on 'Economy of Effort', a masterful way of saying limited manpower and resources. The operation's first phase, with Inkerman Company securing a crossing over the canal to capture the village of Abdul Walid Kalay to the north of Chah-e Anjir, took place between 8 and 11 February. Clearing the patchwork of IEDs was essential to the mission's success and, despite the presence of a village elder to alert them to the unusual, a counter-IED team lost its commander, Warrant Officer (Class Two) Markland from the Royal Engineers.

A good example of intuition born from experience was the alertness of Lieutenant Richard de Gama who saw a British Army Bergen rucksack by his vehicle. The Grenadiers' battlefield discipline would have their Bergens clipped to the outside of their vehicle. Richard backed his instincts. It was a carefully prepared booby-trap operated by a tilt-switch.

The Inkerman Company was involved in 128 enemy contacts during their tour. The minimal use of heavy firepower won the local population round. No civilians had been killed, though good tactical appreciation and accurate shooting accounted for 28 insurgents. The secured population doubled to 8,000 and over 4 miles of roads were re-opened, reducing the journey time from Nad-e-Ali to Chah-e Anjir to 40 minutes. Chah's market flourished once again, as did a school for 600 children.

Major Ed Boanas, who was later to command the Irish Guards, had one tricky issue to deal with. A Guardsman, high on heatstroke, went AWOL from the patrol base and threatened a local child with a knife. Everything that the Grenadiers had worked towards was about to go up in a puff of smoke. The Guardsman fortunately came to his senses. Colonel Roly, who had every confidence in his company commander, put Major Boanas on the spot and asked him to call and run a 'Shura' (a meeting, Shura co-operation is a basic Islamic principle) with the locals and put their minds at rest. He did so with consummate professionalism and tact. In fact, he did such a good job that a village elder presented him with a map with all the Taliban houses marked.

The Grenadier tour was an undeniable success. Indeed, it was probably one of the most successful tours of any regiment in the British Army during the whole campaign, a testament to the best of counter-insurgency warfare where the aim was not to kill as many insurgents as possible but to establish a secure environment for the local nationals. As Colonel Roly was later to write, "in a counter-insurgency, the commander's role is that of the principal agent of the counter-insurgency so that you have the authority to speak to the people and to promote and develop a partnership with the ANA and ANP [Afghan National Police], even if you knew Taliban scouts were listening to your every word at a Shura."

Colonel Roly Walker is now a general. Amusingly, he remarked that he was lucky to have been a subaltern in the Irish Guards, but glad he commanded the Grenadiers. "That was the best of both worlds," Colonel Roly remarked. He remembered his first briefing to the Battalion on pre-deployment training and asking at the end if there were any questions. There was silence. Regimental Sergeant Major Darren Chant took him to one side afterwards and said, "Sir, The Commanding Officer's briefing is not an invitation for discussion."

Perhaps his most important legacy, however, was the generation of young Grenadier officers in whose development he took a great interest. A number remained in the Grenadiers with significant Army careers ahead of them. They would point to his inspirational leadership and belief in their potential. Colonel Roly was to say that "mentoring the young officers was the thing that in some ways gave me the most pleasure during the tour. The Grenadier warrant officers were wonderful in gripping them if they were going astray, but it was up to me and the company commanders to be their trusted and experienced advisors on how to lead Guardsmen." It was a sentiment echoed by another experienced Grenadier officer, Colonel James Greaves, who remarked on his time with the Regiment in Iraq and Afghanistan, "There was no learned helplessness."

Perhaps the last word on the Grenadiers tour should go to Dr Theo Farrell who wrote in his book *Unwinnable, Britain's War in Afghanistan 2001–2014*: "Nad-e-Ali in the spring of 2010 was transformed ... people could stroll freely ... the compound was a hive of activity, at last everyone was working together for a better future."

Battlefield discipline, how men conduct and look after themselves on operations, became a sensitive subject. For Guardsmen returning to the main British Army base at Camp Bastion, it must have stuck in their craw to see rear echelon soldiers – no doubt doing an important job – strolling about as they if were going to the beach. Many soldiers returning from operations thought they had to make a point, unshaven and bedraggled, dark glasses perched: "I've been in the field sticking it to the Taliban whilst you lot have been tucking into pizzas."

General Sir Richard Dannatt, Chief of the General Staff 2006–09, was no martinet but he knew that any lapse in personal discipline could lead to sloppiness on operations. A Household Division general who was Deputy Commander ISAF in Afghanistan in 2010 drew a disheartening comparison between the turnout and personal discipline of the US Army and some British military units. Some senior officers were taken aback when visiting some Army forward operating bases at how they had gone "rogue": young officers and their platoon sergeants calling each other by their first names; the wearing of flip flops, T-shirts and puffa jackets; a lack of direction and routine which one Household Division Regimental Sergeant Major said was "shocking to see". "If you do the basics well," he said, "you'll be professional on operations. I never turned a blind eye however tough things had been."

Colonel Roly Walker took a contrarian view: "not shaving didn't matter, fire discipline and proper fire control orders were much more important, single aimed shots at identifiable Taliban." He had served in the Special Forces, however, where innate self-discipline is a matter of course.

Lieutenant Colonel Piers Ashfield DSO, who was Captain of the Queen's Company on Op *Herrick* 16, remembered his time in an earlier Op *Herrick* tour when he was in the Brigade Reconnaissance Force: "water was at a premium, certainly not enough for shaving, we were all bearded up and probably thought we all looked the business but back in camp we quickly re-calibrated and went to the cookhouse looking as a Grenadier should do."

On balance, the Household Division Regimental Sergeant Major had a point: "the army is one of tribes, you pass on the customs and traditions, the respect you show to others, the standards that never waver in the Household Division. They can see the high standards and that's what they expect from us."

No doubt there were lapses in the Household Division from 2006 to 2013 but nothing that could not be gripped by a Guards or Household Cavalry warrant officer.

As the campaign in Afghanistan reached a critical point, it is worth reflecting on battlefield strain. Many officers and Guardsmen completed several operational tours of Afghanistan. The IED threat placed huge stress on soldiers: an invisible enemy, ever present, bringing death and hideous injuries. It is worth remembering Field Marshal Sir William (Bill) Slim's words in *Courage and Other Broadcasts*, 1957:

All men have some degree of physical courage, it is surprising how much. Courage you know is having money in the bank. We start with a certain capital of courage, some large, some small, and we proceed to draw on our balance, for, don't forget, courage is an expendable quality. We can use it up. If there are heavy, and, what is more serious, if there are continuous calls on our courage we begin to overdraw. If we go on overdrawing, we go bankrupt – we break down.

Bill Slim would have been only too familiar with battle fatigue or what people referred to in the Great War as 'shell shock'. He would have been less conscious of the idea of Post-Traumatic Stress Disorder (PTSD). It was a different era. But you do not have to be on operations to start overdrawing on your bank of courage. Painful memories are hard to erase and PTSD has, over the last two decades, received the recognition it deserves; and, more importantly, the help and support it merits.

Eighteen months after returning from Op *Herrick* 7 in 2008, the 1st Battalion Coldstream Guards returned to Afghanistan. Op *Herrick* 7 had been a frustrating tour for the Coldstream. Fortunately, they had lost no one, but the brigade commander in his operational assessment decided to split up the Battalion across the entire task force. Once again, much of their time was taken up working with, and mentoring, the Afghan National Army and Police. Whether this was a reflection of the stereotyping of Household Division battalions as 'good at that sort of role', or concerns that public duties had dented their operational readiness, remained ambiguous. But it was vexing for a battalion which had trained hard to fight as an all arms battle group.

Op *Herrick* 11's deployment was couched in similar confusion. With an election looming, there was a lack of political will to deploy more troops to Helmand although it had become pretty clear that more troops would be needed to hold ground taken after Op *Panther's Claw*. Lieutenant General James Bucknall, a distinguished Coldstreamer and overall commander of all British forces in Afghanistan from August 2010, was quick to emphasise the need to maintain momentum saying, "progress is not irreversible, we are yet to make it so. But we are certainly on the right track."

After warning orders to deploy to Iraq, Afghanistan, Kosovo, even as a lead element in Britain's quick reaction 'Spearhead' battalion, the Coldstream under the command of Lieutenant Colonel Toby Gray was, to its satisfaction, to be a ground holding battle group in Babaji. No 1 Company under Major Toby Till was switched from relieving the Fusiliers in Musa Qal'ah to Patrol Base 4 in Babaji. For No 1 Company, this was to prove a tour of singular achievement tempered by the loss of four killed in action (two succumbed to their wounds several years later) and eight others losing limbs.

Major Toby Till was an officer of forthright views based on his considerable military experience. He had been the close observation platoon commander in Londonderry and had commanded the

Pathfinder Platoon in 16th Air Assault Brigade in 2006 on Op *Herrick* 4. He was later to write:

> At this stage of the campaign it was evident that we still had a huge amount to learn and if we were all honest with ourselves we were only just scraping the surface of the complex issues that would underline all future deployments to Helmand Province, particularly the tribal dynamics. The previous Op *Herrick* 10 had been overstretched and under resourced. Op *Panther's Claw* was flawed as the follow-up, the holding of ground, was not done effectively.

His experience was to stand him and No 1 Company in good stead. No 1 Company was deployed to Patrol Base 4 which could only be supplied by helicopter and air drop. It was one of the most austere UK patrol bases in central Helmand. His predicament was not unusual. The lack of manpower and surveillance equipment meant that the insurgents had the freedom to plant an IED minefield on three sides of the base. It would take them close to three days to clear a route so that the Royal Engineers, just 1 mile away, could build proper sangars to observe and dominate the ground with direct fire weapons.

Early on in their deployment towards the end of October, Guardsman Chris Dunn, a general purpose machine gunner, recounted his first contact with the Taliban. He was engaged in his first Company operation some 1¼ miles south-west of Patrol Base 4:

> Tensions were high as we listened to the Taliban dick us on our radio scanners. Their messages suddenly died off, a clear signal that they knew where we were and were going to open fire. I suddenly felt a sharp impact on the side of my head, knew I was still alive and got the GPMG [general purpose machine gun] into action firing at likely enemy positions. Once the Taliban had withdrawn, I realised how lucky I'd been. A round had hit me bang in the middle of my helmet, passed through the top of my hairline and out the back. I had to tab around Helmand for a few more days with two holes in my helmet.

By mid-November, No 1 Company was able to push its patrols further out but the insurgents' use of IEDs was all but impossible to neutralise completely. The loss of a much respected and experienced platoon sergeant, Sergeant John Amer, and others very seriously injured, to an IED blast was a grievous blow. The platoon commander, Lieutenant Dougie Dalzell, had a close working relationship with Sergeant John Amer. As Major Till said, "it's difficult to understand what it's like to lose your platoon sergeant, you can't hug a brother officer but I could at least put my arm on his shoulder."

There was frustration too. Everyone recognised the importance of 'courageous restraint' but observing an IED team threading death and disfigurement and using children or locals as cover, and not being able to call in an Apache helicopter, was hard to bear. There was a justifiable feeling that brigade and regional command level interpreted General Stanley McChrystal's doctrine too rigorously.

Similar to the experience of the Grenadiers and Household Cavalry, the major operation of the tour was the joint operation with the US Marine Corps, Op *Moshtarak*. No 1 Company was tasked to push west of Patrol Base 4, dominate the terrain around Walizi, and link up with 2nd Battalion The Royal Welsh Battle Group. A routine patrol before the main operation led to the death of Lance Corporal Daz Hicks, who had been recruited from Penzance in Cornwall. He left a wife and two young children.

For No 1 Company, Op *Moshtarak* began to unravel fast. Based on flimsy intelligence, the Company, supported by the ANA, was tasked with a cordon and search operation on several compounds. More by good fortune than sound judgement, they stumbled across a suicide IED store with Afghan uniforms and Pakistani currency. A nest of insurgents, roused by the find, engaged the Company with a heavy weight of fire until they were silenced by a Hellfire missile. A courageous Afghan soldier was killed in the firefight.

Much worse was to follow. The next phase of Op *Moshtarak* was to insert a new command post to the west of Walizi village, an essential task to ensure it remained a protected community. Lieutenant Dougie Dalzell's platoon was committed to clearing a compound under fire and with the ever present threat of IEDs. Dougie Dalzell was killed in action. He was a charismatic officer with the brightest of futures. But that, sadly, was true of any number of Guardsmen killed in action. Lance Corporal Daniel Robertson was to lose both legs a few minutes later. Just a few months into the tour, No 1 Company had lost three killed in action and eight had lost limbs.

Op *Moshtarak* was to continue for a further two months. The focus became the completion of Route Trident to link the rest of the Battle Group with Patrol Base 4 and establish new command posts across the area of operations. It was not without further tragedy. On a routine supply of Command Post Walizi, Guardsman Michael Sweeney was killed by an IED. He was the fourth member of the Company to fall in action.

In spite of their losses, Major Toby Till was able to look back on Op *Herrick* 11 with qualified pride. Qualified because to lose four men in action and eight with severe injuries is a high price. But there was unquestionable pride in the valour and resilience shown by the officers, non-commissioned officers, and Guardsmen under his command.

Some injuries remain hidden or emerge over time. Guardsman Jack Davies was to succumb to his wounds four years after the IED strike in October 2009.

Winston Churchill once said that "medals cast a shadow". But they also cast a glow, not so much on the individual awarded a medal but on the collective memory of those who have been together and fought together. Members of No 1 Company received four Military Crosses, a Mention in Dispatches, a Member of the British Empire, and several Joint Commanders' Commendations for their actions around Patrol Base 4.

Major Toby Till and his colleagues in No 1 Company to this day have a wellbeing WhatsApp group. They keep in constant touch from all corners of the UK and abroad.

Major Toby was later to remark, "Op *Herrick* XI was the most violent tour witnessed by the Regiment since WW2. We lost seven members of the Battlegroup and many cruelly maimed and injured. The memories I have, both bitter and sweet, will stay with me forever."

The Household Cavalry Regiment, D Squadron, had already distinguished itself on Op *Herrick* 4 under 16th Air Assault Brigade in the spring and summer of 2006 as the Brigade's reconnaissance squadron. D Squadron had also been provided for Op *Herrick* 8, once again under 16th Air Assault Brigade. It had become only too familiar with the Taliban-dominated town of Musa Qal'ah.

The Household Cavalry Regiment Battle Group on Op *Herrick* 11 was commanded by Lieutenant Colonel Harry Fullerton. Colonel

Harry was an experienced officer who drew on his time in the Mounted Regiment as well as his operational background in Iraq and Afghanistan to lead the Household Cavalry Regiment Battle Group as 11th Brigade's reconnaissance regiment. It was a job that demanded both patience and agility. The Household Cavalry found itself, as it often did in Iraq and Afghanistan, fulfilling a myriad of roles: helicopter insertions, dismounted patrolling, cordon protection, establishing forward defensive rings around the brigade's patrol bases, and partnering the ANA on operations.

The parallel between mounted and operational soldiering may not seem obvious at first glance. The bond between horse and soldier is no different from the bond between a soldier and his vehicle. And in Musa Qal'ah, the Household Cavalry Regiment Battle Group had to master and deploy four different vehicles each with different attributes: Mastiff, Scimitar, Jackal, and Panther. Like a good infantry soldier who has a sound eye for ground and fieldcraft, a good soldier with mounted experience developed, in Colonel Harry's words, "ground sign awareness", an essential skill in spotting where IEDs may have been planted. Technology played an important part but so did intuition. Troopers in the Battle Group found and neutralised 17 IEDs.

The Household Cavalry Regiment Battle Group, despite the winter months, experienced a high tempo of operations. To the south of Musa Qal'ah was an area of high ground dominated by the Taliban. It allowed the insurgents to overlook Patrol Base Minden where A Company 2nd Battalion The Royal Welsh, armoured infantry equipped with Warrior, and attached to the Household Cavalry Regiment Battle Group, were based. In a combined Household Cavalry Regiment Battle Group operation with the ANA, elements of the Battle Group took the high ground and established permanent observation posts.

The Battle Group mounted a similar operation in the north close to Mount Musa Qal'ah. Here A Company 1st Battalion The Royal Anglian Regiment was based at Patrol Base 'Gallipoli' so named because of its unnerving similarity to the look and conditions of the 1915 Dardanelles campaign. Fortunately the similarity ended there. The Battle Group assaulted and took the high ground, known as 'Horseshoe Ridge', once again with ANA support. Both operations afforded the Household Cavalry Regiment Battle Group much greater freedom of manoeuvre to stabilise the Musa Qal'ah region.

The Household Cavalry Regiment Battle Group tour had coincided not only with the new philosophy of 'courageous restraint' but also the US surge of significant additional troops. Op *Cobra's Anger* was a US-led offensive to disrupt Taliban supply and communication lines in Helmand's Zad valley. A, B, and C Squadrons of the Household Cavalry Regiment Battle Group provided a blocking force and reconnaissance screen for the main attack. Twenty vehicles were hit by IEDs but with no fatalities. The Mastiff vehicle proved itself worthy of its name, large, protective and reassuring. There was one grievous blow, however, and that was the loss of the Battle Group ammunition technical officer (ATO, or bomb disposal expert), Captain Daniel Read, in an IED explosion. Colonel Harry wrote, "Captain Dan Read had become, in a short space of time, a trusted comrade and friend whom we had relied upon a great deal."

The Brigade Reconnaissance Force, even by the extraordinary endeavours of 2009/10 in Helmand, had an outstanding tour. The force was largely made up of B Squadron, Household Cavalry, with a number of officers, non-commissioned officers, and Troopers made of the right stuff. Major Gus MacGilivary, Royal Regiment of Scotland and an SAS officer attached to the Household Cavalry Regiment Battle Group, was awarded the Military Cross; Captain Robin Bourne-Taylor, the Second in Command and a three-time Oxbridge Boat Race winner, won the Conspicuous Gallantry Cross.

As was the case for the Grenadier and Coldstream battalions, Op *Moshtarak* was the signature operation of Op *Herrick* 11. A Squadron, under Major Tom Giffard, which had been attached to the Grenadier Guards, reverted back to its parent Household Cavalry Battle Group and with a troop of Danish Leopard tanks cleared the routes between Lashkar Gar and Nad-e-Ali.

The Household Cavalry was to serve two further tours of duty: D Squadron as part of 16th Air Assault Brigade on Op *Herrick* 11, and the entire Household Cavalry Regiment as the Brigade Reconnaissance Force for 1st Mechanised Brigade under the command of Lieutenant Colonel Jim Eyre on Op *Herrick* 18.

In December 2010, ISAF had reached its peak of 131,000 troops from 20 NATO and 28 non-NATO nations. A total of 90,000 were from the US. The British Army strength was just under 10,000. At the height of the conflict, the British airfield at Camp Bastion was as busy as Manchester Airport.

The resupply needed by forward British bases in Afghanistan required Combat Logistic Patrols of between 150 and 200 vehicles every week. They were treated as combat operations with sizeable escort forces, counter-IED teams and punchy fire support. They were not unlike the Atlantic convoys of the Second World War except there were no wolf packs. The Taliban did their best to disrupt the vast amounts of freight on 'Jingly' trucks coming from Karachi over the Khyber Pass into Afghanistan.

Huge sums of money were spent and wasted, and probably ended up in the Taliban hands to ease safe passage. To reduce the numbers of troops deployed, extensive use was made of contractors to deliver supplies to military bases. As the war progressed, increasing numbers of civilian contractors filled other logistic roles 'behind the wire'. For example, the British base at Camp Bastion had contractors providing catering, repair and support of equipment, and maintaining unmanned aerial vehicles.

ISAF made extensive use of contractors to provide security for civilian officials. Whilst this reduced the total numbers of troops on the ground, many contractors often displayed highly aggressive behaviour. Their use of lethal force often seemed unconstrained by any rules of engagement. In Afghanistan, this resulted both in avoidable civilian casualties and in increased humiliation. This further damaged the legitimacy of international forces.

There was no let-up in the intensity of operations, nor indeed the threat, during Op *Herrick* 12. Right Flank of the 1st Battalion Scots Guards had already distinguished itself on Op *Herrick* 7, pioneering the use of the Warrior armoured fighting vehicle, supported by No 2 Company Coldstream Guards as dismounted infantry. Right Flank were known as 'Desert Devils' by the Taliban on Op *Herrick* 7. They were the natural choice as the armoured infantry company on Op *Herrick* 12. There was only one Warrior-borne company in Helmand and Right Flank deployed to Helmand to fulfil the role on the cusp of Op *Herrick* 11 and 12, some time before the rest of the Battalion whose role was, as yet, undecided.

On Op *Herrick* 12, the ambition of the commanding officer, Lieutenant Colonel Lincoln Jopp, was to be a ground holding battle group. Colonel Lincoln had commanded Scots Guards platoons and companies on operations and had won the Military Cross in Sierra Leone. He had trained the Battalion hard in Canada. Its appointment as Regional Battle Group South under 4th Armoured Brigade was fully deserved. But as many had come to realise in Helmand, uncertainty was the only certainty. The job was then given to the US Army as part of its 'surge' in the south and the planning for Op *Moshtarak*.

It looked as though the Battalion's carcass would be picked over for parts. It was not uncommon in Helmand or any other campaign where operational needs regularly took precedence over a battalion's preferred roles. Frustrating though it was at first glance, the Battalion took on the job as Afghan National Security Forces Development Headquarters. Given the change in focus from the US-led Afghan 'surge' to Afghan 'security leadership', it was an astute move. And given how the stars were prone to realign in Helmand, a ground-holding role might easily come the Battalion's way.

As the only armoured infantry company in Helmand on Op *Herrick* 11, it was clear that Right Flank would be used on Op *Moshtarak* in support of the Grenadier Guards under Lieutenant Colonel Roly Walker. It turned out that Right Flank would act as the tip of the arrow in a helicopter assault on the town of Sayedabad in central Helmand. The Guardsmen were excited at the prospect, having worn out themselves and their nerves from the Army's age-old custom of rumour-mongering.

Sayedabad had seen no security force presence for two years and was a haven for insurgents as a command and supply hub close to the ISAF Patrol Base line to the north. Colonel Roly Walker had, for some time, identified this hub as a Taliban weak point. There were no Warrior vehicles in which to travel. This time they were to deploy by helicopter with enough rations and water for 48 hours and ammunition and mortar rounds for eight days' combat.

It was an overwhelming load for each Guardsman to carry. Sleeping bags were discarded. "Aye, nae dramas, we're in Afghanistan, it isnae going to be that nippy," remarked one Scots Guardsman. No one believed that Afghanistan could be so cold. As the Guardsmen lay in ditches at night to observe and dominate the ground where the Taliban might lay IEDs, hypothermia became a real concern.

On the morning of 11 February, supposedly their final day in Sayedabad, a Right Flank patrol pushing to the north close to the patrol base line came under sustained fire. Overwhelmed by Right Flank's firepower, the Taliban were neutralised. But worse was to come. Friendly fire from a Canadian mentoring team over the canal to the west 'shaved' the Right Flank's second-in-command, Captain Murly-Gotto, with a .50-calibre round. The round did not hit him, but such was its kinetic energy it removed half his calf muscle. He survived but with life-changing injuries.

After Right Flank had been pulled out of Sayedabad by helicopter having sustained five casualties wounded in action, the situation soured once again in Kawshhal Kalay and Sayedabad. It was the old principle of holding ground. But with too few troops to do a proper job, and whatever hopes ISAF had of Afghan governance and the ANA/ANP proving to be somewhat of a mirage, Brigade decided to fly Right Flank back to Sayedabad. The Guardsmen, never short on humour, exchanged banter about their walk-in part in a Hollywood blockbuster, *Sayedabad, Part 2, The Return of the Borg*. (This was a nickname given to Right Flank at the time.)

If the insurgents decided to take on Right Flank on its return, it would draw them away from the Grenadiers to the north and the Household Cavalry who were clearing a route towards the US Marines to the south. Right Flank were dropped by night by helicopter; the ground was wet, boggy and freezing. A Guardsman remarked, "It didn't look too bad but with heavy packs, slippery thick clay it went straight up to your knees with every step, the men were toppling over, one into an icy irrigation ditch, hypothermia set in and my mate succumbed to the freezing temperatures. The RAF, to their credit, came straight back to casevac him out."

Right Flank also found that, in their brief absence, an IED belt had been laid. It wasn't long before 1 Platoon came under sustained fire with accurate single shots from a trio of firing points. A Javelin missile was fired at the insurgents. There were no further shots.

On 18 February, the Taliban set an ambush as 1 and 3 Platoons left their base. They were shot at from six points to the south and east. The grim, unnerving cry of "Man down" rang out. Lance Sergeant Davy Walker, shot through the head, died instantly. Guardsman Davy McLellan was shot in the chest. The insurgents had worked out the few options that Right Flank had open to them and had taken the time to set and execute a successful ambush.

Right Flank had played a full part in Op *Moshtarak* which would shape ISAF operations for at least six months. Op *Moshtarak* was tactically successful but building on its success at a strategic level was a different matter. Once again, the Taliban could endure tactical setbacks, mindful of their long-term goal of undermining Afghan governance and faith in the ANA/ANP.

The success of the Scots Guards tour in Afghanistan, bridging Op *Herrick* 11 and 12, would ultimately rest in gaining local people's support and conducting classic counter-insurgency operations.

Wiser and more experienced Guardsmen in Left Flank on Op *Herrick* 12 knew that their actual role in Helmand was always likely to change.

After in-theatre training and acclimatisation had taken place in Camp Bastion – the dummy IED lane gripping the attention of all – the Company Commander, Major Rupert Kitching, briefed his men: "This area is Loy Adera and this is Route Mars which runs through it. Our aim is to hold this ground from seven checkpoints and protect the communities around those checkpoints ... We're strung out because of the road, Route Mars, which is the principal link between Lashkar Gar and Gereshk, Helmand's second town to our east. Frankly, it's probably IED central."

Major Kitching went on, "The provincial governor had asked us to keep open the route to help freedom of movement for the local nationals. It's a key priority now that our strategy has changed to classic counter insurgency – what we used to refer to as 'Hearts and Minds', but really is about switching the campaign's centre of gravity from heavy firepower to gaining the support and will of the population."

Like everyone else, Left Flank had to partner Afghan forces at every level. The Scots Guards quickly learned that they were competent in their own way, but a little wild and often foolhardy. On an early joint patrol, a Guardsman found an IED next to a wall. The rigorous process to neutralise the device took over. It rightly took time. There was no room for error or a lapse in concentration. One of the Afghan sergeants, short on patience but long on luck, picked up a brick and threw it on the IED. The counter-IED team were stood down.

There was one story early on in the tour which demonstrates that battlefield discipline, ceremonial, and the traditional Guards ethos are often indivisible. A Mastiff hit an IED followed up with a heavy weight of fire from the insurgents. Fire was returned with interest. The Scots Guards were accompanied by a platoon from the Royal Welsh. After the firefight, the Royal Welsh noticed a Scots Guards colour sergeant neatly putting the empty bullet cases into ammunition tins. "Only the Guards would start tidying up after a firefight lasting three hours," remarked a Royal Welsh lance corporal.

Second Lieutenant Charles Pearson, six months out of Sandhurst, found himself commanding one of the seven checkpoints, 'Said Abdul', garrisoned by Left Flank's 11 Platoon. Charles Pearson was 24, but of all the things he recalled from the tour what struck him the most was how the experienced non-commissioned officers – his platoon sergeant was just 28 – mentored him and the resilience of the 18/19-year-old Guardsmen:

> You'd go stir crazy over six months if you kept yourself to yourself, there's always a fine balance but Guards non-commissioned officers and Guardsmen know that. If do your job properly and 'serve to lead' as Sandhurst taught us, you'll get along fine. I know in other battalions, things could go awry pretty quickly, people wandering around in flip flops, the platoon sergeant and platoon commander calling themselves by their first name or mate. The Guardsmen and non-commissioned officers were a generation on from the Scots Guards who fought at Tumbledown but they were the same men in character and courage.

Ill fortune and tragedy nevertheless took on a familiar pattern. Colour Sergeant Cameron, who ran Left Flank's fire support group and was on a routine patrol, took a shrapnel blast to his head from an IED close to Route Mars. Lance Sergeant Gary Jamieson lost both legs and an arm. Colour Sergeant Cameron was to die a year later from his injuries.

'Courageous restraint' was beginning to pay off. It took a special sort of soldiering but Guardsmen, adept at switching from ceremonial to operations at short notice, took it in their stride. Social worker, farmer, cultural linguist, diplomat, and policeman were just some of the guises Guardsmen had to take on as the Army re-learned lessons from counter-insurgency. The *Shuras*, which equate in British culture to the Parish Council Meeting, which hitherto had been regarded with a degree of scepticism, took on a greater sense of importance as the village elders saw what the Afghan government and ISAF had to offer. The meetings were not without their moments of alarm as Scots Guards officers and senior non-commissioned officers tried to work out who was genuinely interested in 'Cash for Works' programmes and who were insurgents gleaning intelligence.

Checkpoint Said Abdul was a success and served as a blueprint for army and local population co-operation. Eleven wells were drilled, upgrades to three mosques carried out and new irrigation ditches dug. A community centre with space for three small shops selling basic stuff received funding. It would renew the local economy. There was always a risk – the Taliban were desperate to overrun the checkpoint – but the risk of not doing anything constructive was greater.

Major Kitching had been a good friend of Major Sean Birchall, Welsh Guards, whose initiative to create a protected community at Basharan, south-west of Loy Adera, and a new school had been a model for success. Sean Birchall lost his life when his vehicle struck an IED, but both the Queen's Company Grenadier Guards and the Scots Guards kept the school open. As one local man remarked, "These Taliban offer nothing but trouble. If the bombs are cleared and you get rid of these men, my son can get to school in Basharan."

This became universally known as the 'Sean Birchall Effect' and demonstrated how consent-winning projects would do so much more good than 'mowing the lawn' with bombs and bullets which had so characterised earlier Op *Herrick*s.

The book *Six Months without Sundays* by journalist Max Benitz provides an excellent account of the Scots Guards tour in Afghanistan. The book's strength lies in its detailed description of the Scots Guardsmen's day-to-day life. This is a short passage which describes Guardsman Maclaclan's experience as a Vallon (mine detector) man in Left Flank's 12 Platoon. This was a job which few men wanted and which needed a particular temperament:

Dropping onto his chest, he kept his eyes on where the Vallon had been when it started beeping. He drew his bayonet and began his

IED confirmation drill through rock-hard ground. He could see the pressure plate designed to end him. A bearded man appeared out of nowhere gesturing that he wanted to cross the minefield.

"No, No, IED, IED, don't cross" shouted Maclaclan.

The man shrugged his shoulders and shook his head vigorously as if to say No IED.

The man walked nonchalantly through the IED belt. Later that day, six low-metal-content IEDs were found.

The clearance of Route Mars was complete. But in completing such a complex operation, and as the Rest and Recuperation Plot kicked in, the checkpoints had been left undermanned. Dominating the ground in depth could not be achieved. The insurgents had noticed. And the more experienced Guardsmen noticed that the routines of village life had changed. It was more than just intuition. It was not unlike Crossmaglen in the late 1970s and early 1980s where Household Division battalions had learnt that behavioural change amongst the locals usually heralded a terrorist attack.

There followed any number of contacts. Second Lieutenant Charles Pearson expressed his frustration at the constraints of the British Rules of Engagement or 'Card Alpha'. It was demanding for a platoon commander or non-commissioned officer who desperately needed fire support to get his Guardsmen out of a tight spot. As Charles Pearson said, "Sometimes you just don't have time to request Brigade for fire support heavier than an 81mm round. We understood the importance of courageous restraint but, as so often the case, the army interprets things too rigorously and Staff at HQ whatever level don't get what it's like on the ground. But it was ever thus."

B Company Scots Guards did not deploy as a company group. They provided heavy weapons support to Left and Right Flank, but also took responsibility for the main arterial route east of Lashkar Gar to Kandahar and Gereshk to the north – Route 601. Safe roads meant an economic mini-boom. It was a huge area to cover, the largest company area of operations in Helmand. It hosted 26,000 weekly road users on average, a road to be kept free of IEDs and police corruption. There were always incidents. Unpleasant incidents. Poor fire discipline by the ANA with good intentions but where young children died. It was hard for the Guardsmen to witness.

It was B Company's mission to secure Route 601. They did an unglamorous job from their base at Checkpoint Attal, sharing quarters with the ANP. They carried out their task with perseverance, and though off duty standards were relaxed, the 'what if' slide of slow weeks in suffocating heat was exacting for even the most experienced of men. The Guardsmen endured a relentless routine: three days on standby, Day 4 on guard duty with eight hours on stag (sentry duty). Fortunately, though they had their fair share of unpleasant incidents and exposure to Afghan mindless brutality, they did not lose anyone.

Left Flank had a harsh last few weeks of their tour. An insurgent was sitting in a compound on the end of a command wire attached to a main charge of around 150 pounds of explosive. He was to pull the cord and destroy an ISAF vehicle. Even a Mastiff would have been seriously damaged. He dozed off, awakening just a fraction too late and caught a minibus full of civilians. Eight were killed outright; five seriously maimed. A few were young children. Lieutenant William Tulloch commanding the Mastiff held his nerve in what must have been a scene of utter horror. He was awarded a Mention in Dispatches for his leadership.

The 21st of July was the longest of days. Left Flank were clearing the route of IEDs. It was painstaking work, six hours to clear less than 100 yards. And in such a lengthy time span, the Taliban had time to plan an ambush. Guardsman Kabunicaucau, a 6-foot 4-inch Fijian, took a burst of AK-47 to the cheekbone from what seemed multiple firing points. From then on, the unknown and unknowable took over as those in command tried to make sense of what was going on and how best to regain the initiative.

Everyone responded as they had been trained to do. Guardsman Ritchie Carr fired off 20 rounds in the direction of fire. Lance Corporal Stephen Monkhouse raced up in his Coyote vehicle and with his .50-calibre put down a heavy rate of fire. Lieutenant Tulloch wasted no time with his Mastiff to suppress firing points. Corporal Matthew Stenton commanding an RDG Viking fired into multiple firing points. The pitch changed to single high-velocity shots by the insurgents, or possibly one trained Taliban sniper. Lance Corporal Stephen Monkhouse, Corporal Matthew Stenton, and Second Lieutenant George Cowdry were shot in the head.

In Combined Force Headquarters in Lashkar Gar, reports were coming over the radio. To his utter dismay, Captain Tom Cowdry,

Second Lieutenant Cowdry's elder brother, an intelligence officer, received the news that his brother has been shot. He did not know if he was alive or dead.

A few hours later Colonel Lincoln Jopp came to Checkpoint Said Abdul and gave the sorrowful news that Corporal Stenton and Lance Corporal Monkhouse had died. "Guardsman Kabunicaucau and Mr Cowdry are both stable," he said.

Brigade headquarters declared Loy Adera the most violent part of Helmand. The minibus carnage had given Left Flank a chance to push their message that they were there to support the local population and let the economy thrive once again and that the insurgents, in the era of 'courageous restraint', were now the enemies of progress. Not everyone agreed. As one village elder said, "No infidels, no insurgency, and you cannot defeat them with 42 nations and the Afghan Forces as well."

On 1 August, Sergeant Dale McCallum was shot dead in the super-sangar at Checkpoint Said Abdul. He was one of the Battalion's best snipers and exposed himself for just a few seconds and a few inches above the sangar's parapet. It was clear that the gunman who had shot dead Lance Corporal Monkhouse and Corporal Stenton was probably one and the same.

For Left Flank, their priority remained keeping Route Mars clear as the upgrade to Route Trident continued to the east. The battle against IEDs was relentless. The IED cells knew their ground and where the Guardsmen could and could not see. On 12 August, an IED factory and drugs cache was found. On the way out, the patrol, led by Afghan commandos, came under fire. Maybe the patrol had become tired, frustrated at their losses over the last few months, and 'courageous restraint' had palled somewhat; an A-10 tank buster was called in by the Afghan commandos' fire controller. The firing stopped. Five died on the spot, three of whom were children. One of the wounded was pregnant. Responsibility for those deaths was firmly not with the Scots Guards but on every level it cast a shadow.

Free of provincial-level roles, the Battalion had finally got what it wanted in the last month of the tour as a ground holding battle group. The Army likes names which translate into easily remembered acronyms. 1st Scots Guards Battle Group became Combined Force Lashkar Gar. But it had paid its dues in blood and memories which would never be shaken off.

From the start of the Scots Guards tour, the whiteboard in the operations cell had "18 September 2010: Parliamentary elections". The elections, it was hoped, would be a visible sign of progress in security and governance in Helmand for Op *Herrick* 12. The Taliban issued a direct threat to all those involved. Despite the widespread security presence, there were 120 incidents that day. In a province of around 1.2 million people, only 36,162 votes were cast. Thanks to apathy and intimidation, the elections were not a victory for the Afghan government.

"Influence," as the Commanding Officer said, "never takes a day off." Headquartered with brigade headquarters, Combined Force Lashkar Gar sucked in a huge number of visitors. If high-profile visitors were visiting the Scots Guards, Colonel Lincoln would walk out onto the helipad without body armour or helmet. The visitors would outrank him by a country mile but they would be wearing full body armour. His nakedness immediately cut them down to size.

Visitors were a necessary evil. Some came for the bragging rights back home; most, however, because they genuinely wanted to see for themselves the reality of Afghanistan and how they could assist. Most politicians were noticeably poor in engaging with soldiers, resorting to clichés about rations and living conditions. But if it took time and rehearsal to host a visitor, it came naturally to Household Division battalions to present themselves in such a way that a visitor would say, as one did on return to the UK, "I visited the Guards, immaculate as one would expect."

Op *Herrick* 12 ended for the Scots Guards like all Op *Herrick*s, with a sense of relief foremost, and, except for just a very few, an extraordinary maturing of character. This took time to show. 'Decompression' in Cyprus after the tour helped the Battalion come to a kind of understanding with what it had had to witness but the system of justice back in the UK was unforgiving. As one magistrate remarked to a Scots Guards platoon commander defending a Guardsman who had got into trouble after the tour, "I don't want to hear ever again that a Guardsman was a fine GPMG gunner or could throw a grenade with pinpoint accuracy!"

Those Scots Guardsmen killed in action could at last be properly mourned, their families cared for and the wounded looked after as well as humanly possible. There was comfort in that.

Many of the Scots Guards' five fatal battle casualties and their families (these included Corporal Matthew Stenton, Royal Dragoon

Guards, attached to the Battle Group) and 36 non-fatal battle casualties will live with the scarred memories of their time in Afghanistan until their last day. But as Lieutenant Charles, now a successful businessman, remarked 12 years on, "I'm still in touch with many and now consider a number of non-commissioned officers who helped me avoid the usual pitfalls of an officer fresh from Sandhurst as good friends. I know it's a bit clichéd to say there is an unbreakable bond, but like many clichés it has more than a kernel of truth."

The Irish Guards were the last of the seven Household Division regiments to serve in Afghanistan. Many Irish Guardsmen had served with distinction attached to other Household Division battalions, or on the Staff, but September 2010 was its first deployment as a Battalion. In a letter to the Irish Guards Regimental Adjutant, Brian O'Gorman, the commanding officer, Lieutenant Colonel Christopher Ghika, wrote on 27 September 2010:

> 1IG assumed responsibility for the Brigade Advisory Group at 10am local. I have spent the last week permanently on the road. I have travelled north into the Upper Gereshk Valley to Forward Operating Bases (FOBs) RAHIM and KARNIKAH, where Nos 2 and 4 Companies will be based, then down to an area near Gereshk where Nos 1 and 3 will be. I popped into Lashkar Gar to the Scots Guards whom I know well from my time with them a few years back. Isolated patrol bases in Afghan compounds, often under constant attack are the norm, the amusing thing is the Micks prefer living there, taking pride in it all and don't want a more comfortable life.

Colonel Ghika wrote 24 handwritten letters to the Regimental Adjutant over the course of Op *Herrick* 13. They are a remarkably candid account of a tour: poignant but never plaintive, proud but never boastful, and gently humorous where humour was to be found. Given the commitments, the 'unforgiving minute' of a commanding officer's life in Afghanistan, the letters reflect the relationship between an operational Household Division battalion and the wider family back home whose principal link with the front line is the Regimental Adjutant.

The Irish Guards tour was memorable in many ways. Remarkably, it was only the Battalion's fourth operational tour outside the UK since Aden in 1966/67.

The lack of operational experience did not show. The Irish Guards company command plot had been developed to give an exceptionally strong deck of officers: Majors Adam Willis, Alexander Turner, Matthew Collins, Mickey Stewart, James Coleby, and Robert Money, all of whom were ideally suited to the nuanced counter-insurgency now being conducted in the campaign.

Training and institutional memory mattered. Rudyard Kipling, whose son, John, served with the Irish Guards and was killed in action in 1915, wrote about 'The Soul of a Battalion'. Since the Irish Guards' highly successful tours in Kosovo in 1999, Op *Telic* 1 in 2003, and Op *Telic* 10 in Iraq in 2007, the Battalion's preparation under Colonel Ben Farrell followed by Colonel Ghika had been thorough. The Battalion was over strength, competition to secure a place in the operational order of battle was fierce, and the Irish Guards knew they had much to offer. They were determined to show their mettle.

There had been a step change in the way the Army had prepared for Afghanistan since the first Op *Herrick* tours. Keeping fit, shooting straight, and basic infantry skills were all within the reach of a public duties battalion but there were few, if any, opportunities to train Guardsmen in the nuances of fighting as an all arms battle group. The Irish Guards had deployed to Kenya at the beginning of the year numbering 1,200 as a battle group supported by Armoured Engineers, a battery from the Royal Horse Artillery, air assault troops, and a company from the Kenyan Rifles. The conditions in Kenya were not unlike Afghanistan, austere, rugged, and hot. They also found time to celebrate St Patrick's Day with characteristic zeal.

After Kenya, the Battalion was engaged in 'Mission Specific Training' which, despite its strange lexicon given that the political objective in Afghanistan was never clear, was a testament to the Army's commitment to complete all arms professionalism. For the first time, Irish Guardsmen were calling in airstrikes in Otterburn and patrolling in Afghan villages and compounds that had been carefully created at Thetford. In a 'Regimental Perspective' on Op *Herrick* 13, Major General Bill Cubitt, the Irish

Guards Regimental Lieutenant Colonel, wrote, "The Commanding Officer, Christopher Ghika, said he believed the Battalion to be the best prepared and equipped that it has ever been for an operational tour. This was true and credit must go to Colonel Ben Farrell and Colonel Christopher – a totally committed and skilful officer."

Major Alexander Turner, a gifted officer and military historian who commanded No 2 Company on Op *Herrick* 13 and is still serving, wrote:

> Whilst the operating environment in Afghanistan was probably every bit as challenging back in the 19th and early 20th centuries, I would stand by my claim that the training burden facing Guardsmen today covers a breadth of skills and equipment that a soldier from the 1st, 2nd and 3rd Afghan wars would marvel at. We have over ten separate weapon systems in No 2 Company from 60mm mortar to shotgun and pistol. We have trained on over eight types of vehicle, four different night vision aids, biometric testing, two types of counter IED metal detectors and four separate radio systems from satellite to personal role devices, training in two languages, Pashtu and Dari, and we need to link in with our Danish colleagues.

Appearances and promises aside, the only true test of the Micks' preparation for fighting was during the first enemy contact. Lieutenant Ralph Gore, commanding 5 Platoon, wrote:

> My multiple was trudging through the high corn fields with the sun beating down. A beautiful walk in some forgotten world but then rounds smash into the ground around us. Everything clicks into place, those endless platoon attacks, ceaseless physical and appreciation tasks at Sandhurst, your mind clicks into a gear that you never thought you had and you can't help but smile to yourself that the last 18 months have worked.

It was far from a conventional tour. Nos 2 and 4 Companies were attached to the Danish Battle Group (wonderfully well equipped and true to their Viking heritage), and given free rein to operate in small groups, train and influence the ANA, engage with the local communities, but at the same time bring overwhelming firepower to bear at the right time. Much of what was required of them would have been the preserve of Special Forces in times gone by. No 1 Company was deployed to mentor the ANA Kandak (battalion) charged with the security of Highway 1 as it passed through the UK's sphere of operations. No 3 Company mentored the 3rd Kandak of the 3rd Brigade of the ANA's 215th Corps in the challenging Upper Gereshk Valley, including Gereshk city's commercial hub.

The Battalion's headquarters was based in Camp Tombstone – the name a throwback to American humour and link to the old Wild West. It was nestled into the corner of Camp Shrorabak, the home of the 3rd Brigade, 215th Corps. The Battle Group's sign outside the camp read 'Brigade Advisory Group'. In reality, Battalion headquarters was a mere transit camp presided over by the Quartermaster as Irish Guardsmen passed through to forward locations. But it did at least give Colonel Christopher the chance to do what any good commanding officer should do and get out as much as humanly possible and see for himself what was going on.

There was no longer any disquiet about the mentoring and training role in Afghanistan. If anything, it had begun to assume even greater importance. Although Ops *Moshtarak* and *Hamkari* (a huge intelligence and 'hearts and minds' operation to win over the residents of Kandahar) had been a clear success in pushing the Taliban out of key districts in Marjah and Kandahar Province, it did reveal serious weaknesses in Afghan governance. But the transition to Afghan security leadership was becoming an increasingly important priority. The West was growing tired and UK public support, never robust from the outset, was wavering in the face of the seemingly endless pictures and media coverage of soldiers killed in action and the sorrow of the repatriations at Wootton Bassett.

Some regiments found the mentoring role frustrating. The cultural differences were too stark. But for the Irish Guards with their healthy sense of the absurd and innate good humour, it was a task well within their grasp. More importantly, they were aware of the cultural limitations which Lawrence of Arabia knew only too well: "Do not try to do too much with your own hands, better the Arabs do it tolerably than you do it perfectly. It is their war and you are there to help them, not to win it for them. Actually, under the very odd conditions you'll find yourself in, your practical work will not be as good as you think it is."

341

The Battalion's tour enjoyed a number of early successes. It planned and supported an ANA Brigade operation. Op *Omid Char* brought security to an area long held as a Taliban stronghold. Nos 1 and 3 Companies worked their own brand of Mick magic to the business of developing the long-term skills of the ANA Brigade but also taking the fight to the Taliban. The Americans in particular seemed very taken by the Jackal vehicles, which most of the Battle Group used for fire support and manoeuvrability: "You guys must have no fear, do you actually fight in those things?" Despite their intended humour, it was a quip which came back to haunt the Irish Guards at the tour's end.

The first half of the tour had its fair share of tragedy. Guardsman Christopher Davies was killed in action from small-arms fire on 17 November. A further 16 Guardsmen had been wounded, many severely from IEDs. Major General Cubitt attended the repatriation of Guardsman Davies at RAF Lyneham: "The bearer party was immaculate and steady, few things are more moving than seeing young Guardsmen carrying a fallen comrade, the Association turned out in full as did the local community and Liverpool Branch at his funeral in St Helens. Those who say there is no sense of civic pride or community any longer in Britain should have seen this extraordinary event."

Equally, there were moments of happy memory. During Colonel Christopher's Rest and Recuperation, he received the news that His Royal Highness Prince William was to take over as Colonel of the Regiment. The new Colonel wrote: "It is with great pride that I take over as the 10th Colonel of the Irish Guards. It has been a firmly held aspiration of mine to be associated with the Micks. Ours is a unique family Regiment: a combination of the matchless traditions of the Foot Guards and that indefinable spark that marks out the Irish Guards, one of the world's great fighting regiments. God speed your safe return." To a Guardsman enduring the trials of life in a forward operating base in Helmand Province, the Prince's words were a terrific tonic.

The philosophy of 'courageous restraint' was now paying off. For No 2 Company in the Upper Gereshk Valley, the period from January to April 2011, the second half of the Micks' tour, was intense. First, they had to take the fight the Taliban. This they accomplished successfully. Secondly, they then had to establish secure compounds allowing the local population to carry on with their lives under a security umbrella. Local people assisted – unpaid – in the compounds' construction. They realised the sea change in military tactics and that the British Army was now doing everything possible to allow them to flourish as a people, but at the same time crushing the Taliban as they sought to continue the climate of fear and despair.

The IED threat remained, however, intimidating. Of the four Vallon operators in 4 Platoon, only one avoided an IED strike. Guardsmen had to steel themselves each time they went out on patrol.

The best counter-IED asset by some way was the local farmer. Most locals would mark an IED. Of 70 IED finds on the tour, 66 were discovered through local intelligence. It was a testament to the Micks' ability to engage with local people and their sensitivity towards them which helped them win trust – that all important factor in classic counter-insurgency. Given the ferocity of the campaign, it is somewhat surprising that they were able to achieve this. It was also in stark contrast to the British Army's experience in Northern Ireland, particularly South Armagh, where local intelligence was hard to come by for fear of hideous reprisal.

An Irish Guards sergeant summed up how he felt as an ANA advisor: "Being an advisor was a frustrating but rewarding task. It was an honour and privilege to have worked so closely with a totally different culture. I have been humbled by people who have so little yet would give you so much." He went on to say, "I believe the ANA with the right guidance will continue to improve and our exit strategy is not too far away." His words in 2011 were premature. The sentiment was right – the Army did its utmost – but deep-rooted characteristics of Afghan governance put paid to any hopes of Afghan security leadership.

As the prospect of the tour's end filled the Irish Guards with optimism and relief, tragedy struck on 23 March 2011. Major Matthew Collins and Lance Sergeant Burgan, both serving with No 3 Company, were killed when their Jackal vehicle was caught in a blast from a roadside IED as they returned to FOB Price.

The Irish Guards suffered 27 casualties on Op *Herrick* 13. Three were killed in action. Two other soldiers attached to the Battle Group, a Royal Engineer and a non-commissioned officer from the Royal Army Veterinary Corps were also killed in action. Six sustained life-changing injuries. 'Life-changing' is a redundant phrase for all those who served in Afghanistan. In some way, physically, mentally, or emotionally, everyone's life was changed through their experience in Helmand Province.

In a letter dated July 2010 to 'Families and Friends of the Regiment', Major General Sir Sebastian Roberts, the then Colonel of the Regiment, wrote:

> The Armed Forces are suffering more serious casualties than at any time in the last half-century, and the brunt is being borne by the infantry. The average battle group has been losing five to ten killed and ten times that number wounded. It is said that only one triple amputee survived during the whole of the Second World War; one a month now survives because of the huge advances in medical care and Guardsmen's overall fitness.

Colonel Christopher was awarded the OBE for outstanding command of the Battalion and Major Alexander Turner the Distinguished Service Order for "displaying a very rare combination of deep understanding, personal gallantry, flair and energy throughout the tour". There were three Mentions in Dispatches, two Queen's Commendations for Bravery and four Joint Commanders' Commendations. Sergeant K. Tomlinson was awarded the Estonian Silver Cross of Merit for his support to the Estonian Patrol Base Wahid.

The Mention in Dispatches awarded to Guardsman Tobin was typical of an Irish Guardsman's fortitude after a traumatic event. "On 2nd February 2011, Guardsman Tobin was on patrol when a Guardsman in front of him struck an IED suffering a traumatic amputation to both legs. Guardsman Tobin administered first aid that saved his brother Guardsman's life. Once the casualty was evacuated, Guardsman Tobin insisted that he should take over as lead man in the patrol sweeping for further IEDs as he went."

The last word should go to Colonel Christopher Ghika:

> Indigenous force development – the ANA – is hard to appraise. Self-assessment really of little value. Nevertheless, our training wing was in the words of the Afghan Brigade Commander one of the best training wings in the country. All of this work was, of course, useless unless it generated an invigorated force to conduct operations

against the insurgent. This we did, planning and executing three such operations with the ANA. The enemy was no longer at the gates of Helmand's commercial hub in Gereshk.

It was clear that Op *Herrick* 16 was going to be the high-water mark of British Forces in Afghanistan. As the Department of War Studies at King's College London said at the time, "Western forces have become much better at waging counter-insurgency. The problem is in the politics of this war. Across NATO, the public and politicians are increasingly war-weary. Life inside the Taliban may be grim right now. But with NATO on the way out, safe havens in Pakistan, and a fragile government in Kabul, Taliban prospects look bright."

The challenge was to sustain momentum in the transition to the ANA but at the same time crush the insurgents' ability to undermine society in the protected communities.

In the spring of 2012, the Taliban declared an offensive campaign to push back ISAF and Afghan forces. This failed but they still had a lot of fight left in them and the audacity to mount surprise attacks against seemingly well-defended bases. One such attack in 2012 saw a squad of well-led and determined Taliban fighters attack the joint UK–US–Afghan base in Helmand. They dressed in US Army uniforms and got close enough to lob grenades at US Marine aircraft. The attack led to the sacking of two US Marine Corps generals held accountable for the security breach. An inquiry by the UK House of Commons Defence Committee found the UK chain of command and role in the base's security confusing. No UK officer was ever held accountable.

The additional 33,000 US 'surge' troops deployed in 2010 withdrew by the late summer of 2012, leaving 68,000 US troops alongside 32,000 from other nations, including around 9,000 from the British Army. The Afghan Army took an increasing lead with the majority of its brigades operating independently of ISAF. Insurgent attacks in 2012 remained at the same level as 2011. What was encouraging, however, though of little comfort to a Guardsman about to go out on patrol, was the reduction in IED attacks by 20 per cent. Nevertheless, just under half of NATO fatalities were from IEDs. But this amounted to 80 per cent for the Afghan Army. ANA casualties also doubled in 2012 to 1,056 killed in action.

Another worrying trend was the 40 per cent increase in 'insider attacks' when 60 ISAF troops were killed in such a way. The Taliban claimed it was their 'plants' but the reality was that many Afghans would 'snap', often as a result of a minor grievance or provocation. In such a complex culture these were sadly the norm. Institutionally and intuitively, Guardsmen were as adept as any in reading others and their motivation, but Afghanistan was to test even the most culturally aware.

This was to be the Grenadier Guards' last tour in Afghanistan. Their previous tour had ended only 18 months before. But they were in good hands. The commanding officer, Lieutenant Colonel James Bowder, had been a company commander on Op *Herrick* 6, and a brigade chief of staff on *Herrick* 11. It seems trite to say they were battle hardened veterans but their collective memory mattered. Colonel James could draw on a wealth of experience, pretty well at every level of rank.

In the light of this, Brigadier Douglas Chalmers, commanding 12th Mechanised Brigade, had no hesitation in appointing the Grenadiers as one of the principal manoeuvre units: the Nahr-e Saraj North Battle Group; the Nad-e-Ali Battle Group was the responsibility of another outstanding regiment, 1st Royal Anglian; the Nahr-e Saraj South Battle Group was the Yorkshire Regiment supported by The Prince of Wales's Company Welsh Guards.

It seemed an inordinately short time between the Grenadiers' last two tours, but for political reasons at the end of 2011 the Danes reduced their long-standing military commitment. The Grenadier Battalion headquarters left early to act as a bridge with the Danes before they left. Nahr-e Saraj North covered some 385 miles. The city of Gereshk, which the Irish Guards had done so much to keep free from insurgent activity, remained the key economic centre, its security dependent on the perimeter defences of the 'Kamarband' and Highway 1.

Colonel James, now well versed in counter-insurgency, saw the situation with clarity. "The first two months, we fought the break-in battle. That means building understanding and trust in your lateral relationships to a point where you do more good than harm." There were setbacks but not of their own making. In early June, 18 civilians were killed in a night-time airstrike on the village of Sajawand. Nine young children were among the dead. The incident triggered significant damage to ISAF's reputation.

The brigade commander was quick to emphasise the new mindset as '*Primum non nocere*', 'First, do no harm'. They were now in the final phase of NATO's involvement, setting the conditions and tempo of the ANA's medium to long-term success. Disasters like the bombing of Sajawand were as costly to the West's credibility as the torture and prisoner abuse of Iraqis at Abu Ghraib in 2004.

Colonel James summed up his approach: "On the one hand, it was the Queen's Company working in depth from Patrol Base Clifton drawing the insurgents away from the places that mattered most to Afghans; and on the other Inkerman Company and No 2 Company increasing the will and capability of the ANA with whom they worked alongside."

For the Queen's Company, it was a never-ending series of operations as it sought to wrestle the initiative away from the insurgents who sensed that they too were at a critical stage of the insurgency. Lieutenant Fred Moynan, commanding 1 Platoon, commented, "Early on we were introduced to the weapon that defined this war, the IED. The bone-crunching bang, 'Man Down!' Waka Waka Waka, the inbound MERT Chinook to take the casualty to Camp Bastion. The unforgiving game of luck that we played – 30 Guardsmen had walked past that IED and yet it was one Guardsman's misfortune to take the wrong step."

The day of 21 June 2012 was to witness a typical firefight with the Taliban. A Taliban IED team was engaged in placing devices. The Queen's Company set about neutralising the Taliban, but first it had to win the firefight. A Guardsman lost both legs when he stepped on an IED. Others were badly wounded. Captain Brian Jordan, flying a US Marine Corps Venom, dangerously low on fuel and knowing a casevac Chinook was 30 minutes away, landed under insurgent fire and flew the casualties direct to Camp Bastion Field Hospital. He was later awarded the Distinguished Flying Cross by the British ambassador in Washington.

Taliban snipers, not as gut wrenching to a Guardsman's psyche as an IED, remained an ever-present threat. The Queen's Company Second Captain, Captain Olly Holcroft, whose father Lieutenant Colonel Patrick Holcroft was among the first to deploy to Northern Ireland in 1969, devised a strategy to winkle out snipers. By inserting a Royal Anglian reconnaissance platoon by night into a known Taliban firing position, he then sent out a Grenadier patrol (brave men to a man) to draw in the Taliban sniper. The Taliban sniper appeared only feet away from the Royal Anglian reconnaissance platoon. Pursued by grenades and machine-gun and rifle fire, the gunman somehow escaped, much to the platoon's embarrassment, as he shimmied and spirited himself away through the adjoining compounds.

Major Piers Ashfield, the Captain of the Queen's Company, who was awarded the DSO after the tour, challenged the conventional wisdom at the time that night operations were difficult to carry out:

> Logistics and resource meant that for a lot of the time we had to remain static in our patrol bases. But this just gave the Taliban time to sow IED belts. If you made a concerted effort to breach the belt, and good targeted intelligence was key here, then night operations were quite manageable. We crossed a much-heralded IED belt at night, crossing tributaries of the Helmand River before surprising the enemy. All tall Guardsmen keeping their heads above water but that's The Queen's Company for you.

The Queen's Company received a Commendation from a US Marine Corps two-star general commanding Regional Command South West in Bastion for its performance throughout the whole tour.

No 2 Company, commanded by Major Chris Sargent of the Welsh Guards, was no less in the heat of battle. Their record was best exemplified by their actions at the end of May and early June which led to the awarding of the Victoria Cross to Lance Corporal James Ashworth and the Military Cross to Captain Michael Dobbin, the reconnaissance platoon commander, who at the time of the action was attached to the Company.

The Company was based in Patrol Base Rahim on an escarpment above the Helmand River in the notorious Upper Gereshk Valley. In the summer months, half-way through their tour, the trees, crops, and poppy fields gave the insurgents plenty of cover. As the summer took hold, there was an obvious build-up of insurgents to the south in the area of Knowja Morad.

To allow the insurgents to create momentum of their own was unthinkable. But at the same time No 2 Company had to address a growing issue of manpower in the face of relentless patrolling to keep the insurgents off balance and the trickling effect of casualties (fortunately none yet fatal). This meant that Guardsmen were doing stags of at least seven hours. No 2 Company was determined to win back the momentum.

A Taliban sniper team in Mohamad Za'i, a small hamlet but a nest of IEDs and insurgents, had become a serious threat. A helicopter assault was launched to clear the area. Resistance was fierce and it was during this operation that Lance Corporal James Ashworth won the Victoria Cross at the cost of his own life. This extraordinary action is covered in the book's prologue.

The principle of 'courageous restraint', adhered to in both spirit and letter by the Grenadiers, took a knock through no fault of their own on account of the number of civilian casualties caused by IEDs. Five children were caught in a blast in mid-July. Two died instantly and one little girl lost both legs and an arm. For Guardsmen, losing a colleague is bad enough but they know at least they can honour his sacrifice and his memory. The senseless slaughter of innocent civilians, particularly children, affected them all.

The remainder of No 2 Company's tour continued in the same vein of success tempered by ill fortune and the vagaries of fate. As their tour ended, the company commander, Major Sargent of the Welsh Guards, remarked that it had been a blessing to command a Grenadier Company adding, "Whether we did enough will remain to be seen."

The Inkerman Company, under Major Dom Alkin and based in Patrol Base Clifton, was tasked to hold the Kamarband line to the east of Gereshk which ran along a north–south track that split the fields on the Helmand River's northern bank. In the minds of the Afghans, the line marked the extent of their control. Outside that line was seen as disputed territory. It was here that the Inkerman Company focused their efforts to close with the enemy but at the same time build the ANA's confidence that they could (and should) engage the enemy on their own terms without Grenadier support.

Inkerman Company's experience of the tour followed an all too familiar pattern: successful operations, lucky escapes and, sadly, the ghastly misfortune of IEDs and gunshot wounds to six Guardsmen, a Marine and a Bombardier attached to the Company.

The bare facts of the Grenadiers' last tour of duty in Afghanistan bear witness to the Taliban's willingness to continue the fight. Tactical setbacks meant little to them. They knew the West had had enough and the ANA were hollow men behind Western optimism. During 239 days in Afghanistan the combined Grenadier, Danish, and Afghan Battle Group were engaged in 402 enemy contacts, and suffered 117 IED strikes and a further 241 IED finds. A total of 28 men were killed in action including five Guardsmen, and a further 149 were wounded. The Regiment was awarded one Victoria Cross, one Distinguished Service Order, two Military Crosses, six Mentions in Dispatches, one Queen's Commendation for Bravery and one Order of the British Empire.

Colonel James, like any commanding officer who has lost men killed in action or severely wounded, had mixed feelings: "The tour wasn't about getting rid of the insurgents. Certainly, we prevailed in the battle of wits and will. The Kamarband was to a large extent secure and violence in Gereshk at a three-year low. But the principal measure of success was that, by the time we left, the ANA felt capable of taking on the close battle against the insurgents." It was a statement of guarded optimism.

A poignant postscript to a tour where five Guardsmen lost their lives, Sergeant Karl Shadrake, a platoon sergeant in the Queen's Company, gave a moving eulogy at his brother, Guardsman Shadrake's, funeral at St Mary's Cathedral, Wrexham. Guardsman Shadrake, also serving in the Queen's Company, had been killed on 17 August.

The Household Cavalry completed their final Op *Herrick* tour, Op *Herrick* 18, from May 2013 to October 2013. By then the failure of Afghan security leadership was becoming only too clear. It was just a matter of time before the Taliban were able to run down the clock. As the Department of War Studies at King's College London said in 2013, "in the West expect to see the rapid development of governance so we can get out. But, of course, you're in a part of the world where corruption and incompetence are the norm. The Afghan government had political and financial interests in not reforming; neither had they the will to provide security leadership. Their interests will far outweigh any leverage that foreign powers can bring to bear."

Between 2012 and 2014, Taliban offensives were usually defeated but, after the withdrawal of US and NATO forces from combat roles and the marked reduction in air support to Afghan forces, the security situation steadily worsened. The Taliban's capture of Kunduz in September 2015 spelt out the one truth of the campaign: time was always on their side and if they bided their time well, Afghan corruption and inadequate strategic leadership by the West and wavering public support would be no match for a determined insurgency.

Colonel Jim Eyre, whose father, also called Jim, had been the Major General 1983–86, had the honour of commanding the Household Cavalry Regiment on Op *Herrick* 18, their final tour of duty in Afghanistan. It was the last of six regimental deployments to Afghanistan, two more than any other regiment in the Household Division. Of course, not all were full regimental deployments. Sometimes it was just a squadron or so, but it did represent a notable feat of arms, a more or less unbroken period of operations from Northern Ireland, the Falklands campaign, Kosovo, Bosnia, Iraq, and Afghanistan.

Colonel Jim was sanguine about his Regiment's achievements during the tour. He was right to be so. But it was tempered by a recognition that the tour was a shrinking in the Army's involvement: "We were on the way out, the moral justification weighed heavily on us as we did our very best to give the ANA the wherewithal to make a go of things."

The Household Cavalry certainly made a go of things. For the first time they were given responsibility for the Intelligence, Surveillance, Target Acquisition and Reconnaissance Group (ISTAR Group) as part of 1st Armoured Infantry Brigade at Lashkar Gar. In short, they were the eyes in the sky and ears on the ground to glean vital information on what the Taliban were up to.

It was a role with an exceptional span comprising the Brigade Reconnaissance Force, Brigade Troops Echelon; Danes with Leopard tanks; an Estonian reconnaissance troop, tough and determined; No 2 Company of the Irish Guards under Major Jonathan Palmer; and Badger Squadron from 2nd Battalion The Royal Tank Regiment: five nationalities in all, and at least 19 Household Cavalry officers serving in a variety of roles across the theatre of operations. There had always been a blue-red-blue thread in Afghanistan from the outset but it was noticeably strong in the summer of 2013.

By the end of the tour in early October 2013, they had conducted 85 planned operations. It had been a wide remit from disrupting the movement of explosives, weapons, and ammunition in central Helmand to providing a security buffer for the Royal Engineers tasked with the closure of five patrol bases. But they were still very much in the arena and carrying the fight to the Taliban. "Wily as ever," remarked Colonel Jim Eyre as the troops under his command in the group manoeuvre role assumed the dangerous and often daunting role of taking on the Taliban in areas they controlled with their menacing maze of IEDs.

It had taken time and a lot of political and Ministry of Defence feet dragging, but by now the quality of protective equipment afforded to the Army was nothing short of superb. An example was the Mk VII helmet which saved at least two Household Cavalry Troopers from direct hits.

It is a questionable measure of success, at least in the Warrior mindset, to sustain no fatal casualties during an operational tour. But Colonel Jim Eyre was right to take pride from his valedictory words, "We brought everyone home."

It was left to Lieutenant Colonel Toby Till, now commanding the 1st Battalion Coldstream Guards, to complete the final Household Division tour of Afghanistan. Colonel Toby had commanded with great distinction, though at some cost, No 1 Company on Op *Herrick* 11. This final tour, Op *Herrick* 20, was as far removed from his previous experience in the winter of 2009/10 as a training exercise in Thetford was from a desperate firefight. The British Army, driven by Western political expediency, along with its NATO allies, had reached the end game in Afghanistan. In essence, this was intended to be an honourable withdrawal, with the Afghanistan government confident and secure in its own leadership.

The Coldstream deployed in February 2014. No ground holding battle group role, no principal manoeuvre unit or Brigade Mentoring and Advisory Group, just the quietly reassuring role as Kabul Support Unit. It was force protection to all UK forces within Kabul as the country prepared for elections, a new president and the withdrawal of all NATO forces with the exception of training and advisory teams.

In September 2014, after one or two dummy runs with ballot papers mislaid or in need of a recount, President Ashraf Ghani was elected as president. On 28 December 2014, NATO formally ended ISAF combat operations in Afghanistan and transferred full security responsibility to the Afghan government.

By August 2021, some would say that the only unqualified success of the wars in Iraq and Afghanistan was the killing of Osama bin Laden in 2011. The US decision to invade Iraq in 2003 and the British government's tacit encouragement of such a course of action must stand as one of the worst political decisions of the 21st century.

The 2001 destruction of Afghanistan's Taliban government and its forces succeeded in getting rid of the majority of Al Qaeda from Afghanistan. But the failure in late 2001 to hound down the Al Qaeda fighters in the Tora Bora Mountains allowed the movement to bide its time and regroup in the safe havens of Pakistan. The fighters returned with a vengeance in 2006.

The 2003 attack on Iraq destroyed Saddam Hussein's government. But the justification for the attack, the so-called Weapons of Mass Destruction in Hussein's possession, proved to be false.

Within both wars there were multiple political, ethnic, religious, and economic conflicts. It all became hideously complex, a complexity that Western politicians were unable to understand let alone grasp. As Lieutenant General Sir Graeme Lamb remarked in 2007 when he was the deputy commander in Iraq, "this is as complex as anything I've ever done ... three-dimensional chess in a dark room." It certainly gave lie to that old quip that war was too important to be left to soldiers.

Iraq and Afghanistan were, nevertheless, a lot more than 'nation-building under fire', a phrase used by many senior British officers. There was a political dimension, often right down to the tactical level. The 24/7 news flow with the eye-catching but often meaningless strap line of 'breaking news' meant that the 'narrative battle' was sometimes more important than the armed conflict itself. This created a great deal of undue nervousness in Her Majesty's Government and the UK population.

The West often struggled to achieve moral legitimacy in the world's eyes, particularly with Muslims. Abuse of detainees at Abu Ghraib and Bagram by the US, the killing of Baha Mousa in British Army custody in Basra, counter-productive tactics, and the needless killing of civilians by resorting to heavy bombing meant that the West never quite won the propaganda war.

Both Iraq and Afghanistan demonstrated that without a strategy to achieve national objectives, military success at an operational or tactical level cannot guarantee strategic success. It took far too long for both the US and UK to acknowledge the inconvenient truth that they were fighting well-organised insurgencies. Both Iraq and Afghanistan deserved better strategic leadership. As for the British Army, it deserved much better than for all the sacrifice, money and metal to be turned to dust.

For the men and women of the Household Division who fought so valiantly during those two decades, there will be mixed feelings. Most would say they would not have missed the experience for anything, and that they grew immeasurably as human beings; others, understandably, would point to the humiliating events of August 2021 when the Taliban swept to power.

After Iraq and Afghanistan, the Household Division never stood higher in the eyes of its peers. Some very fine officers and non-commissioned officers now fill significant positions in the Army. Those who decided to leave would bring wisdom and leadership to civilian life. And for those who watched the bearer party from the Queen's Company 1st Battalion Grenadier Guards at the Queen's funeral, just a few days back from Op *Shader* in Iraq, they would see the unbreakable link between operational and ceremonial excellence.

Epilogue: Op *Shader* in Iraq and the Beat of the Drum

In 2009, the British Army's presence in Iraq, Op *Telic*, drew to a close. The Household Division along with the rest of the Army believed that they had seen the last of Iraq. It was a view based on optimism rather than a cold, hard look at a region of the world that is a prisoner of its geography and history.

As Op *Herrick* began to draw breath in the summer of 2014, news began to filter through of an extremist Islamic group called ISIS (the Islamic State of Iraq and Syria). Its Arabic acronym was 'Daesh', and swathes of territory in northern Iraq and Syria were now falling under their hold, with towns being overrun. Systematic brutality, designed to terrify the local population and horrify the international community, was widespread. There was a real threat that Baghdad would be taken.

The West had become tired. Iraq and Afghanistan had taken their toll and there was little appetite for further involvement in a region that had cost so much in resources, money and, above all, lives.

In August 2014, the US deployed the headquarters of 1st (US) Infantry Division to Baghdad to coordinate the international military contribution of 35 nations, Op *Shader*, and to stop the advance of ISIS. Brigadier Christopher Ghika was the one-star deputy commander of the US forces. Before he became the Major General, he was appointed deputy theatre commander in 2018/19, well placed to observe events as they unfolded and the contribution of the Household Division to Op *Shader*.

The objectives were threefold: first, destroy the enemy when in plain sight, international special forces would hunt down and destroy ISIS when not in plain sight; second, assist the government of Iraq in containing the threat; and thirdly, train and develop the Iraqi forces to deal with the threat themselves. This last objective was where the Household Division added conspicuous value.

The effort was spread across Erbil in northern Iraq, Taji in western Iraq, and hastily re-purposed coalition bases from Op *Telic*. The training audience varied from individuals to brigade-sized groups. The Household Division tours, along with the rest of the Army, fell into familiar six-month rotations. The ISIS presence was reduced dramatically and by 2018 they could no longer claim to hold any territory in Iraq or Syria.

Op *Shader* may have had more limited objectives than Op *Telic*, but for many Guardsmen it offered, if not the real friction of combat, then at least a demanding theatre of operations. This was a much-valued prize for any professional soldier. The operation was not risk-free; the 1st Battalion Irish Guards were subject to continued and accurate rocket attacks as late as March 2020, when Lance Corporal Brodie Gillon, an attached medical assistant, was killed. Two officers were also badly wounded and repatriated to the UK.

Even among the strain of the unknown and in trying living conditions, there is always an opportunity to live in as civilised a way, bringing some home comforts where feasible. The Household Division has always displayed style in this respect, both on exercise and on operations around the world. Rex Whistler, a talented artist who served in the Welsh Guards in the Second World War and was killed on his first day in action in Normandy in July 1944, used to paint murals and pictures wherever he went to brighten the lives of the Guardsmen, helping them to escape the anxieties of war. The 1st Battalion Welsh Guards on Op *Shader* recreated a familiar scene from one of Whistler's paintings in a large sangar in the Zorbash compound in the Kurdistan region of northern Iraq on Op *Shader* 13. They drew great comfort from this salute to the regiment's past in Normandy.

Op *Shader* was the last operation undertaken in the Middle East. One of the overriding themes of *Those Must Be The Guards* is how effective the Household Division is in playing to its strengths, how it is always able to conduct itself with restraint, and train others with thoroughness tempered by style and humour. This has become part of its collective unconscious, inherited and passed down by generations of Guardsmen. And while the image of a tall Guardsman standing on Horse Guards might convey a sense of stereotype, the reality is different. Guardsmen are individuals with their own idiosyncrasies, and there is always a place in the Household Division for the rather unconventional officer or soldier. The same applies to the regiments that form the Guards. They all have their own traditions and unique characteristics, but it is their collective motto that brings them together: *Septum juncta in uno*.

The past 55 years, the period covered in this book, has been as busy as any in the Household Division's long history. Leaving aside the constant and unrelenting drumbeat of soldiering, including ceremonial duties from the routine to the exceptional, the Guards have been closely involved in the many events that could not have been imagined back in 1969. Wars and conflicts, by their nature, often begin when least expected, and invariably last longer than first thought. Back in 1969, no one could have predicted, sensibly, that the Northern Ireland Troubles would last for some 30 years; that the Cold War would end suddenly in late 1989; or that British troops would fight in the Falklands, Iraq and Afghanistan, conduct peace enforcement operations in the Balkans, and carry out numerous tasks at home from delivering babies, to firefighting and Covid-19 testing; and perhaps, most unexpected of all, help to train and equip the Ukrainian Army in a war against Russia.

If there was uncertainty about the future in early 1969, that short moment of relative calm before yet another storm, then nothing has changed over half a century later. 'Expect the unexpected' is the mantra by which any decent army keeps itself ready and capable for the next challenge, although this basic principle is not always understood by others, including politicians, who prefer the biblical phrase about armies beating 'their swords into ploughshares, and their spears into pruning hooks'.

However, nothing has changed since 1969, nor indeed since the Guards were formed in the mid-17th century, to suggest that armies are no longer required or that they can be allowed to shrink to the point where they are unable to face the unexpected. All armies need a Praetorian Guard, and for the British Army it is the Household Division, a steadfast band of men and women who serve their Colonel-in-Chief and the nation, on the streets of London, at home and around the world.

Acknowledgements

In writing the history of the Household Division from 1969 to 2023, we should like to thank the Trustees of the Household Division. In particular, we owe a debt of gratitude to Major General Sir Christopher Ghika, KCVO, CBE, who not only commissioned the writing of the book, but who has been unfailingly supportive, in reading the manuscript and making many helpful comments, and agreeing to write the introduction.

We are also indebted to the staff of Headquarters Household Division, in particular: Colonel Jeremy Bagshaw, CBE; Colonel Guy Stone, LVO; Lieutenant Colonel James Shaw; Major William Style; and Garrison Sergeant Major Andrew 'Vern' Stokes, OBE, MVO, who have all gone out of their way to help us in the research and writing of the book.

Each chapter has its mentors and markers. We would like to thank General Sir Redmond Watt, KCB, KCVO, CBE, DL; Major General Sir Robert Corbett, KCVO, CB; Major General Mike Scott, CB, CBE, DSO; Major General Peter Williams, CMG, OBE; Brigadier Iain McNeil, OBE; and Colonel Charles Bremner.

Particular thanks for advice and written or face-to-face interviews go to: Lieutenant General Sir John Kiszely, KCB, MC, DL; Lieutenant General Sir Bill Rollo, KCB, CBE; Lieutenant General Sir Roland Walker, KCB, DSO; Major General Sir Evelyn Webb-Carter, KCVO, OBE, DL; Brigadier Ben Barry, OBE; Brigadier James Ellery, CBE; Brigadier Christopher Wolverson, OBE, DL; Colonel Piers Ashfield, DSO, MBE; Colonel Sir Brian Barttelot, Bt, OBE; Colonel Simon Falkner, OBE; Colonel Harry Fullerton, OBE; Colonel James Greaves;

Colonel Charlie Knaggs, OBE; Colonel Sir William Mahon, Bt, LVO; Colonel Sir Alexander Malcolm, Bt, OBE; Colonel Richard Taylor, DSO; Colonel Toby Till, MBE; Lieutenant Colonel Chistopher Anderson; Lieutenant Colonel Lieutenant Colonel Robert Cartwright, LVO; Lieutenant Colonel John Cargill; Lieutenant Colonel Crispin Black, MBE; Lieutenant Colonel Ray Evans, MBE; Lieutenant Colonel Simon Soskin; Lieutenant Colonel Tim Spicer, OBE; Lieutenant Colonel Giles Stibbe, OBE; Lieutenant Colonel Tom Thorneycroft; Major Sir Hugh Robertson, KCMG; Major William McLean; Captain Mark Coreth; Captain Rupert Uloth; Captain Waldo Upperton; Regimental Sergeant Major Dean Bailey; The Hon Ralph Assheton; Christopher Mackarness; Charles Pearson; and Max Benitz for his outstanding book on the Scots Guards in Afghanistan, Six Months without Sundays.

On the nature, ethos and values of the Household Division, we should particularly like to thank: Field Marshal Lord Guthrie of Craigiebank, GCB, GCVO, OBE, DL; Lieutenant General Sir James Bucknall, KCB, CBE; Lieutenant General Sir George Norton, KCVO, CBE; Major General Sir Bill Cubitt, KCVO, CBE, DL; and the late Major General Sir Sebastian Roberts, KCVO, OBE.

There are many other Guardsmen, both serving and retired, who have given their time, recounted stories and anecdotes, and suggested areas we should cover in the book. We thank them all, both those mentioned in the text and those who are not.

We have relied heavily throughout for the advice and enduring patience of Marcus Cowper, Editorial Director at Osprey Publishing, part of the Bloomsbury Group. On a personal note, we would like to thank our families. For Paul: "My wife, Georgina, my sons, Guy and Hugh, and springer spaniel, Waldo, have all kept me perked up during the writing of the book." And for Simon: "The patience and support of my wife Charlotte throughout the time that this book was being written."

For both the authors, the opportunity to write this book has been a most rewarding experience, and any errors or omissions remain ours alone.

Index